Gus Wortham

Gus Wortham

PORTRAIT OF A LEADER

By Fran Dressman

FOREWORD BY STERLING C. EVANS

TEXAS A&M UNIVERSITY PRESS
College Station

Second printing, 2014

The paper used in this book meets the minimum requirements of the American National Standard for Permanence of Paper for Printed Library Materials, Z39.48-1984. Binding materials have been chosen for durability. ♾

Library of Congress Cataloging-in-Publication Data
Dressman, Fran, 1945 –
Gus Wortham: Potrait of a leader/ by Fran Dressman.
p. cm.
Includes bibliographical references and index.
ISBN 13: 978-0-089096-580-1 (cloth: alk paper)
ISBN 13: 978-1-62349-154-3 (paper: alk paper)
1. Wortham, Gus S., 1891-1976. 2. Businessmen–Texas–Biography.
3. American General Life Insurance Company. I. Title.
HC102.5.W67D73 1994
368.3'2'0092—dc20
[B]

93-31049
CIP

Contents

Illustrations

ILLUSTRATIONS

Foreword

I am pleased to present this book which has been written about my friend, Gus S. Wortham of Houston, Texas. He died on September 1, 1976, but his position as a leader in Houston circles is still very important.

The book was written under the direction of Dr. Joe Pratt, Professor in the History Department of the University of Houston. The research and writing were done by Mrs. Fran Dressman, also of Houston. Both of them are to be congratulated on a fine piece of work.

In 1915, Mr. Wortham and his father, John L. Wortham, started a general insurance agency business in Houston. In 1926, they organized the American General Insurance Company, which became one of the outstanding companies in this field. He later bought a life insurance company and established a company known as the American General Life Insurance Company, Inc., which is rated very high in the insurance circles all over the United States. For a period of more than forty years he directed the affairs of the Company. He did a great job in selecting good insurance men to help in this regard. He first brought in Mr. Ben N. Woodson, who became President of the company, and when the latter was looking forward to retirement, Mr. Wortham picked Harold S. Hook from a company in California as President and Chief Executive Officer. He directed the affairs of the company that they organized in 1926 with an operating capital of $300,000 and which has grown into an organization with assets of over $44 billion and equity of 5.1 billion.

We were partners in the farming and ranching business for a period of more than twenty-five years. At one time we had lands in Louisiana, Texas and New Mexico totaling more than 350,000 acres. In the liquidation of our partnership, all our ventures proved to have been successful.

He was quoted in one of his many interviews or writings: "Liquor, if you can handle it, puts a spring in an old man's step!" He was the only individual I ever knew personally who had this philosophy and he lived up to it in grand style.

Before his death, Mr. Wortham provided for the establishment of a Foundation, the primary purpose of which was to serve the cultural and civic interests of the people of Houston. He selected Allen H. Carruth, a prodigy of his, to be the person who would direct the affairs of The Wortham Foundation. He had known Allen for a long time and had him promoted to take his place as Managing Partner of John L. Wortham & Son. After giving away many millions of dollars, the Foundation is now worth $177,000,000.

Mr. Wortham had an interesting philosophy about several matters in life. One was on dollars. With the business dollar, it was immoral not to make money and one had to make sure to receive full value. With the pleasure dollar, if one could afford it, enjoy it and never look back.

—Sterling C. Evans

Preface

Many Houstonians have a vague recognition of the name "Wortham," perhaps from attending the ballet or opera at the Wortham Theater Center, jogging by the fountain on Allen Parkway, or seeing "Wortham" listed among donors' names at the art museum, the zoo, or the park department. But relatively few know who Wortham was or what he did, or, more importantly, how his life made an impact on the city in which they live and work.

Gus Sessions Wortham was a native Texan who came to Houston in the years before World War I and organized an insurance agency. He later formed a fire and casualty insurance company which grew into American General, a multimillion-dollar financial services corporation. He was a leader in community activities, particularly the Chamber of Commerce and the Houston Symphony. In later years, he became well-known for the agricultural and financial success of his avocation: ranching and the raising of purebred cattle. He was among a handful of members of the "8F crowd," Houston's mid-twentieth-century business elite which wielded great influence in local, state, and even national political and governmental circles.

It is important that people know about the Worthams in their history. Such business and civic leaders are part of an ongoing historical process that continues to influence physical, economic, political, cultural, and intellectual conditions. The effects of Gus Wortham's actions in his various spheres of influence are still being felt. This story of a successful American businessman focuses on the impact he had on his society.

This volume is primarily an institutional history in that it concentrates on Wortham's involvement as a creator and sustainer of the economic, civic, and cultural institutions of Houston. Through this approach to Wortham's life, the development of Houston can also be measured. As the facts concerning the creation and growth of these institutions are presented, three major themes emerge, themes that explain the directions Wortham took.

First, Gus Wortham was a good businessman. Through his father's influence he chose a career in the rather conventional, respectable world of insurance. He favored the financial and investment aspects of business life and was particularly adept at discerning trends and directing his enterprise into economically advantageous situations.

Part of being a good businessman, Gus Wortham knew, was being active in the civic life of the community. He was intent upon getting his name known by actively working for whatever fostered a sense of community pride and contentment and, ultimately, good business conditions. A prosperous environment—a place where business was not only courted, but cared for—was important and Wortham worked for this through the Chamber. In addition, he used his business skills at financial management to shape high-quality cultural institutions which, in their turn, created the kind of city he sought.

Central to his business ability and essential to his approach to institution-building were Gus Wortham's connections with people, which is the book's second underlying theme. Again from his father, Wortham inherited contacts and learned the value of such men—mentors who became friends and associates. He had a talent for choosing people who could do the job he wanted done and inspiring in them trust for his vision. He understood how important these relationships were to successful institution-building. Wortham's life and work were intertwined with those of his many friends and business colleagues; this "networking" was critical to the development of many Houston business and civic empires.

The third major theme of Gus Wortham's life is the importance of land. "They aren't making any more of it," he often said; so he bought it, developed it, and built a business with it. The presence of land permeates all aspects of the life of Wortham, who grew up in a rural tradition in Texas, where the land is paramount.

Ultimately, these three themes of business acumen, connections with people, and love of land shaped Gus Wortham's life. They propelled him in the directions that made him an influential man in the history of Houston. Like his adopted home, Gus Wortham was a blend of southern manners and values and western, sometimes specifically Texan, virtues and actions. He was from an upper-class family, but one that migrated to the West for opportunity. Land ownership was a constant for the family, but his grandfather was also an astute merchant who persuaded the railroad to run through his rural county. His father, displaying the courtliness of a gentleman, was an avid business trader and a thoroughgoing political wheeler-dealer.

From this dichotomy evolved Gus Wortham's self-image as a "southwestern gentleman." While holding fast to certain habits, manners, and customs ordained by who he was and where he came from, Wortham also maintained a strong belief in himself as an individual with the God-given right to succeed as he could.

Wortham's Victorian-era forbears were from the old South of the Carolinas and Alabama, where the idea of an aristocracy, a small number of ruling families who held the land and wealth, was well established. Stability, continuity, and noblesse oblige were the ruling tenets of this class, although there was social mobility as "men on the make" moved to more profitable cotton lands. There the cavalier myth and the ideal of the gentleman were solidified. East Texas, as well as the counties on its edge to which the Wortham ancestors migrated, was settled in the antebellum period and was closely tied to these traditions through its economic base and because it was peopled with these same southerners.[1]

But they had chosen to become Texans. Texas—raw, unclaimed land that was not even a part of the United States (indeed, it was part of a wholly different culture). Even its original settlement, orchestrated by a group of land developers or empresarios, was a harbinger of a new, more open, and perhaps riskier existence. To pull up stakes and come to Texas was certainly an act that required confidence in self, a firm desire to try whatever might succeed, and perhaps an acceptance of a new individualistic spirit.

While the South held onto its chivalric ideal, it was modified after the Civil War as the region sought to rebuild and fit into the new commercial and industrial American mainstream. Now the "gentleman" was a "new model capitalist," who combined energy and boosterism with fine manners. Daniel Singal in *The War Within* describes the man as "ambitious not acquisitive; energetic, not predatory; competitive, not cutthroat"—a "philanthropist first and capitalist second."[2]

According to historian Joe L. Dubbert, after the war the country admired the individual and action over introspection. Then, with the advent of the "Bull Moose" mentality of Theodore Roosevelt, the westerner—the man who sought fame and fortune on the frontier—became admired as the true American. The rule was belief in progress, and the businessman—probably for his willingness to venture—was linked with the intrepid "real American" outdoorsman.[3]

Looking into Gus Wortham's involvement as a business builder, as a civic leader, as a cultural backbone, as a political motivator, as a force that shaped Houston's institutions, we will find a man who sought to embody the spirituality of the southern gentleman—what he must be—with the sensibility of the Texan—what he might do. This blend of values and mores produced a generation of men courtly in behavior, sure of their place in society, firmly directed toward the ethics of progress and economic success, and conscientious in their duty to lead.

Many of these men were Gus Wortham's mentors and business associates in Houston. Together they sought to build the city into the "right" sort of world. That, of course, meant one where they could succeed financially. It also meant one that offered and sustained a certain quality of life—through public policy and institutions—commensurate with their ideas on what was best for their city from their class perspective.

But these men who styled themselves as southwestern gentlemen are all gone now. And, ironically, it is largely because of one of the main principles Wortham and his friends sought so eagerly in their own and their business empires: growth. Houston is no longer a southern city on the way to becoming a southwestern metropolis. Instead it has become, in one of its own favorite terms, a "world-class" megalopolis.

Acknowledgments

My debt of gratitude extends to many people for their assistance and support during the researching and writing of this manuscript, from my professors and fellow graduate students to the employees and management of the American General Corporation.

There are four people to whom I am most indebted:

I must thank Mr. Sterling Evans, Gus Wortham's friend and partner, whose idea it was to create this work and who provided the financial support for it. Second, I am grateful to Dr. Joseph A. Pratt, Cullen Distinguished Professor of History and Business at the University of Houston, who chose me to do this project under his direction and was its final editor. Thanks are also due to Mrs. Judy Brumbelow, archivist at American General, for her guidance and access to the corporate archives. Finally, I owe a huge debt to the late Kenneth Fellows. Not only did I make extensive use of his 1976 manuscript, "The Baby Is Born," but before his death, Mr. Fellows allowed me complete use of his own personal notes and research on American General and Gus Wortham. Without his research and writing, this book would not exist.

Others I must thank for their research assistance, insights and memories, reading and comments on the manuscript, and their friendship, include Nancy Boothe, Allen H. Carruth, Dr. Christopher Castaneda, Dr. Louis Marchiafava, Suzanne Mascola, Dr. Martin Melosi, Lois Morris, Patricia Neighbors, Dr. Elizabeth O'Kane-Lipartito, Dr. Robert Palmer, Lester Randle, Barbara Snyder, Dr. James Tinsley, Dr. Lee Winderman, and Benjamin N. Woodson.

I also owe thanks to the staffs of American General Corporation; John L. Wortham and Son; the Metropolitan Research Center at the Houston Public Library; Woodson Research Center, Rice University; the University of Houston; and the Wortham Foundation.

My family, of course, made it all possible. My daughters, Maura and Clare, provided me with a constant incentive to achieve my best. And to my husband, Dr. Michael R. Dressman, goes my greatest thanks for his advice, encouragement, confidence, and love.

Gus Wortham

CHAPTER ONE

The Greatest Boy in Texas

My Dear Dad,

I have just wired you that my orders are in.

Don't grieve or worry over my going, for I am coming back some day all the better fitted for the battle of life, and I hope, with a record that will make you proud of the sacrifice you made in consenting for me to go.

I know you would not have me stay at home when the duty of every young man calls him to the aid of his country. . . .

It is hard, much harder than you know or than I anticipated to leave you, but I am going, believing that you and I will again be together, but with the happy knowledge that should this not come to pass, my father was the best friend I ever had, and left me with a heritage more to be desired than all the riches in the world; and it will be my effort through life to keep the sacred trust you have left me untarnished.

If, when I have finished my course in life, I can look back and know there was nothing that was not worthy of you, I will indeed be happy.

I have never heard anyone, friend or foe, say aught against John L. Wortham. I am proud to be your son and to bear your name. . . .

With love to every one of you, I am, devotedly,

Gus[1]

In June of 1918, a twenty-seven-year-old son writes to his father from Wright Air Field, Dayton, Ohio, as he prepares to ship out for war in Europe. This is not an uncommon kind of letter; neither its sentiments nor its somewhat formal tone are unusual. But the contents and circumstances of this letter stand as an explanation of the influence that this father, John L. Wortham, had upon the career of his son, Gus.

As the father's reply shows, the respect of the son for the father was mutual: "I am pleased beyond expression, great and most deserved compliment to you. Have felt the choicest fruit was in store for you because of your rare ability, well-rounded poise. Your great letter fully restores my strength, injects youthful vigor and determination to see your return crowned with distinction."[2] In addition to his letter's fervor, John Wortham's choice of "well-rounded poise" is most striking. For despite his youth, Gus Wortham was already recognized for a certain demeanor that inspired confidence and respect.

These two letters accurately reflect the close relationship of the two men, suggesting that Gus Wortham's life was predicated on the outlook, expectations, and confidence infused in him by his father. The values John L. Wortham imparted to his son would determine much of what the son would accomplish in his life. John L. Wortham's loyalty to his friends, sense of duty to his state, and aggressive pursuit of material success tempered by respect for tradition were traits passed on to Gus.

Throughout Gus Wortham's young adulthood, John L. Wortham, a gregarious southern gentleman devoted to Texas and his friends, had guided his son's path. One reason for the close ties of father and son may have been that Gus was the only son—his brother, Dickie, having died young. Correspondence which remains suggests that Gus and his youngest sister, Catherine or Cad, were the father's favorites. Gus had the benefit of John L.'s patience and unflinching confidence. Through his father he also had contacts with a great number of influential people in government and business whom his father had met in his various careers and political undertakings. Gus would build upon these connections, creating for himself a place in the heart of the ruling elite of Houston and Texas in the first half of the twentieth century.[3]

This branch of the Wortham family was part of the vast exodus of white southerners into the new state of Texas in the 1840s. Originally from North Carolina, John's father, Luther Rice Wortham, had lived in Graves County, Kentucky, prior to 1837, when he moved to Maury County, Tennessee, and married his distant cousin, Sarah (Sallie) Hall Wortham. After the birth of their first child, Jim, Luther and Sallie moved to Texas in 1848, settling in Woodland in the Tehuacana Hills region of Limestone County in east-central Texas. After trying their luck at farming for a year or so in nearby Navarro County, they finally settled back in Freestone County (created from Limestone County in 1850).[4]

John Wortham began life in the shadow of an older brother, Captain John Lee Wortham, called Jim. Jim died of disease in July, 1862, while with the Confederate forces stationed in Galveston. That same month, another son was born to Colonel Luther Rice Wortham and his wife Sarah and given his dead brother's name. John Lee was the youngest of six children, but after his birth a brother, Edward, and a sister, Mary Jane, died, leaving only young John and two sisters, Henrietta and Emma.[5]

The colonel, known as Dick, was a prominent citizen of Tehuacana, officially named Long Bottom in 1871. He was a farmer and also the area's first merchant, dealing "in staple and fancy dry-goods" and as a "commission, receiving and forwarding merchant."[6] He was active in politics and educational matters, serving as a county commissioner before and during the Civil War. According to a family history, the "colonel" title was probably honorary because there is no record of military service. (John would also be called "colonel," although there was no documentation of military service for him either.) During the war, in 1864, Colonel Dick donated some ten acres of land for a boys' college, church, and the cemetery in which his eldest son had been buried. In 1871 he was instrumental in the negotiations for bringing the Houston and Texas Central Railway Company through the county on land owned by Robert Longbotham. A deed records his gift of land to the railroad in October, 1871, and in 1874 the town was renamed Wortham to honor the civic leader's work in capturing the railroad for the area.[7]

This part of Texas, endowed with rich black soil, was a favored area of settlement for transplanted southerners like the Worthams and their kin, the Kirvens and Sessionses. These were not poor, subsistence farmers but relatively wealthy and well-educated people who were taking advantage of an opportunity to own more land than they could hope for through family ties back home. Many were cotton planters who owned slaves; thus the end of the war signaled a very different kind of life for them. They suffered political and economic hardships through Reconstruction, but not total defeat. They rose to power again with what they would call the Democratic "redemption." Their fates were tied into major industries like cotton, lumber and the railroads.[8] By the time he died in 1874,[9] Luther Rice Wortham owned much land. His estate, including his store and its contents, and over a thousand acres of land, was valued at fifteen thousand dollars. Some of this land was sold by his widow.[10]

Although his father died when John L. was twelve, and his mother seven years later, the youngest Wortham managed to attend Baylor University at Independence, Texas, between 1877 and 1879. He then returned to Freestone County to farm, probably on what was left of his father's land. In 1886, John L. Wortham married Fannie Carter Sessions, daughter of a prosperous cotton planter Gustavus Adolphus Sessions, whose plantation, Sessions Place, was the center of the social life of Woodland settlement in Freestone County.[11]

Both Sessions and his wife, Martha Carter, were natives of Alabama. Gustavus had been orphaned early upon his arrival in Texas in 1848, but had made his own way. Martha, whose family had been leaders in the Alabama migration to Texas, had inherited her father's plantation, which became known as Sessions Place at the time of her marriage. Sessions added more acreage, eventually buying a thousand acres in Freestone County, and became one of the largest cotton planters in the county.[12]

Sessions fought in the Civil War at the battle of Vicksburg, and later was a member of the 1876 Texas Constitutional Convention. "Mr. Gus" (a nickname also later used for his grandson) was described as "a man of quiet strength and benevolence, often serving as judge and jury for whites and blacks. . . ." He taught Bible lessons to his servants and field hands, and local history says that

Fannie Sessions Wortham. Courtesy American General Corporation.

Portrait of John Lee Wortham. Courtesy American General Corporation.

during Reconstruction he hid from the federal troops and was defended by a former slave named Tom Cox who, although threatened with the loss of his life, swore never to tell the whereabouts of "Master Gus." In 1887, two years after Martha's death, Sessions divided his estate among his children. Fannie and John L. Wortham received the "Tom Kirven place," some 150 acres, and the 110-acre Sessions Ranch. John owned and traded sizeable amounts of land in both Freestone and Limestone counties during the early years of this century, thus validating Gus's later claim that his father loved to buy and sell land.[13]

Gus's mother, Fannie, a year older than her husband, and described in one family genealogy as "a vivacious person, of high good humor, though of decided opinions . . . a highlight of the large Sessions household." Family lore even says she was once "churched" for dancing. According to another family member, Fannie was somewhat domineering and her only brother, Carter, would leave when she was expected for a visit so she could not fuss at him.[14]

In 1890, John L. Wortham moved to Mexia, in Limestone County, having, as he said, "a limited success in the farming business." There he ran a farm implement and hardware business with his wife's brother-in-law, William Bonner. He also served as vice president of the town's Citizens National Bank.[15]

On February 18, 1891, Fannie gave birth to a son whom they named Gus Sessions Wortham after his maternal grandfather. Perhaps as an omen of his future business success, Gus Wortham was delivered by—and in the home of—Dr. Jasper Gibbs. In time, Dr. Gibbs's daughter, Mary, would marry one of the most famous entrepreneurs in Texas, Houston's Jesse H. Jones.

John and Fannie had four children who survived infancy, two boys and two girls. Gus's brother, Dickie, died at the age of twelve from the complications of the bite of a black widow spider. The three remaining children were the eldest, Fan Etta; Gus; and Cad, who was ten years younger than Gus. Throughout their lives Gus and Cad would be called "Bubber" and "the Baby" by their family members. These two would remain close confidants all their lives.[16]

As both the Wortham and Sessions families were among the area's reigning families, John L. Wortham was well connected to those in economic, political, and social power in the community, and himself considered a member of the civic elite. In the southern tradition of the rule of the landed aristocracy, it was not only expected, but considered a responsibility of social rank, for these men to assume the leadership roles in civic life. It was a pattern Gus would also follow in later years. Thus, while living in Mexia, John served as a member of the city council and was on the school board for eight years. He became involved with statewide educational issues and promoted educational legislation.[17]

Probably through his school board duties, John Wortham became friends with R. B. Cousins, who served as superintendent of the Mexia schools beginning in 1887. The Cousins' relationship seems to have been one of the many social-political liaisons built by Wortham. The extent of his statewide political involvements can be found in a 1902 letter John Wortham wrote to his sister's husband, Captain William R. Davie, making reference to the extent of his political activities: he had been organizing the county "for Prince" (R. E. Prince of Corsicana was Speaker of the Texas House of Representatives) and vowed this would be the end of his political activity.[18]

Even as the son of one of the town's more prominent and public-minded citizens, Gus Wortham had a normal, rural Texas boyhood, growing up surrounded by relatives who lived nearby in Freestone County. Fannie Wortham was the disciplinarian of the two parents, who, according to Gus "knew how to handle children." When in trouble, Gus and his siblings always went first to their father. But Fannie was outgoing, a "doer" who loved to play cards. Gus conceded that she was "a practical and fair-minded person" who "believed in helping only those who would help themselves."[19]

Gus was probably much indulged, as evidenced by his own favorite story of "free" ice cream. He told of his uncle, Carter Sessions, who kept a running "tab" with the local pushcart vendor of ice cream for his nephew; little Gus did not know until he was nine or ten that ice cream wasn't free. For excitement, Gus could sneak down to watch the brawls at the local saloons with his cousin, J. R. Sessions, who was just a few days older than he. Gus later recalled that it was the fancy sign of an insurance company on the window of a Mexia business establishment that first interested him in the insurance business.[20]

Although his own business career started out like his father's, in the farming and mercantile trades, John L. Wortham's career was profoundly shaped by his friendship with and support of various Democratic candidates for political office. He was thoroughly involved in statewide Democratic politics. Several times he was sent as a delegate from his native county, Freestone, even though he had moved away. Freestone County sent him as a delegate to the 1890 Texas Democratic Convention that nominated Progressive candidate James Hogg for governor. Wortham claimed to have attended all state conventions at least through 1913. He served as chairman of the Democratic County Executive Committee of Limestone County and, as he said, oversaw its "restoration" to "the Democracy." He was certified as a presidential and vice presidential elector from Texas in 1900. In an open letter written in 1912 in preparation for a political race, Wortham talks of his pride that he had never "scratched a Democratic ticket from constable to president."[21]

For his service to the party, Wortham was rewarded with an appointment by Governor Samuel Lanham (1903–1907) in 1903 as financial officer of the state prison system. Obviously Wortham was an important operative, for, as Texas penology historian Donald R. Walker points out: "It is difficult to overstate the importance of the prison system to the political structure of the state during the late nineteenth and early twentieth centuries. In choosing persons to staff the prison, governors placed a premium on previous political service and the potential for continuing effort on behalf of the Democratic party and the incumbent elected officials. . . ."[22] The last governor from the old Confederacy, Lanham reversed the progressive thrust of Hogg's administration and returned Texas to more conservative times.[23]

When Wortham was appointed to the prison system it was just beginning a period of reform, with agitation for the total abolition of the convict-lease system.[24] But during his four years as financial agent, there was little movement toward ending the lease system, although some additional land was purchased for state-controlled share farming by the prisoners. This was considered by most officials to be a more humane solution to employing the prison labor than the lease system. The prison foundry at Rusk, which had seemed so full of possibilities, came to be unprofitable as new methods of making pig iron became feasible. Despite advice that it be shut down, more money was allocated during Wortham's time for its further development. It was finally closed in 1909.[25]

Wortham was proud of his record as financial agent, noting that he had found the system "depleted" but had left it with a $170,000 cash balance four years later and no debts. But, according to a political study of the prison system by Herman L. Crow, "careful audit of the prison records revealed that the profits were obtained primarily from a more extensive leasing of convict labor to private contractors and not from the two walled penitentiaries which were actually losing money during this period."[26] An investigating committee reported in 1910 that the financial records had not been well maintained, no daily records of the industries kept, and "very little coordination existed between the outside campus and financial agent's office so that, in effect, neither knew what the other was doing."[27] There is no mention of whether any of these problems were the result of Wortham's tenure, his successor's, or a combination.

Given the politicization of the prison system and Wortham's heavy involvement in conservative party politics, it is probably safe to assume that John L. Wortham looked upon the task of financial agent as one that required him to make as much money as possible. His job was not to seek change for a public who believed "that prisoners should serve as a source of revenue to the state."[28]

John L. Wortham supported the appointment of his friend, Ben Cabell, to the newly formed prison board created in 1911 as part of a new prison law. Wortham's old job and that of superintendent were abolished in favor of this professional board which, unlike under previous administrations, actually oversaw the prisons. Cabell was a former sheriff of Dallas County and mayor of Dallas, and like his fellow appointees, experienced in law enforcement matters. The new commission finally abolished the convict-lease system.[29]

The Wortham family lived in Huntsville during John's years with the prison system, and, among the many friendships made during these years, one would prove especially important to his son. James A. Elkins was a hardworking young lawyer who became county attorney and then county judge, and in 1926, would become a chief investor in Gus Wortham's fledgling company. Local legend had it that young Gus Wortham was Elkins's "first criminal case." When Gus and some other teenage pranksters were charged with breaking the window of a Huntsville widow's house, John Wortham took Gus to Elkins, who negotiated a settlement with the widow. Apparently the young man was able to escape punishment because Elkins told the widow he was "a bit tetched in the head." Although Elkins often delighted in telling this story in later years, Gus would counter that it was not exactly true.[30]

When Governor Lanham left office in 1907, John L. Wortham did too, going to Dallas and opening a mercantile establishment that likely dealt in hardware and lumber like his store earlier in Mexia. Dating from 1909 at the latest, he also had his own investment business located in the Wilson Building in Dallas. When Wortham and his son met Jesse H. Jones[31] is not known, but in 1911, John, who by then resided in Austin, was listed as a vice president of Jones's Texas Trust Company of Houston. N. E. Meador, another Wortham friend from Huntsville, may have been the connection. Meador was involved in organizing Texas Trust as well as an official of Jones's lumber company. The Texas Trust Company had been formed by Jones in 1909 to lend money on real estate and Jones merged it with Bankers Trust in 1911. John L. Wortham stated

The Kirkettes, John Tarleton College Football Team, December 20, 1907. Gus Wortham is second from left in middle row. Courtesy American General Corporation.

that in 1910 he "became connected with one of the largest business institutions of Houston." It is also probable that John L. Wortham was a friend of John T. Jones, Jesse's older brother, who lived in Dallas until 1920 when he moved to Houston and became president of the M. T. Jones Lumber Company, in which John L. Wortham subscribed for forty thousand dollars' worth of capital stock.[32]

While his father was in Huntsville and later when he entered private business in Dallas, Gus attended high school. Although he did not receive a high school diploma, in 1907 he matriculated to John Tarleton College in Stephenville, located about ninety miles northeast of Waco. Tarleton was a small, eight-year-old junior institution that offered two years of high school and two of college. It was the youngster's first time away from home. Although he stayed at Tarleton only about a year, Wortham was pictured as a member of the football team in December of 1907.[33]

In 1908 Gus went to the University of Texas at Austin. He stayed until 1911, pursuing engineering, law, and a formidable social life as a member of

Sigma Nu fraternity. Engineering looked promising as a field of study, based on Wortham's ability at "figures," but calculus and higher mathematics proved too difficult. Quite naturally for a young gentleman of his class and acquaintance, he thought of the study of law, tried it out, and found it "too theoretical, just the opposite of engineering." He would reflect in later years that "[i]t is too difficult to know what the answer is in law . . . even though you have to prepare information and come to some kind of a conclusion."[34]

In the summer of 1909, Gus responded to a newspaper advertisement recruiting players for the semiprofessional San Angelo Colts baseball team. It was a good summer job, paying sixty dollars a month. Gus played second base. He was not a big hitter but his fielding won the attention of the cartoonist of the local newspaper.[35] Wortham remained a baseball and football fan throughout his life, but these early experiences seem to have been his only attempts at an athletic career. He returned to college in the fall.

Meanwhile, his father, although no longer a public office holder, was still heavily involved in politics and political connections continued to shape John's life career. Gus often commented on his father's vast array of friends and acquaintances, including the most influential politicians in the state.

Prohibition had taken center stage in the drama of Texas politics during the early part of the century and John L. Wortham was an involved "wet." A 1908 letterhead lists him as the manager of the North Texas Business Men's Democratic Anti-State Prohibition Committee, with headquarters at his office in Dallas.[36]

The elder Wortham was also a supporter of Texas' controversial U.S. Senator, Joseph W. Bailey. By the early 1900s, Bailey had become a cause in his own right for his involvement with Standard Oil interests in Texas. In 1909 Wortham and others were planning a rally where Bailey could speak in reply to the recent speech of William Jennings Bryan on the Payne-Aldrich Tariff. Bryan and the 1908 Democratic platform supported free raw materials while Bailey believed raw materials should be protected—a position favorable to city businessmen, entrepreneurs, and the majority of the Democratic party in Texas. Wortham's positions against Prohibition and for the tariff mark him as not of the Progressive mold. His old line Democratic conservatism would be echoed in his son's political leanings in later years.[37] In 1920, when Joe Bailey ran for governor as a conservative Democrat, vowing to preserve true Jeffersonian democracy from the socialist and progressive elements in the party, John Wortham supported him. Wortham feared that Bailey's defeat would mean control of the state, perhaps the nation, by the labor unions. Bailey was the last holdout of the old conservative, antiprohibition wing of the Texas Democratic Party.[38]

As Gus grew to manhood, his father encouraged him to become politically involved, too. Gus had acquaintance, through his father, with men of political power such as Bailey and Congressmen John Nance Garner and Sam Rayburn. But his father wanted him to work actively for candidates. He urged Gus to support William P. Hobby of Beaumont for lieutenant governor in 1914, telling Gus that Hobby had been "active" for him (John). Dutifully, Gus pledged to Hobby the support of thirty-five young men in Travis County.[39]

John L. Wortham's political friendships were important business connections as well, such as with millionaire lumberman John Henry Kirby of Houston. A politician himself, Kirby was also one of Bailey's chief supporters. Kirby was close to John and was "the first big businessman" Gus Wortham ever met.[40]

It was obvious that with his many connections, John L. Wortham would not stay out of government service long. And in 1911 he was appointed to the Texas Railroad Commission by Governor Oscar B. Colquitt (1911–15), filling Colquitt's own unexpired term on the commission. Although a former Hogg man, Colquitt was a conservative antiprohibitionist, who was supported by "corporate interests." Wortham's loyalty to Hogg and Colquitt was rewarded by this appointment.[41]

The Railroad Commission, a reform measure of the Hogg administration, was created in 1891 following a constitutional amendment. Designed to act as a regulatory body on the unchecked economic dominance of the railroads in Texas, it faced much political opposition. Texas was the thirty-third state to set up such a regulatory commission and one of a minority to give it strong regulatory powers, even stronger than those of the federal Interstate Commerce Commission. The U.S. Supreme Court upheld the commission's authority to regulate fares and rates. But the dispute over the strength of the commission split the Texas Democratic Party.[42]

In 1912, John L. Wortham ran for election to the Railroad Commission position to which he had been appointed by Colquitt. Correspondence saved by his son includes a letter from C. S. Fiero of Webb County offering Wortham the county's primary vote if Wortham would see that the local railroad station was repaired. Wortham has written across the top of the letter "I ignored this letter. The solid vote went (*sic*) to [Allison] Mayfield. I guess he made the promise. J. L. Wortham 7/18/12." Wortham was not reelected to the Railroad Commission.[43] But Colquitt appointed him secretary of state, after Colquitt's own reelection in 1912.

While his father was moving in powerful state political circles, Gus's life had reached an impasse. In 1911, not liking engineering or legal studies, Gus left the university at Austin without a degree and with no clear career choice in mind. He was grateful for the patience of his father, who took the position that whatever his son wanted to become was fine, as long as he wanted to become "something."[44]

Gus Wortham never voiced any regret about not completing his college education. In later life he expressed the need for education to be practical and give specific skills for making a living. But perhaps because of his father's example, Gus Wortham retained a reverence for education and its institutions. And surely John was influenced by his own father, Luther Rice, who had been one of the original trustees of Freestone County's Woodland College.

As a school board member in Mexia, where R. B. Cousins was superintendent, John praised the schools as being the best in the state. Given the area's historical support of educational institutions (both male and female colleges flourished before the Civil War), his claim may have some merit. John Wortham remained involved in educational issues his entire life, especially concerning the development of higher education in Texas. He had friendships with the leadership of the University of Texas and Texas A&M College, and he worked for the establishment of the state's teachers' colleges. His friend Cousins went on to become president of the Texas State Teachers Association and held other high-ranking state educational posts.[45]

Loyalty to friends, as exhibited in his relationship with Cousins, was the trait that most endeared John L. Wortham to his supporters. He helped Cousins in employment matters several times, including hiring him as assistant financial agent for the prisons when Wortham moved from Mexia to Huntsville in 1903. In 1904, Cousins won the race for state superintendent of public instruction, serving until 1910, when he became president of West Texas State Normal College in Canyon. When Cousins resigned from West Texas State to become vice president of the Kelly Plow Company in Longview in 1918, Wortham offered him advice and consolation. John told him not to get discouraged; that the "first month [after the founding of John L. Wortham and Son] Gus and I took in $8.50." In 1921 Wortham was very active in getting Cousins elected superintendent of the Houston School District.[46]

On August 12, 1913, the *Houston Post* reprinted an editorial from the *Denison Herald* celebrating Wortham's steadfastness in supporting his friend Ben Cabell for the prison commission: "He is a man who has never turned a deaf ear to the call of a friend nor his back upon a foe. Impulsively, yet generous to a fault, he will go the limit to serve his friend, even at the risk of his own personal interests."[47] Another story of his fidelity to friends relates how John Wortham spent the night at the side of Houston attorney John C. Williams, who was in fear of his life from a litigant in a civil lawsuit.[48]

In a eulogy to Wortham's friendship which Cousins wrote and which was reprinted in papers around the state, he called Wortham "a high priest in friendship's holy temple" and a partisan and generous friend, "who went to the last ditch with every man whose cause he espoused." Cousins spared few superlatives in celebrating John Wortham's loyalty and devotion to friends.[49]

In personal dealings with his son, too, John Wortham always seemed to know just what was needed. It was at John's suggestion that Gus, after leaving college in 1911, spent some months of 1911 and 1912 at the Box T, a twenty-thousand-acre ranch in the Panhandle, owned by a cousin of the Wortham family. Although he did not describe it romantically in later years, the experience of doing hard, physical work out of doors clearly appealed to the young man and gave him "time to think." Fulfilling what must have been something of a boyhood fantasy, he rode the range, wrestled calves for branding, and even tried to ride a wild horse. One skill he remembered being forced to master was cooking—it taught him how to get along with people. But the life of a lone

Gus Wortham (*right*) at work at the Texas Fire Rating Bureau, circa 1912. Directly behind him is E. R. Barrow. Courtesy American General Corporation.

cowpoke was hard, too, and Wortham did not especially care for it. He remembered his cousin's library, for reading was all the leisure-time activity the ranch afforded. Gus enjoyed reading Dickens and "the sorts of things . . . people thought you ought to read"—for instance, *The Rise and Fall of the Roman Empire*. "I didn't read all of it," he admitted sixty years later, "because God knows it was too long." Wortham acknowledged that he learned a lot about people and how his time at the Box T exposed him to a real "competitive spirit," both attributes that would make him a successful businessman.[50]

In the fall of 1912, Gus Wortham returned from his ranching sabbatical and began working at the State Insurance Board in Austin at a job arranged through his father's connections. The State Insurance Board was the direct descendant of the State Fire Insurance Rating Board, which had been formed in 1909 to monitor fire insurance rates. Local agents in Texas were upset that rate competition from the larger companies meant they had to charge smaller customers—their friends and neighbors—higher premiums to make up for rebates to the larger, out-of-state companies. The Fire Insurance Rating Board's job was to authorize rate reductions or increases, with no allowances for "discriminations or variances from the stated rates. . . ." When this new system was abused, a 1910 law gave the right of rate-making to the State Insurance Board, guaranteeing "a certain amount of protection in the matter of competition with larger out-of-state firms" for Texas home companies. Thus insurance premium rates came increasingly under governmental scrutiny, and by 1913 rates were promulgated and published by the State Fire Commission, which replaced the State Insurance Board. This system of state promulgation of rates was unique to Texas.[51]

Gus Wortham never forgot his reception in the small state insurance office; chief clerk E. R. Barrow exclaimed, "Here's another political lout; what in the hell am I going to do with him?" Wortham earned sixty dollars a month as a clerk for the board. His job was mostly statistical, and he prided himself on promoting the use of new technology—a double-carriage adding machine—to reduce the "hand work." Wortham felt that this experience was invaluable, because he learned and got involved in insurance rate-making, even helping to re-rate the city of San Antonio.

This job was a major turning point for him. Besides honing his business skills, it provided the opportunity to forge relationships with people who would become central to his future. His coworkers included chief clerk Barrow and as rate clerks Barrow's brother, Tom, and Marvin Collie; all would play important roles in Gus Wortham's later career.[52]

But it was with B. F. Carruth, E. R. Barrow's assistant, that Wortham would develop the closest bond. This strong personal relationship was as central to Gus Wortham's career as were such friendships to his father's. Wortham described Carruth as simply, "the smartest insurance man I've ever met." But although Carruth was possibly Wortham's closest friend during this period, little data remains about their personal relationship. The son of a military man, Carruth was the youngest of nine children, and often joked that his family called him by initials because they had run out of names. He began his career in 1910 with the C. B. Roulet Fire Rating Board in Dallas, before joining the State Insurance Board. Wortham and Carruth each served as best man at the other's wedding.[53]

As Gus settled into his insurance job, his father began a short-lived tenure as secretary of state. John L. Wortham was bonded for the position in December, 1912, and he held it until June of 1913. There is no clear indication of how close Wortham was to Governor Colquitt, how influential he was during his tenure as secretary of state, or why he held the post for just six months. Wortham's chief clerk, who later became secretary of state, was D. A. Gregg. Gregg and John remained friends, for in January, 1914, Gregg wrote Wortham that he missed him and would see him when Wortham's Lubbock Irrigation Company had its annual board meeting. Gregg was also involved in securing a good price for Wortham on the "old Ellis homestead" in Austin.[54]

After his tenure as secretary of state, John L. Wortham laid the groundwork for a campaign to serve again on the Railroad Commission. Apparently he accumulated enough supporters to feel the need to place a newspaper notice when he withdrew from the race for business reasons.[55]

John Wortham's next venture involved him in the business of owning and managing land. He had always owned land and bought and sold parcels throughout his life; this was another interest and value which he passed on to his son. At the turn of the century, John had purchased grazing land in West Texas for about two to four dollars an acre. When the land values increased he sold it. In his land dealings, he found out about the discovery of artesian wells at Lubbock and bought land there owned by the San Augustine School District in East Texas. Around 1914 John organized the Lubbock Irrigation Company, an experimental farming project. Such projects were quite popular and relatively modern ventures taken on by private developers. But there is doubt about the success of Wortham's farming venture after twenty years away from agriculture. In a letter to his friend R. B. Cousins in October, 1914, Wortham remarked that he had sold the Lubbock Irrigation Company and "saved" his life. This despite an earlier letter to Gus in which he talked about working hard and eating well, although "hungry" to see his son. In November, 1914, John L. Wortham was "winding up" affairs in Lubbock and had some business dealings regarding selling land owned by others. Surely by this time, he and Gus had begun making plans for a new business venture in which they both would be involved.[56]

It was partly at John Wortham's instigation that Gus ventured in a new direction and left his rather secure position at the State Insurance Board. John believed that a man should work for himself. In December, 1914, Gus asked his father's opinion about advice he had received from their friend, N. E. Meador, who was encouraging Gus to come to Houston to pursue a job prospect there. "I think that every young man should get into business for himself as soon as he can and rely upon his own efforts," John wrote to Gus. He believed Meador, with "influence" and "high standing," could be of great help to Gus.[57]

According to Gus, it was Carruth who was first offered the job at the John R. Young Agency in Houston, but turned it down to remain in Austin because of his impending marriage. He recommended his friend.[58] The plan would be for Gus to establish himself with an agency in Houston in which he might buy an interest. The Young job, at the same salary of $100 a month to which he had advanced in Austin, seemed like a good opportunity. And Gus had already decided he did not want to "remain always in the employment of the state."[59]

Certainly much of what Gus Wortham would become was well established by the January day in 1915 when he first arrived in Houston. As he stepped off the train and headed for a bed at the YMCA, Gus Wortham may have been apprehensive about what lay ahead. But he knew he wasn't adrift in a cold and friendless city. He had a job waiting for him, acquaintances with certain important people, and the one thing that propelled him more than all the rest, a sense of belief in himself.[60]

Gus Wortham's first residence in Houston was a boarding house at Chenevert and Walker owned by Betty Gaines Sears, the young widow of Judge Sears. Gus and his roommate, Frank C. Smith, saw little of one another because they kept different hours, but the two became neighbors many years later after Smith had become president of Houston Natural Gas.[61]

Later, Gus said he had been "attracted to Houston" and knew of it by virtue of having lived close by in Huntsville. There had long been a strong connection between the two cities and many young men seeking their fortune migrated from the small community to Houston in the early years of the century, including James A. Elkins. But Gus Wortham also chose Houston because he was offered a lucrative position.

Gus stayed with the Young agency for about six months. His father had joined him in Houston in April and together they began to think about ownership of their own agency. Overtures were made to buy the Young agency, but John Wortham was of the opinion that the prices being asked for partnerships in Houston were too high, and then someone—Gus, his father, or a third person—suggested they form an agency of their own. Just seven months after he had arrived in Houston, Gus Wortham went into business for himself. John Wortham made an investment of five thousand dollars to found the firm, but he also gave it his greatest asset—his well-known name. John L. Wortham and Son began operations in Room 416 of the Union National Bank Building, employing only a forty-dollar-a-month secretary.[62]

Exactly how or when B. F. Carruth became a partner is not known, but there is some evidence that Gus and B. F. had planned their eventual partnership while both were still in Austin. According to company lore and documents, however, Carruth is listed as one of the three original partners as of July 26, 1915. Wortham and Carruth would later form a business partnership together in the 1920s, which owned stocks, bonds, and land.[63]

John L. Wortham and Son's first policy was sold to Williams, the attorney for whom John had stood guard, for insurance on household goods. The fifteen percent commission earned the firm $1.88 on the $12.50 premium. Apparently, Colonel Wortham expressed some doubt at this point about the viability of the firm. But they had entered business just before the massive hurricane of 1915 devastated the Gulf Coast area. Cotton stored around Houston sustained much water damage and the court appointed a custodian to protect the cotton from further damage. Setting a pattern for the future, the custodian was a friend of John Wortham's and so the young firm got the business. Gus was able to broker the "less-than-esteemed business with every agent in town who could place a line," and thus John L. Wortham and Son earned over a thousand dollars in commissions.[64]

In September, 1916, the Worthams moved to offices in the new ten-story Gulf Building, built by Jesse Jones in 1914 (later renamed the Rusk Building after Jones built a new Gulf Building in 1928). At the same time, B. F. Carruth moved to Houston and became a full member of the firm. Agency business was divided equally among the three, except for the surety bonding business which the Worthams retained.[65]

While Gus was the driving force behind the agency, his father certainly was a part of its early operation. John's major role, of course, was to draw business through his name and reputation, and this he did. In 1916, Governor

B. F. Carruth. Courtesy American General Corporation.

James Ferguson invited the two Worthams to visit his suite at the Rice Hotel, where he was staying following a dinner in honor of Colonel Rienzi M. Johnston, then publisher of the *Houston Post*. When the governor inquired and found that John L. Wortham and Son did not directly represent any surety firm, he recommended they call the state resident manager for the National Surety Company of New York. Eventually, all Natural Surety's business in Houston, some eight to ten thousand dollars' worth, was turned over to the Worthams. Gus recalled that when reports of the governor's intervention on their behalf got around, the agency garnered surety bond business on many state jobs. And because of the affiliation, the agency wrote its own first surety bond, for $165,000, for McKenzie Construction Company on a building at Texas A&

The Rusk Building, Houston, an early home of John L. Wortham and Son and American General's main address from 1929 until 1965. Courtesy American General Corporation.

M. This business may also have been garnered because of John L. Wortham's acquaintance with so many prominent educators. Other important business followed, like that of Colonel Jacob Wolters, a Houston attorney and old political crony of John Wortham's. Chief lobbyist for Texaco and head of the Texas National Guard, Wolters gave all his fire business to John L. Wortham and Son.[66]

Sometime in 1916 or 1917, the fledgling firm opened a San Antonio office, where Gus spent the better part of a year. It had some difficulty, and was later closed. There is some evidence it was manned for a time by Marvin Collie, who had worked with Gus in Austin.[67]

When the United States entered World War I in the spring of 1917, both Gus Wortham and B. F. Carruth sought to enlist, but it was decided that Gus should be the one to go, because B. F. was married and had a family.

Gus volunteered for active duty with the air corps in the fall of 1917. Slight nearsightedness kept him from going into pilot training, but he did seek ground training at Kelly Field in San Antonio. Wortham obtained letters of recommendation to the Kelly Aviation Camp from several influential people, including Governor W. P. Hobby, Texas Supreme Court Chief Justice Nelson Phillips, and the state fire marshall and insurance commissioner. All of the letters were written in December, 1917, and refer to Gus as a resident of San Antonio. In his letter, Phillips, an old family friend, cites Wortham as an example of the "good blood" of "pioneer strain" that made Texas great.[68]

Despite these recommendations, Wortham was sent to land school at Georgia Tech in Atlanta and afterward to Wright Field near Dayton, Ohio. There he was commanded by a disagreeable captain who, chagrined that Gus was really no engineer despite his one year of college training, made Wortham keep a minute-by-minute account of each day's activities. Connections paid off for young Wortham even here, however, for he ran into an officer from Houston who saw that Gus was transferred to aerial gunnery school. Since General Pershing had immediate need for additional gunners at the front, the group received concentrated instruction in Allied and enemy guns and bomb sights: Wortham remained amazed all his life from this experience at how much a person could learn under pressure.[69]

Sometime before he left Texas, perhaps before he even went into training, Gus Wortham had made a serious business blunder in San Antonio. Whatever the problem, it involved deception of some sort, and from correspondence between father and son, it was clear that it could have been serious had not both Worthams finally been forthcoming and honest with the other parties involved. Most of the early 1918 letters John L. wrote to Gus contain messages of forgiveness and not admonition. The father wanted his son to know that part of being young was making mistakes and learning from them, and that he would always stick by his boy no matter what. Above all, John L. Wortham did not want Gus to worry about his misstep and he assured Gus that he had his father's confidence.[70]

Gus was sorely disappointed when he and a fellow second lieutenant, Albert Kearney, were passed by as the rest of the company embarked for Europe. Wortham, who had ranked quite high in his artillery studies, never knew whether it was planned or just by accident that he and Kearney were left behind, but the pair managed to salve their disappointment with an "unofficial" leave of absence in Dayton, Ohio. Kearney, a native of Rhode Island, remained a life-long friend. The two exchanged greetings yearly on Armistice Day, for which Kearney would write a new poem, recounting some of their war experiences. Among the collection of war memorabilia Wortham saved were two copies of the company paper, *The Fly Paper,* which Kearney edited, and Kearney's sweet, sentimental ode to the war dead.[71]

Finally, the two were sent to France, where they were housed in barracks originally built by Napoleon. It is hard to say which impressed Wortham more about the place—its history or its discomfort. But he did save a snapshot of it. Here he did some "casual" instructing in aerial gunnery and, as he said, "followed orders and learned not to ask too many questions." Word reached him that his father was ill and strings were being pulled to get him home, but it was all quashed by a Colonel Wolf, who had Wortham reassigned as the commanding officer in charge of an aerial repair squadron. This was to be Gus Wortham's war.[72]

The squadron was composed mostly of men skilled in the building trades who were older than Wortham and had been in the service quite some time. Still a second lieutenant, Wortham was overwhelmed by this assignment and vividly remembered the cooks' sit-down strike as the event that would make or break him as a leader. Bringing the cooks before his hungry men, Wortham admitted he knew they were trying to embarrass him. But, he said, he had had breakfast at the officers' mess and it was really the men who were suffering. So he challenged the troops: "You decide the punishment." Wortham always believed that incident helped secure his men's respect.[73]

Wortham also gained the men's gratitude by acknowledging the importance of their work and their contribution to the war effort, which was often overlooked because they were not fighting at the front. He reviewed each man's file and bargained for advanced rank and pay for several men. Finally, through his contacts with other officers, he arranged for the company to return home after the war ahead of their original schedule.[74]

Wortham well recognized that his time in the military had given him leadership experience, including self-assurance and resourcefulness, but through it he also "uncover[ed] an ability of which I seemingly had been unaware, to work with men—to lead them, to gain their respect, to inspire them, to make things go."[75]

The elder Wortham took leadership of the firm while Gus was overseas during World War I, as evidenced by correspondence written shortly after his son's departure. He told Gus that the company got a "nice bond from the Houston Construction Company," and in another letter noted that Carruth had gone to Austin "to try and get the bond on the Insane Asylum at Wichita Falls. Colonel Johnston told me last night when he left the Club that he would see that we got the bond. It is a $500,000 bid." Wortham also wrote that he had gotten the Rice Hotel bond schedule renewal through friend, N. E. Meador. The elder Wortham exhibited his skill in meshing political friendships with business success. Later that summer Carruth wrote to John L., who was at a Georgia health spa, about trying to capture the agency business for the Standard Accident Company of New York, and filled John L. in on the recent primary election outcome.[76]

A 1919 letter, before Gus's return, also spoke of John L. Wortham's business dealings. He bragged to Gus about "land[ing] all the text book bonds but the small ones," with thirty percent of a $5,400 premium. In the same letter he reported that both fire and surety business were good during the first two months of the year and that he had written a $460,000 bond for Smith Brothers Construction of Crockett, Texas, and another on a Houston building. He credited his cure from pneumonia to his desire to see Gus and even considered meeting him in New York so that Gus could meet "our fire insurance and surety people."[77]

Just a year after his departure, in June, 1919, Second Lieutenant Gus Wortham returned to Houston and his firm. One of the souvenirs that Wortham would keep from his service days was a calling card reading: "Gus Sessions Wortham, U.S. Army." It was not uncommon for officers to carry these during the Great War. But it also directly identifies Gus Wortham as a gentleman soldier—one of the young men of good family and education who set out to save the institutions of democracy during World War I. The card is a symbol of Wortham's social standing as a polished, capable man, ostensibly at the brink of a successful career. His ancestry and his own presence, the impression he made upon people, had already catapulted him out of the ranks of those who would struggle in life.[78]

Much of what Gus Wortham had become was due to his father's influence. The three passions of John L. Wortham's life—business, politics, and land—would also play a large part in Gus's career choices. On top of these, John Wortham left Gus a myriad of connections in the three areas and a personal reputation that would give the son a lead in these endeavors. Gus appreciated and learned his father's skill with people; his ability to be a friend and his loyalty to his friends. These were major components in the father's success and would make the positive difference in Gus's career.

And along with his interest in land and politics and his abilities in business, John Wortham gave his son an even more important commodity: self-confidence. It is the kind of belief in oneself and one's abilities that perhaps can only be bestowed by a parent, based in unqualified love and approval. "Gus is the best boy in the world," John wrote in 1924, "and loves me as a child." "He is the biggest man of his age I ever knew. I love him of that love that only you can have for an infant." He praised him to all, even including Gus in a letter in which he talks mostly of business matters: "I am feeling better than in years. My health is good. I am happy. My son Gus is the greatest boy in Texas."[79]

Finally, one thing that is striking in much of the correspondence of John L. Wortham is the great admiration that so many of his friends had for Gus. Often this reflected on the father, such as in the comments of Senator Bailey, who upon receiving a copy of Gus's letter, quoted above, said: "Nothing that boy could do would surprise me, unless he did something wrong; and that I am sure he will never do. He is the right kind, and he could not be otherwise since he is your son."[80]

CHAPTER TWO

Coming into His Kingdom

Gus Wortham was not immune to the changes that come to men who serve in wartime armies. While his military duty did not affect the direction of his career, it uncovered for him his abilities to evaluate and to lead people. His brief stint in the military gave him a new self-confidence. It also marked the beginning of Wortham as a man of accomplishment and sparked his growth into a man who was building a successful life for himself, creating, as it were, his own kingdom.

When he returned from military service, John L. Wortham and Son was still housed in the two-room office in the Gulf Building they had occupied in 1916, employing a bookkeeper and a typist. The partnership was divided between the two Worthams and Carruth. Gus returned to his leadership role in the firm.

In July, 1919, he hired Carle Aderman, a man he had met when Aderman was the night clerk at the Rice Hotel. He was the orphaned son of German immigrants, self-educated, and a most industrious soul who had become manager of the Bender Hotel, and then gone into advertising. His hiring was somewhat typical of the way Wortham acquired staff, often choosing able people he had observed in other jobs, regardless of limitations in education or training. Aderman began as a straight commission salesman at the agency, eventually becoming production manager and a director of AG.

In October, Mamie Pace (then Mrs. L. V. Loving) became part of the group. She was a good find because of her ten years of experience at W. L. Moody's American National Insurance Company. In addition to accounting and bookkeeping, Pace did personal business for John L. Wortham and balanced Gus's checkbook. In 1923, when the firm finally began to keep books, Pace set up the accounting department with the help of B. F. Carruth.[1] Tom Barrow, Wortham's former coworker in Austin, joined the firm in May of 1923 and was put in charge of the fire insurance department. Also joining the firm in 1923 was Harriet Stewart, another young woman who would devote her life to Gus Wortham's institution, as a sixty-dollar-a-month typist. Later, she became the backbone of Gus's favorite, the bonding operation.[2]

By this time, John L. Wortham and Son already had a respectable reputation; the contacts of both Worthams had attracted sizable clients. By 1920, the agency was handling the surety bonds of John Henry Kirby, and at that time or soon thereafter, the casualty insurance for Kirby Lumber Company. Additional early customers included Smith Brothers Enterprises, owned by the Worthams' friend Jim Smith of Crockett, with offices on San Felipe Road in Houston; Houston Lighting and Power, the city's electric company; and the interests of Jesse H. Jones. An early oil account was Humphrey Oil owned by Colonel E. A. Humphrey of Mexia, where oil had been discovered in the early 1920s. Already in surety and bonding, John L. Wortham believed the day of their becoming the general agency for National Surety Company "made them all [other agencies] sit up and take notice." In addition to National Surety, the firm also represented Liverpool and London and Globe and the United States Fire Insurance Company, and in casualty, The Employer's Liability Association Corporation, Metropolitan Casualty Insurance of New York, and the Maryland Casualty.

Although John L. Wortham and Son had several corporate accounts, the bulk of their business was in "personal lines," property insurance on homes and belongings, including the automobile. This included the personal coverage of prominent Houstonians like Kirby, who insured his mansion with the firm for $80,000 with $200,000 to $300,000 "additional that will come along through the year as it expires." Less than ten years after its founding, the agency had achieved a reputation for respectability befitting a much older establishment.[3]

A story about a customer survives as an agency myth used to illustrate the founders' ingenuity as well as the uncertainties of the insurance business in these formative years. It seems a local farmer-rancher had struck oil and, to celebrate and show off, had purchased a luxury-model car with red leather upholstery. He asked John L. Wortham and Son to insure it "from hell to breakfast," covering every possible contingency. Of course, the one contingency not conceived of occurred. A billy goat climbed in the empty car parked at a well site and chewed up the expensive upholstery. The client was not worried because he had insured his vehicle so thoroughly, but the firm had some trouble finding, in the sheaf of policies issued, any references to goats and upholstery. He was finally paid out of the firm's own pocket under a "comprehensive automobile physical damage claim." Not until the 1930s did insurance companies underwrite such a comprehensive automobile physical damage coverage, an indication, if by accident, of the firm's leadership in the industry.[4]

John Wortham's presence was still a drawing card for the insurance agency. His name, along with those of Gus and Carruth, was featured prominently in a June, 1923, newspaper advertisement announcing the firm's move to new offices just across the street at 228–37 Bankers Mortgage Building, on

The Bankers Mortgage Building in Houston, American General's home from 1926 to 1929. Courtesy American General Corporation.

the corner of Main and Capitol. The large ad invited visitors to see their "increased facilities," for "all forms of insurance, fidelity and surety bonds," and listed fire, surety, and automobile departments, as well as production, accounting, and claims and all their respective employees.[5]

Although their agency was successful, John L. Wortham and his son were still interested in new business enterprises and, after the war, often discussed organizing some kind of finance or insurance company. As always, John Wortham's political friendships and business affairs meshed constantly and in 1920 he organized the Automobile Investment Company, to finance cars which he and Gus also insured. The firm's letterhead listed John Wortham, president; J. A. Elkins and N. E. Meador, vice presidents; and G. S. Wortham, treasurer. John Henry Kirby and Jesse Jones were listed along with Elkins, Meador, and the elder Wortham as directors. But the company was not profitable, probably because of a minor depression in the early 1920s, and was eventually liquidated.[6]

John L. Wortham had always promoted the ideal of a man's working for himself: "You can take off when you want, as long as you're responsible." That belief, coupled with the admonitions of one of the agency's customers to "keep the insurance premiums in Texas," spurred Gus, his father and Carruth to consider seriously the formation of their own, indigenous insurance company. Pushing for the firm's establishment were their old friend and customer Jim Smith of Crockett and San Antonio businessman John Bennett, who was related to Carruth.[7]

But it was Gus Wortham's interest in bonds that inspired the innovative idea that finally made it possible for him to form his own insurance company. The creation of the system of twelve Federal Land Banks in 1916, one of which was located in Houston, provided a profitable outlet for Wortham and Carruth's business ingenuity. Supervised by the Federal Farm Loan Board, the banks initially made long-term loans to farmers and farmers' cooperatives, and during the farm crisis of the 1920s, the banks' loan system was enlarged. The twelve banks and their hundreds of employees located around the country provided an enticing market for a surety bonding enterprise.[8] And in the early 1920s, Gus and Carruth developed a special fidelity or honesty bond to insure the employees of the federal land banks and their subsidiaries. The two worked with Luther Mackall of the Metropolitan Casualty Insurance Company of New York to develop an innovative "blanket bond," one that would cover all bank employees, "from president to janitor," and did not require specific employees to be named as previous schedule fidelity bonds had required. In summing up their case to the land banks, Wortham and Carruth declared their blanket bond would "give to the officers and directors a feeling of security and safety, which is absolute and which they cannot otherwise secure."[9] The bonds were written jointly with Metropolitan Casualty (no connection with Metropolitan Life), U.S. Fidelity and Guaranty Company of New York, and the Maryland Casualty Company (a firm that would loom large in Wortham's corporate future).

The Wortham-Carruth bond was controversial because it included provisions for "faithful performance," or assurance of employees' reliability at their jobs. It also provided a hundred-thousand-dollar bond for each employee, a greatly increased coverage, at a cost "very little in excess of the rate carried on the former bond."[10]

Support came from M. H. Gossett, the president of the Houston Federal

Land Bank, who encouraged the farm loan commissioner, former Governor R. A. Cooper of South Carolina, to approve the blanket bond. Gossett also wrote each of the banks' presidents, introducing Wortham and Carruth (one or the other visited each bank) and asking the banks' help in lobbying the Farm Loan Board for approval of the blanket bond. Gossett, a contemporary of John L. Wortham, was a former state legislator and a prominent Dallas attorney. He lived at the Rice Hotel, belonged to the Houston Club, and was active with the Chamber of Commerce.[11]

The approval of these blanket bonds for use by the federal land banks had to come from the Federal Farm Loan Board in Washington and necessitated travel by Carruth and Wortham to work out the agreements with board authorities. A story about the trip to Washington and final sale of the bonding idea to the federal government became another tale that said a lot about the relationship between the two men. It happened in June, 1924, just after Wortham and Carruth had made the successful presentation to Governor Cooper, convincing him to accept their specially designed surety bond. As they were leaving the building, Carruth remembered his hat, and wanted to return for it. Wortham stopped him, with a reminder of a cardinal rule of salesmanship: Make your sale and "leave while they still love you."

By July, 1924, Wortham and Carruth had secured the business of the banks at New Orleans, Omaha, Wichita, St. Louis, St. Paul, and Houston for the blanket bond. They would later add two more, possibly the Massachusetts and Baltimore banks, for a total of eight of the twelve banks. Part of the bond agreement included a reserve fund for the commissions made by the agency so that the firm would be able "to carry the premiums due on the surety bond if the banks suffered any severe losses," because Governor Cooper did not want the banks to have to pay premiums if any such loss occurred.[12]

The first year's commission of ten thousand dollars from the federal land bank bonds was the largest earned to that date by any Houston insurance bonding agency. The money earned from the sale of these bonds was put into the reserve account as stipulated, but Wortham and Carruth also considered that this money might be the capital to start their own insurance company. Eventually, that account did provide the thirty thousand dollars for the foundation of American General.[13]

Metropolitan Casualty and John L. Wortham and Son also developed a similar blanket bond form for the banks in Texas, which the Texas Banking Commission approved. They even hired a former banking commissioner to sell the bond to the banks in the state. They faced a fight, of course, from other agencies and their companies. The New York insurance companies tried to put pressure on Metropolitan to withdraw the form. Wortham appeared before the New York Insurance Association, telling them that the state of Texas would look unfavorably on any interference and convinced the New Yorkers to just tell its members not to sell such bonds. This left John L. Wortham and Son and the Metropolitan with all the Texas bonding business and no competition.[14]

Similarly, the Towner Rating Bureau, the industry's rating approval authority, opposed the agency's Federal Land Bank bonds, saying the form was not an approved form. Eventually, it was agreed that the land bank bonds as written would stand, but there could be no more business written this way. Although it ended the future of this bond, John L. Wortham and Son had a de facto monopoly on this Federal Land Bank business.[15]

The creation and sale of the Federal Land Bank blanket bond by Wortham and Carruth was the jumping off point for Wortham's business career development. Not only did it provide the seed money for the foundation of his own insurance company, but it was a prime example of Wortham's style: quick and broad origination and assessment of any financial deal, ability to form a consensus among parties, and complete trust and confidence in his own abilities. It also showed how he used the network of political and social leaders of which he was already a part.

But abruptly and sadly, future plans were delayed by the death of John L. Wortham on November 5, 1924. His and Fannie's estate totaled about forty-three thousand dollars, including one-third of the John L. Wortham and Son agency, valued at around thirty-five hundred dollars. Of far greater worth were the personal values and business connections he left to his son.

Although John's death delayed the planning for the foundation of an insurance company, Gus Wortham clearly had assembled a dedicated and accomplished core group of people and established a firm foothold in the Houston and Texas insurance market. In early November, 1924, E. R. Barrow joined his brother, Tom, as a member of John L. Wortham and Son. Barrow, as chief clerk of the Insurance Board, had been Gus's boss. Then he owned his own firm in Austin and did agency work in San Antonio before joining Wortham's firm. Nearly fifty years later, Barrow would recall those early days when the firm had ten employees, a payroll of thirty thousand dollars, and one Model-T Ford which his brother Tom drove to work, picking up B. F. Carruth and E. R. on the way while Gus walked to work from his home in the Rice Hotel.[16] E. R. Barrow became another of Gus Wortham's trusted confidants, and in time, his closest associate in the company.

Familiarity with the fire and casualty business through his work in Austin was the main reason Gus Wortham chose to begin a fire insurance company, although he later called his desire to start a company "the fervor of youth." The fire and casualty business had always been a risky endeavor, one in which losses could not be carefully determined and where there could be no planning, as with life insurance. But Wortham had no experience with life insurance, and, more importantly, a property firm would be unique to Houston.[17]

Nationally, eastern business interests dominated the insurance industry. New York was the largest insurance market, and following the complete investigation and cleaning up of its insurance regulations in the early 1900s, dictated how the business was run to the rest of the states. Texas led opposition to the northeastern domination, and in 1907 passed the Robertson Law requiring life insurance companies to keep seventy-five percent of their reserves invested in the state where they were subject to taxes. In response, twenty-one of the forty-six non-Texas companies left the state. By 1910, one of its results was that "many strong home companies have been organized which will further tend to keep Texas money in Texas." Some believe the law was based as much upon Texas' dislike of non-Texas institutions as reform, although other states had passed such legislation. Even by 1925, though, most of the two million dollars in insurance premiums collected in Houston went out of state.[18]

Attitudes toward "foreign"—that is, out-of-state—insurance companies presented opportunities for Texans such as Gus Wortham. Regulations specific to Texas, coupled with the Robertson Law, made the founding of a local company a potentially profitable idea. Wortham's earlier involvement with the state fire insurance regulatory interests in Texas gave him much-needed legal and business knowledge, as well as contacts at all levels within the state insurance bureaucracy. This involvement also fired his desire to begin a Texas firm that could take advantage of a burgeoning market and favorable regulatory conditions, and to make a contribution to the building of the state itself by keeping the money from Texas insurance in the state.[19]

Armed with $30,000 from the land bank bond reserve fund and another $45,000 provided by John L. Wortham and Son, Wortham and Carruth's next task was to find the rest of the estimated $300,000 in capital needed to launch the company. Here Wortham's connections proved decisive; he successfully appealed to three of Houston's wealthiest and most powerful men: builder Jesse Jones, banker-lawyer Judge James Elkins, and developer-financier John Wiley Link, Sr.

Wortham first approached Link, one of East Texas' moneyed elite. Link had made a fortune in Orange, Texas, in lumber and paper, through a friendship with John Henry Kirby. After moving to Houston, he took over the management of the Kirby Lumber Company and other related ventures. At the time of his involvement in the founding of American General, Link was president of a stocks and bonds firm, owned the Polar Wave Ice Company and Ice Rink, and was a director of several banks and corporations.

Link's son, J. W. Link, Jr., had helped his father organize the Link-Ford stock brokerage, housed on the same floor of the Bankers Mortgage Building as John L. Wortham and Son. The Links and their brokerage business each invested seventy-five thousand dollars in Wortham's enterprise.[20]

Judge Elkins, who had owned oil leases with John Wortham, probably thought it very natural to become a business partner of a man he had known from boyhood. Since migrating from Huntsville to Houston in 1917, Elkins had built a successful law firm and established the Guaranty Trust Company. Vinson, Elkins, Sweeton and Weems invested $50,000 in the venture, and Elkins encouraged several people in his law firm to buy stock.[21]

While Jesse Jones's share in the actual stock ownership was listed on the company's original charter as twenty-five thousand dollars, Wortham and others have stated many times that Jones gave seventy-five thousand to help Wortham found his company. Certainly, Jones was given a central role in the story of the company's founding because of his tremendous influence—and because he liked young Wortham. Although this was before his celebrated years in Washington during the 1930s and 1940s as head of the Reconstruction Finance Corporation (RFC) and later as secretary of commerce, Jesse Jones was already "Mr. Houston." Several versions of how Wortham obtained Jones's backing were told; all stressed Jones's ability to be a "hard trader" and his confidence in Wortham. Gus Wortham's version details his going to New York to see Jones, who was raising money as treasurer of the Democratic Party. "If you'll take a building, I'll take it all," Jones replied, but Wortham said he couldn't use a building without money, so Jones agreed.[22] Another version has Jones cutting off Wortham in the middle of his presentation, giving him a curt yes, and countering Wortham's surprised confusion with: "I don't need to know about the company . . . I know Gus Wortham." Wortham recalled that Jones told him to "deal me in" with the admonition that the money be available if Jones needed it back in a hurry.[23]

Almost forty-five years later, Wortham would say matter-of-factly that stock in his company had never been sold to the public; he and the other major stockholders had offered it to men they "thought might be interested."

Among these was Wortham's friend and business mentor, Colonel Joseph W. Evans, another Kentucky "colonel" who came to Houston in 1901 and became one of the state's foremost cotton merchandisers and exporters. Wortham often cited Evans as one of the founders of American General, although his initial investment was not large. This may have been because of their close relationship or because of Evans's influence in Houston, which probably set an example for other investors or clients.[24]

Another smart money man whose advice Wortham valued was Sam Taub, partner with his brother in their father's wholesale tobacco firm and a major director of Jesse Jones's National Bank of Commerce. Taub was well-known for his financial expertise; Jones called him the "finest judge of credits I've ever known."[25]

While Gus Wortham (and his father) were respected members of the economic elite and their agency was considered well run, he was not yet in the same league of financial power as these other men. But certainly they saw in him a man whose business ability and values fitted well with their own; he was a young man to be mentored, one who would carry their mantle. Despite the age differences, Wortham was considered a contemporary of Jones, Evans, and Elkins, to be supported as he created a solid new institution for Houston.

Even if Wortham felt, in hindsight, that he had taken a great risk in founding this enterprise, there was no doubt that he was resourceful enough to create a special niche for it. The company was to be a "general" firm writing policies in "multiple lines," including both fire and property/casualty underwriting. This was possible because of a 1925 ruling by the Commission of Appeals of Texas, upheld by the Texas Supreme Court. American General's ability to do both kinds of underwriting made it the first insurance company in Texas organized to write multiple lines of insurance.

Although multiple-line underwriting was not authorized as such, this loophole in the Texas legislation made it possible for Wortham to found such an enterprise in an era when other states forbade such business. As noted by one of Wortham's partners, this multiple-line ability was significant in streamlining business affairs for it allowed one investigation and one settlement in the event of a loss involving property as well as casualty. From the beginning, there was already an indication of Wortham's knowledge of the insurance business in Texas and his own sense that his insurance company stood ready to meet the changing and expanding business climate.[26]

In choosing a name for his company, Wortham wanted something that would make people think larger than Texas. He was also concerned that the name reflect the company's ability to write multiple lines, wanting the name "to be something which includes the words 'general insurance.'" Carle Aderman then showed Wortham the manufacturer's logo on the inside of his Thoroughbred brand hat: George Washington on horseback. "Here's a general for you, Mr. Wortham—George Washington, the first American General. How about that for the name of your company, American General Insurance Company." This picture, a reproduction of "Washington Receiving a Salute on the Field at Trenton," painted by Englishman John Faed, was used on the letterhead and early advertisements which emphasized not only American General but the company's roots in Houston and Texas. It was also noted that George Washington had the same initials as the boss.[27]

American General Insurance Company was officially chartered by the State of Texas on May 8, 1926. Corporate lore includes a story about the company's official founding, a story that once again confirms Wortham's place in the Houston business hierarchy and his ability to attract loyal associates. Judge Elkins's first legal work for American General was overseeing the maneuverings of the company's charter through the various state governmental channels. He and Wortham took the Southern Pacific sleeper to Austin on Friday, May 7, arriving early on Saturday morning. Houston writer Ken Fellows, in his 1976 unpublished history of the company, "The Baby Is Born," relates the story as rendered by those who experienced it or who heard it recounted:

> Saturday morning dawned sweaty-hot and muggy in Houston. The outside temperature climbed to 95 degrees by three o'clock that afternoon and only a stir of air created by the long-bladed ceiling fans in the . . . offices of John L. Wortham and Son made the long wait bearable for a tense little group of men, all important to the future of the infant company. B. F. Carruth, J. W. Link Jr., T. G. Barrow and his brother, E. R. Barrow, sat uneasily about the office, their minds in Austin, trying to anticipate what news would be forthcoming from there. Suddenly there was a knock on the door. Mr. Carruth pulled it open and accepted the yellow envelope from the Western Union messenger. He tore it open as the

> others crowded around. It was signed by Judge Elkins. Four words told it all. It read, "The baby is born!"

It is not known whether Wortham or Judge Elkins coined the phrase. The favorite—and very fitting—tag for this story is that Elkins, destined to become one of the most powerful business-political operatives in Texas, did not charge Wortham for these services, and his firm remained the company's chief legal agent for a very nominal retainer.[28]

The prominence of the men involved in the organization of the new firm, its novelty as a "general" insurance firm, and the fact that this was an era when business was king all combined to make American General's founding newsworthy. The principal stockholders were "some very prominent figures in the business world . . . including 14 of the leading local insurance agencies." The *Houston Post-Dispatch* reported it was

> . . . said to the be the only Houston stock company ready to do a general insurance business here. And, though a certain number of Texas companies are now in operation there is in excess of $2,000,000 in insurance premiums annually collected in Houston, of which a large majority is taken out of the state. The new company plans to invest its assets principally in Houston and Texas properties, thus keeping local capital at work within the state as far as possible.[29]

And Wortham explained to the press his faith in the benefits of his new enterprise for the city and vice versa: "Houston and Texas are entering upon an era of new growth which will need the sound aid and support of able financial concerns and . . . this company was organized to fill a place in the insurance world, keeping up with the progress in other lines of endeavor."[30]

Wortham surrounded himself and Carruth with a board of directors made up of those men who had made major investments in his company: Elkins, Evans, Jones, Link Sr. and Jr., Sam Taub; F. A. Smith of Crockett (brother of Jim), and insurance man Henry Robinson, who was to represent "the agent's viewpoint" on the board. To these names Wortham added Link's partner, R. W. Ford, who was also comptroller of the Beaumont Shipbuilding and Drydock Company; John T. Jones, Jesse's older brother and president of Jones Lumber Company; and Wortham's business hero, John Henry Kirby. All of these men except Kirby had bought stock to found the company. The group elected as chairman J. W. Link, Sr., who had the most prestigious reputation in legal, civic, and business circles—except perhaps Jesse H. Jones.[31]

At the first board of directors meeting on May 13, 1926, there was no surprise in the election of company officers: Wortham, president; vice presidents, Carruth, Ford, and J. W. Link, Jr.; Carle Aderman, secretary of production; Tom Barrow, secretary-treasurer; and E. R. Barrow, assistant secretary.

To get the company moving, Wortham took advantage of the structure already in place at John L. Wortham and Son by using a management contract. It was a somewhat obscure device employed in the foundation of new enterprises and based on the manager's or general agent's contract, by which insurance companies designated a general agent for a particular territory. These agents would handle everything from underwriting and collecting premiums to paying losses for the company. Under the management contract dated July 14, 1926, John L. Wortham and Son would do this for Wortham's fledgling insurance company. The agency was "to have complete control of the entire Underwriting of all classes of Insurance and of Surety business engaged in, or undertaken by the Company, including the appointment and discharge of Agents and acceptance and rejection of business." For this, American General paid the agency a commission of ten percent, later raised to fifteen percent, over and above the amount of commission allowed agents. The original management contract agreement contained a three-year expiration date, but with a motion by Elkins, seconded by Jones, such limitation was dropped. Wortham may have included this loophole to test the board's response to the idea of such a contract or because he was apprehensive about how it would work. The agency provided the company with employees, office space and equipment, administrative support and management expertise, and paid everything except agents' commissions, claims expenses, and taxes. Whether the insurance business came from another agency or John L. Wortham and Son, the latter was credited with a commission.

Thus, American General's only employees in the beginning were those who handled claims. The desire, of course, was to run the business with as little expense as possible, and the results gave American General one of the lowest cost ratios in the fire and casualty business. While the concept was not a new idea in the formation of a corporation, its use at American General was unusual considering the length of time it was in force.

This system was possible because both the agency and the company were relatively small and grew together and there was a centralization of power. Because the agency was also chiefly Gus Wortham's preserve, the arrangement was not acrimonious or especially competitive. The contract was part of the operation of the fire and casualty end of the business until American General's merger in 1964 with Maryland Casualty.[32]

From the beginning, building the business of American General took precedence over the affairs of the agency in the minds of Wortham, Carruth, and the other partners of John L. Wortham and Son, and in the actual direction of business affairs. This emphasis, reinforced by the management contract, lasted until after World War II.[33]

Banking on the stature of the Wortham name and the respectability of the agency, Gus had no doubt he would find agents and customers for his insurance. Indeed, the *National Underwriter* noted in its May, 1926, announcement of the company's formation that "[s]ome of its stockholders being owners of large industrial stocks in Houston, it promises to write a comfortable share of the business in the very beginning." No time was lost in getting the company into the thick of the insurance market. In June of 1926 (business formally began on June 7), even before the approval of the management contract, John L. Wortham and Son gave American General its first fire insurance account, followed in July by the first casualty business. In the fall the company began to write fire, theft, and tornado coverage on automobiles. In July, when the management contract was approved, Wortham also announced that the firm had negotiated a contract with Great American Insurance for reinsurance business. This contract was important for the company, allowing it to take on more extensive risks than it otherwise could have, given its own capital and surplus. In December, Wortham called the board together to get approval for the company to qualify to write surety business, requiring the deposit of fifty thousand dollars in securities with the State Insurance Department. Wortham's selling point was that this business would engender additional revenues.[34]

During the early years, most of American General's business was fire, automobile, and tornado coverage. Because of Texas' multiple-line ruling, it had a definite advantage in being able to write one automobile policy, rather than two, to cover all hazards and this business was emphasized. But the company also did a sizable surety bonding business, especially highway construction. This business was from the various construction projects of the Smith Brothers and, in later years, the fledgling Brown & Root Construction Company. At the first annual meeting, February 10, 1927, an auditor's report praised the company for "progressive and conservative management." The year's total losses were $3,368, mostly attributable to compensation to the Smith Brothers Construction Company for hay lost in a barn fire near Crockett. The hay was feed for the horses and mules the company used in road and tram railway construction.[35]

Gus Wortham had begun to build his business kingdom and the formation of the company signaled a transition in his life. With the promising completion of American General's first year, Wortham went from the successful younger man who ran a local firm to the dedicated business entrepreneur and serious institution builder. He was, in a phrase he later used to describe younger men he mentored, an "up-and-coming" Houstonian.

The transition also affected his personal life, for in 1926, thirty-five-year-old Gus Wortham decided to marry. Both of his sisters had married already and Gus and his mother, Fannie, continued to live at the Rice Hotel. Gus was financially successful, socially well connected and no doubt a "good catch." Piercing brown eyes, a rakish mustache, and perfect sartorial taste were the highlights of his modishly handsome appearance. Although caught up in taking his place in Houston's business aristocracy, Gus Wortham found time to play. From his mother, he and his sisters inherited a great love of card playing; he was especially adept at bridge and poker. Gus loved gambling and was a well-known denizen of the quasilegal establishments in Houston and Galveston. He would organize parties of young men and women to spend a weekend on the island, a fairly wide-open town in those days.[36]

Perhaps it was during one of these weekends that Wortham made the reacquaintance of a woman he had known as a student at the University of Texas, Lyndall Finley Davis. Davis was a native of Sherman, Texas, had gone to Galveston, married, and was now a very eligible widow. She and Wortham were married on October 4, 1926.[37]

As the head of a growing Houston-based company, Gus Wortham was a logical choice to serve on the boards of other major Houston enterprises. In 1927 he received an appointment that signified his growing status: he became a member of the board of directors of Jesse Jones's National Bank of Commerce. His business ability had captured the attention of Houston's most famous citizen. By the end of the decade Gus Wortham had moved into the narrow circle of Houston elite.

When elected to the National Bank of Commerce (NBC) board in July, 1927, Wortham was the bank's youngest director. He would remain on the board for forty-four years. Elected along with J. W. Link, Jr., Wortham was nominated by his father's old friend, N. E. Meador, who became NBC president in 1929, when Jones became chairman. Other NBC board members included Judge Elkins, John T. Jones, Sam Taub, J. H. Smith, and Fred Heyne, Jones's chief financial assistant. All were original stockholders in American General and all but Heyne were AG board members, as was Jesse Jones. These men knew that Gus Wortham subscribed to the same philosophy about how business should be done and money allocated, and had the same vision for Houston. Certainly, they valued Wortham's judgment about investments and people. Wortham was also a big customer of the National Bank of Commerce, having $150,000 in loans, direct and indirect, in November, 1927, shortly after he joined the board.[38]

During the 1920s Houston's banks boomed along with the remainder of the economy, which was spurred on by a highly profitable cotton trade and a growing oil industry. Although the oil business created many local fortunes, most of the major oil companies' long-term financing was done through the large eastern establishments. But the heads of the oil firms became Houston bank directors. More availability of money and credit meant flush times for the banks, many of which were founded on what one banker called "jazz banking" principles—high-risk, high-yield loans.[39]

In the 1920s the National Bank of Commerce aggressively expanded; its deposits increased by 104 percent between 1922 and 1929, and NBC became Houston's fifth largest bank with deposits of $12 million.[40] Walter Buenger and Joseph Pratt, in their history of the bank, *But Also Good Business*, point to the financial backing of Wortham's insurance venture—as the bank lent him money, his company grew, along with his deposits in their bank—as a sign of Jones's "willingness to take calculated risks in new fields." Also, by this time, Jones knew Wortham well enough to predict a profitable future for his company and to recognize that Wortham had the kind of financial acumen that Jones needed on his board of directors.[41]

Wortham regularly attended the monthly NBC board meetings and participated in making motions. In 1929 he became a member of the board's "examining committee" along with Will F. Miller (an original American General

Lyndall Finley Wortham on her wedding day, October 4, 1926. Courtesy American General Corporation.

stockholder), merchant Simon Sakowitz, and W. G. Winters. The committee examined all the bank's loans, securities owned and held, the trust records, and all holdings to see if the records were correct. Wortham served on this committee for several years, at least.[42]

Jones's bank was just one of a myriad of business interests for Gus Wortham. These included private investments and land ownership. One of his most astute investments in land was the purchase of some five acres on Buffalo Bayou in Houston in 1928 for forty-eight thousand dollars. West of Lincoln Street, it was the former site of the Butler Brick Yard. The land was a good investment, its chief attraction being its proximity to the large Sears, Roebuck retail store. But when the area proved to be flood-prone, Sears chose to build a new store on South Main Street and this facility became a warehouse. This land was held under the company name of Atlas Realty with no specific future plans. Wortham also formed Bayou Land Company, which bought land to the east and west of the Atlas acreage. Eventually Wortham owned some twenty-five acres on this site a mile from downtown. The stock in these land holdings and various other stocks and bonds were the primary investments of a partnership between Gus Wortham and B. F. Carruth, begun sometime in the late 1920s and liquidated in 1937.[43] Wortham's private business ventures, interest in investing, and fascination in land continued throughout his life.

But despite these interests, his insurance company was paramount in Gus Wortham's career. The late 1920s were profitable for American General. By December, 1928, the first dividend was declared on its stock: one and one-half percent quarterly to begin in 1929—and a quarterly dividend was consistently paid for the company's lifetime. The directors' minutes from December, 1928, give a good indication of the financial conservatism of the board as well as the company's prosperity. The executive committee was selling enough securities to buy $350,000 worth of government securities. The stocks they were selling included Standard Oil, U.S. Steel, Standard Oil of New York, General Electric, Gulf Oil, Sears, Roebuck, Montgomery Ward, and Continental Can. Two months later, Wortham declared a capital stock increase of $200,000 with the par value going from $100 to ten dollars per share. By the end of the decade, gross premiums rose from over $49,000 to $485,000.[44]

In 1929 the company and agency moved again, back across Main Street to Jesse Jones's Rusk Building (formerly the Gulf Building). They would occupy a growing amount of space in this building for the next thirty-six years.[45]

The depression was "mild" in Houston compared to other parts of the country, but Wortham admitted that the company had hard times. He believed it was the management contract that saved it from worse, because expenses were dependent upon volume; no business meant no expenses. In later years, Wortham explained that, "although almost all securities had dropped way down in value, the Insurance Commission issued an order that securities of certain high class ratings could be carried on the books of the insurance companies at cost rather than market value. Loss ratios generally were bad, but ours were held down because we operated frugally and had the buffer of the management contract."[46]

All agency and company efforts were put into the development of the company. One device Wortham used was the special agent, several of whom were sent throughout the state to sell the company to insurance agencies. In 1929, Wortham had subscribed some eight hundred shares of American General stock to a group of trustees to be used for agency development and sold to AG agents to increase their interest in the company. The proceeds of the stock sale went back into agency development. Wortham's "continuing awareness . . . of the need for strong agency development was exceedingly significant" and another example of his business acumen.[47]

By June, 1931, there was no doubt about a stiff economic downturn: premiums were down, claims up, and the stock was worth less. But still there was a profit of about $18,000—and a dividend was declared. By December, the company showed a profit of over $24,000 for the first nine months and a $42,000 profit in interest and dividends, despite a "substantial" depreciation in the market values of the stocks. A year later the executive committee recommended a plan to finance insurance premiums on an installment basis, thus allowing agents to finance policy premiums. Even with a severe hurricane which hit the Rio Grande Valley, 1933 showed nearly $30,000 in profit for the first eight months.[48]

The 1934 "Report to Stockholders" was Wortham's first detailed written notice that the company was doing well, had passed "through the formative stage" and "established itself as a permanent factor in the business." He boasted that the company had the best average loss ratio of any company doing business in Texas. With 490 agents and premium and investment income sufficient to produce a stockholder profit, Wortham could only predict more success as he believed "we are entering a period of business revival." He attributed the company's success to conservative management, with no "business acquired through excess commissions, or through acceptance of substandard business," and because it owned "no real estate, no collateral loans, and has never borrowed or had occasion to borrow money."[49]

Wortham believed that sensible, old-fashioned values had kept the company in business and made it successful during the early years. These included familiarity with the territory served, the interest and enthusiasm of the founders, and the fact that "we only got money if we sold business. So we did not have any drones. Our money only came in through contracts. Then we had a very small business and did not do very much expanding. . . . The value of a lot of our securities did go down. But we always made a profit in the insurance business itself, with the exception . . . of three or four years. That is because we . . . own stock in it. It helps that all of us had a substantial financial interest in our business."[50]

Gus Wortham had proved himself a good businessman through creating opportunities for his agency and making a promising start with his new company. In coming into his kingdom, Gus was brought into the mainstream of Houston's economic elite, evidenced by the men who helped found his company. Wortham's appointment to the NBC board also signaled not only his acceptance into the group, but his acceptance of the responsibilities of being part of this group. Like Jones and the men on the board, he would be expected to take a leading role in the city's life.

CHAPTER THREE

Houston's Own

Houstonians of the 1920s and 1930s aligned themselves philosophically and culturally with the South rather more than the West. The southern style of living connoted a certain set of manners and values that seemed more noble and elevated. Unlike the old South, however, Houston had a relatively open society. Being a member of the elite in Houston was not founded primarily on ancestry or longevity, but more on the kind of commercial abilities possessed in abundance by Gus Wortham. In addition to being young, male, white, born of "good family" in small-town Texas, and having come to Houston to make his fortune, Gus was "a self-made entrepreneur." The well-born or socially prominent male Houstonian might claim a place among the city's civic leadership, but power flowed to those who made the money.[1]

Business interests proved particularly adept at shaping Houston's politics. According to sociologist Joe R. Feagin's study of Houston's political and economic forces, *Free Enterprise City*, the city's business elite advocated at-large elections over the ward system to control the city government. And, by pushing the Texas legislature in 1904 to agree to a mayor-commission form of government in Houston, they "reinforc[ed] business control of government." It was easier to elect probusiness leaders in at-large elections; a strong mayor with affinity for the business community could control the heads of departments that managed the city's infrastructure.[2]

The backing Wortham received in founding American General and his selection for Jones's bank board certainly made him part of the group of businessmen which controlled many of the city's key institutions: major banks, law firms, transportation outlets, and construction companies. Others were active in the cotton and oil industries. They served on the boards of each other's enterprises, creating an interlocking network or "economic elite" which held much of the "public decision making" power of Houston. As political scientists

Richard Murray and Robert Thomas point out, because these elites were not necessarily from the old order, they did not necessarily seek to maintain the old order, but often to change it. And change for these economic elite power brokers meant growth. What they thought best and wanted for their city was exactly what they sought for their businesses: prosperity through growth.[3] In the mid-1930s, coincidentally with the growth of Wortham's company and his reputation as a business power, the business elite of Houston was entering its period of greatest influence over civic affairs. Wortham fit in nicely.

The way Wortham's relationships with Houston's economic elite developed is evidence of how much contact these men had with one another in a variety of settings and situations. Their closeness was partially based on the fact that Houston was still considered by the locals a small city in 1920 (about 140,000 people, forty-fifth largest in the United States). It was also abetted by a style of living in apartment-hotels that encouraged the mingling of social and business lives and interests. Although quality residential areas were springing up in Houston—especially Potter and Hogg's innovative suburban River Oaks—apartment-hotel living was the long-standing, preferred housing choice for many of Houston's upper-class families in the early part of the century. The Jones, Elkins, and Wortham families had lived for years at the Rice Hotel.[4]

It was fitting that when Gus and Lyndall Wortham returned from their honeymoon in December, 1926, they moved into the fashionable Warwick Apartment Hotel.[5] Located on Main Street, the Warwick's "backyard" was 545-acre Hermann Park. Across the street was the new Museum of Fine Arts and one of the city's most exclusive residential areas, Shadyside. Warwick suites from one to six rooms were available, furnished or unfurnished, and patrons could have their own kitchen or eat in the hotel dining room. The monthly rent for a one-bedroom "apartment de luxe" was $110 to $165. After settling first on a lower floor, in 1928 the Worthams moved to the eleventh or top floor where one of five new apartments was "converted into a charming Spanish home for Mr. and Mrs. Gus S. Wortham." Gus liked the convenience of hotel living; he probably enjoyed the access to other men of "substance" with whom he might do business, in addition to the fact that his mother and his sister, Fan Etta, and her husband, Dr. James Hill lived there.[6]

Like most of her peers, Lyndall Wortham did not have a job or career outside the home. She had been raised in the tradition of the southern belle and, although she had been a teacher before her first marriage, after marriage to Gus, her career became that of wife of an accomplished man. She was expected to make sure the home ran smoothly and that it was tastefully, but practically, appointed; and to involve herself in suitable social and civic activities such as garden clubs, literary groups, or charities. Lyndall made a place for herself in the social community, hosting a number of luncheons and card parties.[7]

During the early years in Houston she was active with the local chapter of her University of Texas (UT) sorority, Kappa Kappa Gamma. She often returned to Austin to visit the house and hosted parties and events for the chap-

Lyndall Finley Wortham with her mother, 1920s. Courtesy American General Corporation.

ter in Houston throughout her life. Lyndall was an active UT alumna, serving as an officer in the Houston chapter of the Texas Ex-Students Association. She also worked for the Women's Building Association, a group trying to establish a club where Houston's "prominent women" could house their various activities. Fan Etta Hill was vice chairman of the organization, which was headed by Oveta Culp Hobby, wife of the ex-governor.[8]

Gus Wortham was himself a member of several of Houston's prominent social clubs, yet another realm frequented by the economic elite. Wortham joined the Houston Country Club, although he never played golf, and the Houston Club, a men's club chartered in 1894, of which Jesse Jones was an early member. By the 1940s, Wortham also belonged to Houston's Ramada Club and the Metropolitan Club in New York. Feagin notes that membership in these clubs, along with the residential patterns, helped create the network of business elites. Clubs were places where economic and political ideas and plans were discussed and developed. It was a sign of Wortham's arrival into the elite that he held memberships in these organizations.[9]

As Gus Wortham took his place among Houston's notables, he wanted it known that his company, too, moved in those circles—that it was a solid and high-tone citizen of Houston. Its slogan, "Houston's Own" (also being used by Houston's Seaboard Life), was introduced at a dinner on September 12, 1935, where even the dessert cakes were imprinted with it. The "Houston's Own" campaign encouraged people to have their insurance written by hometown folks. Wortham wanted to make Houston the "insurance center of the South" and to "offer Texans a better and quicker insurance service."[10] In the mid-1930s, as part the "Houston's Own" campaign, American General produced a mailer to homeowners that gave a most stunning impression of the company as a Houston institution. From a simple letter format, it folded out into an arresting skyline panorama of Houston's downtown. Some two dozen major buildings are labeled as insured "wholly or in part by American General—Houston's Own Fire Insurance Company." These included Jesse Jones's Gulf Building, Rice Hotel and Chronicle Building; several banks and government buildings; the electric company, the City Auditorium, two movie theaters, three department stores, and the Farmers Market. The mailer stressed that this was a company run by a group of "conservative, dependable Houston business men who take a keen personal interest in the affairs of the company." Most importantly, and like most of the company's advertisements, it included a list of its prestigious directors.[11]

The presence of the business elite on American General's board secured for Wortham the image of responsibility and respectability he thought desirable for an insurance establishment, especially as it included two of the Texans most famous nationally, Jesse H. Jones and John Henry Kirby. In 1928, Wortham increased the board to seventeen by adding four more men: National Bank of Commerce executive and old Wortham friend, N. E. Meador; Vinson and Elkins lawyer, Wharton Weems; cotton factor and exporter, J. W. Garrow; and

Carruth's friend, the president of Standard Trust in San Antonio, John M. Bennett.[12] It is indicative of Wortham's loyalty and desire to keep company ownership engaged in the enterprise that all these directors were also original stockholders.

Gus Wortham appointed two kinds of people to his board: those he liked and those who were good businessmen. In many cases, the chosen men had both qualities, but four of Wortham's directors stand out not because of their service to the board, but because of Wortham's special relationship with each of them. They were role models and friends for Wortham, and they epitomized the men who were the social, economic and, therefore, political leaders of Houston.

Texas' first captain of industry, John Henry Kirby, was for Gus Wortham two men: the hard-nosed businessman and the magnetic, mythic tycoon. And Kirby was fond of his friend John's son, for in 1925 he wrote a letter of introduction for Gus which Wortham kept for the rest of his life, bundled with the tender letters his father wrote to him during the war. Although he had fallen on hard times by the late 1920s, Kirby was a valuable source of advice and information because of what Gus called his "behind the scenes contacts." Wortham probably admired Kirby as a generous friend as much as he admired Kirby's business acumen and political involvement—all attributes he sought for himself—if in somewhat moderated dimensions. And Kirby was an ebullient, gregarious man who gave lavish parties at his Houston mansion. Wortham's remembered vision of Kirby, in white suit with a red carnation in his lapel, is almost a stereotype of the grand old southern planter/politician.[13] Gus Wortham was so taken with Kirby that years later, in 1962, he commissioned a Kirby biography by Houston newspaperwoman Mary Lasswell.

Jesse H. Jones's relationship with Gus Wortham was not unlike that of a revered older brother or uncle, who is both friend and mentor. He, too, had known and worked with John L. Wortham. Jones was also in the mythic tradition of the Texas entrepreneur, for he began his fortune through the adventurous practice of borrowing money which he invested in land. Gus Wortham called him "the best businessman I've ever known." In his turn, Jones admired Wortham's business abilities, testament to that being that the only corporate board Jones ever served on besides those with family connections was that of Wortham's American General. Unlike Kirby, Jones was not a hail-fellow-well-met. Large of stature with a full head of white hair, he was an imposing man with a deep voice. He was friendly but somewhat standoffish, and he never had partners for any of his business dealings. But Jones was committed to building Houston. It was his personal check and political influence that brought the 1928 Democratic Convention to Houston. A 1930 biography called him the "most outstanding citizen of Texas today." As proof of their close affiliation, Wortham was often called upon in later years to introduce or honor Jones.[14]

The third of Wortham's board members who held a special place in his esteem was Colonel Joseph W. Evans. Evans was a lot like John L. Wortham—

a personable, social man, involved in business and politics, who never forgot a name or a face. And he was devoted to Gus Wortham. Fourteen years older than Wortham, Evans was both business advisor and friend. He was one of the few AG board members whom Wortham consulted for advice before a business transaction. Evans was also a man who could have a good time the way Gus Wortham liked to; he was an expert bridge player and he loved to go to the horse races. Evans was the "town crier," serving as the master of ceremonies, after-dinner speaker, and spokesman for a variety of Houston institutions and events, and his involvement in civic activities was legion.[15] His love of Houston and commitment to its development certainly rubbed off onto Wortham.

Like the three others, James A. Elkins, "the Judge," was older than Wortham. He had known Gus as a child in Huntsville before moving to Houston and starting his legal firm just two years after John L. Wortham and Son began. Elkins steadily built both a law firm, Vinson & Elkins, and a bank, City National, skillfully meshing the legal and financial worlds. In addition, Elkins was a political animal, and was partly responsible for involving Gus Wortham in local and state politics. From the time they both sat on the board of Jones's bank (Elkins from 1918 to 1928), Wortham's and Elkins' careers remained intertwined. Both would be recognized as major corporate builders, civic leaders, and political confidants; and when the name of one appeared in any endeavor, the other's was sure to be close behind.[16]

Kirby, Jones, Evans, and Elkins were core members of the city's economic elite power structure. They were Houston men of wealth who owned or ran major business interests and took leadership posts in civic and cultural activities. Their primary goal was to see the city succeed, grow, and become a profitable market. Their standard was: "A good business climate." They truly believed they were doing the best job they could if the city prospered economically; free enterprise was the backbone of the way of life. If business was doing well in Houston, everyone would benefit.[17]

Wortham's membership in this group had been assured by his admittance to the board of Jesse Jones's bank; it was an acknowledgment that he belonged in the ranks of business leaders. And as a full-fledged member, in the early 1930s Wortham began to take his place in the hierarchy of civic leadership. Encouraged by Evans, he became a member of the board of the Houston Chamber of Commerce. Gus was named a member-at-large of the executive committee in November, 1932, and in December he was appointed to a committee charged with raising money to bring the Chamber budget up to its needed $150,000 for the coming year, as the city had not seen fit to give its usual $7,500 annual contribution to the Chamber.[18]

Houston's Chamber of Commerce, founded in 1845 as the Houston Business League, was among the nation's oldest. Clearly, it was the center of the community's power, because the city's business and industrial leaders were not just token members, but wholeheartedly involved in all its forays into economic, political, and civic life. Much more than figureheads, Houston's men of

The Houston Chamber of Commerce meets in the captain's quarters, U.S.S. *Houston*, 1934. *Left to right:* William Blanton, J. M. Lykes, James A. Fite, President Gus S. Wortham, Commander E. P. Eldredge, L. S. Adams. Courtesy Greater Houston Partnership.

substance—like former Governor William P. Hobby; George A. Hill, Jr., president of Houston Oil Company; shipping head J. M. Lykes; and Ray L. Dudley, head of Gulf Publishing—ran Chamber committees whose reports and studies often became city policy. Its oft-used sobriquet, "The Powerhouse of the Community," was an ironically apt name for this group of men who literally ruled the city under the guise of a business fraternity. The Chamber's reputation was best summed up in 1936 by a local banker who called it the "focal point through which all action looking to the development of Houston must be cleared."[19]

Joseph Evans's backing coupled with Wortham's own skill with finances and people impressed the Chamber, for just a year later, in December, 1933, Gus Wortham was elected to the Chamber presidency. In fact, Evans later said (perhaps giving away more than he meant to about how power was handed down in Houston), Gus Wortham had been elected to the Chamber board with the idea that he would be the next logical president of the group.[20]

The *Houston Chronicle* editorial lauded Wortham as a "thoroughgoing Houstonian" who proved "through his many community service campaigns that he is indefatigable in his efforts for the public good." Wortham was "noted for his many friends, distaste for making public speeches and personal publicity and for being able to get things done and to make people want to do things for him."[21]

In January, Wortham announced that the Chamber's most important job for 1934 would be to "take advantage of recovery throughout the nation," affirming that it was the only body able to protect the city "during the coming months of intensive competition." As such, it needed the financial support of Houston's businesses and Wortham threatened to conduct an emergency solicitation drive, like the one held the year before, if need be to keep the city on a course of steady development. Wortham's being called upon whenever fiscal or budgetary matters needed rectifying is part of a pattern that can be traced through all his involvements with civic and cultural activities in Houston.[22]

As Wortham took over the Chamber leadership, the organization was busy on several fronts. The traffic manager was asking the Interstate Commerce Commission and the railroads to reconsider a ruling affecting coffee shipments, because the Chamber believed Houston's "spot" coffee market rivaled that of New Orleans. With less than ten thousand of the eligible voters in Harris County having paid their poll taxes, the Chamber was working with the county's executive committee to get one hundred thousand registrants. And the Chamber and Texas Congressman Joe Eagle were meeting with members of the U.S. State Department to ensure that southwestern products be included in reciprocal trade agreements pending with Latin America.[23]

Houston was beginning to achieve status as an urban center, as demonstrated by its selection as one of eight cities to be visited by a Commission of Inquiry on National Policy in International Economic Relations.

During both of Wortham's terms (he was reelected for 1935), Chamber "goodwill" and trade tours were major events. These were journeys by Chamber members and other local businessmen, newspapermen and politicians to areas of Texas, the United States, and even to Mexico, to establish commercial connections or to "sell" Texas.[24]

A major event during 1934 was the Port of Houston's receipt of over a million dollars in federal Public Works Administration (PWA) monies for deepening of the Houston Ship Channel, an ongoing campaign which the Chamber had vigorously supported. Heading the Port Commission during this period was Joseph Evans, whose cotton business depended mightily on access to a major port. In August, the port finished its sixth consecutive season as the world's leading cotton export port. The port also handled growing quantities of crude oil and refined petroleum products from the booming refining complex located on both sides of the ship channel. The Chamber had a special section devoted solely to Port of Houston news in its monthly magazine, *Houston*, and expressed pride that the fifty-mile channel to the Gulf of Mexico had been created in the early years of the century with public funds matched with federal funds. Chamber leadership understood that the continued upgrading of the Houston Ship Channel was vital to the city's development.

Indeed, helping attract federal funds for local projects was a major job of the Chamber, and in 1934 Houston was named as one of the leading cities in getting funds from Harry Hopkins's Civil Works Administration (CWA). This was due primarily to city planning done by government officials and the Chamber's civic improvement committee. The CWA, considered radical by some because it seemed to sanction the belief that government had the responsibility to provide each man a job, was destined to be phased out in the spring of that year. Despite the conservatism and free enterprise spirit of the local business establishment, it is notable that the Chamber was so active in promoting such federal programs as the CWA, PWA, and especially the National Recovery Administration (NRA), which actively sought to lend governmental control to the entrepreneurial spirit. As sociologist Feagin notes, this ability of the business elites to make use of government funding had a long tradition in Houston, notably in financing public works.[25]

The Houston Chamber had an active presence in Washington. For example, in April, 1934, Wortham and Chamber General Manager William N. Blanton, went to Washington to lobby Harry Hopkins and others on the benefits of Houston as a site for its agricultural-industrial homestead relief projects. Their visit to Washington was combined with attendance at the annual U.S. Chamber of Commerce Convention, also attended by several other Houston Chamber members. The group stayed at the Mayflower Hotel, where Wortham and Colonel Evans paid a "courtesy call" on Jesse Jones, now head of the RFC and a Mayflower resident. Despite some concern at the convention about government running over business, the official Chamber policy for 1934 was complete support for President Roosevelt and belief that the New Deal was mostly "sound." Speeches to the national gathering by Jones and Houston banker F. M. Law, head of the American Banking Association, demonstrated the city's influence at the nation's highest business and governmental levels.[26]

Ensuring Houston's influence in those arenas was the reason for the continuing involvement of both Colonel Evans and Wortham with the national Chamber. Evans, who had been a national board member, was up for reelection in 1934 and Wortham wanted a good showing at the national meeting to get Evans reelected. Wortham had recently been appointed a national councilor representing the Houston district and he nominated Evans, believing that no other official had shown as much interest in the affairs of the country as had his friend. While former Houston Chamber president (1931–32) and director H. R. Safford was elected to the national group, Evans lost by just four votes. However, Evans did succeed in being elected to the board as one of only three members-at-large by the committee on nominations, no doubt through Wortham's efforts.[27]

While the push for more government funding to promote growth took center stage, the local Chamber did pay some attention to the basic necessities of life along the bayou. The city seemed in no hurry to fix a recurring flood control problem, despite a serious flood in 1929, but Wortham did call for a government survey to suggest ways flooding might be eliminated. A water bond vote was held in June. Wortham, somewhat belatedly, had gotten on the bond bandwagon, arguing that Houston could not be the best city in the Southwest if its water system was not expanded. True to Chamber ideology, he cited not only the safety issue but the need for cheap water to attract industries and help the city grow. However, the bond issue was defeated, much to the chagrin of State Fire Commissioner Raymond Mauk (whom Wortham later hired).[28]

During his first term, Wortham did the job he was handpicked to do—hold the Chamber together during a particularly difficult time. He encouraged support through what the press called "his remarkable ability to get Houstonians to go to work for the general welfare of their city."[29] Wortham claimed that 1934 was the Chamber's most active year with some seven hundred businessmen serving on its various committees. Reflecting the group's supreme boosterism, he said Houston was on its way to becoming the greatest city in the region. Wortham's public rhetoric often spoke of a vision for the city, a belief in its preeminence in the Southwest and its manifest ability to grow and prosper.

Gus's feeling of confidence in his city was reciprocated by confidence in him from other civic leaders. They reelected him because of his devotion to the job and their belief that his leadership was "urgently" needed for another year; they had been "fortunate . . . to have the wise guidance and aggressive leadership of such a man." During the previous year he had kept the Chamber in the black (actually saving five thousand dollars over the 1933 budget) and had overseen the city's early maneuvers to obtain government recovery largesse.[30]

So, on December 31, 1934, as the rest of the country shivered under the depression's oppressive economic chill, Gus Wortham began his second term by presiding at a Chamber banquet where nearly seventeen hundred Houstonians warmed themselves with the words of favorite son Jesse H. Jones. It was a group unshaken in commercial fervor—the largest Chamber gathering ever—that met in the Civic Auditorium to hear Jones promise "there was no distress that cannot be relieved" and to hear Wortham give the annual state of the city report. The worst of the depression had missed Houston; during its darkest years, the number of business establishments in the city actually grew; 624 in 1934 alone.[31]

Perhaps the Chamber's greatest achievement during Wortham's tenure was the acquisition of federal PWA and WPA (Works Progress Administration) monies to build a twenty-thousand-seat, million-dollar exhibition hall to replace the old Sam Houston Hall, and to erect the San Jacinto monument in honor of the state's hundredth birthday. These were the two major projects of the 183 funded for Houston and environs out of 319 that had been proposed. When the government requested that Houston and environs form a committee to develop and submit plans for PWA and WPA funds, the Chamber set up the Harris County Planning Board, which Wortham chaired, and even hired an engineer to consult on all technical plans. But to ensure that Houston's well-wrought petitions would not get lost among the thousands that reached Washington, Blanton was sent to make contacts at the bureaucracies and interpret and intercede for Houston. Of course, as David McComb points out in his biography of Houston, Jesse Jones had much to do with the city's obtaining the federal monies. Delightedly, Wortham read a telegram from Jesse Jones to the fifteen hundred attendees at the 1935 Chamber banquet that funding had been approved for an exposition hall "without equal" to be built without cost to the taxpayers. Gus Wortham himself would serve as chairman of the board of managers for the building of the coliseum.[32]

The new coliseum would greatly aid two of the most important local economies to which the Chamber was intrinsically tied: oil and cattle. Shell Oil had moved its St. Louis and Dallas offices to Houston in 1933, and the Chamber claimed Houston was at the center of fifty-seven oil fields. In a 1934 issue of *Houston* devoted to industry, oil and cotton vie for editorial space, with petroleum-related businesses claiming 230 of the area's 989 new businesses. In April of 1935, speaking on behalf of the need for planning and "logical development," Wortham said Houston was now "recognized as an oil center." Beginning to realize just what it had in its backyard, the city had hosted its first oil equipment and engineering exposition in 1933. The new exhibition space would greatly aid in making this promotional event a focal point for the growth of all aspects of the industry in Houston.

As for the cattle industry, Wortham's Chamber was the sponsoring agent of the new Houston Fat Stock Show and Rodeo, begun in 1932 to rival Fort Worth's stock show. Here, too, the new coliseum would allow the show to become the best in the nation, ultimately bringing attention and wealth to the vast livestock industry of the region and Houston as a center for beef production and packing.[33]

Although Houston was bitterly disappointed in losing out to Dallas for the site of the 1936 Texas Centennial, it was Jones again who had interceded with Congress to make sure $400,000 of the $3 million appropriated for the celebration was earmarked for a monument at what some believed the central site of the state's history, the San Jacinto battlefield where Sam Houston had defeated Santa Anna.[34]

In December, 1935, Gus Wortham finished his second term as Chamber of Commerce president, again with a record-setting year that saw eight hundred men involved and an audience of fifteen hundred to hear his annual report. Wortham began with the announcement that the "Chamber of Commerce completes the year with all bills paid," and went on to touch on the year's highlights. But he also listed five major projects he believed the city must begin or continue: attracting visitors for the Centennial and opening of the San Jacinto monument, support for the Fat Stock Show, cultivation of good will between Houston and its surrounding trade area, increasing the Chamber budget, and undertaking a comprehensive flood control program. This last had special urgency because just days before, Buffalo Bayou had overflowed its banks causing severe property damage and several deaths. It was the worst flooding the city had seen since 1929, and the Chamber had been "hammering on this subject ever since," Wortham noted. The booster spirit and Wortham's vision for Houston came together as he pronounced that depression should be an "unheard word" and exhorted the participants to work "not only to build a great city, but one in which it will be a happy place for capital and labor to work side by side."[35]

The evening's main address was delivered by staunch Republican, Winthrop Aldrich, president of the country's largest bank, New York's Chase National. His topic was the current business revolution and government fiscal affairs. Before beginning his speech, however, Aldrich tendered an apology because, although Wortham had so greatly praised the Houston Chamber's job of obtaining federal funds for local purposes, Aldrich was going to oppose that very activity in his presentation. Following Aldrich, Wortham rose to say he wanted to correct any impression Aldrich may have gotten. The Houston Chamber of Commerce, Wortham explained, "didn't endorse the spending of $4 billion. We never have. But we were dealing with a fact, not a theory. The money had been appropriated and our interest was in developing a well rounded program of useful, worthwhile projects in Houston and this county. I, too, am old fashioned and I know there is grave danger of the government going too far."[36]

Wortham's comment may have been a brief manifestation of his heralded ability to be tactful, or, it may have been—and most likely was—a true statement of his beliefs. But it was Houston's tradition to seek the involvement of the government at all levels in what Feagin calls "subsidizing private enterprise." Also it foreshadows the growing suspicion that business was having about the New Deal and the increasing intervention of the federal government in private, entrepreneurial life.[37]

As Gus Wortham's tenure as Chamber president ended, it was fitting that speaker George A. Hill, Jr., recalled the memory of John L. Wortham. Hill praised John's son for being "as staunch a man as ever lived in loyalties and friendship," and cited Gus's devotion to his father as evidence. "A thing of beauty," Hill called the relationship, noting that the firm banner still read, some ten years after the father's death, John L. Wortham and Son. "He was a chivalrous gentleman of the old South, beloved by all who knew him. Gus Wortham is a faithful replica of his father." Before the smartly dressed assemblage of Houston's upper crust, Hill talked of the "abiding affection and love" and the "enduring good will" that all present held for Gus Wortham. Colonel

Joe Evans, who claimed the acquaintance of many Chamber of Commerce leaders as a national director, echoed Hill, saying he did not know a better Chamber head than Gus Wortham.[38]

All of Wortham's work at the Chamber of Commerce as head civic booster was in tandem with the efforts his company was making to become "Houston's Own," an image American General had continued to push. In January, 1936, just after stepping down as Chamber head, Wortham held an "appreciation dinner" at the Houston Club to thank Houston insurance agents for writing their business through AG. Four hundred agents, guests, and civic dignitaries attended the dinner, which got good newspaper coverage for the company—including a mention in "Mefo," *Houston Press* editor Maurice Foster's chatty column, which lauded Wortham as a good Chamber president, who was now able to turn his attention to his "big insurance company."[39]

The dinner was a sort of preview party for American General's continued growth throughout the 1930s. There were lean years and pay cuts, and it did better some years than others, but AG was always building. The field force was increased in 1935 and 1936, giving the company representatives in southwest Texas, Austin, Dallas, Fort Worth, and Amarillo, and the agency plants in Houston were increased to ten thousand dollars for 1936, and the company began to write profitable marine and inland marine coverage. At the end of 1936, a twenty-five percent stock dividend of one hundred thousand dollars was declared, with "10,000 shares of capital stock issued at par value distributed pro rata to stockholders." By March, 1937, Wortham had achieved his goal of having one million dollars in capital and surplus. Nineteen thirty-six had proven the company's best year in its ten-year history; it earned over one million dollars in premium volume. AG extended automobile fire, theft, and collision and marine classes into seven states in 1938 to take advantage of an offer by Appelton and Cox of New York to write these classes under their direction.[40]

Wortham believed his investment committee to be the best in the city, and touted AG's ownership of "high grade bonds" and stocks and no real estate. He was proud that the company was covering its dividends "out of investment income by a much larger margin than . . . New York and New England companies." The committee at this time included Wortham, Carruth, Evans, Link, Jr., J. W. Garrow, and Sam Taub.

Keeping a high public profile, and reflecting Wortham's own interest in sports, AG in 1938 sponsored a sports program on KPRC Radio, a poll to select the All-Southwest Conference team, and published a "Dope Book" for football fans. The company also fielded a number of men's and women's teams in sports from bowling to softball.[41]

While the advertising campaigns no doubt helped to keep American General in the minds of agents and buyers, its prestige among business leaders came from its growth out of the highly reputable John L. Wortham and Son agency and the stature of the men involved with that firm. Not just in Houston or even Texas was Gus Wortham known as a smart insurance man. In 1935, the *Eastern Underwriter* profiled him, making note of how he had succeeded on his own, without exploiting his social position or mentioning his original financial backers. The article praised the "steady growth" of American General even through the depression. This was ascribed to "Mr. Wortham's highly intelligent habit of seeking and acting upon the advice of executives of leading eastern companies." Wortham did have a presence in the powerful East.[42]

And it was not solely in the business end of insurance that Wortham had clout, for he also had stature in Austin with the politicians who made the insurance laws. One indication was the hiring in 1936 of Raymond Mauk as company secretary and head of American General's production department. Mauk had been named Texas state fire insurance commissioner in 1932. Because the state mandated the rates and forms, the insurance companies wanted to maintain close ties to the fire insurance commissioner. Mauk became a good friend of Wortham's, by then an experienced insurance man, and came to depend on Wortham for advice.

When Mauk left state employ, the *Houston Post* took it as a sign of better times that a good man would leave the public sector for private enterprises. The editorial went on to laud Mauk as "able, honest and fair." In hiring Mauk, Wortham also added to his group of American General leaders another who was familiar with the state insurance hierarchy, system, and, by association, lawmakers and others in Austin who could influence insurance regulation. Gus's own insurance board background, coupled with the friendships and contacts gained through his father's tenure in Austin, provided him with a unique resource for influencing insurance regulation and legislation involving the industry.[43]

Beyond insurance circles, Gus Wortham's way into the centers of power had been well lighted by his father. Because of John L. Wortham's connections in the Democratic Party and involvement as a state official, Gus had access to the state's most powerful legislators and administrative officials, including the governors and lieutenant governors. He also had ties to most of the Texans who held national office, including John Nance Garner, Sam Rayburn, and Jesse Jones. Wortham capitalized on these ties himself, making it his business throughout his career to find out about and meet important politicians.[44]

His chief political power stemmed from this background and, as he became part of Houston's economic elite, from his association with a small, rather plain suite in Jesse Jones's Lamar Hotel—8F. This two-room suite with kitchenette was rented by Herman and George Brown and used for a variety of all-male activities from card games to deciding which candidates for state or national offices they would support—or oppose. There is no clear date for the beginning of these regular meetings by the men who constituted the "8F crowd," but the group began to coalesce in the 1930s. The core group of leaders included the Browns, Jones, Elkins, Wortham, and W. P. Hobby and his wife, Oveta. Other "members" included oil-field equipment czar, J. S. Abercrombie; merchant Leopold Meyer; railroad and construction tycoon William A. Smith;

Gus S. Wortham, circa 1935. Courtesy American General Corporation.

Lamar Fleming of Anderson, Clayton, one of the world's largest cotton brokerage firms; and attorneys George A. Butler and Charles I. Francis.[45]

Suite 8F was permanently rented to Herman Brown, whose home was in Austin, but who had business in Houston to oversee. A native of Belton, Texas,

Herman had starting driving mules for a construction job, began his own contracting business around 1919, and then gone into partnership with his brother-in-law, Dan Root. They specialized in road and bridge construction. A few years later Herman's younger brother, George, joined the company and set up a branch office in Houston in 1926. Like Wortham, Herman Brown had connections all over the state and was politically active. There is no evidence of how Brown and Wortham met and began doing business together, but Brown & Root was an early customer of John L. Wortham and Son and later American General. Wortham's companies provided surety bond insurance for Brown & Root's construction projects.[46]

Most of the 8F Crowd were long-time members of Houston's business-social elite. This meant that in addition to their business dealings with each other, they regularly participated in civic groups such as the Chamber of Commerce, held memberships in groups like the Houston Club, and supported the city's chief cultural or educational endeavors. Through these other connections they met and talked often in a week's time. As the group began to come into power, it was customary for members to select and support the local, state, and eventually national politicians they thought could best promulgate their group agenda of support for and growth of business interests.

The first major local politician with strong ties to the 8F Crowd was Oscar Holcombe, who served five terms as mayor of Houston between 1922 and 1957; his second term, 1933 to 1937, overlapped Wortham's Chamber presidency. Early on Holcombe was associated with the civic elite; John L. Wortham had given Holcombe a $250 campaign contribution in 1924. Other early contributors to Holcombe from men associated with American General and 8F included Vinson and Elkins, Judge Elkins's law firm, Ben Taub, and J. W. Link. A real estate developer and entrepreneur, Holcombe had a vision for Houston of unlimited growth—a thrust the business interests heartily approved. During his various reigns, Holcombe pushed through major construction programs designed to improve the city's infrastructure and attract more business, industry, and people.[47] Holcombe was one of many local, state, and federal leaders who would seek guidance first with the businessmen in 8F for many years to come.

Texas Congressman Albert Thomas was another important politician supported by 8F. Thomas attended Rice University with George Brown, served as county attorney in his native Nacogdoches County, and came to Houston in 1930 as assistant United States district attorney for the Southern District of Texas. In 1936 he ran against Oscar Holcombe and was elected to the first of his fifteen terms as congressman for the Eighth Congressional District. For most of that time he was the city's only U.S. congressman. It is probable that 8F backed Holcombe in his race against Thomas, but Thomas was acknowledged to have been elected by the labor vote. Gus Wortham believed that once you had a man in office, you must work with him and support him, even though he might not have been your original candidate or might not always vote your way. Although never well-known nationally, Thomas was a good behind-the-scenes wheeler-dealer and was able to secure many federal projects for Houston throughout his thirty years in the House. Thomas served on the powerful House Appropriations Committee from 1941 until his death in 1966. Surely, Wortham's friendship with Thomas and Thomas's longevity in the national government were testimony to his acceptance by Wortham and the other 8F members.[48]

The most famous Texas politician associated with the group was Lyndon Johnson, who was first elected to Congress in 1937 from the Hill Country district around Austin. Herman and George Brown introduced the 8F men to Johnson, who had formerly worked in Washington for Congressman Richard Kleberg and been head of President Roosevelt's National Youth Administration in Texas. Johnson had taught at Houston's Sam Houston High School in 1930 and 1931, where he achieved a small amount of local fame as the school's award-winning debate coach. Whether or not Wortham or any of the group of civic elite in or out of 8F ever knew Johnson during this period before his work for Kleberg in Washington is not known.[49] As Johnson's power grew and as he moved from the House to the Senate, the political power of the 8F suite throughout Texas no doubt increased.

As the son of a southern gentleman establishment figure and as a man who believed in that entrepreneurial challenge, Wortham was the perfect 8F member. His pedigree and business ability had been amply proven; and with his acceptance of the city's most important "volunteer" post, heading the Chamber of Commerce, he had made his profession of faith to the city of Houston. The city's leaders recognized in Wortham a man who shared their commitment to success through economic opportunity and growth. They valued Gus Wortham for his sense of what was going to work and what was the right thing to do. He was the deal maker, the compromiser, the gentleman who represented their ideals. Raymond Mauk summed up what many people believed about the way that Gus Wortham practiced business and politics: "Mr. Wortham was . . . a politician that . . . got things done that nobody else could. . . . He made you like it. He never did ask for anything that shouldn't be done. He was just plain right 98 percent of the time."[50]

CHAPTER FOUR

New Directions

Gus Wortham's leadership in Houston rested on his business success, and he continued to seek new economic opportunities while fulfilling civic duties. The depression had been difficult but it had not ravaged Houston, and the coming of war boosted the economy. Gus Wortham sought ventures that would take advantage of the renewed prosperity of the Gulf Coast. Wortham was a man who liked games of chance that required skill and he trusted change. Belief in change was a necessary part of a man's philosophy, he believed, and there was no way one could, or should, stop it. The best practice was to be open to it and the opportunities it could bring.

During this period, Gus Wortham branched out into several new areas that he felt would ensure the future of his insurance company; toward a variety of smaller, nonrelated businesses that were taking advantage of the area's economic boom; and, finally, toward an avocation that fulfilled a bone-deep tie to the land. What connected all Wortham's various business enterprises was his faith in Houston's growth.

Wortham's first undertaking took him outside his traditional fire and casualty milieu, but it took advantage of the economic changes brought on by World War II. As the United States emerged from the depression and people's buying power was revived, they began to think about purchasing major items like the coveted automobile. Even more importantly, Wortham recognized, with New Deal financing, millions of Americans could now purchase what their parents had perhaps only dreamed of: a home of their own. Wortham saw his opportunity, then, in the formation of an investment firm to "engage in the making of automobile and mortgage loans."

In the beginning, the new subsidiary, American General Investment Corporation (AG Investment), concentrated on the automobile trade. While the Worthams' Automobile Investment Company in the 1920s had unsuccessfully tried the same operation, now there was a ready market. Houston's car ownership was on the increase, with fifty-three hundred more new cars by the end of 1939 than the year before. Other institutions had already begun offering car insurance and financing as a package deal, siphoning business away from American General. By lending money for new cars, the corporation would be in a position to attract the buyer's accident and theft insurance also. At a special meeting of the American General board on April 25, 1939, B. F. Carruth outlined the capitalization of a subsidiary to make automobile and mortgage loans. From the first, Wortham's plan was to make this a wholly owned subsidiary, so the board was advised to sell the stock to American General stockholders with the proviso that it would be held for the parent company, and purchased by it within two years.[1]

American General Investment Corporation was chartered on June 26, 1939, to Wortham, Carruth and J. W. Link, Jr. (who had resigned as American General vice president in 1935, to found his own insurance agency). The new corporation's board of directors included these three and Judge Elkins, J. W. Evans, and Sam Taub—the core of Wortham's legal and investment coterie. Early major stockholders were Vinson and Elkins, Evans, Herman and George Brown, Jesse Jones, and John L. Wortham and Son. Houston newspapers announced the new firm, billing it as an auto finance company that would purchase loans from dealers and finance cars on an installment basis.[2]

Given the corporation's relatively small capitalization of half a million dollars, it made sense to stress the automobile business in the beginning. But Wortham also recognized that eventually the corporation should be heavily involved in home mortgage financing. The Federal Housing Administration (FHA) and the Home Owners' Loan Corporation, formed during the depression, made possible twenty- and twenty-five-year mortgage loans for homes, making home ownership possible for moderate income families. The new long-term, low-interest loans, coupled with the city's population boom because of industrial growth (an increase of almost one hundred thousand between 1930 and 1940) meant there was a huge housing market in Houston.[3]

In August, 1939, Wortham had the AG Investment's board approve its move into the real estate mortgage business. It also qualified as a mortgagee to handle FHA loans. American General Investment's new division made "all types of loans on business and residential property, including FHA loans to build, repair, and remodel." In November, Wortham appointed a locally respected mortgage banker, R. D. "Buck" Walton, as manager of the mortgage loan division.[4]

Wortham's expansion into mortgage financing corresponded nicely with the announcement that same month that Houston ranked first in the United States in residential building per capita and second only behind Detroit in home construction for the first nine months of the year. The city had less than seven percent of the Texas' population and yet it had built twenty percent of the state's residential buildings. Indeed, 1939 would prove to be the biggest year in home construction in the city since 1928.[5]

Gus Wortham having his shoes shined. Courtesy American General Corporation.

In February, 1940, the corporation made an arrangement with Seaboard Life of Houston for AG Investment to originate loans approved by Seaboard's loan committee and sold to them for a bonus of two percent. Also, AG Investment was negotiating with the Teachers Insurance and Annuity Society for the possibility of handling their FHA loans.[6]

That March, nine months after incorporation, Wortham recommended that the parent company, American General Insurance, approve an increase in its own capital stock from fifty thousand to seventy-five thousand shares, and that AG exercise its right to buy the stock of American General Investment from the stockholders. Some of the purchasers of the newly authorized twenty-five thousand shares of parent company stock issued were the Browns; Vinson and Elkins partner Charles I. Francis; R. P. Doherty of the National Bank of Commerce; and merchant Tobias Sakowitz. Shortly after this, the board of the investment corporation authorized a capital stock increase by fifty thousand shares at five dollars per share.

Initially, AG Investment's auto loan division did well; a stock dividend of six cents a share was declared in December, 1939. By summer, 1940, AG Investment's monthly income from automobile financing was around $170,000. However, the problems of nonpayment and repossession became a continuing burden. Despite the doubling in capital and surplus in April, the board was discussing a "more conservative policy" for management on purchasing installment auto loans.[7]

On the other hand, Wortham encouraged the mortgage loan division to expand its operations, and by September, 1940, the board agreed to "push" this business "from every possible angle." In November, the board resolved that AG Investment should do business with the Reconstruction Finance Corporation (headed by Jesse Jones) under Title I of the National Housing Act. By fall, 1941, the local FHA office had already accepted over $12 million in Title I and Title IV mortgages.[8]

In a board meeting held just two days after the bombing of Pearl Harbor, a review of AG Investment business through July showed improved earnings and a small profit for the mortgage loan operations, which meant an indirect profit to the parent company. By January, 1942, it was clear that automobile production would decrease noticeably because of war production, and the immediate future of the investment firm lay with the ever-improving mortgage loan division.[9]

A business boom, stimulated by war preparedness, had a major impact on Houston. Industrial growth that had begun in the 1930s, such as the burgeoning refining and petrochemical industries, accelerated in the late 1930s and 1940s in preparation for war.[10] As early as February, 1941, the Chamber of Commerce boasted of $256 million for plant appropriations and defense contracts. In 1942 Sheffield Steel and Dow Chemical built major installations and George and Herman Brown's shipbuilding enterprise got a $200 million contract. With the world's largest butadiene plant in nearby Port Neches, Houston called itself the Chemical and Plastics Center. In 1944 *Houston* magazine boasted that of the twenty basic industries in the United States, Houston had nineteen. In May of 1945, the Chamber estimated some $38 million in new or expanding industrial construction for the city. New industries brought new jobs and the population increased by over fifty percent between 1940 and 1950 as the city continued to lead the nation in construction.[11]

What it all meant for Wortham's young investment corporation was people needing places to live. The dramatic rise in home construction through the 1940s, coupled with new federal housing programs, made Wortham's timing perfect for the inauguration of a local mortgage banking firm. To finance its real estate loans, American General Investment had entered into collateral loan agreements with local banks and life insurance companies, such as the Seaboard Life arrangement.

Its first major entry into Houston's postwar building boom came on April 16, 1946, with its consideration of a one-million-dollar loan to Frank W. Sharp, Ben Taub, and Douglas McGregor to finance the purchase of 1,147 acres for Oak Forest home sites adjoining Garden Oaks Addition in northwest Houston and to build four hundred homes in Jacinto City's Industrial Addition. Sharp, the developer, was the brother-in-law of Congressman Albert Thomas and Taub was the brother of board member, Sam Taub. Thomas's friendship with Wortham may explain why he approached Wortham's enterprise for the funding.[12]

All of Texas was booming by this time, and in 1947, AG Investment established a Dallas office that four years later had become "almost a separate operation with some 7,000 loans." Satellite offices, serviced through Dallas, were begun in Fort Worth, Lubbock, Abilene, Amarillo, Midland and El Paso. Wortham's hiring of Walton paid off handsomely in 1947 when Walton negotiated a deal with the insurance giant Metropolitan Life. Metropolitan was venturing into the residential loan market and AG Investment, through Walton's contacts, was put squarely in the center of the postwar homebuilding boom in Texas. AG Investment became Metropolitan's correspondent, its Texas agent to solicit, make, and service loans on behalf of the larger company. Eventually, this agreement would cover the whole state excepting San Antonio and Austin. The corporation received millions of dollars from Metropolitan in allotments, and it then developed the business, primarily using FHA and Veterans' Administration loans.[13]

Through foreclosures or other arrangements, the investment operation acquired enough miscellaneous real estate that its officers organized American General Realty in 1951, and in 1954 took over Atlas Realty, which held Wortham's land on Buffalo Drive, from John L. Wortham and Son. AG Realty was also organized to lend money to purchase, sell, and subdivide real estate and to erect or repair buildings.[14]

Whether or not Gus Wortham consciously planned to begin building a financial services empire when he opened his mortgage banking subsidiary, the symbiotic meshing of the loan and insurance interests of his two companies formed a solid foundation upon which he could and would build. People buying houses needed mortgages and insurance, too. The contacts made by AG Investment were a natural source for the insurance agents and Wortham's insurance business prospered accordingly. During these years, parent company American General Insurance shared in Houston's ever-growing prosperity and continued to attract the interest and business of prominent Houstonians. The year 1939 was one of its best years, with the company's expense ratio still below the national average for fire and casualty companies. Wortham also noted that from 1926 through 1939, during "one of the worst depressions in the history of the company," American General had lost only some $19,000 on its invested assets. By August, 1940, parent company investment assets were up almost half a million dollars over the same period the year before.

During the war, American General's business continued to increase. The company had its largest underwriting profit ever, $451,000, in 1942, which was an unusually productive year. Business in 1943 was about the same as 1942, despite a net decrease in premiums written in 1943 due to the leveling off of government construction projects. The company also opened an office in San Antonio's Milam Building that year.

American General was not left out of the military building boom that came with the war; in February, 1941, Wortham asked the board for authorization for the company to do business in New Mexico in order to handle the casualty business for defense contractors working there.[15]

Wortham himself continued to build his reputation among insurance men in the state and around the country. In 1940, he became the first Houston businessman named a director of Dallas's Southwestern Life Insurance Company. Southwestern, founded in 1903, was the second-largest Texas-owned life company (after the Moodys' American National in Galveston).

Another sign of Wortham's leadership in fire insurance circles was the development of a new Texas standard fire insurance policy. In 1944, Raymond Mauk, the former fire insurance commissioner, had streamlined the policy used by all companies in the state, making the difficult legal concepts easier to understand for both agent and customer. Wortham took Mauk's work, and by good politicking with Mauk's successor, Commissioner Marvin Hall, and gaining the support of other fire companies in the state, got approval of the form. Indeed, Mauk and Wortham's new policy got the attention of the eastern insurance establishment. *Insurance Age Journal* in April, 1944, headlined "Texas shows the way to succeed," saying the policy was more streamlined than New York's new policy, and praised its being somewhat "radical" because it showed Texas had the courage to change.[16] "Now, Mr. Wortham is no passive individual and he has 'told off' some of the Northern fire insurance executives. Mr. Wortham is a very successful individual in and out of the fire insurance circles and . . . endeavored to exhibit patience and cooperation with all interests outside of Texas in connection with many Texas problems."[17]

Gus S. Wortham, 1940s. Courtesy American General Corporation.

The magazine predicted Texas' great growth potential and recommended more cooperation between the two insurance areas and "some new blood in the committee representing the interest of the East and Northern companies in Texas." This attention made it clear that Wortham was a known and formidable commodity to the insurance establishment. Since his early days in the business he had made it a practice to meet and get to know people in the fire and casualty business in the East, building a reputation for his company as well as making connections unlike those of almost any other Texas insurance company.[18]

With the institutional changes he was working in his world, Gus Wortham had to expect changes in the personnel, but one change was unwelcome and unexpected: the retirement and sudden death of B. F. Carruth. In the spring of 1940 Carruth, at age fifty, announced his retirement from the companies. Some people believed that Carruth left, or Wortham asked him to leave, because of "personal problems." The press cited the retirement of "one of the best known and most popular insurance men in Houston." But on October 14 Carruth was found dead in the garage of his Houston home. Wortham took over in helping Carruth's wife settle the estate and, as he was already close to the boy, overseeing the career of Carruth's son, Allen, who was a student at the University of Pennsylvania's Wharton School of Business. Gus was grooming the young Carruth as the "heir apparent" to the insurance business. Allen Carruth remembered how, immediately following his father's funeral, Wortham took him for a walk in the Carruths' Montrose neighborhood, reassuring him that things would work out for the young man. Carruth's death was shortly followed by that of John Henry Kirby, one of Wortham's business heroes.[19]

Among other personnel changes, the American General board had added new members, builder and real estate developer E. L. Crain in 1935, and attorney George Butler in 1939. Butler, who was Jesse Jones's nephew-in-law, was involved with Wortham in at least two other business ventures and was also active in state Democratic politics. In the mid-1940s Wortham promoted his trusted corporate lieutenants, Edward and Tom Barrow and Carle Aderman, to the board. Jesse Jones had resigned in 1942 when he was secretary of commerce, due to the press of his work in Washington and for possible conflict of interest issues. He was reelected in 1950 when he returned to Houston permanently.

Carruth's vacancy in the corporation was filled by J. W. Link, Jr., who had merged his agency with John L. Wortham and Son in 1940, become a vice president, and taken over the leadership of the investment company. Link was as prominent a civic and cultural leader as Wortham, and headed a variety of family business interests.[20]

During the volatile years surrounding World War II, Gus Wortham's career seemed to mirror events in Houston itself. Like the city, he was building on, venturing out, discovering new uses for resources, and finding himself in the middle of an economic boom. The investment company was a departure for Wortham, but it was not entirely unprecedented because of Wortham's interest in finance. He had inherited an affection and an ability for watching stocks and bonds from his father, and had been investing since the early days of his career. Also like his father, Gus Wortham experimented with a variety of business ventures.

So it was that during this period, Wortham went in yet other directions, continuing and expanding his involvement in other companies, many of them very much a part of Houston's new economic boom.

Since 1919, either John L. or Gus Wortham had been involved with the Gulf Bitulithic Company, a Houston street-paving contracting company. In 1942 the company benefited from war production by getting a contract, in conjunction with Texas Bitulithic of Dallas, for runways, taxiways, sewers, and drainage in Travis County, site of the state capital, Austin. The contract was estimated at between one and five million dollars.[21]

Probably through Butler, who was the company's attorney, Wortham became involved with J. H. McEvoy and Company, a manufacturer and dealer of oil-field equipment, and was elected president of the firm in 1939. Renamed McEvoy Company, this small company became a leader in war production and earned highly valued government contracts. By 1941, the 35-year-old company employed four hundred people in manufacturing tripods for U.S. Army machine guns. McEvoy received the area's first prime defense contract—awarded directly with the government and not through a subcontractor. In November, 1943, Wortham was presented with the coveted Army-Navy "E" Award for excellence in production of ordnance material, and McEvoy was cited as the first prime contractor of ordnance material in the Southwest. Through his leadership of McEvoy, Wortham was directly involved in the unique liaison of government and private industry that typified the American wartime economy.[22]

Wortham's wide-ranging business involvements included an interest in the Houston Ship Channel and port. In the mid-1930s, through J. Newton Rayzor, Wortham became involved with a small towing company, Butcher-Arthur, that hauled petroleum on the Gulf Intracoastal Waterway. Realizing it was undercapitalized, the firm had approached Rayzor, head of a prominent admiralty law firm, Rayzor and Royston. Wortham had known Rayzor socially for a long time, and as his insurance business expanded to include marine insurance, it is very likely the two became business associates. Rayzor and Wortham both invested capital in the company, allowing it to expand rapidly. The company formed an affiliate, Commercial Transport, and became active in oil exploration and drilling, forming the Oil Lease Operating Company, a production concern. As with Wortham's other interests outside insurance, the war caused business to expand. Because of the menace to oil tankers from German submarines, oil was shipped over the internal route of the Intracoastal Waterway. After the war, the company further expanded to include equipment as well as oil. Butcher-Arthur also acquired Commercial Barge Lines and a trucking concern, Commercial Carriers, which transported cars by truck and barge from auto plants in the North to Memphis, New Orleans, and Houston. Sometime in the late 1950s, Butcher-Arthur became Commercial Petroleum and Transport. Later still, it was refunded through "Eastern capital," and became American Commercial Lines and listed on the New York Stock Exchange.

Wortham kept his interest in the firm for some forty years, serving as an officer with E. R. Barrow through the 1950s. He gave the firm his financial and investment expertise and was the conduit for "sources of capital." In turn, the company's insurance business was all done through the John L. Wortham and Son Agency. In the early 1950s, Wortham began the Davis Barge Company with his two nieces, Fanny and June, as his partners, in order to make the young women some money.[23]

A major investment in time and money for Wortham during the period of the late 1930s and early 1940s was the Longhorn Portland Cement Company of San Antonio. His ownership of the company came out of an even longer, more complicated involvement in the business affairs of his customer and friend, the late Jim Smith. As a stockholder and creditor of Smith Brothers Properties, Wortham purchased the cement company from the estate in receivership. This was just one facet of nearly a decade's work by Wortham to save and make a profit of Smith's several business ventures after his death in 1930.

Brothers J. H. (Jim) and F. A. (Albert) Smith of Crockett, Texas, had organized Smith Brothers, Incorporated in 1916, and its earliest work involved building tram railroad lines throughout East Texas, which were used by lumber interests such as those of J. H. Kirby and J. M. West in clearing big tracts of land. After the development of a state highway system, Smith Brothers expanded into road construction. Paving operations included work in Kansas and Florida, and they had two offices in Texas, at Dallas and San Antonio. They expanded rapidly into other kinds of construction, especially hotels, and got into ranching and real estate development.

Smith Brothers Properties was formed in 1923 to handle real estate in San Antonio. That year, Jim Smith became a member of the board of Jesse Jones's National Bank of Commerce. Jones financed various Smith Brothers construction projects. Gus Wortham bought twenty-five thousand dollars in the company in 1924, and in 1927 was a board member of Smith Brothers Properties. That same year Smith Brothers began constructing buildings on the real estate owned. By 1929, the Properties' stock increased to $4 million and the Wortham-Carruth partnership owned over sixteen hundred shares of common stock valued at $169,000. Eventually, Smith Brothers Properties had several important pieces of property in San Antonio, including the Plaza Hotel and garage, A. B. Frank Building, Smith-Young Tower, and the Montgomery Ward building, and they began the Republic Portland Cement Company in 1929. They also owned the Plaza Hotel in Corpus Christi.[24]

In December, 1930, because of financial trouble with his businesses, Jim Smith committed suicide, supposedly after securing a big life insurance policy which never paid off. Albert was still alive and a member of Wortham's American General board, but took no active part in the reorganization of the company. Rather, it was Wortham who spearheaded a drive to keep some portion of his friend's businesses going.[25]

Hewing to two loyalties, one personal, the other financial, Wortham vowed to make some money from properties that he believed could be saved, rather than accept bankruptcy and loss of his own sizeable investment. Although it involved businesses in which Wortham had no special expertise, his preoccupation with these enterprises showed his considerable strengths in investment, financing, and manipulation of people. Wortham displayed not only his father's gentlemanly loyalty to an old friend, but also his business acumen in involving several of his current business associates in rebuilding the assets and thus making a profit. The southerner's sense of duty blended well with the southwesterner's willingness to risk new ventures.[26]

Wortham was both stockholder and creditor of Smith's business interests, and one of five trustees of the estate who managed it until it was put in receivership in 1932. The plan was to keep the estate in operation until its proceeds could be disposed of without great loss, but by 1933, the Smith Brothers Properties Company was unable to meet its mortgage, interest, and tax payments. The mortgage and bondholders took over the Properties Company property; the stock lost all value. The principal property of the partnership was the Plaza Hotel in San Antonio, which was experiencing bad times.[27]

Gus Wortham believed the partnership assets should be distributed to the creditors, John L. Wortham and Son being among the largest. The creditors would buy the only major assets of worth, stock in the Properties Company (the hotel and buildings in San Antonio) and the Republic Portland Cement Company of San Antonio.[28] In November, 1936, a group representing the Smith Brothers' stockholders and lienholders formed Century Investment Corporation (CIC) to manage the estate's assets. Wortham, Butler, and construction company head R. W. Briggs of San Antonio were the incorporators. Other shareholders in CIC included George R. Brown, who with his brother Herman, owned Brown & Root construction company, and the McKenzie Construction Company. To raise the cash to purchase the assets, Century borrowed money from the banks owning stock who were original creditors.[29]

This remained the status of the properties until 1937, when a significant mortgage lien was foreclosed. CIC then formed a new company, the Plaza Company, to acquire title to all the foreclosed Smith Brothers Properties, reorganize them, and provide for the air-conditioning of the Plaza Hotel. Each preferred stockholder of Smith Brothers Properties received shares in the Plaza Company.[30]

Century Investment liquidated the assets of Smith Brothers to pay a percentage of the creditors' debts. Among these assets was the Republic Portland Cement Company. Wortham opposed its sale because he saw its future profitability, but when the group decided to sell its stock anyway, Wortham, Butler, and associates bought it.[31]

In December, 1939, Wortham and Butler, Briggs, the Brown brothers, and W. M. Thornton, the cement company's manager, formed WTB Corporation as a holding company, purchasing the interests and stock of CIC and the Smith Brothers' estate and becoming the CIC's single largest shareholder. Jones's National Bank of Commerce, which held the note, became the sixth partner in

1940. Herman Brown became president of Century Investment. The corporation's major asset was its common stock ownership in the Plaza Hotel in San Antonio. Wortham was anxious for the WTB group to increase its stock investment in Plaza, predicting that the increased military installations in the area would expand the hotel's business.[32]

Wortham labored long and hard throughout the early 1940s to reorganize the assets and make profitable loan arrangements in order to make money and reduce taxes for the stockholders of the Plaza properties and for the WTB group. In December, 1942, WTB was liquidated and the Plaza Company stock sold to the WTB stockholders including Wortham.[33]

Meanwhile, the cement company flourished under Wortham's leadership, in part because cement was an important wartime commodity, but also because of Wortham's business and political connections and financial expertise. As a result of these same connections, the cement company was involved with a number of people, issues, and events of importance to Houston and Texas.

Wortham knew little about the cement business, relying on Thornton, who had himself been a contractor. The Brown brothers and Briggs, in addition to having financial interests in former Smith Brothers Properties assets, were the heads of substantial paving and construction companies bound to need materials from the newly renamed Longhorn Portland Cement Company (LPC). Wortham offered the stock to these men at what he had paid for it and, as these men gave their business to Longhorn, the stock's value went up.[34]

During the early years, government and defense jobs were a big part of the company's quota. In 1940, the company was asked to "participate in the dirt work on the Marshall Ford Dam." The construction of this dam on the Colorado River near Austin was Brown & Root's first major government project. In its later stages, additional federal funding was secured through the help of the Brown's political protégé, Congressman Lyndon Johnson. (Wortham may have also been a Johnson supporter by this date.) There is evidence that American General Insurance was involved in part of the surety bonding business for Brown & Root on this project.[35]

War production greatly affected the cement plant's operation; by 1942 its business was almost evenly split between commercial and government customers. And the company actively sought to provide cement for projects such as construction of the Coast Artillery Replacement Center at Alta Loma and the Air Training Base at Victoria. Longhorn bid on work at the Eagle Pass Air Force Base and was supplying jobs at Concho Airfield, San Angelo; Kelly and Duncan Fields in San Antonio; Seadrift at Matagorda Island; and Randolph Field at San Antonio. By the end of 1942, company production passed one and a half million barrels for the year—a goal Wortham would have thought impossible five years earlier. Indeed, Gus Wortham's bet on the cement company had paid off handsomely. In August, 1942, he was named to the National Advisory Committee for Portland Cement Companies, the group that conferred with the Office of Price Administration on price controls in the cement industry.[36]

The company had an "inside track," with two major construction company owners as stockholders, but Wortham also counted on his business and political ties. A hunting party in November, 1942, included Wortham; the Browns; builders Bellows and Briggs; Texas politician Scott Schreiner (a member of the Longhorn board); State Senator Rudolph Weinert; and A. J. Wirtz, a confidant of Congressman Johnson, lawyer for Brown & Root, and former undersecretary of the interior. And Wortham got information from Congressman Albert Thomas in May, 1943, about submitting bids for a 150,000-barrel order for Corpus Christi, for which LPC received half the quota on the bid.[37]

Labor and union issues were volatile in Texas during these years, and the cement company involved Wortham in them. In 1941, a suit was filed against Longhorn with the National Labor Relations Board but later dismissed and in 1943 the company was in litigation with the United Cement, Lime and Gypsum Workers Union over wage increases and collective bargaining. The following year, when the company did not want to give bonuses to hourly wage earners, union trouble was again expected.[38]

Leadership of the cement company also involved Wortham in the plethora of governmental regulations and systems that came with any business producing a commodity deemed necessary for national security. But Wortham found the price structure satisfactory, and, in 1942, admonished Thornton that the company had a "duty to supply as much to the war effort as possible, irrespective of the effect on our business."[39]

The federal government accelerated its antitrust activity during the later New Deal years, and the cement industry was one of its targets, especially its advocacy organization, the Cement Institute. Longhorn Portland Cement and San Antonio Portland Cement were involved with the Texas Attorney General's office in a price-fixing suit in 1939. The case was settled with a fine and a compromise injunction because both cement companies denied collusion to fix prices and stiff competition.[40] In 1944, the company was again under federal scrutiny. Wortham told Thornton that a "commodity like cement, must, in the great majority of all instances, sell at the same price," but added that if the business had always been conducted as it is now being . . . I do not believe the industry would be confronted with anti-trust suits."[41]

In the fall of 1945 Longhorn was an original respondent in a suit filed in U.S. District Court in Denver by the attorney general. It was brought to keep cement companies from violating the Sherman Antitrust Act through the use of the multiple basing price point system. Vinson and Elkins attorney and AG stockholder Charles I. Francis worked to achieve the dismissal of Longhorn from the suit and talked with Attorney General Tom Clark of Texas, a close friend and political confidant of Lyndon Johnson.[42]

Near the war's end, Longhorn sought the business of Houston's growing chemical industry, and Wortham used his connections with an 8F crony, Jim Abercrombie, to attempt to get the cement business of a new gasoline plant in which Abercrombie had invested.[43] Wortham also sought to do business with oil wildcatter Glenn McCarthy, the man destined to become Houston's major postwar personality.[44]

Although a peripheral venture, Wortham's presidency of Longhorn Portland Cement (which he sold to Kaiser Cement in 1965) managed to put him in the middle of many issues important to the American economy in the 1940s, as well as making valuable use of his already high-powered political and economic connections at the state and national level. Its history also is a good example of the way men like Wortham worked: being brought in on lucrative ventures through the network of economic elites, finding competent men to handle the primary operations, while using other resources of the economic and political networks to ensure profitability.

Indeed, Wortham's two decades of work with the Smith Brothers' estate clearly demonstrated that Gus Wortham was a competent and determined capitalist. His aggressiveness and inventiveness as he offered management and financial advice to his partners and his ability to compromise with others are exhibited throughout. A most important aspect of the Smith Brothers revitalization was Wortham's association with men such as Butler and the Brown brothers, who were up-and-coming Houston power brokers, and also with major capitalists and bank owners of Dallas, all part of his network of powerful Texans.

This tie with the Browns helped pull Wortham into ranching, which came to rival insurance as the chief interest of his later years. Wortham had long held a passion for the land, probably born in his father's own farming venture, and nurtured by those months at the Box T. But not until 1944, when Gus was in his mid-50s, did he move to acquire large ranching properties.

Typically, there was no grand gesture in Gus Wortham's first purchase of land that would become a farming and ranching empire. In 1944, he and Herman and George Brown had been casting about for some land in which to invest. He contacted Sterling Evans, president of the Houston Land Bank, about a ranch in the Panhandle that the bank had in foreclosure. Before they could see the land it was sold, and Evans, seeing Wortham's disappointment, called him several days later about another property. The bank had a loan on the place, and Evans knew the owner was in trouble and would soon need to sell. He accompanied Wortham to the three-thousand-acre site on the Little River in Milam County. Despite its rundown appearance and poor equipment, the river bottom land had possibilities, Evans told Wortham. Wortham suggested paying thirty-five dollars an acre; Evans concurred. But, Wortham hesitated; this was a lot of land. He turned to Evans and asked him if he was interested in being a partner in the proposition. Evans was taken by surprise, but agreed if the two would divide the land into two separately owned parcels. Wortham, however, wanted to "work together" on the project as a whole, so Evans agreed.

Sterling C. Evans. Courtesy American General Corporation.

It was the beginning of a partnership of over twenty-five years in which Wortham provided the capital and Evans the ranching management expertise.[45]

Sterling Evans had been in agriculture his whole life. After graduating from Texas A&M in 1921, he had taken a job as a youth club leader for A&M's Agricultural Extension Service. A few years later he became a district agent, in charge of thirty-four county agents for the Extension Service. In 1934 he became the first head of the Bank for Cooperatives, a subsidiary of the Land Bank of Houston, and in 1940 became president of the Land Bank itself.[46]

There is no record of when Wortham and Evans actually made each other's acquaintance, although it was probably through routine business because of John L. Wortham and Son's fidelity bond business with the land bank. Evans started his career in banking in Houston in 1934, and was certainly aware of Gus Wortham, then president of the Chamber of Commerce. Wortham called Evans a devoted friend before their partnership began, and thought enough of him to break one of his "staunchest rules" against partnerships.

On May 4, 1944, Wortham and Evans recorded their partnership investment of a little over twenty-nine thousand dollars in six tracts of land, 3,246 acres, in Milam County; they called it Randle Lake Plantation. They had a Federal Land Bank loan of almost fifty-seven thousand dollars. From the beginning, it was to be a working farm and ranch, so Evans hired a resident manager who worked under his direction. This ranch, and the several others that followed, were an interesting combination of vocation and avocation for Wortham. He did not like to hear his ranching business called a "hobby"; these lands were a business run for profit. But people who observed Wortham at this "business" could see that it was clearly a way for him to "get away," to nurture another part of Gus Wortham. Wortham was not an accomplished rancher, but he had learned from his time at the Box T, and he was able once again to choose a partner whose assets made up for his own deficiencies. He relied on Evans's agricultural expertise but made sure he knew what was happening on the land.[47]

It did not take Wortham long to realize, if he had not earlier, that ranching's main attraction for him was the raising and breeding of cattle. Just a month after they had purchased the land, Evans wrote to Senator Houghton Brownlee of Burnet, on Wortham's suggestion, regarding some Hereford cows the senator had for sale. It was an example of the Texas business-legislative network, and how "the ranch" was another part of that set of connections.[48]

The ranch took shape quickly. Evans expected to plant eight hundred acres in the fall of 1944, including clover, oats, and winter peas. Although he had mentioned some interest in Brahman cattle for the Central Texas land and had considered Brownlee's herd, Evans decided because of a lack of skilled personnel to handle the animals, to purchase some fifteen hundred head of steer cattle. The farm had two tractors and two windmills and, by November, they had begun making hay for winter grazing. A January, 1945, accounting by Evans to Wortham listed an estimated 756 calves worth thirty-seven dollars each and a net expense for the property for 1944 of $10,204. The next summer Evans added bees, honey, and pecans to the farm inventory, new calves, and, at the end of the year, another 145 acres (eventually, the ranch would include almost forty-two hundred acres).[49]

When Evans reported the profit for 1946 at just over thirteen thousand dollars, (the first two years saw losses of ten thousand and five thousand dollars respectively) Wortham said he believed Randle Lake to be one of the best ranch properties he knew, all due to "your foresight in purchase and improvements." By the end of 1948 the farm's livestock included 474 steer calves, 404 yearlings, four milk cows, thirteen horses and ten pigs.[50]

A venture begun in 1949 to raise turkeys illustrates how ranching was a element of Gus Wortham's regular business connections. Evans became interested in turkeys as a preventative to an expected crop devastation by grasshoppers. Not only did the turkeys help save the crop, but in December, 1951, Wortham was greatly pleased to see that the return on an investment in birds had paid off at seventy-five hundred dollars. "Everyone, including Judge Elkins (who had his own ranch), says that you can't make money out of turkeys," Wortham continued. "I am sending a copy of the report to the Judge so that he will be prepared to loan us money on our next year's turkey crop." The ranching operation often came up with Wortham's closest business associates, many of whom themselves had major farm or ranch holdings.[51]

It did not matter if the Texan's fortune was in oil, medicine, or retail; land ownership was almost a prerequisite component for the "complete" successful businessman. Many of Houston's business elite, like Wortham and Elkins, had grown up in rural Texas and as they became successful, purchased ranches or "estates" on which they carried on various agricultural and recreational activities. Elkins's farm was near his hometown, Huntsville. George and Herman Brown owned several parcels of ranch land where they entertained business hunting parties, in addition to a huge estate outside Washington D.C. *Houston* magazine estimated hundreds of such properties around the state were owned by prominent Houstonians such as Cullen, Fondren, Neuhaus, Sartwelle, Bertner, Underwood, and Sakowitz. The fact that Wortham and Evans's relatively new ranching venture received mention in this article was an acknowledgement of their reputations and the quality of their property.[52]

By January, 1953, Randle Lake Plantation was a thriving operation: pastures of oats and clover ready for grazing and then maize planting, "good red heifers," bulls "on the mend," twenty-seven calves with several expected, a new bridge over the Little River, and an abundant cotton crop.[53]

But it was because of his beloved "red" cattle that Wortham's ranch won its highest acclaim. These were the Santa Gertrudis cattle that Wortham and Evans began to acquire in the 1950s. Originated in the 1920s at the King Ranch, the Santa Gertrudis was the first recognized North American breed of beef cattle. A cross between Brahman and shorthorn cattle, the breed was the culmination of an attempt to find an animal that could withstand the high temperatures and long droughts of the South Texas ranch country. Officially recognized in 1940, the Santa Gertrudis breed became popular enough to warrant the foundation of its own breeders' association.

Whether Evans or Wortham first became attracted to the animals is not known, but Wortham believed people liked the "big and serviceable" red cattle more than dairy types. Late in 1952, they bought purebred Santa Gertrudis bulls from the San Antonio ranch of Wortham's cement company partner, R. W. Briggs, and females from C. Hunter Strain in San Angelo. Bulls were also purchased from the King Ranch.[54]

Wortham was savvy and careful regarding the financial operations and repercussions of this business. To purchase the original breeding stock of Santa Gertrudis, Wortham proposed that he loan the Evans-Wortham partnership $27,000 for five years at three percent interest. Aware of tax considerations, he cautioned Evans to set down a careful record of the purchase so as not to cause "the Internal Revenue Department to limit our breeding herd to the Santa Gertrudis Cattle."[55]

To develop their own breeding herd of Santa Gertrudis, Wortham and Evans "sav[ed] back the increase from their own herds" and acquired cattle from other quality Santa Gertrudis herds. Wortham explained that "by cross-breeding dumpy Herefords with long, rangy Santa Gertrudis" they produced a handsome animal that upped the partnership's "meat production for market sale." The key to the quality herd was also one of the wisest cattle purchases Evans and Wortham ever made. It was El Capitan, a bull bred on the King Ranch and owned by rancher Payne Briscoe. Evans had been watching the bull for some time and told Wortham the animal was the best in South Texas and a good herd sire to start the quality herd they wanted to breed. El Capitan was a prepotent bull, with the genetic capacity to produce offspring that looked like him. About 1954 the partnership paid five thousand dollars for a half-interest in El Capitan. "He is what may be termed a magnificent animal," Wortham said some ten years after the bull's death, noting that he'd had a "great head, great style, pride, and a wonderful disposition."[56]

Randle Lake remained the prime ranching property for Wortham until 1955. It was there that in November, 1954, Wortham and Evans held the first of what would become major annual Texas ranching events—their production sales of Santa Gertrudis cattle and quarter horses. The precedent for the sales was probably established by the King Ranch's first auction of Santa Gertrudis in 1950. They advertised in the trade publications, using the "9 bar" brand developed by Evans, and mentioning the ranch's landing strip (a fact which underscores the wealth of their ranching circle.)[57]

There clearly was more to the ranching business for Wortham than overseeing a money-making agricultural concern. Given his commandment that to be in business demanded success, profitability was very important. But underneath lay Gus Wortham's "fascination" with land. One his axioms about land—"they aren't making any more of it"—was his homemade explanation for this pursuit. So he and Evans continued to look for good land to possess, at a good price. Finally, in 1955, after considering land in Arkansas and other areas, the partnership bought two plantations (farms) in Louisiana, where good land was cheap. Crescent Plantation near Tallulah in northwest Louisiana consisted of about 1,750 acres of Mississippi delta land and a stately antebellum

El Capitan, the Nine Bar's famous Santa Getrudis bull. Courtesy American General Corporation.

home. They paid one hundred dollars per acre, a price their land agent thought too high.[58]

In October, 1955, their purchase of the Chopin (renamed Little Eva) Plantation, eight thousand acres on the Red River at Natchitoches, made headlines. Evans and Wortham paid half a million dollars for the property, purported to have been the home of Robert McAlpin, the man upon whom Harriet Bee-

Diana, Lyndall and Gus Wortham at dedication of black Baptist church at Little Eva, May, 1957. Sterling Evans standing at center. Courtesy American General Corporation.

cher Stowe based Simon Legree, the villain of *Uncle Tom's Cabin*. In addition to an antebellum house, the property included the former homes of black sharecroppers and a small black church.[59]

In between the two purchases in Louisiana, Wortham acquired some three thousand acres at Cypress, Texas, about thirty miles north of Houston on Highway 290. Its proximity to the booming market of Houston was perfect for it to become the showplace ranch that Wortham intended, where the truly "top Certified Purebred Santa Gertrudis cattle were kept." He called it the Nine Bar Ranch and although he alone owned it, Evans was its manager. In 1957 he brought El Capitan to the Nine Bar to be the herd sire for the partnership's main purebred breeding operation.[60]

In 1959 the partnership purchased a farm at Crystal City in South Texas and 8,300 acres in Madison Parish, Louisiana, known as Bear Lake. The latter property was clearly purchased as an investment, for Wortham and Evans did not develop it, except to erect a marker at the spot where Theodore Roosevelt had supposedly shot a bear in 1907. Other land purchases followed including extensive holdings in New Mexico. Wortham owned other pieces of ranch and farm land on his own that were not part of the partnership. Randle Lake was sold to K. S. "Bud" Adams, Jr., in 1962 and other properties were sold in the years following, but by that time the Nine Bar Ranch at Cypress had become the zenith of the Wortham-Evans collaboration; an agricultural, business, and society-page success.[61]

Land for Wortham symbolized something of permanence. His ranching and other properties near and in Houston tied him to the area in a way that his financial empire did not, offering him the chance not only to own part of the city, but also to leave something of himself in its formation. Land ownership allowed him to test his own hypothesis about Houston's future growth; indeed it endowed him with a certain power in the determination of that growth, and he looked for "good locations" where growth was a possibility. Whatever Wortham felt about Houston's potential to become bigger, more important, more prosperous, and however much he felt population and business were keys to its future, underneath—the basis for it all—was land.[62]

American General Investment, involved with land and homes, and Wortham's ranching operations were tangible proofs of these desires, as by the late 1940s he saw them begin to succeed. They also fulfilled a need for change in Wortham. This change was always based on Wortham's confidence in the ultimate goodness of growth. Also, his investments of expertise and money in a myriad of smaller, nonrelated businesses fulfilled yet another need in Wortham. Often in partnership with fellow members of Houston's civic elite, these ventures gave him the opportunity to use his finance and people skills.

But despite moving in a number of new directions during these years, Gus Wortham was in no way bored with insurance. Indeed, for his beloved company, American General, he was considering a new direction; again, a change tied to growth. And this new venture would be in insurance itself, not a related subsidiary.

Even if the opportunity to acquire a viable life insurance company located in Houston had not come along, Wortham would have looked elsewhere for a life firm. He saw the life field as "profitable" and "predictable," with a very positive future. Since the government's establishment of the U.S. Government Life Insurance Program in 1919, the demand for life insurance had grown dramatically.[63]

Wortham finally focused on "Houston's Own," Seaboard Life, a company that shared not only American General's slogan, but also two of its directors and much of its business philosophy. By the time Seaboard was founded in 1925, life insurance, although considered somewhat of a luxury for all but the upper middle and upper classes, was a solid and conservative business venture.

Aged forty-six when he began Seaboard, Burke Baker had already had two successful careers, one in Houston working for Jesse Jones, the other out of state. When the president of Southwestern Life of Dallas suggested that Baker and his father, Colonel R. H. Baker—himself a successful former insurance executive and businessman—headquarter a company in Houston, Burke found a solution to his search for a solid business in a city he loved.

Seaboard's founding was similar to American General's, including the subscription of stock by Jesse Jones and J. W. Evans. Like Wortham, Baker surrounded himself with a board made up of prestigious Houston businessmen. By 1944, under conservative direction and investment, Seaboard Life had blossomed into a solid, somewhat self-righteous ("Insurance is a public trust" was the motto) institution with a reputation as a small company of real quality. Central to the company's strength was its investment policy which allowed carefully guarded mortgage and real estate investments and high-quality bonds; no stocks. In 1931 it was the first company in the United States to receive an "A" rating from Alfred M. Best of New York, and Dun and Bradstreet of insurance. Even during the depression and throughout the war, the company reported increased sales and by early 1945 had over $45 million of life insurance in force.[64]

Seaboard's reputation of being "impeccably run," plus its position in the booming Texas market, made it a good target for acquisition by other companies. This was obvious to a group of Houston investors who tried to put a plan together and to Benjamin Woodson, executive vice president of Commonwealth Life Insurance Company of Louisville, Kentucky. Prior to joining Commonwealth, Woodson had served Seaboard as a consultant from the Life Insurance Agency Management Association and was well acquainted with Burke Baker. Woodson wanted Seaboard for Commonwealth, but Baker and Seaboard vice president Davis Faulkner were not at all interested. Not only did Baker not want to sell, he definitely did not want to sell to a "foreign" company; he believed Seaboard's future was in Texas. Woodson did not pursue the acquisition, but his inquiry stirred some activity in other quarters.

Colonel J. W. Evans, a member of both Baker's and Wortham's boards, knew of Woodson's proposal too, and it was probably he who told Wortham. Meanwhile, Baker was giving serious consideration to Seaboard's shareholders, whose investments in the company had increased, but who, because the stock was not publicly traded, could not realize a profit on them. The company's sale would change this. Evans and Sam Taub (also a member of both boards), despite Seaboard's fine reputation, were "dissatisfied" with its "progress." Most reports say it was Evans who supported a merger for Seaboard and told Baker that it was needed for capital and leadership. And, Evans reasoned, if it had to be in Texas, the only sensible merger was with Gus Wortham's firm.[65]

Discussions with the two board members of both firms, whose financial advice Wortham highly valued, encouraged him to approach Baker and Seaboard about merging the two companies. On June 4, 1945, Wortham presented

Burke Baker, founder of Seaboard Life Insurance Company. Courtesy American General Corporation.

a proposal for merger to a special committee of directors of Seaboard Life. Its first paragraph emphasized the trend toward "company organizations that . . . offer facilities for writing all forms of life insurance."[66]

Seaboard's assent to the merger came quickly, for it was announced on June 15 in an American General press release which emphasized the prominence of the boards and stockholders of each of the companies, as well as the new company's ability to write "fire, life, automobile, casualty and surety insurance"—the only company in the South with facilities to do such. The institution formed would have surplus and capital of over $3 million and assets of $12 million. In a memo to American General stockholders, who were to give final approval on June 26, Wortham called the merger "one of the most important and profitable [steps] in the history of the company."[67]

With this addition, American General became one of the first fire and casualty companies to go into the life insurance business. State insurance laws prohibited companies from writing both kinds of insurance, but American General helped pioneer the plan whereby a parent organization owned the separate companies. Like his earlier initiative with multiple-line underwriting, Wortham again stretched the boundaries of what was possible in the business by combining life and property-casualty-fire under the same corporate entity, although American General and Seaboard Life were separate companies. Beyond the profits to be made in the growing life field itself, Wortham was no doubt aware that the addition of a life company could open up new fire and casualty profit sources.[68]

In the merger negotiations, Wortham had stressed the familiarity of the people involved: "We know its officers and directors, and they know the people affiliated with our company." These connections made possible certain baseline assumptions about ways of conducting business that would not have to be negotiated. Seaboard's directorate was as socially elite, civic-minded, and economically influential a group as American General's, and both companies, "numbered among their stockholders some of the most prominent business interests in Houston and the Southwest." One group of Houston's elite was merely joining another. Wortham pointed out that when companies' leaders could agree on such a plan, a majority of the stock should be handled as a unit. Because of this and a desire to benefit stockholders in both firms, Wortham was able to devise a simple exchange of stock in which Seaboard stockholders would receive twelve and one-half shares of American General for every one share of Seaboard. Wortham had pointed out in his proposal that the market reaction to the proposed merger had caused American General's stock to increase in selling price, if any investors wanted to sell their AG stock. Wortham also warned that a decision needed to be made quickly, or the worth of Seaboard's stock would be in jeopardy.[69]

Perhaps the most striking element of the merger was the clear statement that there would be no drastic change in management; Baker and his "key personnel" would continue in the organization, in their same positions. This may have been predictable, given the closeness of the people involved and the relative lack of expertise in life insurance by Wortham and his staff, but it was still important that this be stated so explicitly. It was to become one of the hallmarks of American General mergers in the future.[70]

The decision to make no drastic personnel changes with the new component went together with a purposeful downplaying of the term "merger" by

Wortham. Wortham wanted no statement that American General was "buying out" the Seaboard; rather, "from the beginning we want to create a spirit of unity." It was such an amicable joining that it was remembered in company lore as just a natural sort of amalgamation.[71]

Although Seaboard's leaders remained in their positions, there was no doubt that Wortham was ultimately in charge, despite his unfamiliarity with the intricacies of life insurance. Insurance was insurance. He wasted no time in being briefed on company progress and setting out on his planned expansion program for Seaboard: "Present economical operating plan has held back the development of additional agents and territories and has not permitted the necessary increase in annual premium volume. The answer to the problem seems to be a material increase in business in force in order to lower the percentage of fixed expenses to insurance in force."[72]

Another area that needed improvement was investment returns, a field where Wortham's competence was well known. Low interest and dividend rates caused a problem. Seaboard had very little stock in its investment portfolio and Wortham asked Baker to consult with other life men about their preferred stock investments.[73] Home mortgages had long been considered a safe investment for insurance companies and Seaboard had been most conservative in choosing its mortgage investments. With the merger, Wortham offered Seaboard the chance to buy most or all of American General's own mortgages, but he was careful to reassure Baker that this portfolio was of high quality. He asked Baker to think about the life company taking the whole list of mortgages at par value.[74] Wortham's involvement with the new firm was at all levels, and his leadership style firmly established his position while not impinging upon the responsibilities or capabilities of his senior officers.

Apparently Seaboard's executive committee had some questions as to just how involved the American General leadership was to be. Wortham said he believed that the guarantee of his and J. W. Link, Jr.'s active participation in company matters had been a major influence in the board's decision to merge. The board and committees were looking to them to "take the lead in the formulation of new plans and policies that would result in a substantial expansion of the company's business." Once again, he emphasized that this could happen "without detracting from the position of anyone in the Seaboard organization." Wortham made clear his vision for the merged companies as "really one institution" and that those who had questions about the lines of authority should read and discuss his memo.[75]

Perhaps it was the excitement and expectations of new ownership, but whatever, even as early as that fall, there was tremendous growth of over half a million dollars in new business over the same period in 1944. Wortham wrote Vice President Davis Faulkner how much of a "kick" he got out of this news, but also stressed the importance of production and the "crying need . . . for the development of more good salesmen," putting in a good word for the hiring of returning servicemen.[76]

If there was any question that Seaboard Life had become an American General entity, it was settled when the life company changed its name four months after the merger to American General Life Insurance Company. Burke Baker assured his employees that the change was not "taken hurriedly" and was made with his approval. He waxed slightly eloquent about the worth of a name versus the "character, management and reputation" of the firm, all of which remained unsullied. He said that good business sense, plus the fact that American General was spending some thirty-five thousand dollars a year on advertising, just made it the thing to do. With over five hundred agents in Texas and offices in several cities, the American General name would open new doors to the life company all over the state, he said.

Baker also announced that a half-million dollars in cash was being added to the company's capital and surplus account. Obviously, Wortham wanted the Seaboard people to know that he was serious when he promoted growth for the company. This influx of funds made the company one of only eight life insurance companies in Texas "with surplus protection to the policyholders of over one million dollars." Nineteen forty-five was the life company's most successful year in history.

By early 1947, American General Life was involved in a serious expansion policy. In his "Report to Directors" Wortham noted increases in new paid-for business from $9 million to over $22 million and in total insurance in force from $48 million to $65 million. There was the addition of three managers, twenty-eight full-time and forty-eight part-time agents, and increases in equipment, office space and salaries, but Wortham stressed confidence that "the new business acquired last year was worth considerably more than it cost."[77]

Nine months later, in December, Wortham again touted AG Life's growth. Since the merger, the insurance in force had increased seventy-nine percent to $80 million. The ratio of new business to old, from 1945 to 1946, was forty-three percent, the highest percentage increase of any U.S. company, and he expected the company to write another record in 1947, at more than $20 million. The number of agents had more than doubled, three new district offices were opened, and invested assets had increased forty-two percent. He concluded that staff and salary grades had finally reached acceptable levels and office space was adequate for the next few years. Again he stressed his "pride" and assurance that the expenses had been worth it.[78]

The merger with Seaboard Life was not only to be the model for all American General's future mergers, but was itself the symbol for the direction of Wortham's business career—growth through merger. And, in many instances, the mergers also meant new directions. Gus Wortham had taken a chance, albeit a safe one, on change; a change from his familiar background.

The important component again was progress through growth. For Wortham, as for the rest of the leaders of Houston, growth was a sign of success. During the late 1940s, the Chamber of Commerce dutifully recorded the city's delight in the expansion of new industries, new construction, and new investments. What happened to Gus Wortham's career in the period surrounding World War II, how it changed courses while continuing to grow, is imitative of what was happening to Houston—precisely because Wortham was intimately part of that change, diversity, and growth.

And while Wortham promoted internal growth in his business, he also, reacting to the growth of Houston, sought other opportunities for becoming bigger and better. His acquisition of and participation in new ventures, some affiliated with his insurance company and some not, were the ways he served the growth ethic.

A key symbol of the growth ethic for Wortham was now land. It was the crux of his new mortgage company, his ranching partnership, and his other growing land holdings, besides being an essential aspect of the image of a "southwestern gentleman." But Gus Wortham also understood that as commercial activities and opportunities in Houston burgeoned under the growth ethic, they must be accompanied by expanding civic amenities that would give the city status and quality of life—and would attract more change and growth.

CHAPTER FIVE

Noblesse Oblige

The title "civic leader" had been appended to Gus Wortham's name for many years, even before he had achieved true financial prominence. Much of this was due to Wortham's social rank, and part of it can be explained by his background and upbringing. His air of quiet confidence left little doubt that Gus Wortham knew how to handle anyone and any situation to the best effect.

Houston was more open socially than many southern cities in that it paid at least as much attention to a man's own successes as to his family background and class. But once you achieved membership in the social and economic elite, you were expected to assume certain responsibilities, traditional for the ruling classes. Following the example of the nobleman or landowner who took care of all aspects of "his people's lives," it was viewed as the duty of the upper class to take charge of the public good and manage civic projects and concerns. There was little heritage of local government involvement in such institutions in Houston. They were to be founded, funded, and led by men like Wortham, who in turn recognized their duty to make sure that these activities thrived for the greater good of the city in which they had built their business empires.[1]

Gus Wortham brought his skills at finance, organization, and people motivation—plus some political clout—to work in the civic and cultural arenas. And although some of his peers may have been involved in a greater variety of civic undertakings, Wortham was among the top echelon of leaders—one whose participation in an event usually warranted attention from the media and commitments from Houston's other prominent economic interests. His abilities were celebrated because he could make others understand what he wanted, achieve compromise, and run a thorough but short meeting.

Thus Wortham's job as a president of Chamber of Commerce was merely his initiation into the ranks of the major civic "doers" who were counted upon to provide leadership, support, and money to cultural, civic, and humanitarian

Gus and Lyndall Wortham in costume (*right*), possibly for annual Houston Symphony event. Annie Cochran is at left. Circa 1940. Courtesy American General Corporation.

causes of all types. Indeed, given the symbiotic relationship between Houston's business and political orders, Wortham had held a quasipolitical office as Chamber head. Immediately after his presidency, he oversaw the management of construction of the coliseum, and had two other minor involvements which continued this business-government link for him. One dealt with labor relations, the other with the new federal housing programs.

On several occasions in the 1930s, city leaders selected Gus Wortham to help mediate relations between the area's business/industry leadership and organized labor. It was a volatile era for labor throughout the nation, as the workers of such major industries as steel and automobiles sought unionization. The fear of slowing down economic progress or even of losing potential industries and businesses encouraged the Houston City Council and the Chamber of Commerce to seek ways to help improve relations, encourage negotiation, and avoid strikes.[2]

A labor group formed by the Chamber of Commerce in May, 1939, was headed by Wortham. This was at the height of a strike by the National Maritime Union against "Standard Oil of New Jersey (now Exxon), Socony-Vacuum Oil, and three other oil and shipping companies"[3] There had been recent violence and threats of violence, and the Chamber felt Houston's reputation would suffer greatly if this continued. The minutes from a May, 1939, meeting, leave no doubt about this group's priorities: "A condition had developed which no one liked, responsible interests connected with labor, least of all. If this city was to continue to progress, it was essential to develop a friendly feeling between all elements of citizenship, coupled with mutual confidence and respect and a desire to work together for the common good."[4]

Several of those attending the meeting told of violent confrontations between labor organizers and corporations. There were tales of companies that had changed plans to open operations in Houston because of its labor troubles. Former Governor William Hobby spoke up about the need for "vigorous action" to keep "law and order," noting that it was only logical that "labor agitators" should choose a prosperous city like Houston. The group was urged to appeal to the local civil authorities, but if nothing was done, the only recourse was to go over their heads to the state authorities.[5] Chamber leaders feared that the growth and influx of new business—progress, which they so highly prized—might be stunted or even reversed by these agitations.

Wortham's group promoted the formation of a committee from the community at large, and he and the others were certain that the city's "sane labor leaders" would want to join. Considering the basic intolerance for union agitation in Houston and by the Chamber in general, the stress on improving relations, rather than cracking down on union agitators or members, seems remarkable. Any evenhandedness in their approach might be partially traced back to Wortham, who was respected for his ability to resolve differences between seemingly irreconcilable forces.[6]

There is no evidence of Wortham harboring violent antilabor feelings, but it is clear from correspondence, specifically regarding the Longhorn Portland Cement Company, that he was not particularly sympathetic to unions. In the 1950s he was opposed to unionization of workers in his insurance enterprises. According to a former American General lobbyist, Wortham did not believe in workers being forced to join a union, even if the majority were for it. Another indication of his leanings was his friendship and partnership with the Browns, who were extremely antiunion and successfully worked for antiunion state labor laws. There was a traditional southern aversion to unions among the business elite. Even if these groups Wortham served were designed more to control than to mediate the local labor situation, his appointment shows that his negotiating skills were valued.[7]

Wortham's other public-governmental service consisted of brief tenure on the board of the Houston Housing Authority (HHA), from February until July of 1941. The Houston Housing Authority was organized in 1938 in response to federal and state legislation designed to improve housing for the poor.[8] By 1940, with a promised $10 million from the federal government, Houston was involved in "seven slum clearance projects at a total cost of $12,185,000," including the construction of at least four extensive public housing facilities.[9]

The major piece of controversy during Wortham's tenure was over fifteen acres located across Buffalo Bayou from the newly built, PWA-funded Sam Houston Coliseum. Negotiations had been going on for almost a year and a half between the city and the HHA over the city's proposed purchase of the land, valued at $250,000. The authority had decided not to build upon this parcel, choosing instead land nearer Jefferson Davis Hospital. The city was eyeing the site as a possible exposition park. E. M. Biggers, chairman of the HHA, suggested there were "a number of businessmen in this town with enough interest in the matter to finance the purchase of the land for the city," and stated he knew of several who had offered. Clearly, there was no misunderstanding about the power of the business interests when they wanted something done. Mayor Neal Pickett explained that the city's hesitancy was due to the fact that the sum would not cover all the parcels of land in the area; several were not owned by the HHA. There were also battles regarding jurisdiction and use of funding between the authority and federal housing officials.[10]

Wortham was not a very involved member of the HHA, missing more meetings than he attended. But when he did attend, he seems to have been vocal, making and seconding resolutions and especially in seeking solutions to disputes. His replacement on the board was real estate developer J. R. Stirton, who had recently spoken out against the city building any more public housing.[11]

Public housing raised "uncomfortable" race-related issues. Houston was still a southern city in which the separation of the races was unquestioningly accepted by the white populace and enforced by their power structure. Existing almost literally side-by-side with upscale, white Houston society like the Worthams were the twenty-two percent of Houston's citizens who were black. The city adhered to the strict code of separation of the races in all areas, and by the 1930s blacks in Houston remained thoroughly segregated and disenfranchised. Blacks developed their own economic, social, religious, and civic structures which ran in tandem to the white ones. Where the two intersected, such as in the public schools, the white leaders and their viewpoint took precedence. "Separate and unequal" applied to all areas of life for black citizens. As sociologist Joe Feagin pointed out, whites cherished stereotypical views of blacks as childish and needing white supervision. There was no question that a man of Gus Wortham's background and position would follow the unwritten rules of the white establishment in his dealings with blacks.[12]

Like the rest of their peers, the Worthams had always had black men and women in service as cooks, maids, valets, and chauffeurs. Although blacks were allowed to work in some trades, such as bricklaying, stevedoring, or transportation, and there were some black professionals, the majority of Houston's black citizens were self-employed in small service businesses, worked as common laborers, or were in service to whites.[13] There were no black employees in Wortham's company or indeed in most white-owned financial businesses, except in the same kinds of personal service work they would be employed for in the home. It would have been unthinkable for Gus Wortham to socialize with black people or treat them in any way as equals. Wortham's set would have found it both gauche and mean-spirited to abuse or insult someone because of his or her race in public, but racist jokes and stories in private groups of whites were accepted—by the whites. It was a paternalistic relationship in which a white man of social standing was at once protector and advisor as well as employer of his black help. Black employees would come to him with serious problems or needs and he would use his wherewithal and contacts to take care of them. For their part, the blacks employed in white homes were expected to lead respectable lives, show deference to their employers, and be circumspect and uncomplaining workers.

To be sure, there was tension between the races. Many could still remember the race riot that had occurred in 1917, when after weeks of harassment by Houston police, black soldiers stationed at Camp Logan, ignited by a rumor, participated in a riot that left over thirty people dead. Blacks, no doubt, were sobered by the fact that it was no longer ago than 1928 that an angry mob had lynched a black prisoner, and since the early 1920s the Ku Klux Klan had seen a revival in Texas. Most damaging and demeaning was the fact that blacks had no real voice in the Texas electoral process, having been prohibited from voting in the Democratic primary elections, the only election that really counted in one-party Texas.[14]

But despite tremendous legal and social barriers, personal relationships did develop, especially among those blacks who worked closely with their white employers, such as cooks, nannies, or valets. Sometime in the late 1930s, the Worthams hired as a driver for Mrs. Wortham a young black man named Lester Randle. He would stay in Gus Wortham's employ for almost forty years, most of them spent as Wortham's personal driver and valet. Sometime in the 1930s, Wortham built a house for Randle and his wife, Lonnie Mae (who worked for the Carruth family), on a lot they owned in Acreage Homes, a black subdivision outside the city on the far northwest side. Later, Wortham built a second home for Randle, in Houston's Third Ward, so that he would be closer if Wortham needed him. These were gestures of need, mingled with duty and friendship, for Wortham.[15]

Wortham had a close relationship with Randle, especially after the latter became his own chauffeur and went downtown to work personally for Wortham—American General's first black employee—around 1946. While it was not startling to find a black janitor, maid, cook, or chauffeur on a company's payroll, Wortham warned Randle before he came downtown that things might be difficult but that he was not to talk back—he should just come to Mr. Wortham if any incidents occurred.[16]

In the Randle-Wortham relationship there was no racial tension because each accepted the "rules" of the white-dominated, segregated social structure. From that base there developed, however, a bond of trust. Wortham provided for others of his staff—black and white—in similar ways, but the ties between him and Randle were deeper. Wortham felt cared for by Randle and used him as a confidential sounding board. Some indication of how Wortham felt is in the inscription on the back of a photograph of Randle taken in May, 1957, at the dedication of the church at Little Eva Plantation: "Lester has been with me 25 years and I don't know what I would do without him."[17]

Randle was intensely loyal to Wortham. Of all the men who were close to Wortham, perhaps no one knew as much about what went on in Lamar Hotel suite 8F as Randle did. He often worked there, serving drinks and making his famous hamburgers. Yet at Wortham's request, he never discussed what went on there.

Wortham probably never saw himself as a racist; he was merely conforming to laws and mores that went unquestioned by whites in Houston. For them, the black community was almost another world. Wortham, as part of the "ruling" class, had learned how to treat those of the underclass, especially blacks. Segregation continued the paternalism and so-called chivalry of an earlier time. Gus Wortham's behavior toward blacks was all an unspoken and unquestioned obligation; his attitudes were shared by the most "enlightened" of the Houston elite.[18]

Other civic and cultural obligations mandated by class came to be seen by Wortham as necessary service for the betterment of the city of Houston. This clearly describes his work on behalf of the Houston Symphony Orchestra, the one Houston cultural organization with which Wortham's name was most closely associated throughout his life.

Although it was not until the fall of 1939 that Gus Wortham was elected a director of the Houston Symphony Orchestra Society, he had regularly attended such cultural events as Houston offered since coming to the city. Attendance was expected of him because of his position in the city and because it fostered the kind of environment that attracted people and business to the city. For Houston to grow and become a significant metropolitan region, it required certain social and cultural necessities.[19]

The Houston Symphony was the oldest of Houston's arts organizations, founded in 1913 by a group of prominent women led by the venerable Ima Hogg, daughter of Texas' famed Progressive governor, James S. Hogg. "Miss Ima" was Houston's First Lady. Over the years, through the determination of Miss Ima and a loyal group of musicians and music lovers, the group had survived. With the appointment of conductor Ernst Hoffman in 1936, however, the orchestra came of age and even achieved some national attention.[20]

A lavish Symphony Ball was inaugurated in 1939 by the Symphony Society for publicity and funding purposes. The theme for that first ball was a recreation of the court of the Emperor Franz Joseph with various prominent ladies of Houston appearing as members of the court. Princess Meternich was none other than Lyndall Finley Wortham, whose husband was serving his first term on the large Houston Symphony Society board.[21]

Gus Wortham's substantial involvement with the Houston Symphony Society came as the result of a meeting of businessmen called by oil man Hugh Roy Cullen to generate financial backing for the Symphony. Although by the 1940s the orchestra was receiving some critical acclaim, the level of financial support was not rising with its reputation. For years the Symphony had depended on the pocketbooks of wealthy individuals, and had not heavily canvassed either the Houston business community or the citizenry.

During the war years Cullen served as president of the society and the body's chief benefactor and booster. During the 1944–45 season Cullen donated some $125,000 to keep the orchestra out of debt. But Cullen also demanded his due, including that serious attention be paid to his suggestions or even demands for the orchestra. One persistent media rumor said that, to please Cullen, the Symphony would play "Old Black Joe" before concerts he attended.[22]

Cullen lessened his involvement, becoming Symphony board chairman after the war, but he remained a major financial backer. In 1946, a falling out over the appointment of a new conductor caused Cullen to resign. He also threatened to withdraw all financial support unless Miss Ima herself became president. Miss Hogg agreed with the proviso that she have a "strong supporting committee representing the business leadership of the city." For this group she enlisted Gus Wortham, "one of Houston's most powerful men of finance," who became chairman of the board.[23]

In 1947 Wortham also headed the Maintenance Fund Campaign, a fundraising effort begun in 1945 to give the orchestra a source of income over and above operating income. The operating monies, from box office receipts, never completely paid the bills and the orchestra often depended upon large donations from private citizens to balance its books. Wortham believed the maintenance fund should provide forty percent of the orchestra's budget, as was the case with the country's major orchestras. He wanted to turn it into a major segment of the fundraising activities and to broaden the Symphony's donor list beyond the rather circumscribed group of the very wealthy patrons.[24]

The building of the Houston Symphony Maintenance Fund Campaign was Gus Wortham's shining hour as a civic leader. It was doing what he could do best: managing people who were managing money—precisely why Miss Ima had selected him. He had the civic "clout" and a gift for attracting people to himself. The general feeling among city leaders was that if Gus Wortham got behind something, it probably was a sensible and needed endeavor. Wortham's leadership in this particular cultural appeal set the standard for other groups to follow. His ability to organize, educate, and enthuse was emulated. Especially important, in an era when cultural fund-raising was becoming big business, was his emphasis on training volunteers like sales professionals, making sure they knew about their "product." No longer was fund-raising in Houston to be done solely as a favor or on a friendship basis; it was to be handled in a businesslike way.[25] Expanding contributions from the community at large would raise money from new sources and increase awareness of the Symphony.[26]

And it was not only in training volunteers that Wortham excelled. He also knew how to get public backing for his cause by highlighting just the right issue. As the fund drive was set to begin, Wortham told the press that the only way the orchestra could be self-sustaining was to raise prices to eight or ten dollars apiece. But, of course, he concluded, that would keep many citizens from attending the concerts at all. Before the campaign even began, newspapers headlined how Wortham "says Houston Symphony is for all" and "Symphony prices kept low so everyone may attend." They quoted his belief that raising ticket prices would defeat the orchestra's whole purpose, that it was not established to make money in the first place, and editorials praised his foresight and magnanimity. This was the end of August—the fund-raising drive for a hundred thousand dollars was scheduled for September.

Paul Hochuli, a much-read *Post* columnist, called Wortham a "stable businessman, who knows values," who had made studies of other symphony orchestras and was well aware of the costs of musicians' salaries, hall rentals, guest artists, and crews. Hochuli believed Wortham was correct: higher ticket prices would defeat the Symphony's purpose. Besides, both San Antonio and Dallas had raised over a hundred thousand dollars for their orchestras the previous year. Lastly, Hochuli emphasized that none of the monies raised in this campaign would go to pay campaign expenses; those monies were coming from a private source.[27]

This was only the beginning of a media blitz to raise symphony subscriptions. A brochure calling the orchestra the "singing voice of a dynamic Houston" said it was "'Big Business' with all the problems and none of the profits"—wording designed to capture the prospective capitalist donor's interest.[28] Another adept fund-raising move was to have a quarter of the funds already in hand when the campaign began, mostly from long-time supporters.

The papers covered Wortham's address at the main workers rally on September 7, where he called the Symphony a "cultural force" for Texas that "added much to the prestige and importance of Houston in the eyes of the nation," and which now found itself at a "turning point."[29]

Wortham's biggest triumph in the campaign was in his handling of the women's annual drive, which he expanded. He told the women he wanted to create a "blueprint" that could be used in later years to handle the annual campaign. He organized three hundred women, primarily society matrons, into small teams which reported to a leader who in turn reported to the campaign head. The two-week long campaign "create[d] a feeling of responsibility." Each worker was expected to collect at least $150 from as many of her seven prospects as possible.[30]

Ironically, Gus Wortham did not care for classical music and he never pretended that he was an expert in music. In the late 1950s, when he sat for society portrait painter Robert Joy, Wortham told the painter: "Young man, I don't profess to understand music. I'm not even sure I like it, but it's a damn fine thing for the community." Wortham's interest and involvement in the Symphony stemmed from his sense of duty and his respect for Ima Hogg, whom Wortham called a "very convincing and charming person . . . [who] thinks it is not possible to build cities only with concrete and smokestacks." He would continue to support and sustain the group for many years thereafter, heading its finance committee and, in many seasons, privately donating funds to help the group break even. Of course, a "fine thing" for the community, for Wortham and the other civic elites, assuredly meant something that would promote growth and help business flourish.[31]

But, if Gus Wortham's motives were not culturally the purest, his ability to raise funds and keep the Symphony going were right on target: the Wortham-managed maintenance campaign of 1947 collected $102,750. More importantly, pledges had increased from just three hundred the year before to 1,373, achieving Wortham's goal of a much broader base of support. It is doubtful that many of the cultural groups of the city would have ever gotten beyond the stage of being mid-level regional groups with just a glimpse of greatness had it not been for the expertise and civic clout of men like Wortham. His own participation and rally cry told business leaders that this was an appropriate and necessary avenue of involvement, and led to the opening up of cultural institutions to the revenues and expertise of Houston's business community.[32]

It is not surprising that Gus Wortham was able to work well with the women's group, for he was a man who admired women and enjoyed their company. He, like most of the men of his class and generation, believed in the Victorian notion that women's realm was centered around the home, not in the worlds of politics or business. A proper extension of this was volunteer work for civic or cultural entities; things that advanced the "quality of life."

Lyndall Wortham, like many of the women who had served as fund-raisers in Wortham's Symphony Fund Drive, was a woman whose main job was to be the wife of a prominent businessman.[33] But, although Lyndall had been raised as a society "belle," she was no shy, retiring southern blossom—she was vivacious, attractive, outgoing, and often outspoken, and got attention for these attributes as much as for her civic involvements.

Mrs. Wortham very much lived the life of a wealthy socialite wife of the era and she clearly relished that role. She openly admitted knowing little about Wortham's insurance or other business ventures and was not terribly interested in his ranching properties either, although she was at his side for all social business and ranch functions. She continued to be active in her college sorority and was also a member of another sorority, Beta Sigma Phi, whose local chapter met for twenty-eight years at her house. Through Beta Sigma Phi, she became involved with Girlstown, U.S.A., a residential facility for girls located fifty miles west of Lubbock; she contributed funds and later became a board member and president. Probably her most significant charitable involvement was with the Houston Speech and Hearing Center, which she served as an officer for many years. She also volunteered for the American Cancer Society and the women's auxiliary of the county hospital. She later held prominent board positions with the opera, ballet, and other cultural institutions.

While she was active and well-known, Lyndall was not in the civic forefront, as was her husband. In 1961 she did head a group of 132 "prominent clubwomen" who were drumming up support for a bond election for the building of a domed stadium. (A year later, Gus and W. A. Smith led a group to support passage of another bond issue for the stadium.)[34]

In 1963, however, she received an important honor when she was the only woman appointed to the University of Houston Board of Regents by Governor John Connally. The new board was the first selected after the local college had become a state institution, and Lyndall was aware that her appointment was a great coup for the unknown school when she candidly told the press that the university got two regents for the price of one. "When I get any problems, I take them home and get Gus to help me work them out," she said. Gus Wortham was a long-time supporter of Connally.[35]

Her social and civic activities obviously did not fulfill Lyndall Wortham totally, for in 1941 the Worthams privately adopted a baby girl through a local hospital. They named her Lyndall. In 1944, they adopted another daughter, Diana, reportedly from somewhere outside the city. Whether the Worthams were biologically unable to have children of their own or chose not to when they married is not known, but it was Lyndall who decided to proceed with adoption. Gus and Lyndall were fifty and fifty-one respectively and many thought them too old to be proper parents to very young children. Although the children were clearly wanted, the age gap did present problems for the family, especially when the girls were in their teens.[36]

Partially because of the children, Lyndall decided the family needed to move out of the Warwick, and in 1950 the Worthams purchased the Sterling Mansion at 1505 South Boulevard in Houston's Broadacres neighborhood, just a few blocks from the hotel. The purchase was symbolic of Gus Wortham's stature in the community.

The house was originally built in 1925 for $200,000 by Frank P. Sterling, cofounder with his brother (and later Texas governor) Ross Sterling, of Humble Oil. Part of the lot on which Sterling built the house had been purchased from Seaboard Life's Burke Baker. The architect was Alfred C. Finn, who had designed many edifices for Jesse Jones, including the Rice Hotel and the Gulf Building. When finished, the Mediterranean-style house was the largest and most expensive in Broadacres.

Sterling died in 1938, and in 1948 the house was given in his memory to

Wortham family at the beach. *Back:* Gus, Lyndall, unidentified. *Front:* Little Lyndall and Diana. 1950s. Courtesy American General Corporation.

the Museum of Fine Arts (MFA). But its size and the neighborhood restrictions made it a liability for the museum, and in 1950 they put it up for sale. The museum was glad to take Gus Wortham's offer of fifty-one thousand dollars in March, 1950. Although the museum board wanted to make more, it could afford the property no longer. Wortham, despite his beneficence to other cultural groups, his intimacy with many MFA supporters, and his later membership on the museum board, made no attempt to make this a philanthropic transaction. He did pay cash, however, putting up five thousand dollars' earnest money prior to the sale and at its consummation writing the museum a check for forty-six thousand dollars.[37]

Mrs. Wortham spent the next year having the house completely renovated, but before they could move in, it exploded and burned. Lyndall remembered Gus answering the phone in the early morning hours of January 31, 1951, and then turning to her, saying with shocked understatement: "Mrs. Wortham, your house has just blown up and it's burning to the ground." It had been a bitterly cold night in Houston with a hard freeze; fire had also broken out in several stores downtown, the worst fire in that area for twenty years. The explosion was attributed to the gas heat left on to dry the freshly painted rooms. Lyndall decided to redo the house just as she had done it the first time and the Worthams finally moved into it in 1952.[38]

Gus Wortham's financial expertise as well as his abilities in dealing with people made him an attractive choice for civic leadership roles. It was for this strength that his friend George Brown tapped him for service in the management of Houston's Rice Institute. Although he had attended Rice for only two years, Brown was deeply devoted to the school. When he saw its prestige threatened, during the years following the Second World War, he determined to do something about it. This included the naming of many prominent men to the Rice Board of Governors, such as Wortham.

Wortham's appointment to the institute's board in 1946 was influenced not only by his financial acumen, but by his close relationships with Brown and J. Newton Rayzor. (Rayzor, Wortham's barge company partner, became the first Rice graduate appointed to the board in August, 1949.) Throughout his life he remained somewhat awed by "one of the great honors to be bestowed in this community." Wortham had come to be acquainted with Rice Institute's first president, Edgar Odell Lovett, whom he greatly admired. Perhaps it was from his father's example of involvement with higher education that Gus developed a devotion to Rice and felt it a special privilege to be associated with the school. It is only too true that, unlike at the Symphony, Wortham felt quite at home at the Rice football games. Like the other members of the 8F group, he always had season tickets and would often attend other Southwest Conference football games, sometimes on the same day.[39]

Wortham's appointment was part of a plan to position younger members on the board while easing out the older directors to emeritus positions.[40] This, in turn, was part of a much larger ten-year plan, formulated in 1945, to build Rice into a school of national repute. Academic and physical revamping and expansion meant a more active and agressive financial portfolio for the institution. Wortham's expertise would be much valued in this area.[41]

Appointed to the Finance and Loan Committee with Brown, Harry Hanszen, and William Kirkland, Wortham had the American General accountant, H. D. Reynolds, audit the school's financial reports.[42] Early in his tenure as a board financial director he carefully studied the school's investment policy and the management of its endowment and recommended changes based upon his successful management of American General. "Inflation has always been a way of life," Wortham explained in later years. "It was quite clear to me from the outset that the endowment of Rice needed to expand toward more flexible securities like common stock—securities that could be expected to rise, hopefully, faster than the spiral of inflation." Southwestern entrepreneur that he was, Wortham favored an investment policy tied to his belief in growth.[43]

He advised on the acquisition and retention of stocks, and perhaps by his calm example helped quell the fears of some of the more conservative Rice leaders. But he kept in mind the reasoning of those former board members, whom he called "very cautious men of the highest civic caliber who took the trust placed in them very seriously." By January, 1947, the Rice Institute held stocks with a total market value of almost $7 million in such blue-chip companies as AT&T, R. J. Reynolds, U.S. Tobacco and Sears, along with those of regional interest such as Gulf, Humble, Standard of New Jersey, and Texas Gulf Sulphur. By August, the end of the fiscal year, the expansion in investments, gifts, and oil income came to an $8 million increase in total assets for Rice over the previous year.[44]

Wortham personally knew or dealt with most of Houston's business leaders and he shared his skillful assessments of these people and his advice on working with them with the Rice leaders.[45] From the late 1940s through the early 1950s, Wortham spent much time working on retirement and pension arrangements for Rice's faculty and staff, including chairing the 1946 committee that set a mandatory retirement age of seventy and provided for an annuity fund.[46]

Wortham's interest in land investments was put to good use on the Rice board. He helped the institution take advantage of good, high-yield mortgages that were available after the war. He was involved in a proposition with F. W. Woolworth for Rice to participate in a loan for the building of a store on prime downtown land at Main, Travis, and McKinney, near the new Foley's department store site.[47] Rice steadily became a partner to the postwar commercial development of the city of Houston. The Institute already owned a fair amount of prime Houston real estate. C. W. Malone of the Second National board wrote Hanszen, Brown, and Wortham regarding leasing land the bank and Rice owned at the corner of Lamar and Travis. Wortham praised Malone's real estate savvy but suggested leasing the land after completion of the new Foley Brothers' store to ensure the highest possible income. Wortham later advised against Rice purchasing the Sterling Building at Texas and Fannin because while it was then in the middle of downtown, it was not in the path of the city's growth. Wortham's advice showed his good business judgment, his ability to foresee the city's growth, and probably his insider knowledge as a member of the 8F group.[48]

In addition to his investment foresight, Wortham's fund-raising skills were also put to use on the Rice board. When in 1947 it became apparent that more money would be needed to finish the Fondren Library, Wortham encouraged chairman Hanszen to impress upon the other trustees the size of the amount to be raised and the necessity of their involvement in contacting fifty people.

But it was for the Rice Stadium project that all Gus Wortham's abilities in investment, fund raising, and people skills came together. In 1949, as the chairman of the Stadium Option Drive Committee, Wortham oversaw the financing of the seventy-thousand-seat football stadium that perhaps best epitomized Rice's "arrival" into major academic leagues—and in many ways, along with oil man Glenn McCarthy's nearby Shamrock Hotel, signified all the city's postwar boom boosterism.[49]

A new stadium for the city had been a source of much debate for at least a decade. In late 1948, Mayor Oscar Holcombe and the city council had proposed a giant stadium—the largest in the world—seating 110,000, but agreement was hard to reach on funding. Rice Trustee and City Councilman Kirkland assured Holcombe that both Rice and the twenty-year-old University of Houston (UH) were interested in such a project. The stadium proposal grew to include a baseball field, swimming pool, and track, in hope of attracting the Pan American Games. The plan was to raise private money by selling seating options for ten or fifteen years. The Chamber of Commerce eagerly endorsed the plan, even recommending that an armory be built as part of the complex. By February, 1949, the stadium idea had burgeoned to include a coliseum for the city's annual Fat Stock Show on land owned by the show on South Main Street, adjoining land Glenn McCarthy would donate—in all, a 315-acre fairground.[50]

In April of 1949, Wortham and Brown, on behalf of Rice, attended a meeting with Holcombe and two city councilmen; lawyer W. B. Bates, representing UH; and an anonymous donor who pledged underwriting for the sale of $3 million in bonds. The key seemed to be how much of the revenue the schools would keep and how much the stadium would use to pay expenses. But by that fall, enthusiasm for a giant community stadium had waned. McCarthy, the secret underwriter, decided to take his underwriting and his land back. UH and Rice had decided to go their own ways, "killing the deal," Holcombe said.[51] Thereupon, Rice announced that it would build a fifty-thousand-seat stadium on land west of the present stadium, to be completed in time for the next season's opener, September 30, 1950. The Rice trustees called the new stadium a "community asset" that would be available for use by other schools. Wortham, quoted heavily in the *Chronicle*'s report, explained the plan to finance the stadium through a seat option drive of one hundred dollars for each twenty-year option. Wortham and Rice President, Dr. William Houston, also emphasized that the new stadium was part of the school's updating of its athletic facilities and an answer to rumors that Rice would deemphasize athletics.[52]

Wortham rationalized Rice's desertion of the citywide stadium plan as the realization by the board that the size of the schools Rice was scheduled to play necessitated a bigger stadium by the coming fall. The Owls were the reigning Cotton Bowl champions for the Southwest Conference.[53]

The story of Gus Wortham's idea to sell twenty-year seat options to pay for the building of the Rice Stadium often has been embellished in its retelling. George Brown, who headed the Stadium Committee, recounted in 1970 how he and Wortham had discussed the stadium over lunch at the Houston Club one day late in 1949. Wortham suggested that Rice sell seat options; Brown questioned the interest that could be generated by such an idea. Whereupon the two men, realizing they were sitting amidst many of the city's leaders, turned to other diners and did a quick opinion survey. Brown, stating that "without Wortham there would not be a Rice stadium," recalled the overwhelming positive response from the men there to the plan.[54]

In reality, Wortham had thought or learned of the plan much earlier, most likely through correspondence in December, 1947, with Lenn Kelly of Douglas Sulphur Company regarding the funding of the expansion of Texas A&M's stadium which included details of a twenty-year seat option plan. But Wortham wasted no time in getting the subscription drive for the seat options going. With the Stadium Committee headquarters located in the Rusk Building, Wortham's offices and staff became a virtual command station handling everything from the sale to assignments of the seats.[55]

Just after the seat option drive began, Brown & Root agreed to build the stadium at cost, saving Rice from $200,000 to $250,000 on the fifty-thousand-seat stadium. Like George Brown, the members of the architectural firm designing the stadium and the mechanical and structural engineer were all alumni of the institution. Wortham was one of the few working on the project who had no personal ties to the school. Falling in line, other area industries offered the concrete, paving, and public address system for the new stadium at cost.

The *Chronicle* reported a "brisk business" in ticket sales as preliminary construction preparation began at the site. Wortham's reputation with local bankers proved invaluable when they agreed to an easy-payment plan for the purchase of the seat options. By the end of the year, the board voted to give the building committee another $400,000 to raise the stadium's capacity to seventy thousand.[56] Eventually the option plan raised $1.6 million, with the remaining $500,000 coming from the institute's athletic monies. Because of the donations, it was estimated the school got a $4 million stadium for only $2.1 million.

On September 30, 1950, the Rice Stadium opened for the first season game, pitting the reigning Cotton Bowl champs against the Orange Bowl champion, University of Santa Clara. The *Chronicle* quoted one fan who summed up the stadium's importance for at least a portion of the community: "This is what Houston's been waiting for." Wortham admitted to the press that he was surprised at the way people bought seats. And he wanted to make sure the community understood that Rice was not beholden to anyone for the stadium—it was all voluntary and paid for.[57]

The stadium's completion symbolized the achievement that Brown, who had become chairman of the Rice trustees, Wortham, and the others had sought for the institution. At the end of December, 1950, the group announced that most of its ten-year program had been completed—in five years. Five new buildings and the stadium had been erected, the board of governors reorganized, the student-teacher ratio lowered, faculty salaries made competitive, and course offerings expanded. All of this had hinged on the increased funding which Brown had said was his primary goal when he became chairman.[58]

Brown, Wortham, and the other Rice trustees took the initiative to build the stadium, putting the needs of this essentially elitist institution above those of the larger city. It is true that they did believe it was important to keep Rice ranked the best in all areas; that a city needed to have top-quality educational and research facilities like this to attract the right kind of growth. But the decision also demonstrated the power of Brown and Wortham to decide to go ahead with the project, in effect taking the impetus away from a city group unable or unwilling to make a compromise with another power broker, Cullen, who was "pushing" his own institution, the University of Houston. Brown and Wortham were perfectly willing for the other institution to use the Rice facilities, but a stadium needed to be built and it would be best if they did it. While these men did not seek to impose their will on the political leaders, neither did they defer to the larger Houston community's need or desire for an all-purpose sports/entertainment complex.

Gus Wortham remained on the Rice board until 1961, when he reached age seventy, the mandatory retirement age. As with the Symphony, he had served as head of the board's finance committee during most of his tenure. He was named a trustee emeritus and his support of the school did not abate. In 1967 he donated stock in Gulf Insurance Company and recommended and arranged for the purchase of additional shares by the school which gave the endowment fund a capital gain of over a million dollars.[59]

In the histories of these two Houston institutions, Rice and the Houston Symphony, Gus Wortham is among the revered. Typically, Wortham was asked to serve in civic and cultural positions because people saw how he could better their organization; but he stayed with them because he felt they were important to Houston.

Wortham's work for these groups flowered in the late 1940s, a time during which he became quite visible as a civic patron. And, by the early 1950s, Gus Wortham's renown as a civic booster had grown to the point of his receiving laudatory comments in the local social pages where he was celebrated for his role in fostering the growth of Houston's institutions: "Gus Wortham (who without fuss or fume, is one of the city's prime movers in charity and civic fund raising). . . ."[60] And he continued to take on new duties with other groups, although these were not as extensive as his Rice and Symphony connections.

His only significant involvement with the burgeoning Texas Medical Center in these years was his appointment to the Board of Trustees of Texas

Children's Hospital from shortly before the hospital's opening in 1954 through 1967. Though there is little documentation about any of his activities on behalf of the organization, Wortham's investment expertise as well as insurance connections were used extensively. The hospital was the special project of James S. Abercrombie and Leopold L. Meyer, both 8F members.[61] Probably because of Mrs. Wortham's involvement, Gus Wortham, along with J. S. Cullinan III (grandson of the founder of Texaco), was instrumental in expanding the Houston Speech and Hearing Center in the Medical Center. Wortham did not endow major Medical Center institutions like his friends, although he gave sizeable donations to some institutions in later years, including Dr. Denton Cooley's Texas Heart Institute and the Neurosensory Center at Methodist Hospital.

Wortham was an early board member of St. John's, a private school founded in 1946 which his daughters attended. He was also a board member of the Community Chest (and later the United Fund), originally founded in 1922 by a group including Joseph Evans. Wortham's documented involvement in the group was not in a prominent role; his participation in the Chest began in 1934 and lasted until the 1960s.

He was also a board member of the Houston Fat Stock Show, which the Chamber of Commerce began in 1932. Although involved as Chamber head, he did not take an active public interest until the late 1940s and early 1950s. Sterling Evans was also a director and served on the executive committee at various times during this same period.

Wortham often chaired civic events which required a well-known citizen to be spokesman. In 1953, he and James A. Elkins, Jr., headed Houston's fourth annual Armed Forces Day celebration at which the U.S. Army Chief of Staff was the main speaker. He was also named to a committee of fifty-five community "leaders" in 1954 by Mayor Roy Hofheinz to study and devise a plan for Houston's growth. The group, which read like a who's who of the elite, angered city councilors, one member calling it a "rich man's organization intended to strengthen the mayor's influence in the city government." Wortham and the other 8F members had supported Hofheinz in his mayoral bid in 1952 against their perennial candidate, Oscar Holcombe.[62]

In 1958, in a repeat of his Rice stadium role, Wortham, R. E. "Bob" Smith, and L. F. McCollum led a campaign to get a $20 million revenue bond passed for the Harris County government for the funding of a civic stadium (which would eventually become the Astrodome). Wortham prophesied that the city "could build something unique which will attract international attention." The group's work paid off and the voters approved the issue of the revenue bonds; but in 1962, Wortham and William A. Smith cochaired the effort to promote passage of a $9.6 million dollar bond issue to finish the domed stadium. In accepting the task, Wortham displayed his constant civic boosterism: "There may be some who still think of us as an oil town on a bayou—and not

Lyndall and Gus Wortham on opening night of the Houston Symphony season, October 29, 1957. Courtesy American General Corporation.

as one of the world's truly great cities. The fact is that we are reaching for the heights in every field. . . ."[63]

Wortham's reputation as a financier, fundraiser and people motivator made him an attractive choice for these kinds of positions. Even though he only served in an advisory role, his name lent stature to the whole endeavor. Wortham was the 8F member generally noted as the "public" person of the group; he was more affable than either Elkins or Herman Brown, younger than Jones, and perhaps an understudy of sorts to Colonel Evans, whom Wortham admired for his ability as a pro-Houston spokesman. Wortham was often a speaker or master of ceremonies for events; photographs of him and Lyndall appeared frequently in the newspaper and his persona as a kindly, gentlemanly mogul made him a most attractive "point man for the Houston establishment."[64]

As with his other undertakings, Wortham's civic service to Houston illustrated the three themes that infused his other activities. His ability to manage and motivate people made him a successful leader, his business acumen raised funding levels, and his interest in land gave him a sense of the importance of civic work to future growth and development.

All these activities took place while Wortham was enlarging his insurance business, managing various smaller companies and private ventures, and beginning a ranching empire. This involvement in so many enterprises was possible because the lives of men like Wortham were intertwined in social and business networks that made it possible for business to be conducted in a "by-the-way fashion" if it was necessary. These men knew each other from residence hotel lobbies, from boardrooms, from golf courses, from symphony boxes, from club rooms, from their wives' garden and book clubs. They were comfortable with each other in this cozy and secure world. To be sure, they worked hard to stay in it, but they knew it was safe and solid because men like themselves oversaw not just the commercial, but the political, civic, and social institutions as well.

CHAPTER SIX

Mixing Politics with Business

By the late 1940s there was a new Houston. Oil, transportation, and World War II had transformed the city which was rapidly throwing off its southern reserve and small town aspects. Month after month, the Chamber of Commerce publicized seemingly endless increases in commercial and home construction. It bragged of a $100 million medical center, massive industrial complexes built by major oil and chemical companies, the announcement that Prudential Insurance was building a regional office, and that Foley's, the city's major retailer, would build a $10 million store on Main Street. Houston's inland port was the country's third largest and still reigned as the country's top cotton port.[1] Houston was poised to take advantage of a postwar boom which would push it into the ranks of the nation's largest cities.

Critics such as New York writer John Gunther, famous for his *Inside* books, decried Houston as "reactionary" and a place "where few people think of anything but money, where the symphony orchestra is the feeblest" and as having "a residential section mostly ugly and barren. . . ." But he could not deny that Houston had grown overnight to a city predicted to "have a million people in fifty years."[2] Gus Wortham and his 8F counterparts ignored such criticism; they were much too busy orchestrating Houston's development through their economic and political activities.

There are no archives that describe what happened in 8F, Herman and George Brown's famous Lamar Hotel suite where the power brokers met, but in 1978 journalist Harry Hurt, a chronicler of Texas' elite, portrayed the group as gathering "to relax—drink and play poker—but also to talk politics, exchange ideas, make business decisions, and choose the candidates they would support for public office. . . . Their blessing was the blessing of 'The Establishment.' Their rule was virtually unchallenged and—they would emphasize—very 'civic-minded' gerontocracy."[3] Another journalist, James Conaway, described the

Herman Brown and James A. Elkins, before 1962. Courtesy American General Corporation.

8F crowd as "millionaires, self-made, and of similar opinions. During the 1940s and 1950s they exercised a concerted influence in Texas that was unparalleled. Not only did they raise a great deal of money for candidates, but the endorsement of the 8-F Crowd meant that a candidate had the general approval of the business community, was the establishment's anointed."[4]

Gus Wortham rented apartment 7F in the Lamar just below the Browns; Wednesday and Saturday afternoons there were reserved for cards; usually two tables for bridge and poker.[5] The traffic between the two suites was steady and others in the group had their own suites in the Lamar. Wortham recalled some "raucous" 8F afternoons when the group often got home late for dinner, but he also acknowledged that "[t]here were a lot of serious things about the 8-F Crowd, too. We talked about public affairs, exchanged ideas. . . . Herman [Brown] was an excellent conversationalist, when he wanted to talk. He was extremely positive in his views, never doubting that he was right."[6]

As a member of the 8F crowd, Gus Wortham helped shape postwar events in Houston. Although none of these men ever ran for office, they had great influence over those who governed because of their economic power and social prominence. Philosophically, southern tradition demanded leadership from the wealthy, high born, and better educated. Those who met regularly in 8F had invested their fortunes and lives in the city; they were both responsible for and dependent upon its future. They asserted influence over local and state politics in order to assure what they considered a "healthy business climate." Their economic power gave them considerable political power within the region and the state. Also, because of the preeminence in national politics of Texans such as John Nance Garner, Jesse Jones, Sam Rayburn, Will Clayton, Lyndon Johnson, and Albert Thomas, their power extended into this realm.[7]

Whether in 8F or 7F, the group mixed pleasure with business. They discussed issues and people, finding out each other's beliefs and desires, the deals and projects they were working on, and trying to come to a consensus on what, as they saw it, was best for Houston. Aspiring political candidates paid court, seeking the 8F crowd's approval as *the* man for the job. According to historian Don E. Carleton, the 8F members formed a "general committee" to study and recommend on a particular issue or election based upon the interests of the members. This committee would split into two groups, one to nominate candidates, the other to raise money. Generally, the group was of one mind.[8]

Although the 8F clique was thoroughly ensconced in power by the 1940s and well-known to Houston insiders, it probably first became known to a broader public when it supported and then backed away from Mayor Roy Hofheinz in the mid-1950s. One of the proofs of Wortham's local stature and his place at the center of the 8F crowd was his indictment as one of the "fat cats" by Hofheinz in November, 1955. In 1952 the group, chiefly led by Judge Elkins, had chosen the feisty young county judge to run for mayor, instead of backing Oscar Holcombe. But by 1955, when Hofheinz sought reelection, he had run afoul of the group through a push for a possible property tax readjustment and a telephone rate increase (Elkins's law firm represented the phone company), among other issues. Scandals at city hall and a resultant feud between the city council and Hofheinz were making daily headlines. The 8F group persuaded Holcombe, "the Old Gray Fox," to come out of retirement and run for his eleventh term.

The *Chronicle* (Jones) and the *Post* (the Hobbys) both backed Holcombe. In a blistering "open letter" (which the papers refused to run), Hofheinz attacked them and the group of "fat cats," which included the Browns, Abercrombie, Elkins, and "Gus A. Wortham, multi-millionaire American General Insurance operator and vast land owner, subdivider and home mortgage banker." Wortham's office had been the place where the 8F group had told Holcombe they were supporting Hofheinz instead, and Wortham had also set up a later meeting where the group asked Hofheinz to change police chiefs. Wortham had no comment about Hofheinz's tirade; the rest pled forgetfulness. After Holcombe won, he reportedly received a gold tie clasp in the shape of a cat with ruby eyes and a pearl ball, inscribed, "to the Old Gray Fox from the Fat Cats."[9] How Wortham really felt about the "fat cats" incident or Hofheinz was never publicly known, but he did come to the aid of the former mayor when the Astrodome project needed to raise monies in 1958 and 1962. Wortham supported the Astrodome because of his "good-for-Houston" rationale, above and beyond any personal feelings for or against Hofheinz.[10]

Like his father, Gus Wortham had always made it his business to know politicians and become involved in politics. He had an acquaintance with John Nance Garner and the two U.S. senators from Texas, Tom Connally and Morris Sheppard, during the early years of his business life. He also had a closer relationship with Representative (later Speaker of the House) Sam Rayburn. While not as publicly active in the Texas Democratic party as his father had been, Wortham was influential behind the scenes and financially supported a number of candidates at local, state, and national level. He also attended a number of Democratic national conventions.

Gus's prominence, enhanced by his father's previous friendships with so many politicians throughout Texas, gave him a tremendous advantage in dealing with everything from specific insurance regulation to legislation affecting the city of Houston. Wortham was a fairly frequent and well-known visitor to Austin for many years, first making himself known through his father's connections, then as a presence in the insurance industry, and later as a kind of senior business expert-spokesman. "Mr. Gus" was close to a number of legislators and enough of an insider to be included in the crowd of legislators and lobbyists who often met to play cards in a local hotel. The group included Lieutenant Governor Ben Ramsey, attorney-lobbyist Edward Clark, Senator Johnnie B. Rogers (later a lobbyist for the insurance interests), and Senator Rudolph Weinert of Seguin—all powerful political forces in the state.[11] During the late 1940s, 1950s and 1960s, and probably before, Wortham had close acquaintanceships with the governor, lieutenant governor and speaker of the Texas House, and many times, all three. Wortham was a phone call away from the Texas governors, beginning with Beauford Jester, who reportedly knew Wortham at the University of Texas. How close he was to most of them is uncertain, except for John Connally, whom he had known and admired since Connally had worked as an aide to Lyndon Johnson in the 1940s. He was very close to Ramsey, arguably Texas' most important politician, who served for twelve years during the administrations of Shivers through Connally.[12]

Wortham and the 8F men knew they could also depend on a côterie of Austin legislators to push their basic probusiness agenda. As candidates, many of these lawmakers were backed by the 8F group. Wortham and the 8F men chose the people they backed based upon their own ideas of what was good for Houston, especially the business community. This could be translated into lower taxes, minimal regulation, and constant attention to the needs of business as regards growth and development. Gus was a conservative Democrat and supported candidates whose views matched the 8F philosophy, although he was always willing to work with whoever was in office, even if a liberal.[13]

An example of the kind of candidate backed by Wortham and other 8F members was State Representative Searcy Bracewell. A Houston attorney, Bracewell decided to run for the Texas legislature even before he was back in the United States after World War II, and financed his 1946 campaign out of his own savings, spending about sixteen hundred dollars. His platform was mostly conservative; he was a strong believer in states' rights. He favored redistricting, the submission of the poll tax to the voters, and the establishment of a black university. Later, he was one of eighteen House members who voted to abolish the death penalty.[14]

In 1948 he ran in a special election for Harris County's seat in the Texas Senate. Wortham praised Bracewell's performance in the legislature and gave him a check for several hundred dollars, but added that he could not promise to vote for Bracewell, because he might "have a kinsman running or something."[15]

Wortham felt it important to get a good man into office, one who shared the same basic philosophy, and keep him there over time so that he would gain seniority and influence. But if this group disagreed with a candidate on an issue or with a legislator on a particular vote, it did not necessarily mean that the politician would lose their support.[16]

The Texas Senate itself was a small, close-knit body, and Bracewell remembered that the thirty-one senators often worked together, across philosophical and party lines, on votes needed to pass a bill. It was understood that certain members who might support a bill would not vote for it because it would hurt them politically. While the politicians "recognized" the power of 8F, Bracewell believed that the candidates were not in any way owned by them. Bracewell felt the 8F men got what they wanted because they were "players" who knew the political ropes and had empathy for the politicians. He knew they would understand if he could not vote for a bill they supported, or perhaps even one he supported, if it were going to hurt him. Wortham would have told him it was acceptable not to vote for such a bill; as far as Wortham was concerned, it was more important to keep Bracewell in the legislature than to worry over any single specific vote.[17]

Bracewell kept in close contact with the 8F men and the Chamber of Commerce leaders during his ten-year tenure in the Senate. When he left office he became a kind of "front man" for them, especially in looking for more business-oriented conservative Democrats to run against the strong labor-liberal faction. He was paid a fee by Elkins, George Brown, and Wortham for almost a year in which he sought such men, organized support behind them, and helped them raise money. As sociologist Chandler Davidson, an expert on Texas politics, points out, Bracewell went on to become one of the state's foremost conservative lobbyists.[18]

In the papers of Benjamin N. Woodson, Wortham's successor at American General, it was documented that Wortham met or talked often with legislators and the executive branch of Texas government concerning the insurance business. This would be expected because insurance was regulated by the states. Also clear is that Wortham was familiar with the men who served as insurance commissioners and directors of the commission. And this familiarity with power was surpassed only by his friendships with the political leaders who selected them.

A good example that demonstrates the depth of Wortham's influence with these politicians as well as his beliefs regarding the relationship of government to business was demonstrated in his response to the Southeastern Underwriters Case and decision.

In 1942, the attorney general and the U.S. Department of Justice successfully secured a grand jury indictment of the Southeastern Underwriters Association (SEUA), an Atlanta association of 197 fire insurance companies, of which American General was not a member, for violations of the Sherman Antitrust Act. The government claimed that the association fixed rates and agents' commissions and used coercion of insurers and customers. The SEUA claimed that the nature of the insurance business made some of these practices in the public interest. But SEUA's chief defense rested on a long-held ruling that insurance was not interstate commerce, and therefore did not come under the Sherman, Clayton, or other federal antitrust statutes. When a federal district court ruled in SEUA's favor, the case was taken to the U.S. Supreme Court, and in June, 1944, the court upheld the attorney general's decision that insurance was interstate commerce and that Congress had the right to regulate the insurance business. The court's ruling surprised Wortham and most other insurance company leaders because it reversed the seventy-five-year-old decision keeping insurance regulation the job of the states.[19] As the case was being considered and federal control seemed possible, Wortham and other insurance executives labored for congressional passage of a law that would put control of insurance matters firmly at the discretion of the states and disallow application of the Sherman or Clayton antitrust acts to insurance.[20]

Wortham's response to the SEUA case demonstrates how he cultivated people in politics and insurance at all levels and then worked, usually successfully, to bring them to his viewpoint. In September, 1943, Wortham wrote a memo, which he sent to Judge Elkins, on a bill he favored to be submitted by U.S. Senators Josiah Bailey and Frederick Van Nuys in tandem with an identical bill in the House. The bill would give insurance regulation back to the states and not subject it to the antitrust statutes. A supporter of the measure was Texas Congressman Hatton Sumners, chair of the House Judiciary Committee. Wortham had gotten his information from the head of the Insurance Executives' Association, New York lawyer Edward L. Williams, who was in contact with Senator Bailey. Wortham asked Elkins to talk with Texas Senator Tom Connally, chair of the Senate Judiciary Subcommittee (which was considering the bill) about attending a meeting of legislative supporters of this bill.[21] Wortham also wrote to Judge D. F. Strickland of the Rio Grande Valley about the Bailey–Van Nuys Bill, hoping Strickland would contact Congressman Milton West. In the letter, Wortham revealed his concern about federal regulation: "[I] firmly believe that it would be the death bell of all sectional companies. . . . The State is the proper place for insurance regulation because they can take into consideration local conditions and further, the property laws of the various States enter into the insurance picture."[22] Wortham was anxious to involve

West in his cause because of the latter's power in Congress and his abilities as "one of the best advocates of States' rights."[23]

In the meantime, Wortham had enlisted his legion of Houston agents to write letters to the senators and congressmen, and was planning to be in Washington when the bill was considered by the Judiciary Committee.[24]

Wortham wrote to other congressmen, including Albert Thomas and Lyndon Johnson. His letter to Johnson is much more familiar than the others, referring to a recent luncheon conversation the two had had in Houston about the insurance bill. In Washington Wortham visited Johnson and many members of the Texas delegation. In form letters to Texas congressmen, Wortham stressed his belief that if federal regulation should occur it "would be finis for our company and all other local or sectional companies." Thomas replied promptly, assuring Wortham that he was generally in favor of states keeping jurisdiction over "all matters which they can reasonably be expected to supervise." On November 15, Wortham sent congratulations to Senator W. Lee O'Daniel for taking a "courageous position . . . with reference to Federal bureaus, adding "[t]he closer we can keep the government to the people, the better it will be for everyone. Local self-government is the best government that anyone has ever devised." Clearly, Wortham knew that the thought of more government intervention would rile these conservative Democratic legislators.[25]

Wortham corresponded and worked with representatives of the large New York firms and was sent hearings transcripts by one representative so that he could discuss the bill with Speaker of the House Sam Rayburn.[26]

By May, 1944, Senator Connally had resigned from the Judiciary subcommittee and was replaced by Senator Joseph O'Mahoney, who seemed to favor more study of the insurance situation. But when the Supreme Court decision came down in June, Wortham corresponded with Connally about the necessity of passage of some kind of legislation to regulate the insurance business, now that the state regulation was nullified by the ruling. While Wortham expressed his basic conservatism and fear of federal government encroachment into what he considered private matters, it is evident that he was also cognizant of the problems a state of regulation limbo would bring on the industry.

> [T]his condition largely nullifies state regulation and causes a chaotic condition in the business. While I am opposed to federal regulation, and am convinced that it cannot properly take into consideration local conditions and the varying hazards in the several sections of the country, such regulation is better than none. Without regulation, unbridled competition will cause insolvency, and tremendous loss to POLICYHOLDERS.[27]

Wortham wired Connally requesting his attendance at a special judiciary committee meeting on the bill scheduled for June 22, appealing for "some form of legislation that will permit the temporary continued use of rating organizations developed under state regulation. . . . [It] is in my opinion vital to the insurance business and is definitely in the public interest." When Senator Connally later replied that he had attended a committee session and urged prompt action on the bill, Wortham sent the message to Williams, showing his understanding for the politician's need for confidentiality in cautioning Williams not to make Connally's position public, as "he does not like for others to discuss how he is going to vote." In this letter Wortham also blamed the insurance business for part of the muddle in which they found themselves and gave a good capsule statement of his view of industry practices:

> We have made a complicated business out of a very simple business. We do unnecessary things and incur substantial expenses. . . . The executives in the business are too "steeped" in the old practices and traditions to ever initiate any changes on the broad scale. . . . I . . . hope that you will not [think] that I am a radical. . . . I primarily want to cut out unnecessary expense, and broaden coverages to produce more losses that can legitimately be paid and that will serve an economical purpose. It is only through loss dollars that we get expense dollars![28]

Although the House passed the bill identical to S.1362 later in June, 1944, the Senate did not complete its hearings. The case was not decided until the following year, in March, 1945, when Congress passed Public Law 15 recognizing federal jurisdiction over insurance but granting a moratorium, giving the states time to readjust their laws. Ultimately, this allowed the states to continue to regulate and tax insurance as they had done before.[29]

Much of Wortham's and American General's involvement in state governmental regulation was done through a company lobbyist in Austin. The first man who occupied this position was the former fire insurance commissioner Raymond Mauk, who was replaced by Paul Benbrook in the mid-1950s; Benbrook was the company's first lobbyist required to register as such. Wortham also hired attorney Edward Clark of Austin. In addition to representing the insurance interests, among others, Clark was lawyer-advisor to Herman and George Brown and a political advisor to Lyndon Johnson. Chandler Davidson has called the Texas lobby the "most visible means of Texas' business-class influence," and named Clark the premier Texas lobbyist in the post–World War II era, followed by Bracewell. Certainly, the lobbyists in Texas were legendary—for their numbers as well as their unabashedness in conniving to make deals favorable to their clients. Through these men, Wortham made his position clear and known to individual legislators (many of whom knew Wortham themselves) as well as to the governor and lieutenant governor.[30]

Edward Stumpf followed Benbrook as the company's lobbyist in Austin. Stumpf became active in statewide Junior Chamber of Commerce circles and, thus, had a wide acquaintanceship with businessmen throughout the state. Serving until 1973, Stumpf worked with Clark's law firm and the other lobbyists representing insurance interests. And when the legislature was in session, he talked with Wortham daily. Stumpf remembered Wortham's special interest in getting two laws passed by the Texas legislature that greatly helped business in Texas, especially his insurance concerns. The first was a bill specifically allowing Texas insurance companies to have authorized and unissued stock. Before, insurance companies could only have that number of shares approved and issued by the insurance board, unlike insurance companies in other states, which were allowed to have such stock available. The passage of the measure allowed American General to grow by having a number of shares which it could use in a stock swap agreement. This legislation was passed sometime before American General made most of its early acquisitions. The other piece of legislation, passed sometime in the early 1960s, had more general economic repercussions. This was the holding company bill, allowing banks and insurance companies in Texas to form such concerns. Wortham considered such legislation part of creating a "good business climate" in the state; giving "business an equal opportunity to compete."[31]

While Wortham went to Austin to talk privately with the governor, lieutenant governor, or selected legislators on business matters, he was also appointed to several public groups. For example, in 1949, Governor Shivers appointed Gus to head a Houston committee studying the needs of state institutions in the city, especially Texas State University for Negroes (later Texas Southern University), M. D. Anderson Hospital and Tumor Institute, and the University of Texas School of Dentistry. In 1956, Shivers appointed him to the eight-member Texas Security Advisory Committee. The group was to review the revised securities act and another act creating an insurance securities division. And in 1960, Governor Price Daniel made Wortham a member of the State Financial Advisory Commission.[32]

Wortham also went to Austin to testify in person on behalf of certain issues he felt strongly about and for which his presence on behalf of the industry or representative companies would lend strength to their position. He often attended the fire insurance rate hearings in Austin before the board of Board of Insurance Commissioners. In March, 1957, Wortham spoke against a flexible rating system, before Senator Bracewell's committee on behalf of the Texas Association of Fire and Casualty Companies. Wortham led the opposition to flexible ratings for casualty and auto coverage, saying the system would not give Texans lower rates but rather would lead to the writing of "100 different kinds of policies . . . and produce higher rates for more people than lower rates for people." Wortham believed that a company could reduce rates by making dividend payments. Since the insurance commission fixed the minimum rates that could be charged, it is certain that Wortham disliked the legislation because it would bring to Texas increased competition, in the form of companies (especially the larger, national fire and casualty concerns) charging lower rates. Wortham believed the old system protected the insured against a company's failure and that unscrupulous types would be attracted to start companies by a flexible rating system.[33] This testimony came shortly after the state had been rocked by financial scandals involving a number of insurance companies. Wortham testified again in 1959 before the Senate Insurance Committee against another such bill. Texas at the time was the only state without some kind of flexible rating or price competition, but Wortham and opponents said that Texas buyers already had low rates.[34] In earlier testimony before the Texas House, Wortham, representing twenty-three companies of the Association of Fire and Casualty Companies, said it was "unbecoming of them [the National Association of Independent Agents who favored the bill] to come down here and mislead the people of Texas when these same companies are charging higher rates in other states."[35]

At the same time, another issue, that of the establishment of a merit rating system for insuring Texas' drivers, was also being debated. Most Texas companies favored the system. American General's lobbyist represented the Association of Texas Fire and Casualty Companies at these hearings. In 1960, Wortham again represented the Texas Association of Fire and Casualty Companies, against compulsory liability car insurance, because he believed such mandatory coverage written would reduce incentives for safety laws and produce higher rates.[36]

State insurance matters, although of major import to his companies, did not limit Gus Wortham from seeking a voice in the national political arena. Although the extent of Wortham's involvement in the national political scene in the 1940s and 1950s is unknown, he traveled often to Washington. Some indication of Wortham's early involvement in Democratic party politics can be gained by a document left in his income tax files. It is a receipt for a contribution of one thousand dollars to the Democratic National Campaign Committee, dated October 15, 1940. For the time this was a significant donation and may have been an expression of his support for President Franklin Roosevelt seeking an unpopular third term. The chief fund raiser of the 1940 Democratic Congressional Campaign Committee, which in reality was the same as the National Committee, was Congressman Lyndon Baines Johnson. The financial solicitation to Wortham may have come through the Browns. It may also have come as the plea of Sam Rayburn who was trying to keep the Congress under Democratic control.[37]

By 1941 Wortham was actively backing Johnson. Wortham chartered a bus to take employees—almost the entire John L. Wortham and American General staffs—to San Marcos for a Johnson rally. Johnson lost the close—some believe stolen—election race against Governor W. Lee O'Daniel to fill the U.S. Senate seat.

Wortham and American General had a history of major business dealings with Brown & Root Construction Company, including a surety bond for a Brown & Root project in 1935 in Maverick County. In 1940, Wortham's Longhorn Portland Cement company was tied in with the Lower Colorado River Authority's Mansfield Dam project, the event cited by historians as the beginning of Brown & Root's ascendancy. It was Brown & Root's attorney, the powerful former state senator, Alvin Wirtz, who had helped them get the job; Wirtz was a close associate of Lyndon Johnson. With Johnson and his associates making things possible for his good clients, Brown & Root, Gus Wortham would also support Johnson.[38]

Wortham felt close enough to Johnson himself, however, to ask for favors and make recommendations. In March of 1941 Wortham and Congressman Johnson communicated on HR 3360, a proposed bill cowritten by Congressman Fritz Lanham of Texas regarding patent infringement rights. Later in the month, Wortham corresponded with Johnson's chief aide, John Connally, about some kind of appointment for which Wortham had probably written a letter of reference. Johnson lauded Wortham's "quality . . . [of] always being there at the right time and saying the right thing at the right time."[39]

There is no indication that Wortham was involved with the "Texas Regulars," the conservative, anti-FDR/New Deal group that was formed in 1944, although it was headed by Wortham's business partner and AG board member, George Butler. This group was primarily antilabor, anti-*Smith vs. Allwright* (the Supreme Court decision that abolished the Democratic white primary) and anti–wartime bureaucracy. Butler was the State Democratic Executive Committee head. Another Texas Regular was Wortham business partner, Wright Morrow, who later became Democratic National Committeeman. Texas political scientist George Norris Green also cites James A. Elkins as one who went along with the "rich elite of the Regulars," such as Hugh Roy Cullen, who opposed Governor Beauford Jester's backing of Truman in 1948. Morrow and many Regulars supported States' Rights Party presidential nominee Strom Thurmond, governor of South Carolina, that year. Whoever he voted for, Wortham did contribute to the campaign of incumbent president Harry Truman in 1948.[40]

However, when Lyndon Johnson ran for the U.S. Senate in 1948, Wortham went all out in his support. He called together a number of his younger executives at John L. Wortham and American General and explained to them that he and some other prominent men in town were supporting Johnson and were looking for campaign workers. If they were interested they were to report back after lunch. According to one account, there was to be no pressure and no one was ever chastised for not returning. Those who worked were given a leave of absence and assigned certain counties to canvass for Johnson. This work included talking to voters, putting up posters, and collecting contributions. In 1953, Johnson wrote to Wortham about getting a list of friends in Houston, saying "that both in 1941 and 1948 you did about as much for me as anybody in the state."[41]

Wortham's reputation as a political "godfather" was that of a man generous to candidates with his money because he supported their ideology or program in general, not because he sought a definite objective. There is no doubt, however, that he did expect attention. Historian Don Carleton in *Red Scare!* quotes a 1950 letter to Senator Johnson from Wortham, in which Wortham explained that he never helped candidates financially in the expectation of "special privileges," but he did hope for the candidate to pay attention to his views. Johnson's reply, Carleton reported, showed his cognizance of Wortham's power, as Johnson apologizes for a misunderstanding of Wortham's position.[42]

One piece of correspondence between Wortham and Johnson during this era provides some insight into the political climate of Houston and Texas during the 1950s. In 1953 Wortham wrote to Johnson commenting on the Bricker Amendment, a constitutional amendment then being debated. "Designed to give Congress a dominant role in foreign policy and to prevent American participation in broad international agreements concerning human rights that might offend one or more of the states," the proposed amendment was backed by states' rights advocates and isolationists.[43] According to Carleton, whose book is a chronicle of the pro-McCarthy excesses in 1950s Houston, it also became a cause for Houston's branch of the ultraconservative anticommunist organization, the Minute Women, and was supported by Jesse Jones and a letter-writing campaign in the *Houston Chronicle*.[44] Senate Minority Leader Johnson himself was publicly ambiguous on the amendment proposal. The issue generated a great deal of mail from constituents. To be against it was to be un-American, but to be for it might severely limit presidential powers, which neither Johnson nor President Eisenhower wanted.[45]

Other Wortham correspondence with Johnson demonstrates Wortham's interest in a number of legislative issues. In 1956, Wortham asked Johnson to support the merger of the Production Credit Corporations into the Federal Intermediate Credit Banks as part of the Farm Credit Act of 1956. Apparently this was a cause of Sterling Evans, who was still president of the Houston Land Bank. In 1959, Wortham contacted him about HR 4245, a bill concerning federal taxation of life insurance companies; the bill may actually have been drafted by Benjamin Woodson who was running Wortham's expanding life insurance companies. Interestingly enough, the telegram expressed support for the bill "in principle, even though, it increases our tax liability enormously and considering that it is a substantial step in the direction of sounder taxation of life insurance companies." Wortham and Woodson's telegram expressed an objection to part of the bill which taxed some tax-exempt income.[46]

Wortham's relationship with Johnson continued, but most of his business correspondence with Johnson dealt with very specific issues or votes, and in later years, their discussions revolved around their mutual interest in ranching. But a short note written by Wortham to Johnson in 1958 indicated the depth of Wortham's behind-the-scenes political involvement with Johnson and Texas Democrats. Wortham warned that if something was "not done and quickly Frankie Randolph and her crowd [were] going to control the Harris County Delegation" and maybe the state convention. Wortham was helping to organize the opposition against Randolph, a Houstonian and leader of the Texas liberal Democrats.[47] It was also in the spring of 1958 that Governor Price Daniel invited Wortham to a "strictly personal and off the record" luncheon to discuss the upcoming precinct conventions and "the importance of keeping the Texas

Democratic Party in the hands of the majority. . . ."[48] That was the year, too, that Senator Ralph Yarborough, the state's leading liberal Democrat and a nemesis of the 8F contingent, won a "decisive" victory in the general election that signaled a new ascendancy for the liberal wing of the party.[49]

During this same period, the strength of the Republican Party increased nationally and in Texas, but there is no clear evidence that Wortham switched parties. It is not known whether he supported Eisenhower in 1952 or 1956, following the lead of his friend Allan Shivers, then governor, or if he was at all influenced by the appointment of Oveta Culp Hobby as Eisenhower's secretary of health, education and welfare. There was much speculation that Wortham did support the national Republican ticket, but as usual, he never divulged his vote. In the 1960 presidential race he certainly was a Johnson supporter early on, but unlike the Browns, was not upset when Johnson agreed to be John F. Kennedy's running mate.[50]

But Gus Wortham never became a liberal Democrat. An indication of how close Gus Wortham was to a conservative, business-oriented political philosophy can be gauged by his continuing involvement in the Chamber of Commerce movement, locally and nationally. Perhaps no organization stood more for the connections between the country's capitalist philosophy and its politicians than the Chamber. As the chief advocacy group for business interests, the Chamber wielded great influence at all political levels and Gus Wortham continued to be an influential member not only of the Houston group, but of the national body as well.

Wortham had remained an active member of the local Chamber after his tenure as president ended in 1934. From the late 1930s he served on and off on the highway and water supply committees, and most importantly, the nominating committee which chose the Chamber's officers.[51]

Following in the footsteps of his dear friend, Colonel J. W. Evans, Wortham was selected as a director of the United States Chamber of Commerce in 1953 and served on that body until 1958. Now, the *Chronicle* editorialized, the national group truly had a 'man who can speak 'with authority' for and of the business of Texas.' Wortham was taking the place of Evans, who had served the national Chamber as a board member or officer for twenty-one consecutive years, had been vice president for twelve years, and reportedly had turned down the presidency. The *Post* noted that Houston was unique in having such long-term representation at the U.S. Chamber and believed it had been represented longer than any other city on the body.[52]

In 1954 Wortham became a member of the U.S. Chamber's insurance panel of thirty-three members and was appointed to the group's committee on taxation for 1954–55, designed to work with the "Commission on Intergovernmental Relations . . . to help integrate state, local and federal functions and tax sources."[53]

Historian Carleton called Wortham the 8F group's "chief activist" in the Chamber, which served as the group's "forum" and "unofficial spokesman."

Gus S. Wortham in his office, in front of portrait he had painted of his friend, Colonel J. W. Evans. Courtesy American General Corporation.

Carleton closely linked the activities of the local Chamber to the policies fostered by the national group, citing especially the U.S. Chamber's crusade for rooting out "reds."[54]

As Wortham was joining the U.S. Chamber board in the early 1950s, Houston was making headlines in national publications because of its remarkable growth. *Business Week* in January spent several pages on the city it called a "Mecca for Capitalists."[55]

This picture of an open-to-all-comers city was curiously juxtaposed with its ultraconservatism, which also made national headlines. As evidenced by the hubbub over the Bricker Amendment, a sometimes hysterical anticommunist mood overtook Houston and parts of Texas in the 1950s. A large segment of the Houston population felt deeply threatened by any "socialist" tendencies in its institutions, especially its schools and labor unions. Carleton linked Wortham and the rest of the power elite to the Committee for Sound American Education, a group of ultraconservatives who controlled—and terrorized—the Houston Independent School Board for nearly a decade. How Wortham felt about the anticommunist crusade, its leaders, or its tactics is not known, but it is conceivable that he and other business leaders would have felt threatened to the core by a social movement that theoretically wanted to bury the political-economic class to which they belonged.[56]

In 1954, journalist Theodore H. White wrote of the uneasy alliance of wealth, political power and anticommunism in "Texas: Land of Wealth and Fear," a two-part magazine series. White linked the conservative, reactionary movement to the way Texas was governed, describing groups like 8F:

> Texas politics rests . . . on a series of autonomous self-winding groups in each community, consisting of the local aristocracy of enterprise and commercial achievement. These close-knit social groups are the respectable people—merchants, lawyers, bankers, publishers, contractors, businessmen, oilmen, and their wives—who run their cities as if the cities were clubs in which they constituted the nominating committees and the electorate-at-large the herd. Some of these little oligarchies may be . . . corrupt and crude . . . others . . . distinguished by the most extraordinary civic responsibility and honesty. But their common characteristic is a ruthlessness that arrogates to them sole control of political life.[57]

White believed it was the "little" money people who were running scared, while "big" money was concerned with national political issues—especially tax status. This does not apply totally to Houston, for besides being among the "big" rich, the men of 8F were also very much concerned with local issues.

In 1958, Wortham was elected director of District VII of the U.S. Chamber, instead of an at-large member, and was reappointed chair of the policy committee—an appointment that would seem to rank Gus Wortham as a leader in the national Chamber.[58]

How influential the policy committee was to the overall action of the U.S. Chamber and its impact on governmental issues is not known, although Wortham later said, "It is supposed to be their top committee, but I do not like to say that." Wortham said his committee took stands exclusively on "business matters" and "fiscal matters of the government and of the cities. It had no cultural, religious, or educational purposes." Wortham told his interviewer the committee only dealt in political matters when it presented factual matter before congressional hearings.[59]

The U.S. Chamber of Commerce was in many ways the chief cheerleader for what was becoming "the American Century." Unabashedly optimistic, the Chamber was totally for the expansion of business and business ideals, while at the same time seeking to reclaim the values of individualism and free enterprise that it felt the country had lost as government encroached more into citizens' lives. It promoted a laissez-faire attitude toward business and a lessening of government "interference" in all aspects of life. It feared "creeping" socialism, worried over government debt and increased taxes and inflation, hated labor unions, and had supreme faith in free enterprise.[60]

The paucity of information on the specific candidates or causes which Gus Wortham supported during his period with the national Chamber or in his role as a member of the Houston's ruling elite is indicative of the way he operated. An oft-cited remark was Gus's reaction to being asked who he supported politically: "You don't go hunting with a brass band."[61] But there can be no doubt that throughout this period, Gus Wortham employed his energies as a civic and cultural booster and a behind-the-scenes political manipulator to promote a goal he considered loftier than culture or sound government. That goal was to create a nurturing environment for business interests, one that promoted their growth. This would create a thriving city, and if Houston thrived, so would business. And, as Gus Wortham watched the burgeoning metropolis of the early 1950s, he contemplated the possibilities for future growth of his own institution—American General.

CHAPTER SEVEN

Expanding the Business

In 1947, American General was twenty-one years old and Gus Wortham felt moved to reflect to his board on the company's founding: "Looking back, this was rather a bold venture and I can now more clearly realize than at that time, the problems that confronted so small a Company in establishing an agency plant and in acquiring a profitable volume of business."[1]

But it had been a successful chance taken; the company's premium income the first year had been $26,000 and now it was over $4 million. In one of his very favorite comparisons, which would be repeated in company literature for years to come, Wortham noted that an "original stockholder who bought 10 shares of stock at a cost of $300 now has invested $1,200 and owns 100 shares of stock that has a present market value of more than $5,000. In addition, such stockholder has received $910 in dividends."[2] And Wortham thanked his original backers, mentioning the names of Jones, Elkins, and the Links.

The next twenty years would bring even greater success to Wortham. During the next two decades he would lead American General through a series of business transactions that would bring his small, regional company to a position of national notice. With the same spirit, Wortham would also expand his private business interests, especially his land holdings, and his ranching enterprise. Perhaps caught up in the spirit of possibility that swept Houston and Texas, Wortham the southern patrician now paid keen attention to his westerner's faith in unlimited potential and expansiveness. He wanted to capitalize upon and become part of this pattern of growth, beginning by building upon the solid reputation of his company.

As it entered the postwar years, American General had carved out a notable niche as the only insurance company in the South to write all forms of insurance. But at the same time, Wortham had to report that the company had

Gus and Lyndall Wortham. Courtesy American General Corporation.

experienced its first "bad" year in 1946 due to underwriting losses and decreases in securities value. Allowing that "[p]ractically every Company in the business" had an underwriting loss, Wortham attributed American General's to the insuring of old cars (production of new cars had been slowed by the war), and to severe weather. Despite underwriting losses, business was growing and the underwriting loss was turned around in 1947. Nineteen forty-eight was the best year in the company's history and by the twenty-fifth anniversary year of 1951, capital and surplus had increased from the original founding capital of $300,000 to almost $6 million. That year, however, the company experienced bad losses in automobile liability and windstorm insurance, as had been the case in 1946. In 1953, Wortham reported a twenty-two percent increase in net premiums, the largest the company had ever written, although the underwriting profit was small due to "continued bad experience on automobile liability insurance," a problem that plagued casualty insurers throughout this period.[3] American General was a substantial entity, continuing to grow in its own right, but ripe for further development.

Wortham's own influence in state and national fire and casualty insurance circles was considerable, given the size of his enterprise. In the late 1940s, after the Supreme Court ruled that insurance was commerce and new state regulations were passed to bring the industry within antitrust guidelines, Wortham set about forming an advisory group that could legally advise the Texas State Board of Insurance. The group would be made up of representatives of the national insurance companies doing business in Texas, representatives of the Texas companies, and Texas general agents, who were the local representatives for out-of-state companies in Texas.

Wortham knew the leaders of the major New York fire and casualty companies, and he took a leadership role in founding the new entity. The group would replace the Texas Fire Prevention Association, originally organized by Raymond Mauk when he was fire insurance commissioner. Unlike the old group, this new entity would include the large non-Texas companies, which had their own organization in Texas, the Texas Conference. Wortham was concerned lest the new body, acting as an advisory group, violate antitrust statutes, and asked the legal assistance of Judge Elkins's firm in assessing this matter.[4]

Wortham and a group of Texas insurance men were successful in persuading representatives of the eastern companies to come to Texas to meet with the attorney general and state insurance department. It looked as if the easterners would agree to the formation of a new group, and Wortham told his Texas contacts that he hoped—and planned—for it ultimately to be run by the Texas companies and Texas general agents. Wortham believed that the eastern companies had more influence over the state insurance regulatory bodies than the Texas interests did.[5]

Although there was general assent that such an organization was needed, there was disagreement about the particulars, especially about the size of representation of the three groups. Wortham acknowledged that the eastern companies had the most business, and therefore that they should have the majority of members and that an easterner should head the group. As Wortham told R. B. Cousins, Jr., secretary of the Texas Fire Prevention Association: "The people in the East and the people in Texas must understand that the old order of things is past, that if we are to get the job done that we must be united when we go before the Insurance Commission." Wortham knew the non-Texas companies would want to run such an organization with their policies, and that it should look that way, "but in actual operation we [Texas companies] should find a way to take the lead and I think we can do this." The eastern companies urged the Texas groups to join the existing Texas Conference, but that would amount to the Texas companies playing second fiddle to the larger, out-of-state concerns.

Because of dissension, no overall conference was formed until 1946. The new organization, formed of the three combined interests, was the Texas Insurance Advisory Association (TIAA) and the head of the former Texas Conference, an easterner, was the first chairman. This had been Wortham's plan. He did not want a prominent position for himself because he felt that he could "work more effectively without an official position." In 1951 Wortham served as the fourth chairman of the TIAA and in 1952 was reelected chairman of the executive committee.[6]

Wortham remained keenly involved in the fire insurance business; he was not as involved in the running of his two newest subsidiaries, the investment corporation and the life company, the day-to-day operation of which he left in the hands of trusted subordinates.

Dealing mostly in home mortgages, American General Investment could not help but grow in postwar Texas. In his 1951 "Report to Stockholders," Wortham mentioned that American General Investment "transacted a very large volume of business and is a leader in its field," and 1951 became AG Investment's most profitable year before taxes, servicing twenty-two thousand loans totaling $150 million. Later in 1952, Wortham reported the investment corporation's "earnings . . . to be highly satisfactory" and that despite the decline in government-insured loans, such as those issued by the Veterans Administration, "we are producing the largest volume of conventional loans in the history of the Company." By March of the next year, the total was thirty thousand loans valued at more than $210 million. AG Investment's growth was helped tremendously by its role as a correspondent for Metropolitan Life. When the man who had built the firm's connection with Metropolitan Life, Buck Walton, died unexpectedly in 1952, Wortham, who had remained the corporation's president, made J. W. Link, Jr., the executive vice president. Link and Wortham, both with years of investment experience and both perceived as social and economic pillars of the city, managed the firm until a former FBI man, Charles Boswell, joined the company in 1954. The Metropolitan, looking for even more expansion in the Texas market, used AG Investment to become active in commercial loans and the company built a sizeable income property loan department. Although the largest, Metropolitan was only one of thirty investors in AG Investment, including American General Life Insurance.[7]

The life company continued the growth spurt which had begun after joining AG. American General Life wrote more than $20 million in new business in 1947 and increased its insurance in force to $80 million, almost doubling that figure in the two and one-half years since the Seaboard acquisition. In September, 1949, American General Life announced that it had passed $100 million in the amount of insurance in force, a major milestone considering the company was licensed only to do business in Texas. The *Post* said it was a goal "only a few Texas companies ha[d] attained without any mergers or consolida-

J. W. Link, Jr. Courtesy American General Corporation.

tions." That November, Wortham asked the parent company to raise the life company's capital to \$500,000 and provide a \$1 million surplus. In 1949 AG Life paid a \$2,500 dividend and the Investment Corporation paid a \$40,000 dividend; Wortham called this a "highly satisfactory result for the year." As with the investment company, the life company was of great benefit to the parent company in 1950, with capital of \$1.9 million and insurance in force of \$115 million. In March, 1953, the life company produced \$7,700,000 worth of new business—"the largest writing in any one month in the history of the Company." Gus Wortham had made the right decision in joining the small, strong Seaboard Life to his tiny insurance group.[8]

Considering more expansion, Gus Wortham began to think about growth in the direction of life insurance, despite the fact his background had been solely in fire and casualty. The boom in the life insurance business after the war, coupled with the profits to be made, made it an attractive growth option for Wortham. He wanted expansion of his business, he wanted it to come in the life company, and he wanted the right person to do the job.

In 1952, as Burke Baker approached his sixty-fifth birthday, Wortham asked him to agree to retire, but to wait until his sixty-sixth birthday, to give Wortham a year to find a suitable replacement. Not being a "life" man, Wortham was judicious enough to see he needed to seek someone who was, and who also believed in growth and challenge. Baker, somewhat reluctantly, agreed to the retirement plan. By 1952, Wortham had eliminated Davis Faulkner, Baker's second-in-command, for the head position of AG Life, although, ironically, it had evidently been Faulkner's enthusiasm that had helped convince Wortham and the boards of AG and Seaboard of the viability of the original merger.

Among the several names mentioned to Wortham by the insurance men from whom he sought advice, including Burke Baker, was that of Benjamin Woodson, a forty-four-year-old who had been in life insurance for twenty-six years and had seen the industry from a variety of perspectives.

Woodson had developed an affection for Baker and Faulkner several years earlier. Woodson had worked at the Life Insurance Agency Management Association, a trade-management organization in Hartford, Connecticut. Assigned to Texas companies, Woodson had visited Seaboard several times a year and become friends with Baker and Faulkner. In 1944 Woodson became executive vice president of Commonwealth Life of Louisville, Kentucky, and tried to acquire Seaboard Life, the Louisville firm being several times larger than either Seaboard or American General. Woodson believed his offer stirred Faulkner, Colonel Evans, and others associated with Seaboard to consider merger in the first place, paving the way for the ultimate Seaboard–AG merger.

Wortham had met Woodson briefly before, shortly after Seaboard had been acquired by American General. But by 1953, Woodson had moved again, this time to New York as managing director of the National Association of Life Underwriters and the Life Underwriters Training Council, the country's most prominent life insurance trade association. By this time, Woodson had a national reputation through consulting and publications.[9]

In January, 1953, Wortham sent Woodson a brief letter inviting him to lunch at the Hotel Pierre in New York while Wortham was in town for a few days. The letter and Woodson's retelling of the details of that meeting have become part of American General lore.

When he made that lunch date, Woodson was probably already the prime contender for the job; however, Wortham left himself an escape clause, telling Woodson that lunch would last until 1:30 P.M. because he had another appointment. When no appointment materialized, Wortham admitted that he had invented the excuse in case things were going badly. During lunch, Wortham asked Woodson, as a former consultant to Seaboard/AG Life, to rate three other men Wortham claimed he was considering for the company's presidency. When Woodson had done so, Wortham asked him to rank himself among the group. Woodson coyly ranked himself fourth, because, he said, he was thoroughly suited for and liked his current job. Yet by the end of the visit, he was certain he would be leaving New York for Texas at some future date.

Wortham continued to question Woodson about the other men he was considering and

> what the job entailed and he began to say, "If you could bring yourself to leave this present job of yours, which do you think would be the right way to go forward

> at that point, this way or that way?" . . . Until pretty soon, it was like a fellow and a girl who have come to the point gradually that they realize that they're going to be married or ought to be and it hasn't been said in so many words, but pretty soon, they find themselves saying, "Well, would we want . . . an apartment or single-family house."[10]

The luncheon lasted long into the evening, with Woodson phoning his wife with the news he would be on the last commuter train home and that he had just finished "the most exciting day of my business life." Gus Wortham was sixty-two years old, and this might have been the classic story about the man who has built a respectable and profitable enterprise, and as he neared retirement age, searching for the right man to carry on. But there is little evidence that Wortham was ready to relinquish the American General reins, even in the near future. Rather, it is surmised by most that Wortham wanted someone who would help him make American General expand.[11]

Woodson remembered two major issues upon which negotiations hinged: how Wortham felt about growth by acquisition, and formation of a separate company to operate in New York. Woodson thought acquisition was the best way for a company to grow. As for the New York market, it had always posed problems for companies located out of state. It was the nation's most lucrative life market, yet stringent state laws made it difficult for a company to do business there. Woodson's plan was to create a company just for New York, in New York, and therefore circumvent cost and regulation hassles. Wortham's positive reaction to these two major concerns were crucial to Woodson's acceptance of any offer. But Woodson was also charmed by Wortham and "could see what he and I together could do." It was this possibility that made Woodson leave a job with national stature and come to Texas to head a small life insurance company doing business in only one state.[12]

No time was wasted in looking for properties to acquire after Woodson became American General Life's president in July, 1953. Later that month, Wortham presented to the board of the parent company a proposal to purchase the stock of the National Benefit Insurance Company of Des Moines, Iowa. Wortham hoped this company could help AG enter the "industrial" or "debit life insurance business." The debit system, connected with the sale of industrial insurance, involved the weekly or monthly collection of premiums at the insured's home. Industrial insurance, unlike ordinary life insurance, was usually written on amounts of one thousand dollars or less.

Actually, the proposal was being suggested by David B. Barrow, brother of Wortham's associate, Edward and Tom Barrow. David Barrow was a former chief examiner of the Texas Insurance Department and had formed a partnership as an insurance actuary and consultant and broker in insurance company sales. Beginning at least as early as 1955, he was also a partner with Wortham and Edward (Tom died in 1954) in the R-B-W Syndicate (the "R" was Newton Rayzor), which owned land and oil leases.[13]

Although the National Benefit deal was not consummated, by October,

1954, Wortham and Woodson were proposing to both fire and life company boards the purchase, in cash, of another company, American Reserve Life of Omaha, Nebraska, which was described as "comparable to Seaboard Life at the time we purchased their stock." It had $58 million dollars of insurance in force, compared with AG Life's $210 million, but the biggest factor in the acquisition would be the entry of American General into ten additional states with a plant already in business. (AG Life had recently entered Louisiana.) The company then would operate from the Gulf to the Canadian border.[14]

Ben Woodson had been casting about during his first year on the job for a suitable acquisition for American General, and he and Wortham had already considered and rejected several other possibilities. Woodson had hired Andrew Delaney as the company's first actuary to help evaluate risk and company potential, a step he felt necessary for a life company that was serious about growth. As with many of his subsequent ventures, the possibility of American Reserve came to Woodson through personal acquaintance with its president, Raymond Low, whom Woodson had known since his youth.

Woodson worked out the agreements and then presented the deal—three million dollars cash—to Wortham, who grilled him and sent him to talk to Wortham's chief confidant, E. R. Barrow, who also queried Woodson. When the time came to present the proposal to the board, a nervous but thorough Woodson was gratified when Wortham told the group he concurred completely on the acquisition. The proposal was passed unanimously. At that moment, board member Jesse Jones said to Wortham, "Now that you've got your merger, how would you like to make a million dollars in ten minutes? I'll give you four million dollars for your three-million-dollar deal." Woodson was flabbergasted, and Edward Barrow later assured him that Jones was serious. His offer was a testimonial to a solid, well-made deal.

The entire American Reserve acquisition was orchestrated by Woodson and the consummation of this merger began what Kenneth Fellows called the "decade of acquisitions" for American General. Most were instigated by Woodson. While industrial mergers were somewhat of a trend in the 1950s, their number and the way American General handled them would gain the company the attention of the business world.

The American Reserve was not officially merged with American General Life for two years. Wortham and Woodson decided to keep the home office and key personnel in position for a time, thus following the trend begun with the Seaboard Life acquisition, and partly necessitated by the inability of getting American General approved for entry into the states where American Reserve was operating. It remained a wholly owned subsidiary of American General until the end of 1956, when it was merged into AG Life.[15]

Wortham and Woodson's decision to keep names, locations, and personnel of acquired companies intact for some time after acquisition would become a hallmark of an American General merger, and proved to be a valuable and attractive business policy in dealing with other firms in the future. The obvious benefits for American General in this decision were tax advantages and political clout (i.e., the company could call upon the senators for each state where a subsidiary was located), in addition to public relations value for the takeover agency.[16]

The year 1954 was the most successful so far in the parent company's history. American General's assets increased to almost $20 million and the profit was over one million dollars before income tax—the largest in the company's history. AG Investment Corporation, servicing $250 million in loans, paid the parent company a $200,000 dividend, and AG Life wrote its largest volume during 1954, more than $50 million.[17] Woodson continued to seek out advantageous properties for acquisition. But in July, 1954, Gus Wortham, then sixty-three, suffered what was believed to be a heart attack at his Randle Lake Ranch. Lester Randle rushed Gus to Scott and White Clinic in Temple, Texas. He was later transferred to Methodist Hospital in Houston, where his stay was duly noted by *Houston Press* columnist Bill Roberts, who began his column with the fact that Gus was seriously ill.

Wortham's illness and convalescence concerned Woodson, not only because he and Wortham had developed a close friendship, but because he was afraid Gus might lose his enthusiasm for building the company. But Wortham remained enthusiastic, if somewhat subdued for a few months. A daily nap after lunch became part of his office regime, but beyond that there was no appreciable slowing down in Wortham's behavior after this incident.[18]

In February, 1955, Wortham gave Woodson the go-ahead to pursue business in Hawaii where Woodson was looking at another possible acquisition. And Wortham himself talked of expanding the fire and casualty business, which he did in July by acquiring tiny Texas Standard Company of Marshall, Texas. This purchase kept American General competitive with other Texas companies offering a new, cheaper form of insurance on dwellings and automobiles.[19]

Woodson was attracted to the Hawaiian market while attending an underwriter's conference. There was no doubt this would be a growth area, and Woodson soon found Hawaiian Life, the territory's first domestic life company, which had broken away from a Philippine company. It was a small company, with about $17 million insurance in force and a "modest" growth rate of five or six percent. For just $1.1 million it was a good investment. Woodson worked most of the year on the acquisition; another potential buyer was also interested in the firm.[20]

Concurrent with the Hawaiian deal, Woodson was considering other acquisitions, the possibility of moving more into the debit insurance business, the final merger arrangements for American Reserve, and the organization of a mutual fund for insurance stocks. Woodson and Wortham also discussed legislation authorizing variable annuities for Texas, the possible building of a corporate headquarters on the Buffalo Drive land, and the formation of an American General holding company, though Wortham opposed the latter because it would take money away from capital and surplus.[21]

Wortham, too, was busy with many other activities. During 1955 he acquired his two plantations in Louisiana and the Nine Bar at Hempstead. In addition to his other private business concerns, at this time Wortham was active with land deals in Austin with the Barrows, and in buying the Houston Country Club. He was also enmeshed in Mayor Hofheinz's row with the 8F group, while at the same time being honored by the East Texas Chamber of Commerce and his old college fraternity, Sigma Nu.[22]

In September, 1955, with the Hawaiian Life deal now-on-now-off, Ben Woodson got a tip that another familiar company, Union National Life of Lincoln, Nebraska, for which Woodson's father had worked in the 1930s, was available. One of its founders had died and the other owners wanted to sell. Union National had over $170 million of insurance in force and operated in seven other midwestern states. Its earning powers were "exceptional," Wortham reported to the directors, making more on $171 million than American General had on $255 million.

By November, the Hawaiian Life deal looked more promising and AG Life passed the quarter-billion dollar mark; by Christmastime, the Hawaiian Life deal was a certainty. On December 30, 1955, which Ben Woodson called one the best days of his business life, he went to the 8F suite in the Lamar Hotel to tell Wortham that a deal with Union National had been finalized. He felt the Union National acquisition would put the company into the "big time."[23]

On January 3, 1956, after a thorough going-over of both the Union and Hawaiian deals by Jesse Jones and Judge Elkins, the board approved the issuance of 57,500 new shares of American General stock to acquire the Hawaiian firm and sixty-five percent of Union National. Hawaiian Life was to remain autonomous, a wholly owned subsidiary, and Union National was not to be merged finally until March, 1957. To his directors, Wortham stressed that both the deals were "good bargains," but the most important thing they offered was "their contribution to our growth potential."[24] Even though Union National was not to be merged soon, or Hawaiian Life at all, from the two deals American General "would derive much of the prestige, momentum, and competitive advantages of a half-billion dollar life insurance operation . . . and we can begin to aspire to a billion-dollar life company . . . within five or six years."[25] In ending his report, Wortham noted that with the purchase, the company would no longer be in need of new money, the transactions increasing the net assets by $3,750,00 (for the 57,500 shares)—"equivalent for selling the . . . shares for well over $150 per share. . . ."

The *Houston Chronicle*'s January 9, 1956, headline read "Insurance Firm Buys Big Company," as it announced American General's purchase of the controlling interest in Union National and, a few days later, the *Houston Post* named Hawaiian Life as the company's second acquisition of the week. By February, 1957, American General owned ninety-nine percent of Union National, which was embarking on the formation of a monthly debit insurance force, a move both Woodson and Wortham had wanted to make. Hawaiian Life increased its new business by thirty percent following their purchase in 1956.[26]

American General's good fortune was a welcome bright spot on the Texas insurance horizon in 1956. Several Texas companies were involved in major insurance scandals precipitated by the state's lax restrictions, especially those authorizing capitalization requirements. Second only to the oil and gas industries in its importance to the state, the Texas insurance industry had been having troubles for some time, and by the mid-1950s many companies had failed. Texas, which had just endured a land fraud scheme involving some of the highest-ranking officials in state government, faced another political crisis that would help sully the name and future political prospects of many high-ranking officials. In December, 1955, with the failure of U.S. Trust and Guaranty of Waco, a huge savings and insurance conglomerate with 128,000 investors, the situation was at its nadir. The Board of Insurance Commissioners was implicated, mostly for ignoring or covering up shady or unsound practices for many companies.[27]

By 1957 nearly eighty Texas companies had gone broke, losing half a million dollars for policyholders and shareholders. There was evidence of kickbacks to and incompetence on the part of insurance examiners and commissioners. Crusading liberal journalist Ronnie Dugger of the *Texas Observer* cited the insurance troubles as symptomatic of a "corporate society," where government was "at one with the private controls." He attacked the state for monopoly pricing in the casualty insurance industry, created by the insurance companies with the help of the commission.[28]

While American General was honestly run and solidly financed, it suffered by association, as did all Texas insurance entities. It was well understood that Gus Wortham through his close political association with legislators, Lieutenant Governor Ben Ramsey, and Governor Allan Shivers, probably had some say in the appointment of this group of commissioners. Wortham was well aware of the problematic situation, and evidence shows that he did not condone—and indeed worried over—the involvement of the commissioners in the bad business practices. Wortham and Woodson were upset by the happenings; they knew that things were not being handled properly and that the state's regulatory guidelines were too lax.

Back in 1954, Wortham and Woodson had taken note of the problems within the industry and put together a set of recommendations for the legislative committee meeting on improving Texas' insurance laws. They were especially cognizant of the need for more stringent rules regarding the sale of stock and, most importantly, that the capital requirements to start companies be in cash and bonds. In June, 1954, Wortham, after a meeting with Insurance Board Chairman Garland Smith, was upset over Smith's lack of aggressiveness regarding stronger state laws. Wortham also worried about the commissioner's close association with BenJack Cage, whose Insurance Company of Texas looked as though it was in trouble. He also declined participation in an advertisement in the *Chronicle* in which a number of companies defended the industry; Wortham did not want to be associated with those companies. By the end of the year, Wortham was apprehensive about Smith's attitude, but he felt sure increased supervision over sales of life insurance stocks, restrictions on the markup of real estate, and an increase in the capital investment requirements would be enacted.[29]

With the convening in January, 1955, of a House and Senate conference committee to consider insurance legislation reform, Wortham and Woodson agreed that what was needed most was a legislator who would look out for the public. Wortham also considered using his Austin lawyer-lobbyist Edward Clark to push through needed legislation. State Senator Searcy Bracewell introduced a bill in February, 1955, to strengthen life insurance regulation. It passed later in the spring. The failure of U.S. Trust and Guaranty prompted Wortham and Woodson to ask Clark to make sure that the company, which dabbled in other financial areas, was really chartered as an insurance company. They were distressed because the company had reportedly been in trouble since the previous June.

Wortham and Woodson took no public action during this period, although they considered the formation of an insurance advocacy group which would run advertisements to counter the negative news. Finally, Wortham was called to Austin to consult with the governor and in January, 1956, Wortham suggested that the insurance department instruct the companies to have complete audits. Newspaperman Dugger later sarcastically noted that, when rocked by the failure of giant U.S. Trust and Guaranty, the commission and Shivers had okayed an audit of all Texas companies—done by "private accountants who were chosen, hired and paid by the companies themselves."[30]

But in January, 1956, as American General announced its two new acquisitions, the *Houston Chronicle* praised the good Texas insurance firms in an editorial titled "Insurance Officer Lauds Solid Companies," which cited American General as an "outstanding example" of a company that had grown through proper management. The *Post's* editorial, "Here's Some Good Insurance News," was reprinted in trade journals. It noted that Gus Wortham had been in the news twice because of his company's strength, not weakness. "The strength and prestige of American General is attested to by the array of businessmen connected with it," the *Post* said, reiterating the importance of Wortham's relationships and his role among the city's economic elite.[31]

A few days after this editorial appeared, Commissioner Garland Smith resigned as chairman of the insurance board and Shivers called Wortham for suggestions on a replacement. Wortham talked with Commissioner Byron Saunders and Lieutenant Governor Ramsey and eventually Saunders was made chairman. But by July, Wortham told Woodson how another commissioner, Mark Wentz, who apparently was not friendly to American General, dominated the insurance department. Wortham talked with Saunders and Shivers about the situation. When Saunders resigned in October, Wortham speculated on men he would like to see in the job, including Senator Bracewell, who at the time was considering a race for the U.S. Senate. Lieutenant Governor Ramsey said he would take any nomination okayed by the industry and Governor Shivers, or someone recommended by Gus Wortham. There could be no doubting Wortham's power within the Texas business-political circle.[32]

In January, 1957, outgoing Governor Shivers named his executive assistant, John Osorio, chairman of the board. Shortly thereafter, Wortham had a private luncheon with the new governor, Price Daniel, who asked Wortham to back his opposition to the appointment. Wortham said he refused to do so on the grounds that he had no specific objections to Osorio, although he had thought it unwise for Shivers to appoint a staff member. Daniel and Ramsey were considering various proposals for reorganization of the Board of Insurance Commissioners, but Wortham, despite pleas from Ed Clark and the governor, felt strongly that none of the insurance associations in the state should take any position on the reorganization proposal. In May, Wortham was reluctant to help lobby for Daniel's reorganization plan, because he did not want to incur the wrath of the current commissioners if the plan failed. Wortham was not thrilled by the legislature's insurance package, but told Woodson it was better than nothing. The insurance scandals did not touch Wortham's companies but he knew their potential danger and tried to use his influence carefully.[33]

By this juncture, Wortham and Woodson had developed a good working relationship. Wortham had turned the running of the life companies over to Woodson with his trust and his expectations. Wortham clearly wanted Woodson to be aggressive and look for ways to expand the life business on his own. Woodson, in turn, took hold but never bypassed Wortham's opinions and final approval. Part of their compatibility was based on their ambition and dedication to the same end: growth of American General. Many had wondered just what Woodson, with a national reputation and future, had seen in this small Texas entity. Certainly it was potential, but there was for Woodson also a strong attraction to the person of Gus Wortham. Woodson recorded what a good business mind Wortham had, and although Woodson was given much autonomy, he consulted with Wortham on a daily basis. On Woodson's second anniversary with the company, July 1, 1955, Wortham wrote to his "business associate and friend" Woodson, that his presence relieved "pressures and uncertainties." It had been just a year earlier that Wortham had spent six weeks in the hospital. But he did not talk of retirement from AG, although during these years, more of Wortham's time was taken up with his ranching properties, and Woodson believed that his own hiring had freed Wortham's time for these involvements.[34]

Woodson also believed that the first acquisition, American Reserve, was the most crucial because it established him in Wortham's confidence. If that transaction had turned out badly for the company, Woodson knew there would have been no more. For despite his board and his deference to men like Jones, Evans, Taub and Elkins, Wortham literally was American General, owning some fifty percent of the stock. Wortham knew what he wanted and made arrangements so that those things happened. He did not openly dominate the board, and sought its advice—or at least the advice of his most trusted côterie—on major steps. But in 1956 two of his most trusted board members died: Jesse Jones and Sam Taub.[35]

The death of Jesse Jones deprived Gus Wortham of an irreplaceable source of business counsel and support. Jones's capitalism-for-civic-good appealed to Wortham and was emulated by him. How much advice went the other way, from Wortham to Jones, is unknown, but there is no doubt Jones admired Wortham's business abilities. In January, 1956, just a few months before Jones died, he sent Wortham a letter praising him for his success with his company, and for being "the fine and useful citizen that you are." Wortham replied: "Dear Jesse; I did not know that I could get so much joy out of a three-line letter. Your confidence means a great deal to me. Thanks for your forty years of friendship."

Wortham greatly revered Jones and was often the master of ceremonies at tributes to the man called "Mr. Houston," including Jones's last public appearance on February 22, 1956, when the Houston Chapter of the Sons of the American Revolution presented him with its Good Citizenship Medal. Wortham said "Jesse Jones means Houston and Houston means Jesse Jones," and praised his friend and mentor for building Houston into a "community and industrial empire that is a credit to the Southwest." Two years later, Wortham was again called upon to preside at the dedication of Jesse H. Jones Senior High School. He repeated his statement about Houston meaning Jones and spoke of Jones as the builder of Houston, of his high-ranking government service and the power he had in running the RFC, capping it with: "He loaned more money than any man ever loaned in the history of the world, and what is more he loaned it wisely and well."

Wortham sought to emulate Jones's entrepreneurial spirit, as well as his pride of citizenship in Houston. Wortham wanted to be successful in business, to make money and certainly to have power, but these desires were woven around a tapestry of creating—building—something that would last. Like the others in the business elite, Wortham believed in his vision for the city and sought to impose it on Houston. There was in these men a certain sense of responsibility to a larger purpose of growth and preeminence for the city where they had made their fortunes. They built Houston the way they wanted it, and they did it partially because it was their duty to do so.[36]

Always a "man of sentiment," Wortham appointed *Houston Chronicle* publisher, John T. Jones, Jr., to the American General board. John was Jesse's nephew and the son of another original board member, Jesse's brother John. For the same reason, Wortham also named Sam Taub's brother, Ben, to the AG board.

Before the deaths of Jones and Taub, Edward Barrow had become Wortham's closest confidant inside American General management. A much more conservative man than Wortham, Barrow was often depended upon to give a cautious, even jaundiced eye to proposals with which Wortham, Woodson, Link, or others wanted to proceed. It was only fitting that Barrow should fill the role of Wortham's second, for he had been with Wortham since his days at the State Insurance Board and was one of the original John L. Wortham and Son employees and partners.

As American General celebrated its thirtieth anniversary in May, 1956, it was in the midst of still another best-ever year. It advertised itself as the largest group of insurance companies west of the Mississippi, writing all lines of insurance with one or more companies in twenty states. With capital and surplus at $14 million, the companies wrote $10 million in fire and casualty and had $500 million of life insurance in force. The American General Investment Company, one of the five largest in the country, serviced $300 million in mortgage loans. The group had 1,207 agents, 850 employees and 80 branch offices.[37]

Wortham and Woodson did not stand still with their triumphs; personally and as the leaders of American General, they continued to push the corporate entity in new directions. One of these directions was an innovative and rather controversial one in 1956: variable annuities. The first foray into the field had been the College Retirement Equities Fund (CREF), founded by the Teachers Insurance Annuity Association in 1952 to provide variable annuities to college teachers. While the variable annuity was devised to give the policyholder some hedge against inflation by investing the annuity in stocks, worries about a noncorrelation in cost of living and market value of stocks made the variable annuity a questionable vehicle.

Some felt the variable annuity threatened the life insurance business, but both Wortham and Woodson were solidly behind the principle, as long as it was included in a sound life insurance program. They not only felt that it was proper for life agents to sell variable annuities, but that this business would grow, and they wanted to be in on the ground floor. Woodson noted that the two talked in early 1955 about variable annuities and impending legislation that would allow such companies into the state. Wortham favored the legislation and wanted to get involved, be the first into the business, believing it was "the coming thing." Woodson was in contact with former Texas Congressman Lloyd Bentsen about the legislation. Bentsen would shortly found his own insurance company in Houston. Woodson went to Austin and lobbied for the bill, but no law was passed that year.

In late 1955, the plan had been for American General to make a large investment in the Variable Annuity Life Insurance Company (VALIC), and Wortham talked with Barrow, Sam Taub, and his barge company partners, Newton Rayzor, E. D. Butcher, and Jake Hershey, about investing. It all seemed too complicated, and in the end the group decided to finance their own company in 1956, the Equity Annuity Life Company (EALIC). It was chartered to operate in Washington, D.C., the only place variable annuity companies were licensed at the time. George E. Johnson, who had headed VALIC, was named president and Wortham ("head of one of the largest general insurance agencies in the country") chairman. Woodson, also an investor, was on the board. American General had less than a ten percent interest in the company. Shortly after EALIC's incorporation, American General Life took a public stand for variable annuities by printing a piece by Woodson in his "The Back Page," a monthly column in AG Life's company publication, reprinted and read nationally. Sometime in the late 1950s or early 1960s, Gus Wortham himself also took a public position when, at his installation as a member of Beta Gamma Sigma, a national honorary business administration fraternity, he spoke on the efficacy of variable annuities.

By 1960, EALIC would be one of only three commercial companies formed to offer variable annuities. This was because of regulatory problems with life companies selling variable annuities, having to do with federal or state jurisdiction. Variable annuities were "essentially" specialty insurance policies and insurance was under state, not federal, regulation. However, annuities also have traits of securities, which are federally regulated. The Securities and Exchange Commission involved EALIC and VALIC in litigation seeking to prevent them from selling variable annuities without federal control. Finally, the Supreme Court ruled that a variable annuity was a security, giving the Securities and Exchange Commission jurisdiction. This legal row lasted most of the 1950s and during that period most life companies waited to see the outcome before entering the variable annuity market.

After 1963, however, over 250 life companies began variable annuities sales. Woodson and Wortham had led the way in this development, and continued to support legislation favorable to variable annuities throughout the 1960s. Woodson and Wortham had been far-sighted enough to see the value of variable annuities, and were not frightened by the skepticism of the majority of the insurance establishment.[38]

After the banner year of 1956, American General joined fire and casualty companies around the country in experiencing a dismal beginning of 1957. Many companies—including the large nationwide writers and several Texas firms—experienced underwriting losses. American General did not, squeaking through with a small profit. The income from investments, the investment corporation, and especially the life companies bolstered earnings. Indicative of Wortham's reputation, he received a letter from Clinton Allen, president of one of the giants, Aetna Insurance:

> I see you have done it again. How any one company can show up with an underwriting profit for last year is beyond me. For, without exception, it was the worst year in the history of the fire and casualty business.
>
> You certainly have a right to be inordinately proud of the record of the group of companies which you head. I congratulate you most sincerely on one of the

outstanding jobs of any company in the entire United States for the past year. May your shadow never grow less.[39]

There was no slow down in the life company's growth-by-acquisition process. In August, 1957, American General acquired, ostensibly for investment purposes, nineteen percent of Knight's Life Insurance of Pittsburgh, an old company, doing both debit and ordinary business, with a solid reputation and solid growth rate. But more than just an investment was involved in the $4 million acquisition. Woodson wanted to acquire Knight's Life because it would put AG's life operations over the billion-dollar mark in total life insurance in force and give American General a stronger foothold in the debit area. American General did not have the cash for such a purchase, so the plan was devised to acquire the company by having Knight's Life acquire the AG-owned Union National. The plan called for the placement of pro–American General people on the Knight's Life board and winning over the key Knight's Life people, especially company president, Joseph Hess. Woodson and Wortham both felt that Hess and the others at Knight's Life should be brought openly into the plan and that Hess could be sold on the benefits for his company of the merger with Union National. Wortham presented the idea to his two senior board members, Colonel Evans and Judge Elkins. Both approved and Elkins's bank, First City National, provided the credit for the $4 million investment to buy the original Knight's Life stock.[40]

In the fall of 1958, plans for the merger of AG's Union National into Knight's Life were set. The press announced the formation of a new, $700 million company to be called Knight's Life—two regional companies, as Woodson explained it, forming a national company. To purchase Union National, Knight's Life issued 140,000 more shares to American General, who already owned about twenty-five percent of Knight's Life stock. At the end of 1959, American General had acquired nearly forty-five percent of the Knight's Life stock and added Hess to the AG board. In early 1960, American General acquired the rest of Knight's Life stock and completed the merger with a stock split and an exchange of two American General stocks for one Knight's Life. It was, Wortham said, the "largest single purchase or merger in Texas life insurance history." American General's life operations were now operating coast-to-coast with $1.7 billion of life insurance in force. Wortham, in his civic leader role, used the moment to pump Houston, saying that the merger "serve[d] to point up the growing importance of our city as one of the major financial and insurance centers of the nation."[41]

Concurrent with the Knight's Life–Union National maneuvers, Woodson was working toward other acquisitions for American General. At one point in mid-1957, Woodson was in negotiations with Texas Prudential in Galveston, Home State, and Midwest Life, and was considering future possibilities with Great National, Amicable of Waco, and Texas Life. Another merger possibility was a hometown company founded by Jesse Jones, Commercial and Industrial Life. Meanwhile, Wortham told Woodson he was thinking about merger possibilities with one or more fire insurance companies, especially the venerable Gulf in Dallas.

The Texas Prudential deal had come very close, made even more agreeable by the chance of linking up with the Kempner family of Galveston, the owners of the company. At the last minute, however, Woodson and actuary Delaney discovered the company was currently losing money and was not as valuable as anticipated.

In October, 1958, AG acquired through exchange of stock worth about $4.5 million Home State Life of Oklahoma City. Although the company was sound, Wortham had misgivings about the deal, mainly because of the large amount of real estate, including a home office building, owned by the company. One exchange between Wortham and Woodson during the dealings showed how Wortham allowed and expected Woodson to lead. Wortham told Woodson that he, Woodson, was the life insurance man and he had to make the ultimate decision regarding acquisition of Home State. Wortham said he would not disavow it, but Woodson also had to remember that if the deal succeeded, the board would give Wortham the credit; and if not, Woodson would get the blame.[42]

Like the life company, American General Investment was seizing new sources of growth. During the late 1950s the corporation became heavily involved in commercial loans, as the home mortgage market dropped off somewhat. In 1958 AG Investment made firm commitments on such commercial deals as a $200,000 loan to the doctors in charge of the Diagnostic Clinic in the Texas Medical Center, a $300,000 loan to George Butler for construction of a bus terminal in downtown Houston, a $500,000 loan for construction of an apartment building on Montrose Avenue, $50,000 for an office/warehouse complex at Greenbriar Shopping Center, and $100,000 for an apartment complex on San Felipe.[43]

By the end of 1958 the parent company, American General Insurance, and its subsidiaries called themselves the American General Group. American General Insurance, the original firm, was both an operating company doing fire and casualty business and a holding company, owning one hundred percent of the stock of the other members. These included two fire and casualty companies, an investment company, a realty company, and the six life companies: American General, into which American Reserve had been merged; Hawaiian Life; Home State Life; and Union National, which was about to be absorbed into Knight's Life, in which American General had the controlling interest.

To go with the company's growing national presence, in 1958 Gus Wortham received a national honor when he was named Insuranceman of the Year by the Federation of Insurance Counsels. Wortham had been nominated in 1956 by his friend John C. Williams, executive vice president and president-elect of the group. Williams was the son of John L. Wortham and Son's first customer and the elder brother of Willoughby Williams, a John L. Wortham and Son partner. Since the federation's convention was to be held in the South, Williams wanted a southern recipient, and thought Wortham ideal. He cited Wortham's ability to treat all people considerately and said that, despite attaining business success, Wortham had never "advanced himself at the expense of others." When he received the award, Wortham addressed the group on the growth of all lines insurance; the speech was later printed in *Insurance Advocate*.[44]

American General was still a small to moderate-sized company by national standards, although in life insurance circles it was gaining quite a reputation for its recent mergers. And it had grown. American General's headquarters remained in the Rusk Building in Houston's downtown, where it had settled in 1929. Space had been at a premium for some time, and the various company subsidiaries and offices were scattered at seven locations throughout the city.[45]

As early as 1952, when his companies occupied about two-thirds of the Rusk Building, Wortham was concerned about space. Jesse Jones wrote to Wortham with a plan for him to take a five-year lease on the space he already occupied in Jones's building at four dollars a square foot, and then have the life company buy the building for one dollar with a $2.25 million mortgage at three and one-half percent.

> To reproduce a building of this size and character would cost approximately $2,500,000 and a year and a half time.
>
> Apparently you will continually need more space and within a few years may want to build your own building. In the meantime, you can occupy as much of the building as you need. . . .
>
> Your only fixed obligation would be your five year lease and if and when you desire to build, we can work together on a basis of fairness to each interest.[46]

But early in 1954, Wortham told Jones that he did not want any of the property and had decided to build—perhaps on the Buffalo Drive land, a move Woodson and J. W. Link, Jr., favored. The issue recurred again and again as Wortham considered some kind of solution for a larger home office building. At the same time, Woodson was pushing for the formation of an American General holding company which would buy the Petroleum Building. In September, 1954, AG Investment relocated to a building at the corner of Main Street and Richmond. Wortham met with merchant Leopold Meyer and W. A. "Bill" Smith, both 8F members, about the block at Main Street and Gray for the location of a home office (it had been the site of Meyer's family home).[47]

Finally, in 1958 Wortham made a decision on space. He and Judge Elkins made what was at the time Houston's biggest real estate transaction: the sale of Elkins's First City National Bank building to Wortham and American General for an estimated $16 million dollars. Elkins, who had created the city's largest bank in 1956 by merging his City National Bank with First National, was building his own new building, which the press called a "monument" to one of city's

Judge James A. Elkins with Wortham, possibly when the deal was made for Wortham to buy the Judge's building in 1958. Courtesy American General Corporation.

biggest backers. American General, now with seven affiliates, needed room and Elkins's twenty-four-floor building, built in 1947, seemed the perfect solution. Wortham predicted that American General could put all its home operations under one roof and, even then, would need only about twenty percent of the total floor area of the Elkins's building.[48] Elkins's new edifice would be right across McKinney Street from the old.

Reportedly, Elkins and Wortham had been negotiating the arrangement for the previous few years. *Houston Post* editorial page editor Ed Kilman, who was close to the Hobbys and other powerful Houstonians, used the building story to write a feature article in *Texas Parade* on the "Damon and Pythias" relationship of Elkins and Wortham. Kilman described the linkage of the two men's lives, from Huntsville through the capitalization of American General. The article provided a perfect description of how the business elite network operated in Houston—portrayed as a folksy kind of bartering between two men who had nothing better on their minds than the success of their city through their own success. Kilman suggests that Elkins's decision to build hinged on Wortham's purchase of the existing building.

> James A. Elkins sauntered familiarly into the office and with a quiet "Hi Gus," eased into a leather-covered chair beside Gus Wortham's desk. Without any softening-up preliminaries he said, "Gus, I want to sell you my bank building, so I can put up a bigger one" . . . "Yeah?" Gus Wortham fitted a cigarette into an ivory holder.
>
> "Yeah. It simply hasn't enough bank lobby space."
>
> "I told you that Judge when you built it." . . .
>
> "Well, how could I have known then that we'd consolidate with the First National? . . . Anyhow, you need space as badly as we do. . . . What'll you give me for the old one?" . . .
>
> Wortham's answer topped the question and a little over. He leaned back in his swivel chair, lighted the cigarette, and grinned. "Judge, you know what I'll give you for the building. I'll give you whatever you tell me to.'[49]

Kilman almost certainly wrote a laudatory editorial in the *Post* right after the announcement of the deal, praising it as "tangible evidence of faith in the future of Houston" by "two old friends [who] may sit in their offices and see each other across the canyon—the head of the South's third largest bank and head of the largest multiple line insurance group west of the Mississippi. . . . And the growth of the city will be due to the works with which such men as these back up their faith."[50]

Despite Kilman's ability to turn the Elkins-Wortham building deal into positive publicity for the spirit of Houston business establishment, the deal was not consummated. In August, 1960, the American General board voted to sell the First City National property to Herman and George Brown's Texas Eastern Transmission Corporation, in which both Wortham and Elkins owned stock. The First City building would not be big enough to house the "American General family" after all, Wortham said. With that tidily arranged, in 1960 American General announced it would build a new building, big enough to house American General when it became three times its present size. Part of the need for a new building came from the company's decision to move the western regional office of Knight's Life, formerly Union National, to Houston from Lincoln, Nebraska. Sites mentioned for the new building included some in the downtown Houston area and further out on South Main Street as well as the seven-acre tract the company owned on Buffalo Drive.[51]

Gus Wortham's prestige and power in business circles continued to grow with his business enterprises. He wielded much influence as a senior director of the National Bank of Commerce, in which his company owned perhaps one percent of the stock. In 1951, he was named to the board of the Texas Eastern, a gas pipeline corporation formed from the famed Big and Little Inch Pipelines built during World War II. Wortham had been one of a select group of people chosen by the Browns to purchase stock in their new corporation in 1947. This fifteen-hundred-dollar investment was soon worth almost $100,000. In February, 1956, Wortham was named, along with Houston lawyer-banker Colonel William Bates, to the board of the reorganized Missouri Pacific Railroad. A former Houstonian and president of the Chamber of Commerce, Paul J. Neff, was named the railroad's head. Neff had been chief executive officer for the railroad's trustees since 1946.[52]

Such positions on corporate boards were an important source of unity and shared points of view among business executives. Indeed, "interlocking directorates" cemented business and personal ties; by serving on common corporate boards, the members of 8F and other prominent business leaders met regularly in settings at which regional economic trends were the prime concern.

Wortham's fondness for owning land manifested itself in his private business dealings many times during this era of his corporate expansion. In 1955 he led a group of investors who purchased the former site of the Houston Country Club on the city's southeast side from the owners. The 178 acres were sold to Wortham for an undisclosed price, said to be over $1 million. The eight-hundred-member club had since moved to new facilities on the far west side. It offered its property to the city in 1953 for $1.6 million and the city had been trying to come up with the money ever since. Wortham was the best-known member of the purchasing group, which included E. R. Barrow, J. Newton Rayzor, Butcher, and Jake Hershey. They planned to use the club as a commercial golf course and for private parties. In March, 1958, Wortham and the same group, along with the Brown brothers' Brown Securities, bought a little over a thousand acres in the northeastern part of Harris County.

Another of Wortham's projects was the development of Merchant's Park Shopping Center on the city's growing near west side. Around 1950 Wortham purchased from the University of Texas land which had originally been given to it by Houston developer Will Hogg, brother of Ima. Builders C. R. Brace and E. R. Carruth (no relation to B. F. or Allen) announced construction of a $5.5 million shopping center at the corner of North Shepherd Drive and East Eleventh Street, close to Timbergrove, a fifteen-hundred-home complex also developed by Brace and Carruth. The center would serve nearly one hundred thousand local residents. Construction apparently did not begin until 1954 but by August of that year, eighty percent of the space had been filled, including leases with Henke and Pillot food stores, Walgreen's drugs, and W. T. Grant. "Merchant's Park is the first shopping center of comparable size in the city's new North West area," said Brace and Carruth. The center opened on March 10, 1955, with twenty-one stores, and an addition across the street was begun in 1960. But at the end of 1960, Wortham sold Merchant's Park to stockbroker Milton Underwood for $3.6 million.[53]

Besides the land on Buffalo Drive and the larger parcels noted above, Gus Wortham owned other parcels in partnership with others, including the R-B-W (Rayzor-Barrow-Wortham) Syndicate group, although it is not certain how much land he owned in the 1950s. He did own several oil and gas properties as a member of R-B-W and Group 27 Properties, both groups involving Rayzor and Edward and David Barrow; with lawyer and oil operator, DeWitt Gordon; and with various other partners including James Abercrombie, W. A.

Smith, and E. D. Adams. These included royalties and leases in Texas, Louisiana, Arkansas, and Colorado. There was also another corporate entity, Lyjania Oil, which very likely was owned by Wortham, E. R. Barrow, and Rayzor because the word was a combination of all three of their wives' names: Lyndall, Jane, and Eugenia. Wortham never considered himself an "oil man" and never particularly liked being confused with one. He would say he did not know much about the oil business, which may have been true, but he did count on people who did know, like Gordon, and would invest with them.[54]

Perhaps Wortham's most important land purchase—outside of his ranching properties—was made in January, 1960, when he bought 1,803 acres from Mrs. Mabel Saunders for $1,100,000, or about $600 an acre. The land was near the intersection of two major roads in northwest Harris County, Highway 290 and Farm to Market Road 1960 with the latter running through the property. From the beginning Wortham realized this land's investment potential because he saw it as a future residential or industrial development site. He had been looking at the land for well over a year and tried to interest Herman and George Brown in going in with him on its purchase as an investment. Wortham recommended that the trustees of his children's trusts participate in the deal. He continued to purchase smaller parcels of land adjoining or near this site, including one across Highway 290.[55] Near that same location, in Fairbanks, Texas, Wortham shared ownership with E. R. Barrow of some fifty acres purchased for $1,750 an acre in 1959. This land was next to a fifty-acre tract owned by American General Investment.

Wortham joined E. R. and David Barrow and Newton Rayzor in investing in land in Austin and surrounding Travis County, where David Barrow was now a developer. In 1955 the group owned almost 250 acres of land in South Austin's Travis Heights, fronting on the new interregional highway, representing a total investment by the group of about $500,000. By the end of 1956, the group owned over 950 acres of land in Denton County north of Dallas as well as in Travis County. In 1957, Rayzor deeded his interest in the Austin properties to Wortham and E. R. Barrow for their interest in the Denton properties. David Barrow continued to buy land for the group in Austin and in a 1958 purchase, David Barrow had the land deeded to his brother, rather than to himself or Wortham, "in order to keep down possible curiosity on the part of the seller as to the purchasers."[56]

There was another kind of business investment of Wortham's that demonstrated how the 8F business elite of Houston was tied together in recreational as well as business pursuits, and how they had fun. The investment probably grew out of the yearly trip, beginning in the 1940s, to the Kentucky Derby by a group of these men headed by Colonel Evans and including Wortham, Elkins, the Browns, and others. In 1955 some of the participants—Wortham, Elkins, Herman Brown, W. A. Smith, and Abercrombie—purchased a racehorse, a bay filly named Bluebonnet, for seven thousand dollars. Records last only through 1957, when the horse may have been sold by the group. She raced several

Houston cronies at the races, probably in the 1950s (*clockwise from bottom left corner*): Robert Abercrombie, Naurice Cummings, Wortham, DeWitt M. Gordon, Jr., Eddie Dyer (*behind Gordon*), J. W. Evans, George A. Butler, and W. M. "Fishback" Wheless. Courtesy American General Corporation.

times, but placed second and fourth only in two races at Churchill Downs in 1956. The Kentucky Derby junkets were well known to Houstonians, and became part of the common lore of the 8F crowd. Wortham also ventured often to Louisiana and yearly to California for horse races. These Texans' devotion to horse racing fitted well into the ideal of the southern gentleman as well as that of the western cowboy, and the "love to take a risk" Texas entrepreneur.[57]

Certainly Wortham's wealth allowed him to indulge in such pleasures without worry, but he had a philosophy about money and its responsible use that he imparted to many other men; it became a sort of "principle." Allen Carruth remembered Wortham telling him:

> Buddy, there's two kinds of dollars. There's a business dollar and a pleasure dollar. And a business dollar, if you can't buy for less than it's worth, you haven't done anything. Anybody can buy something for what it's worth. On the other hand, if it's a pleasure dollar and you want it and you can afford it, it doesn't make a difference what it costs, buy it. But the real problem is don't get your business dollar and your pleasure dollar mixed up.[58]

Accompanying the enlargement of his insurance business and his private enterprises was the growth of Gus Wortham's ranching and cattle-breeding business. The Wortham-Evans ranching partnership had grown to include five pieces of property by the late 1950s: Randle Lake in Milam County (sold in 1962); Nine Bar in Hempstead; Little Eva and Crescent Plantations in Louisiana; Bear Lake, an undeveloped eight thousand acres in Louisiana; and Crystal City Farm in south-central Texas. Wortham and Evans had joint ownership of Randle Lake and the Louisiana properties and, although Evans did not own part of the Nine Bar, he managed it for Wortham.

Many Houstonians thought Gus Wortham just as interested, perhaps even more so, in ranching and breeding Santa Gertrudis than he was in the insurance business. Asked in the 1970s, however, Wortham maintained he was still, first and foremost, an insurance man. But he prided himself on running top-quality agricultural businesses. His fondness for these ventures and his stature as a rancher were recognized early by the Houston economic community. In the summer of 1955, when Wortham was purchasing land in Texas and Louisiana for ranching, one of his 8F cronies, railroad magnate William A. Smith, took over *Post* columnist George Fuermann's column. In it he speculated that Wortham's great interest in land and cattle came from his experience as a young man at the Box T.[59]

The Nine Bar became the prime ranching property for Wortham after its purchase in 1955. He moved the Santa Gertrudis herd here and portions of it also to the Crescent Plantation in Louisiana. Wortham had the herd inspected by the Santa Gertrudis Breeders International (SGBI) Association in 1954. Formed in 1951 with 166 members, the SGBI was a close-knit group of breeders, functioning as both a social group and a trade organization. Kleberg, Armstrong, Briggs, and Briscoe were among the influential and wealthy names that appeared on the group's roster. The size of the group was remarkable given that the new breed had been around only thirty years, and in the two years before Wortham joined, the SGBI had already signed 321 members, 241 in Texas. Wortham was also an active member of the Delta Santa Gertrudis Association, operated mainly in Louisiana and Mississippi; the Florida Santa Gertrudis Association, from which he liked to purchase animals; and the Mid-Coast Santa Gertrudis Association, the local Texas organization to which Wortham belonged with several of his close associates such as Allen Carruth and attorney Mayo Thompson.[60]

By the end of 1959, the Nine Bar had five hundred classified Santa Gertrudis cows and there were plans to increase that to a thousand. At Crescent

Nine Bar Ranch sign. Courtesy American General Corporation.

Plantation, the *Santa Gertrudis Journal* reported in January, 1960, Wortham and Evans had a herd of about three hundred cows that were second-cross accredited Santa Gertrudis. This property, where rich bottom land could support a lot of cattle, was being used for a "grading up breeding program" and it was expected that the whole herd would be purebred Santa Gertrudis in a few years' time. At Little Eva, Wortham and Evans used Santa Gertrudis bulls on commercial cows, but planned to have fifteen hundred Santa Gertrudis there eventually. Cattle were rotated among the ranches for the various stages of the grading-up breeding program. The *Journal*'s article highlighted the fact that the Wortham and Evans team were "near the top of today's list of 'most Active' Santa Gertrudis breeders and promoters."[61]

From the beginning, Wortham and Evans also had several thousand head of steer calves which they bought when weaned, fattened up, and then sold a year later to a feedlot. A 1955 letter to the Houston Packing Company says that the partnership had about seven hundred head of "choice" steer calves to sell, averaging around one hundred pounds. Wortham bragged that the previ-

Robert Kleberg of the King Ranch, Wortham, and Evans at Santa Gertrudis sale in 1966. Courtesy American General Corporation.

ous year the lot had been sold to Armour and Company and were graded "choice." He later explained that the feedlot business was risky because it involved high inventory and sales that were subject to market conditions. Interested strictly in a profit-making business, Wortham also clearly understood that he was in the "meat business" and from the beginning tended to prefer crossbred animals because they produced better meat.

All the ranching properties produced other crops that were marketed including grains, cotton, and pecans, but there is no doubt that the operations required a good deal of capital. Evans would apprise Wortham when cash was needed at any one property, and Wortham would deposit it. For example in October, 1957, Evans asked for $10,000–15,000 dollars for Crescent Plantation and in December another $7,500, because circumstances had prevented harvest of the cotton crop. The cattle and ranching operations were expensive propositions. In the first three years Wortham owned the Nine Bar, he paid out over $350,000 on land, cattle, machinery, housing, and expenses for the ranch.[62] An illustration of the esteem in which Wortham and Evans's prize bull, El Capitan—as well as their whole Santa Gertrudis operation—was held, was in the November, 1959, issue of the *Santa Gertrudis Journal*, which featured a cover picture of the recently deceased animal, identifying him as the "noted herd sire used extensively by Nine Bar Ranch . . . and Payne Briscoe. . . . his recent death came with regret to many."

In 1959 the Nine Bar held the Houston area's first registered Santa Gertrudis production sale. The event made as big a splash on Houston's social pages as it did in the farm columns. Guests at the sale included Winthrop Rockefeller of Arkansas, Robert Kleberg of the King Ranch, and a group of West Coast bankers. Evans and Wortham hosted a party at the Ramada Club the night before the sale, a precedent which became a part of the annual sale tradition. The sale itself featured twenty bulls and twenty heifers. Rockefeller was the top purchaser, paying over eight thousand dollars for two animals. The ranch earned an estimated seventy-five thousand dollars from this first sale.[63] In October, 1960, Wortham thanked Sterling Evans for all he had already done to make the Nine Bar a "beautiful" place with "fine cattle" that he was pleased with and proud of. He also expressed his hopes for the ranch:

> What I would really like to do is to have Nine Bar Ranch the very best anywhere around and for us to have the finest cattle and I would like to have a goal to have our auction sale bring prices comparable with those paid for cattle at the King Ranch and the sales at Winrock Farms [owned by Winthrop Rockefeller]. I know this is a big undertaking and that it will be expensive, but it is tax-deductible, except that every fifth year I have to have an overall profit in the farm operation as a whole.[64]

Wortham and Evans's annual Nine Bar sale would become one of the breed's major production sales, a regular on the circuit of sales held yearly and one of the "big four Santa Gertrudis sales," attracting politicians and dignitaries along with the magnificent animals. It was judged the most "citified" of the Santa Gertrudis sales, which included auctions at ranches owned by Briggs, Rockefeller, and, of course, the Klebergs. (As the number of breeders and annual sales grew, Wortham and his Santa Gertrudis cronies would make a yearly round of the various sales, buying animals from each other.)

Wortham had other plans for his prized Santa Gertrudis besides the annual sale and show. In 1958 he and Lyndall set up a small foundation geared toward funding Texas-based projects. At first it was a rather eclectic foundation, giving monies to the Houston Symphony, Museum of Fine Arts, the United Fund, and a few other religious, charitable, and educational projects. Then in 1960, Wortham made the decision to give the foundation a purpose: to fund experimental research in the study of fertility in beef cattle. He told the press he hoped to take a different approach to solving world hunger problems with an emphasis on future food supply. "We want to do something broader than just being interested in individual students or in financing the erection of buildings," he said. Sterling Evans, whom Wortham named to head the foundation, recruited Dr. R. O. Berry of Texas A&M University to direct the research. The program centered on the problem of why certain female beef cattle were infertile. The average calf yield from a female herd was only about

Mr. and Mrs. Gus S. Wortham at the Nine Bar, November 1967. Courtesy American General Corporation.

eighty percent. Berry was the first to transplant ova in farm animals and was studying ova maturation and methods of ova storage and fertility. He worked in a laboratory at the Nine Bar, using Wortham's six hundred breed cows.[65] Wortham stressed to Evans: "I am also deeply interested in the work to be done by the Foundation and Dr. Berry and I would like to see that he has full facilities to carry on the various types of work that we decide will be beneficial in the

Young Lyndall with son Russell and daughter Margaret, with Gus, Diana, and Lyndall. Early 1960s. Courtesy American General Corporation.

accomplishment of our Foundation goal."[66] Both Berry and Wortham held the firm belief that the population explosion would demand a fifty-eight percent increase in calf crops by the mid-1970s, and that by the year 2000, two-and-one-half times more would be needed.[67]

Wortham obviously wanted a lot of attention for this work. He announced the foundation's new focus at a dinner at the posh Ramada Club, attended by, among others, the chancellor of Texas A&M, the chairman of the school's animal husbandry department, the head of the Texas Agricultural Experimental Station, and thirty-six reporters from southeast Texas. Wortham was lauded by the *Post* as "a man of broad vision" for putting into systematic form the philanthropy of the foundation. The paper was certain, based upon his success as a businessman and a rancher, that he would make a success of the foundation's work, especially with the association of Sterling Evans.

The foundation held its first annual symposium on cattle fertility the next spring, 1961, one topic being the pros and cons of artificial insemination, which most breeders' associations did not favor. The symposium would grow in prominence during the next several years, as had Wortham's annual auction and sale.

Whether Wortham thought of the foundation primarily as a way to get certain tax advantages on his ranching operations is not known; there is an indication, however, that this did play a part in its primary thrust because Wortham used his own animals for the foundation's work. But in 1969, Wortham was forced to change the direction of the foundation when the Internal Revenue Service, responding to a decade of changes in foundation tax law, disallowed the foundation's tax-exempt status because Wortham was using his own herds.[68]

With the creation of the foundation, his increase in land and ranch holdings, and the growth of his insurance business, Wortham solidified his standing as a southwestern gentleman; the successful man of commerce who owned and worked the land and was recognized as a civic statesman. It was a good perspective from which to contemplate one's role as community elder. But, at a point in life when he might have considered retirement and certainly had provided well for himself and his family, Gus Wortham was still vitally involved in all his ventures. He was building and enlarging with few thoughts of handing any of it over or slowing down. Indeed, Gus Wortham had plans for his institutions that would require what some could only see as the passions of a much younger man: change and risk.

CHAPTER EIGHT

In Pursuit of Empires

In the early 1960s, as Gus Wortham entered his seventies, he remained an aggressive seeker of new opportunities, in land and in business. The creation of his foundation did not in any way stop his search for more land to own. For some time Wortham had taken long drives on afternoons or weekend mornings to "look at land." Those trips continued now, especially on Sunday mornings with Lester Randle or one of Wortham's associates, often a young protégé such as his cousin Rusty Wortham, a Houston developer, or Charlie Boswell, the president of AG Investment. They would drive around and look at parcels that were for sale, ending up at the Nine Bar where Wortham might drive through the pastures inspecting his beloved Santa Gertrudis.

But the continued building of his business empire held Wortham in even greater thrall. Although he often depended on Ben Woodson's lead in acquisitions, he remained fully the leader of his insurance conglomerate. In accord with his faith in change, he also backed American General's diversification into related financial arenas. In charge and in pursuit, Wortham was moving toward a major corporate acquisition attempt that would raise his conglomerate of insurance and financial companies to the status of a business empire.[1]

As American General entered the 1960s, it was an image of strength and unity that Gus Wortham and Ben Woodson sought for their burgeoning group of companies. They stressed the idea of the parent, American General, as a de facto holding company; the parent of a "family" diagramed in each year's annual report. In the 1961 annual report, Wortham touted the company's stature "among the older and larger groups writing all forms of insurance, and . . . among the pioneers in multiple-line operation."[2]

These were good years for the American General group. In 1961 the group topped the $60 million mark in premium income, and total life insurance in force passed the $2 billion mark in February, 1962, which made the previous year the group's best ever. In 1963 the statutory earnings were up almost fifteen percent to over $6.4 million, despite continuing industry-wide troubles in the fire and casualty business, and loss of the group's largest group life holder. Gradually, Woodson and Wortham had been consolidating the operations of the acquired companies into the parent operations. Knight's Life became American General of Delaware and Home State became American General of Oklahoma at the end of 1962, thus practically if not legally merging the three life companies, although keeping home office operations in Pittsburgh and Oklahoma City intact. Hawaiian Life kept its own identity to capitalize on its status in an unusual market. American General's life companies operated in all but the seven northeastern states of the union.[3]

American General Investment remained "one of the nation's larger mortgage loan firms," with more than 37,000 loans worth over $327 million in 1962. The next year AG Investment earned over $320,000. It had continued to branch into commercial lending and by the early 1960s had gotten into commercial and joint venture projects, such as the Tennessee Gas Building in Houston, for which AG Investment secured a $29 million loan—the second largest real estate loan made by the Metropolitan Insurance Company.[4]

With Wortham's encouragement and advice, Ben Woodson was constantly on the lookout for companies. Other Texas firms, such as Southwestern Life and Southland Life, had acquired companies and American General looked at Amicable of Waco and South Coast Life of Houston. Woodson investigated and mulled over possibilities given to him by brokers or insiders at firms around the country, but at the end of 1962 was disappointed with himself for not having completed a merger that year.[5]

More than disappointment came with the death that fall of two of Gus Wortham's closest confidants, Joseph Evans and Herman Brown. Gus had played cards in 7F at least weekly with the Colonel, and probably saw Brown as often. Brown was not only an 8F confidant but a valued customer of Wortham's and his insurance business. For years, John L. Wortham and Son and American General had provided the fidelity bonding insurance to cover Brown & Root's massive building projects. And Herman Brown was a big influence on the political involvements of Wortham, especially his connections with Lyndon Johnson.

Evans, of course, was one of Wortham's oldest friends, one of the original shareholders and members of the American General board. Wortham depended upon him for advice. And he truly loved Evans for his personable demeanor and ability as a social raconteur. Wortham had a portrait of Evans painted and hung it in his office. Surely, the deaths of these two men not only reminded Gus of his own mortality, but left large voids in his life.[6]

Although there were many courtships in the early 1960s for American General, only two small mergers occurred. In 1963 it added a third fire and casualty company, Oregon Automobile Insurance Company and its subsidiary, the North Pacific Insurance Company. That state's oldest and largest casualty company gave AG entry to the Pacific Northwest market, for life business as well as fire. As before, AG kept the company's management intact.

Negotiations with the late Jesse Jones's Houston Endowment for Jones's Commercial and Industrial Life had begun in 1961, but the deal was not consummated until 1964. The company, founded in 1947 and specializing in group life and pensions, had branches in five states. It was purchased for $10 million in cash. Jones had been Wortham's mentor, financial backer and friend and now Wortham, whose management abilities Jones had praised, was looking after Jones's company. But Wortham did not keep the company intact with its original name: at the beginning of 1965 it became a division of AG Life. The *Chronicle* noted that American General was in the top four percent of the nation's fifteen hundred insurance companies.[7]

But long before the completion of these mergers, most of Wortham and Woodson's energies were centered around the possibilities of a new affiliation with one of the giants of the fire and casualty industry, Maryland Casualty Company. The decision to pursue this acquisition would profoundly affect the future of the American General group.

Established in 1898 to write casualty insurance, Maryland Casualty had added fidelity and surety bonding in 1910, and fire and marine in 1951. It had subsidiaries in New York and New England that handled specialized markets, and a system of branch offices to coordinate its large number of general agencies throughout the country. By 1963 it had an established fire and casualty business in every state, Puerto Rico, the Canal Zone, the Virgin Islands, and Canada. It had 3,900 loyal, mostly long-term employees; and had over ten thousand shareholders. Its home office building, set on twenty-three acres in Baltimore's northern suburbs, bespoke the company's stability and prestige. Indeed, John L. Wortham and Son had represented Maryland Casualty for over twenty-five years.[8]

For American General this was "the big time"; and a big gamble. Maryland Casualty, a company with a national reputation and presence, was, unbelievably, under siege from the little Texas conglomerate with the unremarkable name (a newsman said) of American General. But this was no game; it was a serious proposition. If some saw it as the minnow swallowing the whale, in the plans of Wortham and Woodson the "winner" in a merger with Maryland Casualty would nevertheless be American General. It would be the surviving, acquiring company. But it would be a difficult deal due to the disparity in dividends—two dollars per share for Maryland Casualty, sixty cents per share for AG—and in market value, sixty dollars per share "The Maryland" against AG's thirty dollars per share. At the end of 1963 the two companies compared thus:

	Admitted Assets	Capital and Surplus
American General group	$381,912,000	$ 40,465,000
Maryland Casualty group	$392,841,000	$142,343,000[9]

Unlike most other AG acquisitions, the Maryland Casualty bid was primarily Wortham's idea. Gus Wortham had planned this merger, studying for four years how he could make "The Maryland" part of his group.

> We were doing a nationwide life business, and our desire was to do a nationwide fire and casualty business. If we stayed in fire and casualty only in Texas, it would be so small that we could use our energies better just to concentrate on the life business. We had thought about the Maryland Casualty. . . . It looked like a logical thing. It seemed to be a company that we could help and they could help us.[10]

Wortham explained later.

Wortham professed to have known the president of Maryland Casualty, J. Ellsworth Miller, for many years, ever since Miller had been the "clerk in a small agency in Texas." But it is unknown exactly when Wortham seriously began to consider the integration of Maryland Casualty with his interests. It was clear by late 1962, however, that Wortham had studied the company, for he told Woodson his idea of forming a holding company for three companies and American General, one being Maryland Casualty. He believed the Maryland and the other two would fit well together with AG, and the stock of all three was then selling for less than book value.[11]

Central to Wortham's desire for Maryland Casualty was its business in the East and the desire to make AG a complete "all lines" entity such as State Farm, within the next five years. American General had been one of the pioneers of all lines when it had acquired Seaboard Life in 1945, but this merger would put them in the business of all-lines underwriting in a major way—"that is, the underwriting of all forms of insurance by a single, integrated group of companies."[12]

Through New York broker J. William Middendorf II, American General made the first approach to Maryland Casualty. Middendorf had tried and failed to bring together Northern Insurance of New York with American General the year before. However, he did broker a merger with Northern and Maryland Casualty. He felt he owed a favor to American General, and attempted to try out Maryland Casualty for AG. In June, 1963, American General bought fifteen thousand shares of Maryland Casualty. Wortham told Woodson he was thinking of a merger involving AG, Maryland Casualty and Gulf Insurance, in which Maryland Casualty, with its charter and reputation, would be the survivor while key AG stockholders would retain control through a stock exchange.[13]

Discussions began between the Maryland and American General in mid-1963, amicably at first. As the negotiations began, Woodson and Wortham pushed the idea of a holding company with Baltimore as the home office for the fire and casualty business.[14]

Woodson visited Baltimore twice and Maryland Casualty's leadership met with Woodson and Wortham in Houston. Remarkably, it seemed as if the merger arrangements were working out smoothly; only one item, how long preferred stock should be callable, was in contention. While there was some apprehension, Wortham and Woodson thought they had a deal and Ben Woodson noticed that Gus seemed more enthused than at any time in Woodson's ten years with the company.

Then in the middle of December, 1963, just a week after their visit to Houston, Maryland Casualty management called off the merger negotiations. Wortham and Woodson believed the Maryland Casualty people woke up to the reality of who would be the "survivor" when they came to Houston and saw the massive steel structure of AG's half-completed new home office. And they realized that American General's life insurance business was at least twice as big as its fire and casualty.[15] In the meantime, Woodson had contacted one of Maryland Casualty's largest investors, Insurance Securities Incorporated (ISI), a mutual fund in San Francisco, which very much favored the merger. ISI owned ten percent of both Maryland's and AG's stocks.[16]

Ellsworth Miller told Wortham he did not think it would be a good move for Maryland Casualty, although he still had not talked to his board or the stockholders. Wortham said he did not consider the matter closed, but the next day he and Woodson drove to the Nine Bar and talked; the younger man tried to keep Wortham aggressive about the deal.[17]

On December 27, Miller told American General that a committee of his board had directed him to deny all of the many rumors that had circulated about a possible merger of the two companies. Although discouraged, Wortham agreed to let Woodson have his way and go directly to the Maryland Casualty stockholders if turned down by either its management or board. Success was possible with this move, as the Maryland management had direct control of only around three percent of the outstanding stock of the company.[18]

On January 6, the AG board endorsed the proposed merger and set up a special committee composed of Judge Elkins, George Butler, John T. Jones, Jr. (Jesse's nephew and publisher of the *Chronicle*), and Ben Woodson to consider and help implement any merger action. The next day, a formal offer to affiliate was made to Maryland Casualty. Miller's courteous but formal reply came on January 22, indicating that Maryland Casualty's executive committee and full board of directors would discuss the offer. The board appointed a committee of outside directors to study the offer to affiliate. But when the special committees of the two companies met on March 10 in Washington, Maryland Casualty declined the offer. American General publicly called off the negotiations.[19]

Wortham and Woodson were committed to the affiliation; they would go directly to the stockholders. Lehman Brothers investment banking firm agreed to act as the manager for a group of investment dealers to solicit shares of Maryland Casualty for exchange. Woodson informed Miller of the exchange offering on May 5, 1964, and requested a list of its stockholders. "The request was denied."[20]

American General countered by filling a registration statement with the

Securities and Exchange Commission for 1.1 million additional shares of common stock and 3.4 million shares of newly issued preferred stock, all proposed to be exchanged for Maryland Casualty stock tendered by its stockholders. AG would offer one-third of a share of common and one share of the new $1.80 cumulative voting preferred stock for each of Maryland Casualty's 3.3 million shares. American General did not make its acceptance conditional on a certain amount or percentage received; it was sure that if a controlling interest were gained and announced, the rest of the stock ultimately would be tendered. Its confidence reflected the fact that American General stock was then being traded at 92½, Maryland Casualty's at 60¾. American General added that a joining of the two companies would not constitute a real merger, for Maryland Casualty would retain its home office, personnel, and identity.[21]

Miller urged his stockholders not to sell, saying, "The Maryland will use every available legal means to oppose American General's action, since, in our opinion, the offer is totally inadequate to safeguard your interest." Meanwhile, with the help of Lehman Brothers, AG took its "show on the road," visiting major brokerage houses and stockholder groups across the country.[22]

Its ownership of eleven percent of Maryland Casualty's stock entitled American General to inspect and copy the stock ledger, and on June 1 AG filed suit to force the Maryland to allow it to do so. Maryland Casualty countered by filing an antitrust suit in U.S. District Court on July 7, alleging that American General's acquisition of stock was a violation of antitrust laws and seeking a restraining order preventing further exchange of stock. The restraining order was granted, but on July 27, a Washington judge denied a request for a permanent injunction and, instead, issued an order permitting the exchange offer. But on July 29, the court denied American General's suit to inspect the stockholder list, forcing it to rely on newspaper advertisements and investment dealers to find and contact the Maryland Casualty shareholders.[23]

The Securities and Exchange Commission, however, did approve American General's exchange offer on August 3, 1964, just as AG announced its plans to acquire Jones's C&I Life. The prospectuses were printed and investment dealers began soliciting stockholders. At the same time, Republican Congressman Charles Mathias of Maryland introduced a bill to provide for a federal conference to review antitrust laws to see why they did not stop the AG stock swap. He also claimed that ISI, with over $1 billion invested in various stock insurance companies, was using its power to interfere with the Maryland's management.[24]

But by September 12—two weeks after the exchange offer was made—AG had acquired more than forty-two percent of Maryland Casualty stock, bringing its total to fifty-three percent and "giving American General its long-sought casualty foot-hold in the heavily populated Eastern states." Wortham extended the exchange offer, hoping to acquire eighty percent and making the offer tax-free to Maryland Casualty shareholders. At this time, American General obtained a computer listing of all the company's shareholders.[25]

With working control lost to American General, Maryland Casualty's board and management agreed to discuss consolidation, although they certainly did not want it believed that they had "capitulated" to American General. On October 15 a statement was released by both companies that a "program to affiliate" had been approved. Maryland Casualty dropped its objections to the exchange and withdrew the antitrust suit. The story listed the main points of the agreement: Maryland Casualty would remain a separate entity with its home in Baltimore and the board and executive committee of American General would be composed of an equal number of members from both companies. By November 20, 1964—the first meeting of the new, combined board—AG owned 97.4 percent of Maryland Casualty's stock. Unwieldy, disparate and contentious as it was, Gus Wortham had his national insurance company.[26]

American General had also acquired a new, more aggressive corporate image. Unfriendly mergers were still relatively rare among businesses in this era, and one of this magnitude—the largest contested merger ever to happen in the insurance industry—received considerable attention, augmented by the fact that the fight, as one newspaper said, involved the Securities and Exchange Commission, the state and federal courts, and even the U.S. Congress.[27]

American General was now a nationwide company in both the fire and casualty and the life insurance businesses, and one of the twenty largest insurance firms in the United States.[28] The Maryland American General Group consisted of eighteen separate companies, fourteen of them insurance companies. (The Maryland Casualty merger had brought five subsidiary companies with it.) *Insurance Graphic* described the huge, new entity:

> . . . contracts are held with a total of 9,800 individual fire and casualty agencies . . . operating in 50 states; 200 life insurance agencies spread across 42 states plus a few foreign countries; 1,600 full-time life insurance underwriters. . . . The stock of the publicly-owned company is now held by a total of 25,908 shareholders . . . a total of 7,781,368 shares are outstanding . . . total assets of over $825 million . . . capital and surplus of $187 million. Total income of the group for 1964 was $320 million, and premium income, $190 million. . . . [29]

Moving from a fire and casualty operation in two states to one operating in all fifty, American General faced two unsatisfactory years in the fire and casualty insurance industry. The year 1964 was the worst since 1957, and both AG and Maryland Casualty had heavy underwriting losses. The next year was also bad for the industry, but by then Wortham had launched a program to streamline operations so that there would be an increase in profits from the already sizeable volume of fire and casualty business; and in the life business, to increase the volume of the already profitable life sales. Part of the reorganization also included the sale of Oregon Automobile and its subsidiaries to avoid duplication.[30]

Among the profound consequences of the merger was the dissolution of the management contract under which American General had been administered by the agency, John L. Wortham and Son, since 1926. It was obvious that such a management arrangement would be unwieldy with so large an entity; it was time for the partnership of John L. Wortham and Son to separate itself from its ward, American General. Each of the twenty-five partners of the firm, many of whom were closely affiliated with both entities, had to choose which side of the business they wished to remain attached to; and a fair price had to be determined for the company to pay the firm for the physical properties used by the company and the value of the business. The termination price was decided at $1.5 million. Fourteen of the partners elected to go with the corporation, including Wortham, Woodson, Barrow, and Mauk. Those staying with the firm included Link and Carruth. Consolidating the Texas business of Maryland Casualty and AG, the parent company kept a small amount of property casualty business, but in reality was the holding company for the much-enlarged group.[31]

Almost as if it had been planned to coincide with and reward its new national stature, American General moved into its impressive new headquarters building early in 1965. The nine hundred Houston employees were now housed in the same building—the city's eighth tallest—for the first time in many years.

Building plans for American General's new home had been announced in October, 1962: A twenty-five story, three-hundred-thousand-square-foot building that was the first phase of a multimillion-dollar cluster of buildings on Allen Parkway. There was a three-stage development plan, culminating in seventeen buildings on the twenty-five-acre site.

Wortham, Woodson, and Barrow had been thoroughly involved in all aspects of the $11 million building from choosing the architectural firm through its completion. The new building, "facing the recently beautified Buffalo Bayou," had all the latest amenities including indirect lighting, flexible space, under-floor ducts for the utilities, and automatic elevators.[32]

The building's location was almost as innovative as its design. West of downtown, it was an area with no other comparable buildings and Wortham took a chance not only on whether his business could be run efficiently away from the commercial center, but also that others would follow his lead and relocate there.[33]

The AG building opening was cause for local celebration, and the *Chronicle* and the *Post* published special advertising supplements celebrating the dedication of the building in March, 1965. "The Powers Behind American General," included biographies of Wortham, Barrow, Woodson, Link, and Judge Elkins. The article described the four men as being alike in that they were "quiet, assured men who exude[d] confidence and the intangible aura of success." All four, the article said, had helped in building Houston as well as American General.[34]

A national insurance publication used a similar theme—the tremendous growth of Houston symbolized by the rapid expansion of American General.

Gus Wortham and Benjamin Woodson, then president of American General Life, with sketch of new home office to be built on Allen Parkway. August, 1962. Courtesy American General Corporation.

Like other press about AG's growth, Wortham's leadership was mentioned. The writer said he had attended many insurance events with Gus Wortham and cited his "calmness, his alertness, his fairness and his personal efficiency." *Southern Insurance* said, on the fiftieth anniversary of John L. Wortham and Son in 1965, that Gus Wortham was "an accomplished leader whose name was a byword in the South before it became so in the nation."[35]

Consummating the beginnings of an insurance empire with his Maryland Casualty acquisition and overseeing the building of its new home, Gus Wortham also found time during these years to increase his land holdings, creating another empire in land.

In July, 1962, Wortham and E. R. and David Barrow purchased a 340-acre farm from St. Edward's University in Austin, Texas, for about $1.1 million. The land was on the Southern Interregional Highway and Ben White Boulevard and included a site already chosen as the site for the Internal Revenue Service's data processing operation. The *Austin American-Statesman* in "A New Austin Investor, Or, Gus Wortham's Stake," noted David Barrow's prominence as a real-estate broker and called Wortham "one of the South's biggest landowners." It claimed that in just sixty days one of Austin's biggest contractors, James Odom, won the bid to build and lease the $3 million IRS building on the site, making the syndicate's stake worth about $4 million. The next year, Wortham received St. Edward's University Coronat Award for high ethics in business life.[36]

A prime parcel of real estate in Houston was also available at this time: the San Jacinto Ordnance Depot on the Houston Ship Channel. Wortham and a syndicate including George Brown and William A. Smith bid on the forty-five hundred acres of industrial land under the name of Wortham's corporation, Alert Mart. Their bid in December, 1963, was the only one submitted. The government, which had tried to sell the site five times, rejected it. With John F. Kennedy's assassination and Lyndon Johnson's ascension to the presidency, Wortham and his group decided against resubmitting a bid for fear of attracting criticism of political favoritism.[37]

During this period, too, Wortham and Evans bought ranch land in New Mexico. Big tracts of New Mexican land were leased to ranchers for notoriously low prices—some at five cents an acre—with the proceeds going to the state's education fund. New state administrators desired to change this situation and began to offer the land at public auction. The terms of sale were almost as unbelievable as the rental prices: five percent down with the balance not due for thirty years and a yearly interest rate of four percent. Wortham and Evans planned to use the land for their steer calf business. The auctions were not widely advertised outside the state and when Wortham and Evans showed up to bid, raising the stakes, there was no little consternation on the part of the locals.[38]

Their first purchase of New Mexican land was in September, 1962, when they bid on some twenty-seven thousand acres of state land leased to the Mitchell family in Harding County. They paid twenty-seven dollars an acre on land appraised at fourteen. In October, 1963, they paid twenty-four dollars an acre for over twenty-two thousand acres of the Ortiz y Pino Ranch and the following January, Wortham and Evans were the highest bidders on the Haggerman Ranch, some fifty-nine thousand acres in Santa Fe, Torrence, and San Miguel counties, near the Ortiz y Pino land. This became the heart of their New Mexico Nine Bar Ranch at Clines Corners. The total sales price was $2.1 million. A spirited bidding war went on between Wortham and C. D. Shamburger of Wichita Falls for one 21,500-acre plot. The press reported that since 1962, Wortham had purchased more than 108,000 acres of state-owned New Mexican land for a total of $3.1 million.[39] In April, 1964, the *West Texas Live-*

Ranching partners Gus Wortham and Sterling C. Evans. Courtesy Sterling C. Evans.

stock Weekly published a major article on the history of Wortham's land acquisitions, including the New Mexican purchases (claiming they amounted to some 110,000 acres).[40]

As a Santa Fe journalist pointed out, the land deals were very good for rich investors who could buy the land cheaply and hold it with money that would otherwise go to taxes. They held the land and waited for its value to rise.

A reporter for Scripps-Howard News Service connected these land deals to the many of great wealth who had gone into the cattle-raising business to reduce their taxable income. "Anyone who has watched the recent purchases of land in New Mexico knows that the sales are not going to the old-time ranch families . . . but to a wholly new class of land owner looking for capital gains treatment."[41] Wortham and Evans understood this perfectly and these circumstances, plus the excitement for Wortham of owning large expanses of land, made these deals irresistible.

Then, on October 15, 1964, *The New Mexican* in Santa Fe published a piece detailing how the previous month Wortham had called off a contract "that was costing him $1.29 an acre per year in interest payments" and was now renting the same land from the state for thirteen to fifteen cents an acre per year. He said Wortham wanted to cancel the contract on the Ortiz y Peno land, for which a thirty-thousand-dollar interest payment was due, and have the same kind of rental arrangement with the state for it. Robert Anderson, against whom Wortham had bid, was telegraphing the land commissioner to protest Wortham's being able to lease land he had defaulted upon, asking instead that the land be put up for sale again. Wortham and Evans continued to lease the land.

In the summer of 1967, Lowry Haggerman protested the renewal of a lease to Wortham because he claimed Wortham had not filed his renewal on time. Wortham had bought the land that Haggerman formerly had leased in 1964, had quit-claimed thirty-seven thousand acres back to the state, and then leased it from the state. A news article also pointed out that the group insurer for State of New Mexico employees was American General.[42]

Two more properties would be acquired in New Mexico. In 1966, Wortham teamed up with Charlie Crowder, a land developer-speculator, and acquired land near Belen, New Mexico, just south of Albuquerque; in 1968 Wortham and Evans bought the historic U Bar Ranch on the Mexican border. They sold it the next year when a buyer offered them $3.8 million for the 155,000 acres, giving them a profit of $1.87 million on the deal.[43] In the midst of these huge land deals, in 1965 American General acquired the Agricultural-Livestock Finance Corporation and reorganized it to provide "ranch loans in Texas."[44]

The New Mexican land became just the newest part of Wortham and Evans's already established, profitable ranching and farming business, which now also included leased land in South Texas. The biggest part of the Wortham-Evans operation, at least in sales, was the steer feeding operation, for which they handled between six thousand and ten thousand head a year.[45]

But the Nine Bar Ranch near Houston became Wortham's showplace and the epitome of how a Texan capitalist-rancher operated. Wortham wanted the Hempstead ranch to be the best, with the finest cattle, and an auction sale that equaled those at the King Ranch and Rockefeller's Winrock Farms.[46] After all, he pointed out, it was all tax deductible.

Astronaut Frank Borman, Ambassador (to Australia) Edward Clark, and Wortham at the lavish pre–Nine Bar auction party, April, 1968. Courtesy American General Corporation.

The annual Nine Bar auction, with its lavish party the evening before, became a prominent event on the Houston social calendar. Wortham and Evans hosted the cocktail party at a suitably ritzy Houston location, often the Petroleum Club or one of the private clubs to which Wortham belonged.[47] The auction followed the next day at the ranch, under a huge tent with box lunches, entertainment and the services of auctioneer Walter Britten for the main event.

The 1961 auction, which attracted over five hundred people, some of them arriving in eight airplanes and one helicopter, brought in $116,325 for thirty-eight Santa Gertrudis animals. The take at the 1962 sale of thirty-six animals was $108,275 and engendered a large photo spread in the *Houston Chronicle*, "Big Men, Big Money, Big Day at Nine Bar," touting the sale as one of the country's top three along with those at the King Ranch and at Winthrop Rockefeller's Winrock Farms. Buyers included 8F stalwarts W. A. Smith, Elkins, Abercrombie, and Butler, as well as SGI breeder-capitalists like R. W. Briggs and the Klebergs.[48] In 1963, during serious dealings with the recalcitrant Maryland Casualty, Wortham still managed to entertain four hundred at a lavish pre-auction party at the Petroleum Club that was even attended by Governor John Connally and scientist Edward Teller, in town for a visit. One bull sold for $28,000; reportedly one of the highest sellers in the breed. At the 1964 auction, the King Ranch purchased the top-rated bull for $25,800. The Associated Press covered the auction at which "cattlemen from all over the United States" attended and paid $118,450 for thirty-four animals.[49]

The party and auction in 1965 made an even bigger impact on the social pages, in addition to netting Wortham $229,900 for thirty animals, including ten bulls weighing ten tons. Long-time *Houston Chronicle* society writer Maxine Mesinger announced the 1966 sale, noting "it's always one of the most social events of the season for the ranch set . . ." while the *Post* proclaimed it the social, agricultural, and zoological event of the week. The preceding night's dinner was held at the Warwick and included guests from Hawaii, Australia, and a representative of the world's largest cattle company. The sale attracted seven hundred people. The guest of honor, rancher-Governor Connally, praised Wortham and Evans for improving the livestock business in the Gulf Coast. At the sale, a half interest in Bull 099, the son of El Capitan, was sold for $32,500. The bull remained at the Nine Bar, his frozen semen being sent to the new owner in Georgia.[50]

The buyers among the thousand people who attended the 1967 sale paid $137,000 for twenty heifers and bulls; Robert Kleberg paid $30,000 for one animal. The *Post's* society page gave the sale an even larger than usual photo spread and the *Chronicle*'s *Texas Magazine* dubbed it a "country club picnic." A 130-pound bull constructed of cocoa and lard, rotating to music, was the centerpiece for the 1968 cocktail party and the 1969 pre-party was attended, as usual, by a host of Texas politicians like Governor Preston Smith, Lieutenant Governor Ben Ramsey, and Speaker of the House Gus Mutscher. Former President Johnson attended the sale the next day, along with a thousand other guests. "Other than the Houston Livestock Show, it's the biggest livestock sale extravaganza in this area." The final Nine Bar sale was held in 1974, shortly before Wortham sold the ranch.[51]

It was all great fun, of course, but the cattle-raising was business, too. And Gus Wortham was very serious about the work of the Wortham Research Laboratory and its annual symposium, sponsored by his foundation. Advanced in the study of artificial insemination and with state-of-the-art facilities for processing and storing animal semen, the lab was declared "one of the reasons why Houston was becoming 'one of the world's top cattle producing centers.'" In 1961, the fertility symposium dealt with the use of artificial insemination to produce a hundred percent calf crop, attracting around three hundred participants. The next year the auction sold the first blood-typed animals—buyers could know the "blood factors which . . . indicate hereditary characteristics." They would also know which bulls sired how many calves, without building fences. This novel advancement attracted international attention in the cattle world. Later in 1962, at the second annual symposium, the keynote speaker was a British researcher specializing in cattle milk production and in artificial insemination for breeding. The Nine Bar ranch and lab often played host to a number of international scientists, agricultural experts, and cattle businessmen touring the country, with visits regularly arranged by the U.S. government.[52]

In 1963, Dr. Jan Bonsma of South Africa was the guest speaker at the foundation's fertility symposium. Bonsma had a worldwide reputation for his ability to select fertile cattle by sight. Bonsma was hired the following year by the Texas Department of Agriculture at the ranch and at Texas A&M. Three hundred breeders and ranchers attended the symposium in September, 1964, which got national attention for its fertility work.[53]

Work continued at the lab on blood typing animals to trace the ancestry of cattle—a factor especially important to breeders who used artificial insemination. AI (or the "abominable ampule," as one of Wortham's SG breeder friends called it) continued to be a source of much controversy among beef cattle breeders. In another innovative move, for its 1965 sale the Nine Bar used ultrasonic equipment to evaluate bulls for their lean or fat qualities. Later that year the annual symposium featured a Dutch expert on cattle stillbirths.[54]

After the 1969 federal tax laws disallowed Wortham's use of his own herd for the purposes of the laboratory, the foundation, which was not large, concentrated on more philanthropic projects, with monies going to various mainstream community groups such as the United Fund and the Houston Symphony. Sterling Evans, who had headed the foundation since its beginning, turned over the reins in 1971 to Allen Carruth.[55]

As his empires grew and his life lengthened, Gus Wortham's longevity and activity had earned him a kind of "grand old man" status which he began to acquire in the early 1960s. And he found himself the recipient of many honors. In 1962 Wortham was honored by two Texas institutions of higher education. As he retired from the Rice University board of trustees, he was appointed to its emeritus board of governors; the same month George Brown added Ben Woodson to the Rice board. The University of Texas chose Wortham, Judge Elkins, former Governor Allan Shivers, and former Supreme Court member Tom Clark to receive distinguished alumni awards in 1962. Wortham's brief acceptance speech at the UT awards dinner made news when he reminded the gathering to "remember this school in your prayers . . . and your wills." Clearly, the university was hoping for a remembrance from him, describing him in the publicity as an "educational philanthropist." Also that fall, Wortham, probably through Sterling Evans's impetus, was named to the Texas A&M Century Council, a group of one hundred prominent Texans.[56]

In 1966, Tarleton State College presented its first distinguished alumni award to Wortham. Tarleton had "truly picked a winner," said local columnist Morris Frank, in choosing "the likeable and widely known Wortham" who had "attained success in such various kingdoms" that Frank could not list them all. About five hundred people attended the dinner in Stephenville and heard a Wortham protégé, former Lieutenant Governor Ben Barnes, describe him as a "builder of Texas." This tribute also prompted an impressive feature story in the

Chronicle under the headline, "Gus Wortham: Beauty in a Sunset, A Sonnet or a Financial Statement." The sunset-and-sonnet remark was Lyndall's; the article also quoted her, Evans, Wortham's secretary Jerry Reidy, and cook Edna Ammons. Gus was portrayed as a beneficent business tycoon "with agate-hard brown eyes in a pink-jowled face," who was Jesse Jones's match at poker, thought liquor was fine "as long as you're the master of it," and ate gourmet dishes and steaks but preferred corn bread and soup. But when asked if he was ready to retire, Gus Wortham's reply was, "Hell, no."[57]

And he was not, although he had conceded it was time to let Ben Woodson have a chance. In April, 1966, Wortham stepped down as president in favor of Woodson, although retaining his board chairmanship and status as CEO. In reality, he and Woodson had worked so much together establishing the major direction of the companies that there would not be much difference. And, although it might publicly look as if he was giving up a little, Gus Wortham still held his place as founder and final word.[58]

Thirteen years after Wortham had first discussed it at Woodson's hiring, American General finally got a strong toehold in the New York market in May, 1966, with the cash purchase of Patriot Life from CIT Financial Corporation. But even the company's entry into fifty states and the District of Columbia did not sate Wortham and Woodson's appetites for acquisition properties.

Twice in 1966, an investment dealer informed AG of the availability of shares of one of the South's most prominent companies, Life and Casualty Insurance of Tennessee (L&C). L&C had begun business in Nashville in 1903, selling life, health, and accident insurance on a debit basis. It was still led by a group descended from its wealthy and socially prominent founders, although its controlling interest had been sold in 1959 to Clint and John Murchison, two of Texas' wealthiest independent oil men. This ownership made the original founders and Nashvillians nervous, for, although relations with the Murchisons were amicable and "management was skillful and professional, their ownership lacked paternalism." Even more importantly, the Murchisons were known to be constantly on the make, and there was fear that the company might be sold to a group much less acceptable. The company's current president, Guilford Dudley, a descendant of one of the founders, was a long-time acquaintance of Ben Woodson.[59]

The tips American General had received about L&C concerned a portion of the Murchisons' interest, some fifteen percent of the outstanding stock. A third call offered this stock at an even lower price than previously. Woodson called Dudley who was pleased with the prospect that American General would acquire the Murchisons' shares. Negotiations went ahead rapidly; in just a little over three weeks Wortham and Woodson were meeting with John Murchison and Dudley in Houston to finalize the deal. The final purchase of the Murchison shares was made by AG (thirteen percent) and members of the management of Life and Casualty (two percent) for $21 million. Although Woodson became chairman of the L&C board, he and Wortham, working closely with

Dudley, were careful to affirm that nothing about the company or its operations would change under their stock ownership.[60]

Woodson believed some type of affiliation with an established debit life operation like Life and Casualty would surely make American General a leader in this field. And its joining with yet another established firm, associated with the best of mid-South society, could only enhance AG's reputation. In early 1967, as the stock prices of American General and Life and Casualty rose with the improved economy, Dudley and his team sought a "closer affiliation" with AG. In February, Life and Casualty declared both a twenty percent stock dividend and the beginning of acquisition talks with American General.[61]

Looking back, American General's annual report aptly described 1967 as "one of the most eventful years" in corporation history. Despite losses due to a long, hot summer of urban unrest, business in fire and casualty looked positive again, with the company reporting its largest one-year increase in written premiums. And life sales and life insurance in force reached their highest figures. The imminent acquisition of Life and Casualty of Tennessee was perhaps the year's biggest single event, but there were other ventures pending that would mean as much, and perhaps more, to its future corporate profile.[62]

One of these was the acquisition of the management of an existing mutual fund, the First Participating Fund. This came, as the annual report noted, at the end of a period of opposition toward life insurance companies dealing in mutual funds and variable annuities. The mutual fund, a vehicle for investment whereby monies are invested in a diverse group of stocks of many companies, had achieved great popularity in the 1950s. Woodson had been considering a move into mutual funds since that time; Wortham had been "keeping an open mind" about such an acquisition. AG might have formed its own if one already established in forty-two states had not been available. In September of 1967, American General "activated" American General Management Company to underwrite the mutual fund.[63]

Another acquisition that would have major portents for AG's future was the August, 1967, purchase of half of the stock of the Variable Annuity Life Insurance Company (VALIC) for $12 million dollars. At the same time, VALIC acquired the Equity Annuity Life Insurance Company (EALIC). EALIC was the company which Wortham had founded in 1956 and in which American General owned thirty-four percent of the stock. It was a consolidation of the two pioneer companies in the variable annuity field, and variable annuities were "becoming a big part of the life insurance business." With a 48.6 per cent ownership of VALIC, Woodson became president of the company. A group of EALIC stockholders fought its acquisition by the AG-controlled VALIC; its injunction was later denied. In 1968 VALIC became the first variable annuity company authorized to write business in Texas, the thirty-seventh state to which the company had been admitted. Once again Wortham's firm was in the vanguard, as it had been with multi- and all-lines underwriting.[64]

These acquisitions led American General out from its strictly insurance realm and into the financial services arena. The idea to build a kind of "department store of financial services," as Ben Woodson would later describe the American General group, was a concept that had grown through the years in the minds of Woodson and Gus Wortham. Wortham described it as a "generalized" plan that was open to whatever "develops as you go along"; he did not believe in a rigid master plan, but in being open-minded and ready to accept change. The events that would make American General such an entity began to come together in 1967.[65]

In addition, late in 1967, American General moved speedily toward the affiliation with Life & Casualty. In November and December, 1967, stockholders of both companies approved a stock exchange to make L&C part of AG. This gave the AG group, by January, 1968, total assets of $1.39 billion, combined capital and surplus of $228 million, and life insurance in force of $7.8 billion. It was now the largest financial institution in Houston.[66]

No longer was Gus Wortham's insurance company a brash upstart. It now had achieved a major national presence. At the end of 1967, *Finance* magazine summed up much of what had occurred with American General in the last decade: American General was "driving hard" to live up to the "Lone Star standard" of [b]igness—in aim and in accomplishment." Another indication of how far AG had come was the speculation that it would soon seek a listing on the New York Stock Exchange.

Gus Wortham had indeed reached empire status in his business world, in insurance and related enterprises and with his extensive land holdings. Personally, he was now accustomed to being recognized as one of Texas' great institution-builders. If he had retired eleven years earlier, *Forbes* magazine said, when he was sixty-five, his business would be just another run-of-the-mill company. But Gus Wortham, seventy-six years old, was still not ready to retire; he considered himself "the most progressive one around here."

No, Gus Wortham was not ready to leave American General. Indeed, even with all his accomplishments, he was again intimately involved in another merger struggle with a company that could not only vastly increase his company's power, but establish its future leadership.[67]

CHAPTER NINE

Scope and Breadth

"Insurance tycoon and cattle baron," the *New York Times* called Gus Wortham in June, 1967. No more needed to be said; Gus Wortham had reached national status as a businessman.[1]

And even as the *Times* pictured him at Winthrop Rockefeller's cattle auction, Wortham was engaged in negotiations for control of a life company in California that would put American General in a prominent place in the country's most populous state. Wortham was looking west—actually and symbolically—seeking what as a southwesterner was his guiding tenet, growth. These negotiations were woven throughout American General's history of the late 1960s and early 1970s. And the tenacity shown by Wortham and Woodson in pursuing California-Western States Life (Cal-West) was symbolic of the tough-minded persistence of Gus Wortham with regard to his business and institutional ventures. The pursuit also provided a frame for Wortham's involvement in seeking a financial power base of major proportions. American General had reached beyond insurance into other financial services. During this period it was reaching for greater depth in all areas and greater prominence. The negotiations for the Cal-West also took place among—and sometimes mirrored—the volatile societal and political events occurring during this period.

Beginning in the mid-1950s, Gus Wortham's American General had grown from a gangling child reaching out to establish a toehold in the life insurance business to an adolescent grabbing at stature in its fire and casualty operations. Now, in 1967, it had reached adulthood as a national leader in fire and casualty and, with the impending merger of Life and Casualty of Tennessee, life insurance. But even before the Life and Casualty deal was consummated, Wortham and Woodson's interests had been captured by California-Western States Life of Sacramento.

Cal-West was a fifty-year-old Sacramento firm ranking fifteenth among

Sterling Evans, Wortham, and Winthrop Rockefeller, May 13, 1967. Courtesy American General Corporation.

stock life companies with $4.7 billion of insurance in force in 1966, compared to American General's almost $4 billion in force. It was an important company in an important market. But it was also experiencing difficulties, and that made it a good takeover target.

In early 1967, Robert E. Murphy, president of Cal-West, told Woodson that, although it opposed all merger offers, the Cal-West board had set up a committee to evaluate them, thus obliquely letting Woodson know that Cal-West would entertain a serious offer.[2]

Wortham and Woodson met with the Cal-West committee and in July American General was one of six companies to make a half-day presentation to the group. As part of that program, Guilford Dudley of Life and Casualty described the proposed merger plans between his company and AG and how American General was known for keeping an acquired company and its staff intact. Overruling four no votes, the whole board voted to accept the AG proposal—a $121 million stock swap—and recommend it to stockholders. News reports speculated that both the L&C and Cal-West mergers would make American General the sixth largest stock life company, the fifteenth largest fire and casualty company, and the third largest financial institution in Texas. Woodson and Wortham were introduced to Cal-West's six hundred employees and later the California press. There was much reassurance that Cal-West would remain as it was and in Sacramento.[3]

Shortly after, the four dissenting Cal-West directors formed the "Stockholders Protective Committee for the California-Western States Life Insurance Company" to block the merger. They claimed American General's price was too low, that Cal-West made more profit out of one policy than American General did out of five. They objected to American General being in the faltering casualty business and claimed Cal-West's territory was faster growing than AG's. And they objected to ownership outside of California, even alluding to Wortham's ties to President Johnson, whose popularity in California was at a low point.[4]

As the dissenters predicted that some forty percent of Cal-West's shareholder's opposed the merger, American General stockholders approved the affiliation with L&C . . . and with Cal-West.[5] At the Cal-West stockholders meeting on December 19, President Murphy offered to resign to keep the company together. The vote, with nearly ninety percent of the shares being voted, was close, but the American General affiliation received less than the fifty percent needed to pass. Wortham believed that the fact that a number of shareholders did not vote at all caused AG to lose its $121 million bid.[6]

He praised the campaign that the California-Western Stockholders Protective Committee had put together, especially its appeal to local pride—something he, with his sense of loyalty to friends, duty to Houston and ties to the land, could understand. He also demurred that American General would have never gotten into the situation if they had known there would be a proxy fight, reminding everyone that AG had been invited to make a bid.

Although its head was slightly bowed from the Cal-West rebuff, 1967 had been a momentous year for the company, capped by the L&C deal and its tremendous increase in life insurance business.[7] And in a surprise move to show it was not giving up, in the early months of 1968, AG purchased 9.7 percent of the outstanding Cal-West shares—just for an investment. It was now Cal-West's largest stockholder and entitled to one seat on its board, although Woodson declined the board position. Wortham and Woodson proudly pointed out in March, 1968, that Cal-West's institutional investors such as mutual and pension funds, banks, and investment houses, voted "almost unanimously in favor of the American General offer."[8]

But at this same time (in typical Wortham-Woodson fashion) another venture, in a new financial area but with an old friend, was distracting Wortham and Woodson's attention. Again it was merger and growth that propelled them—the motive permeating all of Gus Wortham's business activities. And eventually this included his membership on the board of the National Bank of Commerce (NBC).

Wortham was the longest-reigning NBC board member, and that, and the esteem in which Jesse Jones had held his friend's business acumen, gave him a tremendous amount of influence, especially during the period when the bank was seeking leadership and growth after Jones's death.[9]

Wortham was also very much involved in the 1964 merger of the NBC with Texas National Bank (TNB); a merger the bank badly needed to stay competitive. It had dropped to third place, far behind the city's number one bank, Judge Elkins's First City National. A merger with Texas National, Houston's fourth largest bank, would not only make NBC a banking power again, but provide future leadership from the young, aggressive bankers running Texas National. TNB was led by Baker and Botts attorney, Dillon Anderson, a former national security advisor to President Eisenhower. Wortham along with John T. Jones, Jr., and Fred Heyne, Jones's right-hand investment man, were important in the negotiations for the merger and in getting other board members to see why such an affiliation was needed. Ben Woodson, who assisted Wortham in an informal financial analysis of the two banks, believed Wortham was the entire impetus behind the deal, and that Wortham showed the bankers how they could effect the merger.

Just as he trusted change, Wortham was a supporter and believer in young men "on the way up." He often acted as a kind of mentor for younger men in his own varied business interests. He believed it was the duty of his generation to seek out and encourage young men who could follow in their footsteps. Perhaps in the forty-one-year-old president of Texas National, William McLean, Wortham saw the future of Jones's bank—perhaps just as Jones had seen that same spark in Wortham forty years earlier. Also, one bank officer believed Gus Wortham wanted the merger more for the sake of growth—he wanted the bank to get bigger like his insurance empire—than leadership. (And this was the same year of the Maryland–American General merger which would bring tremendous growth to his own business.)[10]

The merger was eventually approved in January, 1964, creating Texas National Bank of Commerce. But major problems over management and succession continued. The trouble stemmed mainly from differences in management philosophy and age and experience of the personnel of the two merging institutions. Many of the NBC bankers did not have faith in the Texas National people and tended to view them as "upstarts" who were trying to remake "Mr. Jones's bank."

Although he was close to NBC Chairman Robert Doherty, Wortham had wanted the merger, and it is not known how he voted when Doherty asked the executive committee to approve his plans to oust McLean, the man designated to be his successor. A year later, the final showdown occurred between the shareholders who were NBC advocates and those who supported TNB personnel. The NBC faction, backed by the Houston Endowment's thirty percent share, won a larger participation on the board and the upshot was the resignation of McLean and Dillon Anderson. It is not known how Wortham voted here, either, but the embroglio hurt the bank financially and resulted in bad publicity.[11]

Thus Gus Wortham's affinity for the bank, plus his powerful financial position as stockholder and customer, made American General a logical guardian—and savior—when the Texas National Bank of Commerce (TNBC) encountered another unhappy succession crisis. By 1965, Jesse Jones's foundation, the Houston Endowment, needed to rid itself of the bank stock because of rising political criticism of charitable foundations having control over business enterprises. The endowment sold its bank stock, the *Houston Chronicle*, and the Rice Hotel in a package to oil man John Mecom for $85 million. But Mecom could not meet the cash payment date, and the deal collapsed in 1966. During this period Wortham and Woodson discussed the future ownership of the bank stock and commented on rumors of potential buyers. In early 1968, word leaked out that the endowment was considering selling its bank stock to investors from Ohio. Wortham did not want the bank to go to non-Texans and began seriously to consider a purchase of the endowment's stock in the bank.[12]

In March, 1968, in harmony with his dual business values of duty and opportunity, Gus Wortham's American General announced its intent to purchase about thirty percent, over eight hundred thousand shares, of the outstanding stock of NBC. The purchase, added to its already existing shares, gave AG almost forty percent of the outstanding TNBC stock—working control. Not only was the stock a bargain at fifty-five dollars a share, but the acquisition of such an investment in a bank fitted perfectly into AG's plans to expand its financial services empire.

However, it was made clear to the bank management that AG considered this an investment and not a subsidiary. Bank President John Whitmore asked Wortham if he wanted to head the bank, but at this point Wortham did not wish to replace his friend, although things would be different when Whitmore retired in a few years.[13]

Eventually in 1970, when Gus Wortham was elected chairman of the advisory board, American General's involvement with the bank would come under scrutiny. The U.S. Congress amended the Bank Holding Company Act in 1970 to provide stricter guidelines for companies like AG which owned just one bank, the number of which had grown appreciably in the 1960s. Any company that held over twenty-five percent of a bank's stock was subject to the same strict federal regulations as the bank. In 1971 American General began working on a plan to "terminate" its bank holding company status rather than have the entire insurance conglomerate answerable to the bank holding regulations.[14]

But in April, 1968, the new acquisition of Jesse Jones's bank was surely a topic of great excitement and interest at the American General stockholders meeting, along with discussions of civil unrest, the resignation of Lyndon Johnson, and the country's upheaval over the Vietnam War. Although Wortham's business empire flourished during these years, it was not immune from the larger struggles taking place in society. Wortham told the stockholders that Maryland Casualty faced almost one million dollars in losses due to the civil disturbances that had hit the nation's cities during the summer of 1967. And, Wortham said, estimates of $30 to $70 million in losses for all insurance companies due to the riots was too conservative an estimate. Wortham himself was appointed by presidential aide Joseph Califano to the Riot Insurance Advisory Board of the Department of Housing and Urban Development in October, 1968, to oversee a riot loss reinsurance program designed to protect property/casualty insurers while providing insurance coverage to property owners.[15]

Their involvement with California-Western States led Wortham and Woodson toward still another big acquisition in 1968. A member of Cal-West's board from the investment counseling firm of Van Strum and Towne began to talk to American General about its possible acquisition of Van Strum and Towne's parent, the Channing Companies. This would move American General into mutual funds in a major way.

Van Strum and Towne, one of the country's oldest investment advisory services, had been the nucleus from which the conglomerate of mutual fund and insurance companies known as the Channing Companies had grown.[16]

Its interesting corporate profile brought the Channing Companies to the attention of a number of corporations and unsuccessful takeover bids were made by J. C. Penney and Franklin Life. Meanwhile, thanks to the Cal-West board member's tip, American General had been sizing up the Channing Companies. When the Franklin merger fell through in September, 1968, American General was ready and in December the sale of Channing to American General for $62.5 million was approved by Channing stockholders. By the 1969 annual report, the Channing group had $640 million in mutual fund assets under management.[17]

Tied closely to stock market fluctuations, however, the mutual fund business found it hard going in the uncertain economic times of the early 1970s, compounded by poor sales, bad publicity, and later, high interest rates. In addition to divestiture, American General sought to restructure and streamline the business. Further consolidation of American General's varied financial interests occurred in the 1970s, and Van Strum and Towne, the original investment firm, which had become Channing Management and then American General Capital Management, acquired American General Management, which had been formed in 1967 to manage the investments of the AG Group. Although it ranked among the top ten in mutual fund management groups, American General experienced disappointing returns and by the mid-1970s was considering getting out of the business.[18]

American General's next focus for acquisition in 1968, after the Channing negotiations had begun in earnest, harked back to its insurance roots, a conventional life company located in Texas. That summer, Southwestern Life of Dallas agreed to merge with American General, in a $270 million transaction put together by Woodson and W. Dawson Sterling, Southwestern's president. This would make AG the sixth largest stock insurance firm in the United States and the "culmination of the affiliation also would tighten Houston's grip on the title of financial capital of the Southwest." But the merger was opposed by some Southwestern stockholders and leaders of Fidelity Union Life and Gulf Insurance. Two weeks later AG and Southwestern abandoned merger talks. A major point in the break-up was the opposition of the head of a major Dallas retailer whose family had held Southwestern stock for three generations. The shareholder was most apprehensive about the forty-five percent of the holding company's earnings that were from the volatile fire and casualty market. Again, American General had been thwarted in its attempt to merge with another Texas company. Six months later, Sterling became executive vice president of Patriot Life, AG's New York subsidiary.[19]

Despite these other deals, there was no change in AG's ultimate merger intentions toward Cal-West. Shortly after the Southwestern Life rebuff, AG announced a thirty-dollar-a-share tender offer for California-Western States stock. Cal-West, with a new president and board structure, reiterated that it was not for sale. But the August stock offer and one in November "wooed" Cal-West stockholders, and by the end of 1968 American General had acquired 33.3 percent. The Cal-West management countered by having the state insurance commission and the Securities and Exchange Commission investigate the possibility of a prior leak about the tender offers.[20]

The Channing merger plans in September, for $62 million in stock, made American General's predicted assets $803 million. AG also bought a four percent interest in another California life company, West Coast Life of San Francisco. And, as if this was not enough activity, Woodson announced the company's consideration of an equipment leasing subsidiary. Later that fall, Woodson, in a speech before the Baltimore Bond Club, referred to American General as a "money business department store." The year 1968 ended with American General announcing its decision to seek the NYSE seat; Wortham said the big board listing would mean "increased marketability of American General shares, in addition to enhancing their use in any further acquisition that may be considered."[21]

The year 1968 had been remarkable for its activity and profitability, too, despite the troubled property/casualty business. One of the major problem areas, as always, continued to be automobile coverage. In addition to high medical and repair costs, insurance carriers suffered from an increasingly litigious society coupled with higher jury awards. But for American General, 1968 proved to be the third straight year of fire and casualty underwriting profits. In the annual report published in March, 1969, Wortham announced the sixth increase in dividend payments since 1960 and a tripling of the cash rate in five years.

The American General board had decided that the parent company should become a "general-purpose corporation" in principle, ending its fire and casualty insurance business. Legal obstacles however, prevented the company from giving up its charter, so the company would now act like and be thought of as a holding company, although not one in reality. By this time, American

General Insurance's holding company status was generally accepted in business circles.[22]

The new year, 1969, brought still more opportunities for American General to "add on." The first of these was instigated by the firm to be acquired, rather than the acquirer; and it came because of Wortham and Woodson's reputations, not as ruthless takeover artists, but as saving affiliators. The company was Fidelity and Deposit of Baltimore (F&D), like Maryland Casualty, another prominent, well-respected and long-time insurance force in Maryland, with fidelity and surety business in every U.S. jurisdiction. Despite the company's reputation and worth, however, its stock was listed at only around forty dollars per share on the over-the-counter market. This, coupled with the fact that over half its stock was held by trusts and trustees, made it ripe for a takeover.

Indeed, F&D was in the midst of final discussions for the formation of a new insurance holding company with three other entities. Then, on February 10, 1969, the Security Corporation of Hartford announced an unexpected tender offer for four hundred thousand shares of F&D for sixty-five dollars a share. Not only would this upset the already planned merger, but Security had a poor reputation for harsh dealings with companies it had acquired.[23]

Fidelity and Deposit decided to fight, but not in a way that might have been expected. On February 13, company president Julian Neal called Gus Wortham. Finding Wortham out of town, he talked with Ben Woodson, telling him that F&D's management had decided that "if we've got to dance, we at least want to choose our own partner," and American General, based on its treatment of Maryland Casualty, was the partner it chose. Wortham, who was at a cattle auction in San Antonio, was greatly interested in the deal. Being a "bond man," he was well acquainted with F&D and Neal. An agreement was reached the next day; the affiliation would be done by a tax-free stock exchange.[24]

F&D ran ads touting the advantages of this merger over the proposed Security takeover and encouraging F&D stockholders to tender their shares to AG. Faced with opposition, a tax-free offer and a higher price, Security withdrew.

Another Baltimore firm, the Title Guarantee Company (part of the original F&D holding company deal), which specialized in writing title insurance coverage, was invited into AG's merger plans with Fidelity and Deposit. F&D stockholders approved the AG merger in March and in July, 1969, the F&D acquisition, which also brought along its subsidiary, Maryland Life, and Title Guarantee Company, was finalized.

But even before their finalization, American General's two quick fidelity bond acquisitions in Baltimore raised eyebrows at the Federal Trade Commission and it announced an investigation into possible antitrust violations in the two mergers.[25]

In March, 1969, the *Houston Post's* Sam Weiner attempted to recap the frenzied pace of AG's recent growth. Immediately on tap was the stockholder vote on F&D, the official acquisition of Channing and its eight mutual funds worth $1 billion, and the company's listing on the New York Stock Exchange. At this juncture, AG also owned the controlling interest in Texas National Bank of Commerce and had a $49 million share of Cal-West. But Ben Woodson hinted that AG's acquiring was slowing down; the company was now concerned with consolidating and streamlining its acquisitions and operations and with staying in the finance field, "intend[ing] to be a diversified financial services company."[26]

And good news about Cal-West greeted the AG stockholders at their annual meeting in April. Neither the SEC nor the California Insurance Commission had found any violations regarding AG's 1968 tender offers for Cal-West. A *Sacramento Bee* reporter attended the meeting, reporting that Gus Wortham's mood was much better than the previous year, when he had been glum over "one of his few business setbacks"—the failed Cal-West acquisition. But Gus said he now wanted to concentrate on "developing rather than assembling," thus, as the skeptical reporter put it, "helping allay the suspicions of those who had seen the cover of the *Annual Report* for 1968"—a photo of the earth. The reporter doubted that American General was finished with Cal-West.[27]

AG's listing on the NYSE became effective in May, 1969, and VALIC, in which AG owned fifty per cent, moved its home offices to Houston, assuring better tax treatment than it had received in Washington, D.C. Woodson and lobbyist Edward Stumpf had campaigned hard to have VALIC admitted to the state by the legislature in 1967.[28]

The remainder of 1969 was relatively quiet at American General. One big new business involvement was a joint venture agreement between American General Investment Corporation and a division of construction conglomerate Morris-Knudsen, to develop industrial parks near large cities in the western United States and Canada. As Gus Wortham had become more interested in land development, AG Investment had "accelerated [its] program of equity participating in land development" and F&D head Julian Neal had brought the two companies together.

In his August announcement that net earnings of the company were up from the previous year, Wortham observed that while most newly acquired affiliate companies diluted earnings initially, that had not occurred with AG's new acquisitions, which he attributed to their strong performances. Overall, however, 1969 did not prove as profitable for American General as 1968; earnings were down due to high property and liability claims in the last quarter of the year and the national "economic slowdown."[29]

Just as his company was a huge and varied entity now, Gus Wortham's city was a major metropolitan area. Houston was no longer the small, close-knit southern city that could be run by an elite oligarchy of white men with the same backgrounds, politics, and belief in their own ability to provide for the greater good of the city. There were few left of Houston's old guard, the original inner circle of the 8F group. Judge Elkins was in his nineties and ill, and only George Brown and Wortham of the inner circle remained. There were younger business magnates taking their places in the various leadership roles of the city, but they would not rule like their predecessors.[30]

As sociologist Joe Feagin pointed out in *Free Enterprise City:*

> Between the late 1960s and the late 1970s more than 150 companies moved subsidiaries, divisions, or headquarters to Houston. The magazine *Texas Business* commented that the older movers and shakers in Texas were being eclipsed, in part, by urban-based capitalists from outside and that the "influx of corporations into the state has both enhanced and diminished the power of the business establishment."[31]

But, like Brown, Gus Wortham was still a "player" in political circles. Amidst Lyndon Johnson's tumultuous second term as president, which took him from the heights of public acceptance to the nadir, Wortham remained close. Some correspondence hints at political or issue-oriented discussion, and it was not uncommon for the president to telephone Wortham. In April, 1967, while Ben Woodson was entertaining the heads of the about-to-be-acquired Life and Casualty of Tennessee, Wortham had been called to the LBJ Ranch for an urgent meeting with the president. Johnson did rely on Wortham for advice on insurance matters. For example, before Wortham was named to the Riot Insurance Advisory Board in 1968, Johnson's aide Califano reported to LBJ that the program had been checked out with Wortham. American General already had expressed its desire for governmental underpinning if insurance companies were to continue insuring "marginal areas." This was a prime example of the belief of Wortham and the other 8F crowd members in the efficacy of "government interference" when it "promoted" the good of business.[32]

Much of the written material between Gus Wortham and Lyndon Johnson during this period concerned social invitations, thanks for gifts, or recommendations for appointments. The Worthams were guests at both the 1961 and 1965 inaugural celebrations for Johnson, and were invited to dinner at the White House in 1964 as ambassadors for the Houston Symphony, along with Ima Hogg. They were also the Johnsons' guests when Ed Clark was visiting from his duties as ambassador to Australia in May, 1968. The *Washington Daily News* reported that the Worthams, who owned the "third largest cattle ranch in Texas," had slept in the Lincoln bedroom. Wortham visited the White House and Johnson several times by himself, and often when he was in the city on business, staying at the Mayflower Hotel, Johnson would have his bags transferred to the White House. Wortham was also a ranching confidant of Johnson and discussed cattle and other such matters with him. Although he was not as close to Johnson as the Brown brothers, Wortham was a sort of "elder" for Johnson, a man whom he respected, not just for his financial gifts and his political backing, but for his wisdom and business savvy. Ostensibly, Wortham remained loyal to Johnson's party. When the president chose not to run in 1968, a skeptical Wortham visited Hubert Humphrey in Minnesota.

Coming away much more impressed with the candidate than before, he financially supported Humphrey's campaign. There is no indication of whom he voted for, however.[33]

In Texas, too, during this era, Gus Wortham was still a major political actor and financial backer. A measure of his closeness with Houston's longtime and powerful congressman Albert Thomas was that at Thomas's death in February, 1966, Wortham flew to Washington to escort Thomas's widow, Lera, and the body home aboard a plane belonging to Brown & Root. Thomas was buried on Wortham's seventh-fifth birthday, February 18, 1966. Ironically, before Thomas's death, Wortham had put himself in the position of seeming disloyal to his old friend in order to make sure that a candidate suitable to the establishment took Thomas's place in Congress. When it seemed Thomas would not live to run for office again, Wortham made arrangements for a name to be filed—at the last possible minute—to run against him, with the stipulation that if Thomas lived the other candidate would drop out. However, the liberals managed to file their candidate, Bob Eckhardt, who eventually won Thomas's former seat.[34]

A promising young Texan Wortham heavily supported was Ben Barnes, who was a protégé of Wortham's friend, Governor John Connally. Barnes served as Speaker of the House from 1965 to 1969 and later as lieutenant governor. Some believed Barnes was headed for great political heights, even the presidency, but his fortunes were entangled in the Sharpstown banking scandal of 1971 and his star descended rapidly. Barnes named Wortham and George Brown in an interview with Texas newspaperman Jimmy Banks in the early 1970s as two of his major contributors who never asked for favors for their own interests: "I know he [Wortham] had an insurance bill that he wanted passed pretty badly but it met with a lot of opposition and was killed. . . . He never did even contact me about it." Wortham did not support Ralph Yarborough, Texas' liberal Democratic senator elected in 1957, but he did work for Yarborough's opponent in the 1971 U.S. Senate race, Lloyd Bentsen, the former Houston insurance man and scion of wealthy Rio Grande Valley landowners. Bentsen was the kind of probusiness Democrat Wortham and the 8F crowd wanted in Texas, just as was Bentsen's Republican opponent, George Bush. Bush told Banks that Wortham once said that if he, Bush, were a Democrat, he could be elected governor and Wortham would like that.[35]

Wortham had supported Preston Smith for governor and his successor Dolph Briscoe, a South Texas cattleman from whose relative Wortham had bought some of his first Santa Gertrudis. But Wortham was closest to John Connally, and said in the mid-1970s: "John was the most attractive man I knew. He was sweet, but strong as horse radish. He's not just a promoter, though he is interested in business. We wouldn't have been interested in him if he wasn't."[36] He supported Connally over Price Daniel for the governor's race in 1962, but only after Daniel, whom Wortham had supported in all his races, had told him he was not going to run. There is evidence that Wortham supported

Connally even after he became affiliated with the administration of Republican Richard Nixon. In October, 1971, Connally sent the Worthams one of the first dollar bills printed with his signature as secretary of the treasury, with a handwritten note: "Gus, It was good to see you Sat."[37] In 1972 Connally left his Cabinet post to head what some might have believed to be a turncoat cause, "Democrats for Nixon." There is no indication how Wortham voted in that year's presidential election, but he was one of the VIPs invited to Connally's Picosa Ranch in April, 1972, when Connally hosted President and Mrs. Nixon. In his 1976 book, *The Texans*, former New Orleans newspaperman James Conaway described the party and its guests, which included the Hunt brothers, James Elkins, Jr., H. Ross Perot, George Brown, and Wortham.

> The stocky czar of the Houston insurance empire, Gus Wortham, moved through the ceremony with characteristic abruptness. He had built up American General Insurance from scratch, and still ran it and other enterprises with an iron hand. Johnson [LBJ] had often visited Wortham's cattle auctions at the 9-Bar Ranch while he was President, slipping secretly away from Washington in Air Force One. They frequently talked by telephone in those years.[38]

In 1972, Connally returned to the law firm of Vinson, Elkins in Houston, which he had joined after his tenure as governor. He also joined the American General board.

As a basic conservative Texas Democratic, Gus Wortham was wary of government's growing control in citizens' lives, especially financial enterprise, although earlier he saw the need for pieces of social legislation to protect certain segments of society. There is no indication how he felt about Johnson's "Great Society" programs, but they certainly meant change for his world. John Connally believed Wortham felt the president had gone too far with some of the social programs, such as Medicare, but Wortham did not criticize Johnson.[39]

During this period of social upheaval, Gus Wortham in 1970 consented to do a series of oral history interviews conducted by the College of Business Administration at the University of Texas. Besides the wealth of information they provide on Wortham as a businessman, during these interviews Wortham divulged some of his philosophy and beliefs about the current American scene.

Wortham did not despair of the younger generation, but claimed he looked at the individual: "I do not care what he looks like or what his thinking is. Just so long [as] he has a purpose in life. . . . I do not like the fellow who is against everything. I like people who have positive approaches to things." And he was not particularly alarmed at the student protests. Campus upheaval was not new, Wortham said: "Scholars took over buildings two or three hundred years ago." He believed the radical students of his day "turned out pretty good. They usually had get-up to them. . . . The ones I am most opposed to are those who are opposed to the government. I just do not like this business of denouncing the government. It is part of the freedom of speech though. . . ."[40]

Wortham's true apprehension about left-wing politics had surfaced a year earlier, when he was appointed to the board of regents of North Texas State University. Governor Smith had appointed Wortham specifically to counteract a situation where "a very liberal block of faculty members . . . are preaching a socialistic philosophy antagonistic to the free market enterprise system you and I love so dearly," as one his fellow regents described it. The "situation" seemed to stem from the appointment of a new president at the state-supported school who allowed the Students for a Democratic Society and the black student groups to sponsor activities for students.[41] Wortham's appointment also illustrated his power as a representative of Texas' cultural establishment.

And a very traditional representative he was, retaining all his class consciousness. For example, in his oral history he said college was not for everyone because it made people unhappy to get above their station: "They yearn for something and they do not recognize that they do not have the ability to do it. It is very frustrating. That is one of our troubles with minority groups. We promise them things that are impossible to perform. . . . The ones that can come to the top will come to the top, just like the immigrants who came over here."[42]

But he claimed to dislike intolerance, although saying the country had to solve the "problem of how far can you go with personal liberty. I think we are right where it is touch and go. . . . personal liberty cannot interfere with the mass of the people."[43] And he called Houston a "progressive city" with a lot of southerners like himself, who were not "pig-headed about things."

> You take our racial situation. We have never had any trouble in Houston. . . . These things came along, we got these business people together and opened up these soda fountains, toilets, etc. We decided that racial pig-headedness was a lot of damn foolishness, and we got rid of it. . . . We have a number of Negroes who work here. For the most part they are fine employees and do a good job. . . . They are nicely mannered. We are selective.[44]

Gus Wortham's comments aptly represent the views of the Houston business and civic elite of his era, men who were watching societal changes happen around them, of which they did not always approve, but over which they no longer had control. The "opening up" brought about by the civil rights struggle, the budding women's movement, student unrest, and the protests stemming from the Vietnam War threatened the world order this older generation had created and which they believed was operating pretty well. They certainly resented the increased interference of the national government in their civic and business lives, believing people like themselves—and not the masses—could best make the major decisions affecting the masses.

Lester Randle recalled that the 8F men, including Wortham, were not generally in favor of racial integration, and Feagin reports these men funded many segregationist candidates. Wortham even told Randle not to get "involved" in civil rights activities, that he would "take care" of him. In his way, Wortham did take care of Randle and because people had seen Wortham treat him with respect, Randle received the same kind of courtesy as Wortham's emissary. Randle especially remembered one instance in Wortham's Lamar Hotel suite when one of Wortham's guests had ordered, "Nigger, fix my drink." Wortham, knowing Randle was upset, followed him to the kitchen. When Randle acted as if nothing had happened, Wortham said to him: "Lester, you see and you don't see, you hear and you don't hear."[45]

Wortham suggested that he and other business leaders in the early 1960s had decided it was time to open up the other public facilities to the blacks. However it was really managed, probably with some input from this group, Houston's integration was done with little media attention. Wortham told Randle to let his friends, the "better sort" of black people, know this was going to happen and that it was now all right for them to use what had for so long been denied them.

Obviously the white establishment did not feel comfortable having blacks become part of their prominent cultural institutions, however. Sometime in 1960 or 1961, the Houston Symphony's conductor, Leopold Stokowski, had wanted to use the black chorus from all-black Texas Southern University in a performance. Since the performances were still segregated, his request was refused. Stokowski left the symphony soon after this, and although there were other complaints against him by the management, he cited this incident as a reason for his own antipathy toward the institution. Wortham, as head of the finance committee, could not have escaped some knowledge and probable involvement in this event, although where he stood is unknown. What is clear from this period is that Houston, even in its new persona as a "former southern" city, and its ruling elite were still uncomfortable with issues of racial equality.[46]

Despite the upheaval and major changes of the late 1960s, Wortham professed to be optimistic about the future generation, even hoping they would bring about new awareness and participation of people in the political process. But for Wortham, change and new ideas were firmly rooted in a conservative work-ethic philosophy that seemed to say: "Have a good time when you're young, then settle down and get to work making the free enterprise system grow and serving your community."

This philosophy of free enterprise coupled with community service had been the foundation of Wortham's civic involvement. As his company and his ranching interests mushroomed with Houston in the late 1960s, he, as one of the civic czars, helped it meet expanding cultural needs. In 1966, Wortham joined John T. Jones, Jr., J. W. Link, Jr., and other civic leaders to found the Society for the Performing Arts (SPA), a nonprofit booking company that brought arts attractions to town to lease space in the newly built Jesse H. Jones Hall. Wortham also served on the board of the Museum of Fine Arts during these years and was a benefactor of the fledgling opera. During this period Lyndall Wortham was heavily involved with the Houston Grand Opera and served on the board of the Houston Ballet and Theater Under the Stars.[47]

As "one of the state's most powerful financiers and executive talents," Gus

Lyndall and Gus Wortham, September 28, 1972. Courtesy American General Corporation.

retained his position as head of the finance committee of the Houston Symphony Orchestra, which he had held since 1947. His steadfastness was due partially to his high regard for the others associated with the hierarchy of the Symphony, like attorney Maurice Hirsch, who was its president from 1956 through 1970, and, especially, Ima Hogg.

But in 1969 the symphony orchestra was feeling the reverberations of a society in the midst of social revolution and Gus Wortham was embroiled in a situation of clashing values between the old guard Houston elite and the young director, Andre Previn. At the end of Previn's second season with the Houston Symphony, there were problems. Attendance at his concerts was falling, and Previn had taken on conducting duties with the London Symphony and asked to be relieved of some of his chores with the Houston group—especially touring to outlying towns and small cities. Added to these problems was the maintenance fund deficit of over two hundred thousand dollars and the renegotiations of the musicians' union contract. Hirsch warned that the symphony might have to be closed.

Previn had been given a contract but had not signed it and there was a strained relationship with symphony manager, Tom Johnson. A consideration was also the married Previn's very public romance with actress Mia Farrow, who had come to Houston several times. The Symphony Society's executives met and decided to rescind Previn's contract.[48]

Gus Wortham was very much involved in Previn's dismissal; reports said it was the decision of his finance committee. There was much protestation among the musicians, concert-goers, critics, and, of course, Previn. Many were unhappy to see the city lose Previn's recognized talent and showmanship. "PR Mistakes" were made, the Symphony's executive committee admitted to the press, and "Gus Wortham, head of the all powerful finance committee explained, up to a point, the symphony's position. But only up to a point," claimed the *Chronicle's* Ann Holmes. "Previn was a man we were unable to get along with and that's it" Wortham was reported as saying, admitting his finance committee had made the final decision.[49]

The symphony episode demonstrated Wortham's great behind-the-scenes power as the financial heart of the group, but also the clash of values between his idea of loyalty and decorum versus someone his crowd might consider a cultural "maverick" like Previn, who did not have their sense of loyalty to the institution—an institution formed very much in their own image, and one in which they wanted it to remain.

This incident, too, perhaps marks the end of the kind of devotion displayed by Hogg, Wortham, and Hirsch, for Houston's cultural institutions. Involved on a day-to-day basis with them, they felt a responsibility, because if they did not govern, there would be no institution. They wanted growth and increasing artistic acclaim, but within the realm of their control as designated arbiters of civic pride.

This era also saw changes in the way that government dealt with business—the government was paying attention to the increasingly vociferous critics of the unfettered rule of business. And Gus Wortham's company, with its many mergers and rapid increase in size and power was bound to catch the eye of new, more watchful government regulatory groups. In 1970 the Securities and Exchange Commission (SEC) filed suit against American General, Channing, and VALIC, accusing them of violating federal prospectus requirements by advertising sales offers for mutual fund shares and variable annuity contracts. American General stopped running the ads and agreed to modify all future advertising, but the story made national news. It was the first SEC lawsuit involving an insurance company's offering of equity products, and, although it was dropped in the fall, it had a lasting effect on this business.[50]

Since its 1969 merger with Fidelity and Deposit of Maryland, American General had been under scrutiny by the Federal Trade Commission in its new position as the country's largest surety bond and fidelity underwriter. In February, 1971, the FTC filed a "proposed complaint" challenging the merger as a violation of the Clayton Anti-Trust Act. The FTC said the mergers lessened the competition and that they should be dissolved. The FTC's interest was piqued because, since 1957, more than half the fidelity and surety bond underwriters had been taken over. This FTC challenge to insurance company mergers was another first for AG. Wortham was surprised, but would not divest AG of F&D. The FTC filed a formal complaint to force divestiture in June, but for its refusal to submit to federal jurisdiction, American General harkened back to the McCarran Act of 1945 (which Gus Wortham had supported) that put regulation of insurance companies with the states. In early 1972, the FTC agreed that it did not have jurisdiction over the merger.[51]

These governmental challenges and the changes occurring in regulation did not in any major way inhibit the continued prosperity of Gus Wortham's business enterprise. And the early years of the new decade saw continuing growth and diversity at American General. In September, 1970, AG registered a new kind of bond fund with the SEC, a "closed end" fund as opposed to the "open end" Channing funds, which would "generate interest income while preserving capital." A second fund, American General Convertible Securities, was begun in 1972 and a third was acquired in 1974. These funds would ultimately prove much more popular and profitable than the mutual funds.[52]

In December, 1970, American General announced its aim to acquire more shares of California-Western States Life "from time to time" over the next several months with the goal of increasing its holdings to fifty percent. There was no change planned in Cal-West's operations or personnel; in fact, Wortham and Woodson told the press of their regard for the company's new president, Harold S. Hook, who had assumed the job in August, 1970.[53]

Still, there was an almost fifty-fifty split at California-Western States, on the board and in the company, over the possible American General takeover. And when the time came to seek a new leader for the troubled concern, the main criteria were strength and independence, with no ties to AG, someone who "could and would" keep American General out. In such an atmosphere, the board decided to hire Hook. At thirty-eight, he had already served as president of two life companies in Kansas and New York.

Ironically, in 1966 Hook had been interviewed for a vice presidency by Woodson and Wortham, before taking the New York position. And although the older men were taken aback by Hook's age and experience, Hook clearly came under Wortham's spell:

> They were working half-days on Saturday then and I was down there on a Saturday . . . so I went in and visited with him. I had an image of sort of polished mahogany. . . . and I remember . . . that you fe[lt] like you ought to take your wallet out and put it there on the table because it's safer with him than it is with you. . . . He was just an older person and small and very soft-spoken and yet, there was a power. . . . I mean he had an aura about him.[54]

Wortham and Woodson had signed a letter with the California Insurance Department saying they would exercise no control over the company, even though AG was Cal-West's single largest stockholder. But, as part of his process of interviewing for the Cal-West presidency, Hook stopped by to talk with Wortham and Woodson, to get their approval, but also to get their agreement that he could run the company as he saw fit. Ben Woodson said later that he had clandestinely recommended Hook to the Cal-West people.

Hook believed, however, that Gus Wortham did not approve of Hook's seeking so much power and money. But the Cal-West board had hired the man and there was a noninterference agreement. Hook had his job cut out for him: Cal-West was an ailing company and the acquisition war with American General had not helped. While Hook labored in Sacramento, Gus Wortham in Houston watched.[55]

In January, 1971, Ben Woodson finally joined the Cal-West board and in February the plan to acquire "working control" of Cal-West stock was approved by California's insurance commissioner, although AG said it did not plan to purchase the shares soon. But that summer, American General further consolidated its hold on California-Western States Life when it sold the Agricultural Insurance Company, a subsidiary acquired with the Channing companies, and as payment received stock in Cal-West, raising its ownership to thirty-seven percent. In addition, the Cal-West board chairman resigned to be replaced by Woodson.

At the end of 1971, American General announced its intention to consider offers to buy Cal-West stock, indicating, however that it would not initiate purchases or borrow to buy the stock. A *Los Angeles Times* story said that American General had spent $50 million acquiring its thirty-seven percent of Cal-West's stock, although denying merger.[56]

The year 1971 had been much better all around for American General than 1970. Earnings were up to $1.75 per share versus $1.25 and the all-important fire and casualty ratio was down to 98.6 percent. Woodson called the company a "department store of financial services," stressing that insurance was the foundation and the most important component. American General Investment experienced its best year, earning $1.3 million servicing $600 million in mortgages for twenty-five institutional lenders. And at Cal-West, Harold Hook made a difference; a "turnaround" with earnings per share rising from 53 cents to $1.15.[57]

And 1972, despite some continuing federal regulatory problems, was another good year for American General. The first half was the best six months in the company's history; at nine months the company reported its earnings hit a high of $45 million, the company's best nine months' earnings in its history. In July, ground was broken for the second building in the American General complex. Estimated to cost $8.8 million dollars, it was to have fifteen stories and be named after its main tenant, Riviana Foods.[58]

But that spring and summer of 1972, a number of events occurred which signaled profound changes and new directions for Gus Wortham. In May, Judge James Elkins died at the age of ninety-two. Like the other 8F men, Elkins had never retired, neither from his own bank nor from the American General board, and the final years had been rough ones. Of all these powerful men, it was Elkins who had known Gus Wortham as a young boy and who had most likely nudged the young Wortham into Houston's political and civic scene. In August, the *Wall Street Journal* reported that Elkins's place on the board had been "filled" by the appointment of Harold S. Hook. His appointment, as Hook later observed, was somewhat unusual, given that California-Western States Life was not yet a wholly owned subsidiary, although by the end of 1972 American General had 38.7 percent of its stock.[59]

Certainly Elkins's death had touched Wortham; as, probably, had Wortham's visit in June to his ancestral home. As the guest of honor at a dedication of Texas Historical Markers in Wortham, he met more memories.[60]

Another personal "ending" occurred in 1972—the dissolution of Wortham's great passion outside insurance, his ranching partnership with Sterling Evans. Evans had been seriously ill the year before and the two men just decided "it was time." Evans bought out Wortham's share in the Little Eva Plantation in Louisiana, and the Crystal City farm was sold. The Bear Lake land in Louisiana had been sold by 1966, and the other Louisiana plantation, the Crescent in Tallulah, had been sold to Wortham's daughter and son-in-law, Lyndall and Russell Peterson in 1970. Of the New Mexico property, only the Nine Bar at Clines Corners was kept. The Nine Bar near Houston was not affected by the break-up because it was Wortham's alone.[61]

Whether or not any of these events had to do with his decision, by the end of 1972 Gus Wortham had made up his mind to retire from the company he had founded. Part of the immediate motivation was likely his desire to allow Ben Woodson to have his own significant tenure as CEO and chairman of the board. And, perhaps realizing that he could see himself in no other position but what he had always been—CEO—Wortham felt he had to retire.

Benjamin Woodson, Gus S. Wortham, and E. R. Barrow on the day of Wortham and Barrow's retirement, November 3, 1972. Courtesy American General Corporation.

But another incident earlier that year may have provided a more important reason for Wortham's decision. In August, 1972, when Harold Hook came to Houston as the newest AG board member, Gus Wortham spoke at length with him, telling the younger man that he had been wrong about him. He offered to loan Hook $250,000 to buy AG stock, which Hook refused. During that encounter and in a subsequent letter, Hook said Gus Wortham indicated that he wanted Hook to be (and that Hook would be) his successor after Woodson. Hook did not understand how it was to happen, and he never discussed it again with Wortham or anyone else. He returned to Sacramento and continued to run Cal-West, ostensibly without any interference from American General and without comment from Gus Wortham.[62]

Given Hook's evidence, there is good reason for Wortham having felt he could retire from active affiliation with his company. He did so, making his sudden resignation announcement at the November 2, 1972, board meeting, effective the very next day. The resignation came as a complete surprise to board members; Wortham had to coax them to get someone to propose the resolution accepting it. He resigned from all its subsidiaries and affiliates as well, except as chairman of the board of American General Investment, because of his great interest in land and development.

Also retiring the same day as Wortham was E. R. Barrow, the man inside the company who had shared his career and confidence the longest. J. W. Link, Jr., an original stockholder and board member, was now the only one of Gus Wortham's early team at American General still affiliated with the company. After the meeting, as usual, the board members went to lunch together—all except Wortham, who told Allen Carruth that since he was no longer a board member he should not go.[63]

Very simply, Wortham had explained his unwillingness to leave his business in his 1970 oral history:

> I created this business. I have a different feeling and position in it. It is my baby, so to speak. I still think that I can contribute to it. I have always been able to and will always have to be able to get along with people and to delegate responsibility and authority and not be critical or second guess people. So with that philosophy, you can continue on longer than if your way is the only way to do it.[64]

Although *Southern Insurance* called it "the End of an Era," the local press stressed that Wortham was in no way quitting his business life; he would be at his desk 8:30 A.M. to 6 P.M. every day. And while Wortham had relinquished his own office to Woodson, the thirteenth-floor board room was converted into an office for Gus. It was, Hook believed, not a stepping down at all, for Wortham remained at the power center—and in a bigger office.[65]

Two more events occurred at the end of 1972 that were highly symbolic of the changes that had come to Gus Wortham and his company. The first was the naming of Elizabeth Reap the first woman officer of American General. Reap, who had begun her career as secretary to Benjamin Woodson in 1953, had "worked her way up," achieving her life insurance sales certifications along the way. She was one of the few women in the company's higher ranks; Gus Wortham was an old-school chauvinist and did not particularly approve of women in business. The second event was the death of E. R. Barrow, who had entered the hospital right after his retirement and never recovered. Truly, this signaled the end of one era and the beginning of the next for American General.[66]

A final event, in December, 1972, had much symbolism for Gus Wortham's public life, especially as creator and sustainer of Houston's civic institutions. It was Ima Hogg's ninetieth birthday party held at Jones Hall for three thousand guests with a concert by pianist Arthur Rubenstein. Wortham was honorary chair of the event. His remarks that evening, while praising Miss Ima, were truly an apology for the way he and the men who were part of Houston's older establishment thought of culture in its relation to the city: "No city can be a great city if made of smoke stacks, bricks and mortar. We must have culture." Thus he summed up the duty he and other ruling business leaders had

Gus Wortham, Maurice Hirsch, Ima Hogg, and Dr. Jones at Houston Symphony party for Miss Ima's ninetieth birthday, December 15, 1972. Courtesy American General Corporation.

felt incumbent upon them for their city. Their involvements in the city's political and cultural institutions had left those institutions indelibly marked with their personalities. Now there were few members of that elite group left. He ended his tribute to Miss Ima by saying, "Her like will not pass your way again." He might as well have been speaking of himself.[67]

CHAPTER TEN

Death of a Southwestern Gentleman

Gus Wortham kept an office at American General—in the board room—after he retired because the truth was, he never wanted to leave. He told Lyndall that people did not live long after they retired. And he told his doctor, Lloyd Gregory, that a man should always have an office to go to, some place where he could get away from home, even if it was just to read the paper. And so he continued to come to American General every day, although he spent most of the time on his other business ventures and investments, claiming he tried to stay "out of Mr. Woodson's way." Woodson, who was now CEO and chairman, said he liked having Wortham close by to consult with him.[1]

How Gus Wortham's official estrangement from the two things he loved best in the world—his company and ranching—affected him, cannot be known for certain, but there was no doubt that Wortham's health deteriorated steadily after 1972. There was no recurrence of the heart problems from the 1954 attack, but, Wortham, who had been a smoker, had developed emphysema.[2]

His departure did not slow down activity at American General, however. His surprise retirement announcement was soon eclipsed in the press by other AG events. In December, 1972, the Federal Trade Commission decided to reopen its challenge of the AG merger with Fidelity and Deposit of Baltimore, overriding a previous decision that it did not have jurisdiction in the case. Now the FTC argued that state regulation did not include mergers affecting the national insurance business. Some thought the case might go all the way to the Supreme Court. The case would drag on for several more years, ending finally with AG's divestiture of Fidelity and Deposit in 1980.[3]

The FTC investigation did not deter Benjamin Woodson's eagerness for acquisitions. In January, 1973, the company announced that it was buying the stock of Gulf Coast Savings and Loan of Richmond, which it would acquire pending Federal Home Loan Bank Board approval. This would, in some ways, make up for the loss of the Texas Commerce Bank stock. Gulf Coast had three offices, and after it was merged in July, 1973, opened an office in the American General building.[4]

Finally, too, the California-Western States situation was coming to a head. In February, American General proposed a twenty-five percent stock split and made another offer to purchase Cal-West shares at twenty dollars each. The Cal-West directors rejected it, but chose not to fight, deciding to let the shareholders make the decision. Just twelve days later, the headlines read: "Texas firm wins control of Cal-West Insurance." By the end of the year, American General had acquired 62.4 percent of its stock. A "classic example of corporate patience, mixed with easy-going yet sophisticated approach" was how the *Post*'s business writer, Gerald Egger, described the American General conquest.[5]

The acquisition of its long-sought prize also made Harold S. Hook an official part of American General management, as head of a wholly owned subsidiary. Under him, Cal-West had continued to improve and its first quarter earnings for 1973 were the best in sixty-two years. The California press predicted that Woodson and Wortham had big plans for Hook. Indeed, Hook was among the nineteen chief operating officers pictured in AG's 1972 annual report as under consideration to be heir apparent to Woodson, who announced his retirement for June, 1978.[6]

In April, 1973, American General began a campaign to bolster its own stock earnings by buying its own shares, finally acquiring 2.6 million shares for $51.6 million. Again, in January, 1974, the company acquired almost 1.3 million more shares and purchased 500,000 more shares during the year.[7]

American General Investment, with Gus still chairman, announced a $39 million loan agreement that spring for development of a ninety-nine-acre site in northwest Harris County, not far from Wortham's own land holdings. AG Investment had made the loans for the land and the development for the new Bammell Village at FM 1960 and Kuykendahl Road. In all the investment corporation was involved in twenty-two separate joint ventures.[8] American General and its subsidiaries were in top form.

That spring, Fred Nahas, a well-known Houston radio announcer and social raconteur, devoted his program to Gus Wortham, prompted by Ben Woodson's tribute in the 1972 annual report. Nahas noted that Wortham's initial investment of three hundred thousand dollars had grown to a billion-dollar entity, and how his "talents . . . helped mold the Baghdad on the Bayou into the sixth largest city in America." He quoted directly from Woodson's disclaimer that neither he, nor anyone, could ever take Gus Wortham's place at American General. Agreeing with Woodson, Nahas then painted a picture of the "courtly" Mr. Gus going to a cultural fête with Lyndall, involved with his cattle, and sharing his "wisdom" with so many community endeavors. "But the loudest voice of Mr. Gus," Nahas concluded, "will be devoted to the land of Texas which spawned the opportunities from which he and his father . . . built the Texas success story which rivals many among the concrete canyons of Wall Street." Certainly, by Nahas's description, Wortham had reached the status of the revered elder; he was the epitome of a southwestern gentleman: courtly in manner, talented in business, wise with people, and devoted always to Texas.[9]

Actually, the apotheosis of Gus Wortham had begun some years earlier. In 1967, he had been honored with the Good Citizenship Award by the Paul Carrington Chapter of the Texas Society of the Sons of the American Revolution, the same award Jesse Jones had received eleven years earlier at a dinner over which Wortham had presided. And, in 1968, Wortham had been named Key Houstonian of the Year by the city's Board of Realtors. It was a testament to his and the company's involvement in land acquisition and development. In an editorial, the *Houston Post* said there was "no one who better represented the spirit of his city than 'Mr. Gus'. . . ."[10]

Now, as he achieved this elevated status in the community, Gus Wortham began to put his affairs in order. A top priority was the Wortham Foundation, changed from its earlier agricultural focus, and incorporated in 1971 to provide donations to local civic and cultural groups. In February, 1973, Wortham carefully delineated his vision for the foundation in a letter to its head, Allen "Buddy" Carruth, the only son of his first partner:

> There are two areas in which I am interested: the major cultural activities in Houston Texas—i.e. Symphony society, Houston Grand Opera, Ballet, Art Museum on Bissonet [*sic*] between Main St. and Montrose—City of Houston and perhaps Harris County parks. . . .
>
> Hospitals and schools are being more and more supported by local, state and national government, and should not receive gifts from our Foundation. I believe, based on long experience, that our Foundation should concentrate on assuming that Houston will have first class cultural activities thru [*sic*] well organized organizations and equal if not more help should be given to large parks—I do not like numerous small gifts to the causes that flood foundations with requests. . . .
>
> . . . I thank you for what you have done and will do to see that our estates are used for the people of this area.[11]

While he was concerned about the foundation's future, Wortham had long ago made ample provision for his family. He had set up trusts for his daughters, his nieces (Cad's daughters, Fanny and June), and their children. He also established trusts for his closer kin, Lyndall's relatives, and various members of his household, office, and ranching staffs and close friends.[12]

Shortly after his letter on the foundation to Carruth, Wortham also composed a memorandum concerning the "financial affairs of Mrs. Wortham and me." He estimated their net assets at about $30 to $40 million, but surmised that his land holdings, especially the larger parcels northwest of Houston, would greatly increase that figure in the "next few years." (Wortham told Carruth that he should wait three to six years to sell the land in the estate.) Other land holdings mentioned included a forty-five percent interest on the land and buildings in Austin where the government buildings were built; partial ownership of the old Country Club; Houston Private Homes, a development in northeast Harris County; industrial land on North Shepherd, near the Katy railroad; and a one-half interest in several tracts in Fort Bend County, owned with his friend W. M. "Fishback" Wheless. At this time Wortham still owned the Nine Bar, Cypress, and the Nine Bar, New Mexico. Lastly, Wortham's oil holdings were worth about eighty-six thousand dollars and he had extensive holdings in Texas Eastern Transmission and Texas Gas Transmission, ITT, and Kaiser Cement (to whom Longhorn had been sold in 1965). He also expected American General stock, of which he held vast numbers of shares, to double in value.[13] A wistful reminder that things were changing was Gus's cancellation of his rental of suite 7F in the Lamar Hotel. "For years we had 10 or more in our group but time has taken its toll and we now have a bare quorum. This makes it necessary for us to economize," he explained, hoping the hotel could provide smaller quarters at weekly rent.[14]

Land was still a passion with Gus and he and Lester Randle still took their long rides around Houston, looking at properties. As he had predicted with his own purchases, land west and northwest was in a development boom, and Gus Wortham watched as the value of his holdings rose rapidly. But he came to a new appreciation for the uses of land in these later years, especially the need for park space.[15]

October 16, 1973, was designated "Gus Wortham Day" by Mayor Louie Welch in honor of the renaming of the old Houston Country Club land the Gus Wortham Park. Its major owners—Wortham, Newton Rayzor, and the estate of E. R. Barrow—allowed the city to buy the land from them in a "donative sale" (at less then it was worth), for $3.6 million. This maneuver let them claim a tax deduction while giving the city another park. At the dedication, Wortham spoke on keeping Houston beautiful. Although not the only owner, Gus had the largest single interest in the land and it was named after him most certainly because of his civic stature.[16]

Wortham's beneficence was the subject of many tales of unrecorded loans and donations for various causes, to old family friends, to acquaintances "down on their luck," and to associates for various ventures. The best known story of a Wortham anonymous gift was his bequest in 1959 to buy Houston's historic Nichols-Rice-Cherry house for five thousand dollars, save it from demolition and move it to Sam Houston Park for the Harris County Heritage Society. Wortham had been asked to buy the house at a social event and agreed; his participation was not known until after his death when Lyndall told the press. Of course, there were also his anonymous bail-outs for the Houston Symphony Orchestra.

Although Wortham often gave anonymously, it is clear that he also liked being recognized for his contributions. He recounted to one of his younger col-

At the dedication of Gus S. Wortham Park, the former site of the Houston Country Club, are Lyndall, Gus, and Houston Mayor Louie Welch, October 16, 1973. Courtesy American General Corporation.

leagues a lesson he had learned working at his uncle's hardware store in Mexia. Filling the order of a good customer for a pound of nails, young Gus reached in and added a handful more to the pound, explaining to the uncle that he thought they should treat this customer well. His uncle replied that was fine, but the customer should also know he was getting the extra.[17]

The extent of Gus Wortham's beneficence and what he thought were endeavors worthy of his support can be deciphered from a list of his personal donations, dated 1969. The list includes several contributions to schools of all kinds, including $53,000 to retire the mortgage of the Delta Christian School in Tallulah, Louisiana, where his grandchildren attended school. He gave $6,000 to the Museum of Fine Arts and $1,000 to the Founders Fund for Bayou Bend (Ima Hogg's home, furnished with American antiques); $3,000 to the Houston Grand Opera; and $17,000, including both 1968 and 1969, to the Houston Symphony Society. He donated $5,000 to the United Fund in 1969. Wortham had several long-term pledges, including $100,000 to Dr. Denton Cooley and the Texas Heart Institute at St. Luke's Episcopal Hospital. Another list, from 1968, includes a note to the Houston Symphony Society for $60,000, and a 1966 pledge to the University of Texas for $1,000 a year for life. His gifts were eclectic: $5,000 in 1969 to the Congressional Medal of Honor Society for college lectures by Medal of Honor recipients to "offset some of the speeches being made by minority left-wing organizations"; $500 for the restoration of a memorial to Robert E. Lee in Waco; $200 to the YWCA for Job Corps returnees; and $750 for the Barbecue for Racial Harmony at the Kashmere Gardens Baptist Church. In 1971 Wortham endowed a professorship in architecture at Rice University and in 1973 he pledged $35,000 to the Museum of Fine Arts.[18]

The amount of Wortham's personal contributions and deductions decreased from about $260,000 in 1971 to under $100,000 in 1974, although this does not include the totals of certain pledges. In 1974 Wortham's main personal donations went to Mrs. Wortham's sorority, Kappa Kappa Gamma; the major arts groups, including the Houston Symphony, Houston Grand Opera, Houston Ballet, Theater Under the Stars, and Museum of Fine Arts; Methodist Hospital; and Baylor College of Medicine. This did not include the Wortham Foundation's donations, whose 1974 statement lists its assets at $948,000 and includes significant monies to the Symphony Society, the City of Hope, and Girlstown, USA.[19]

As Wortham was scaling down his personal empire, American General was continuing to expand, including opening life operations in Canada and Great Britain. Clearly Woodson meant to continue moving out, if not away, from insurance and was seeking wider markets for the company. He also sought a place in history for American General when he arranged to have the Newcomen Society of North America, a nonprofit business history association, recognize American General by sponsoring a lecture and printing the company's history. The culmination of the project was Woodson's presentation of the history, written with the help of publicist Kenneth Fellows, at the 1974 Texas Dinner of the Newcomen Society, April 29, 1974. Gus Wortham was the guest of honor. Two heirs of the 8F crowd, Ben Love, president of Jesse Jones's Texas Commerce Bank, and James A. Elkins, Jr., now head of his father's First City National, hosted the reception.[20] Wortham, who was ill, made brief remarks praising his and Woodson's ability to work together to build the company. *Chronicle* columnist and Wortham friend, Morris Frank, wrote a column on the dinner, referring to Wortham as that "venerable, esteemed Houston institution."[21] Another recognition of the Newcomen Dinner was written by the Reverend John Lancaster, pastor of Houston's First Presbyterian Church. Mrs. Wortham was a member of its socially prominent congregation. Although Gus had never joined this or any religious congregation in Houston, he had told Lancaster that he thought of him as his pastor. Lancaster praised American General's growth as a tribute to Wortham's "integrity"; business "flourish[es] where clear moral values are upheld."[22]

If the Newcomen Dinner was the fitting finale for his business career, Gus Wortham's ranching career was summed up at the final Nine Bar sale that October. Pappy Selph's Band played "Turkey in the Straw" while buyers, including some from South Africa, Australia, Argentina, and Brazil, along with famous political faces such as John Connally (now special counsel to the AG board and executive committee) and Mrs. Albert Thomas munched on six hundred pounds of barbecue. Because of their various health problems, Gus and Lyndall rode about in modified golf carts called "Gusmobiles."

That December, Wortham sold his beloved Nine Bar and the Nine Bar at Clines Corners, New Mexico, to Cox Enterprises' Barbara Cox Anthony, heir to the Cox publishing empire and a Santa Gertrudis breeder. The sale of the ranches included both herds, but the estimated sale price for the thirty-two hundred acres near Houston, reportedly one of the biggest ranches in Harris County, was $12 million. For most of Houston's social elite, this truly marked the end of an era. Gus Wortham's lavish party and sale were the epitome of a life-style which Texans thought particularly theirs—the mythic Texas cattle industry overlaid with the charm of southern plantation largesse and hospitality, all made possible because of the savvy risk-taking of a western entrepreneur. *Weekly Western Livestock Journal* cited Wortham's breeding research and land management operations, but also his personal popularity, allowing that he would be "missed as a powerful individual factor in furthering the nation's livestock industry."[23]

As if in sympathetic reaction to the slowing down of its founder, American General had a bad year in 1974, despite its being the company's third best year in consolidated earnings and second best in per share earnings. Property and liability earnings were down by more than a third. American General was getting more attention for its diversified services, although they only produced just over three percent of its earnings. *Fortune* ranked it fourteenth in its list of the fifty largest diversified financial service companies in the country. AG had merged its own investment advisory firm with Channing's Management fund, and by January, 1975, *Financial Trend* predicted that AG would be the sixth largest company in the mutual fund business. Things were expected to improve for AG in 1975.[24]

That summer, American General finally arranged to acquire the remaining shares of California-Western States Life Insurance. It had been part of Woodson's agreement with Wortham and the board to have his successor in place by 1975. The AG board's executive committee, charged with finding a new president, was to make visits to the nineteen CEO's of AG's subsidiary

American General Chairman Ben Woodson, Wortham, and Harold S. Hook, on July 1, 1975, when Hook became American General's third president. Courtesy American General Corporation.

companies. How many visits were actually made is not known; many of these men were in Houston. One visit was made to California, however, to Harold Hook who became president of AG, with Woodson continuing as chairman and CEO. *Insurance* magazine noted an insurance milestone on its cover of July, 1975, picturing Wortham and Hook. At eighty-four, Gus Wortham was turning over his company—grown from a small, Texas entity to a national financial conglomerate—to Hook, forty-three, the consummate professional manager. There could be no need of further proof that Gus Wortham trusted youth and change.[25]

Hook remembered that once he was in place, Wortham seemed to commit himself to a principle of noninterference. He would no longer listen, as he had before, to plans or ideas and by his listening be the de facto decision maker. Now, when Hook came to him with an especially difficult personnel decision that others had told him Wortham would not countenance, Wortham said that he "should know better"; he was no longer involved.[26]

But by early 1975 the company's founder was very ill, requiring constant use of oxygen for his emphysema and spending his days in an exhausting round of visits to doctors and hospital stays to relieve his several other physical complications. A gaunter, older Gus Wortham had his photo taken at yet another

John Connally, Ben Woodson, Gus Wortham, and Nellie Connally at Connally's homecoming to Houston in April, 1975, after being acquitted of wrongdoing in the Associated Milk Producers' scandal. Courtesy American General Corporation.

public tribute, a Rotary Club luncheon naming him Houston's distinguished citizen, with the keynote address by John Connally. It must have given Houstonians a pang to see the newspaper photo of two Houston traditions, Ima Hogg and Gus Wortham, now both old and very frail. Connally's speech to the 750 in attendance cited Wortham's beneficence and the need to protect the "system" so that others could rise from "humble beginnings," like him.[27]

Despite his health, Wortham was still involved politically. In the fall of 1975 he donated five thousand dollars to the campaign of Fred Hofheinz, son of the man who had once labeled him a "fat cat." He was much interested in the furor over rewriting of the Texas Constitution. In 1972 he had been part of a committee backing passage of an amendment which would have had the 1876 document revised by the state legislature, a step opposed by many liberal Democrats. But in 1975, Wortham gave a thousand dollars to the statewide organization trying to stop a proposed revision of the Constitution, as did other prominent businessmen such as George Brown, Walter Mischer, and J. A. Elkins, Jr.[28]

Lyndall Wortham's book, *Around the World on a Frayed Shoestring*, appeared in March, 1975, published by the University of Texas Press. The book was a compilation of the letters she had written for publication in the *Dallas Morning News* during her world cruise in the early 1920s.[29] The book was used as the theme of Houston's annual March of Dimes fundraising ball, honoring her; because of her recent illness she spent the evening in her wheelchair without Gus. The evening's success (raising $100,000) prompted the *Post* to editorialize that "[the] Worthams have meant a great deal to the life of this city for a long time."[30]

One of Gus's last "society page" appearances was at a September, 1975, party thrown in his honor by the Cox daughters, Barbara Anthony and her sister, who had purchased the two Nine Bar ranches.[31] A local society publication, *Houston Town and Country*, featured Wortham in a "They Built Houston" series in December. The piece, "Portrait of an Optimist," celebrated his Texan individualism and status as "one of Houston's most beloved citizens and leaders."[32]

Certainly it was a love of what he had built in Houston that prompted Gus Wortham to choose to be buried in small Magnolia Cemetery at the corner of Montrose Avenue and Allen Parkway (earlier Buffalo Drive)—right next to American General. Wortham had purchased a group of lots at the center of the property and built a mausoleum for himself and Lyndall, a site easily seen from the American General offices. At the same time, American General had made arrangements to acquire the north and south ends of the cemetery and was creating a small park at Montrose and Allen Parkway.[33]

A final grand gesture of Wortham civic beneficence occurred in January, 1976, when Gus gave a million dollars to the University of Houston in honor of his wife's thirteen-year appointment to the institution's board of regents. Some of the impetus for the gift may also have come from the enormous taxes Gus would otherwise have had to pay after selling his property, but it was much welcomed as one of the largest unrestricted gifts received by the university that had originally been founded to serve Houston's working class.[34]

Shortly after this gift was made, Gus began a final round of hospital stays, culminating in the removal of his spleen by Dr. Denton Cooley. He was hospitalized for the last time in August and it was evident that he would not return home. A vigil at Wortham's bedside was held by men like Hook, Connally, oil man Eddy Scurlock, and Lester Randle.[35]

During this period Harold Hook was called often to the hospital because Wortham wanted to see him. Hook sat in the hospital room as Wortham endured blood transfusions and other procedures, all the while talking to Hook about the company. It was clear that, for Wortham, his company came before anything. Refusing other visits from friends and family, he wanted Hook there to tell him "things he felt I needed to know—the obligations and relationships that he thought maybe should be continued; those that had been satisfied."

To Hook, this was a perfect example of the way Gus Wortham held sway over people—not by taking obvious control, but by insinuating in them a sense of how important he himself felt something was. There were no questions or instructions. Wortham simply told Hook that there were issues he would face and he would just have to do as he saw best, without "respect to me or past situations. . . . But the point was it was very clear to me that he knew he could . . . ask for whatever he wanted to, but he was specifically not doing that. And, therefore you felt more obligated than if he had tried to extract [promises]."[36]

Hook felt "bonded, welded into the situation." But while holding on, Hook believed that at the same time Wortham conceded that the younger man was the "man for today" and knew far better than he did what American General needed for the future. "More than anything else he [Wortham] wanted it to continue. . . . it was just a marvelous way to try to extend his reach over another generation. . . . I don't think there's another experience like this in American business where someone has been able to have as much influence on a successive generation without having a blood relation."[37] Gus Wortham wanted to continue to influence his child, his company, and thus ensure his immortality. Both Ben Woodson and Harold Hook remembered that one of the last things Gus Wortham said to them was in reference to his grave site: "I'll be keeping an eye on you."[38]

On Wednesday, September 1, 1976, at 1:10 A.M. Gus S. Wortham died in Methodist Hospital. The funeral was held on Friday, September 3 at the First Presbyterian Church, Dr. Lancaster presiding. A large crowd attended the burial services; fittingly, it rained. The pallbearers included Ben Woodson, James Elkins, Jr., Ben Love, Mayo Thompson, Rusty Wortham, Raymond Mauk (who oversaw much of the Worthams' private business affairs in the later years), and Nine Bar foreman Winroe Jacoby. The papers properly eulogized him; the *Chronicle*'s headline reading "Farewell to a legend," the Galveston paper calling him "Insurance Firm Founder, Politicos' Godfather."[39]

With the daughters grown and living their own lives in Louisiana and North Carolina, Lyndall was alone in her grand home, not in the best of health, but still very much a Houston society doyenne. She continued her work as a regent at the University of Houston until 1979 and served as a board member of the Houston Grand Opera until 1980. When she died in July, 1980, she was eulogized as a "southern belle" who cared about her city. The editorial recounted her life and her partnership with Gus in many philanthropic causes— "a life of rich texture and color, a life well shared," the *Post* said, as if marking the end, for Houston, of that set of southern gentlemen and their "vivacious" ladies.[40] The paper mused about Houston's "southernness" being a way and philosophy of life that was ending. It did not acknowledge, however, that Gus Wortham's life had been one of many that had brought about that change as it incorporated the southwestern into the southern.

After Lyndall's death, the Worthams' household furniture and belongings, including Lyndall's many pieces of expensive jewelry, were sold at auction for $1.5 million, split between young Lyndall and Diana. The house was bequeathed to the University of Houston as a residence for its president.

Because the Worthams had executed a companion will, the foundation, worth about $1.7 million at Gus's death, ballooned to a market value of $15.7 million when Lyndall died. Its first major project, completed while Mrs. Wortham was still alive, caused a bit of a public stir. It was a fountain in Gus's honor placed across Allen Parkway from the American General building. Lyndall had donated $126,000 for the fountain and landscaping in 1977, along with plans for its design, based upon one Gus had seen and admired in Australia. Houston's Municipal Arts Commission rejected the fountain design when it was first proposed after an embarrassing incident in which the fountain was originally accepted by the Parks and Recreation Department without the commission's acceptance. The arts panel called the work a "lollipop, golf ball . . . no better than a plastic-poodle over the mantle," and proclaimed distress at the multiplicity of such fountains mass-produced by an Arizona firm. Later the work was approved, provided a grove of trees was planted around it.

Another grant from the foundation went to the city for the fountains in Tranquility Park in downtown Houston, and still more money for a feasibility study to create a parkway through downtown along Buffalo Bayou. Carruth and the foundation board continued to fund park projects of all kinds in keeping with Gus Wortham's wishes.[41]

But the majority of funds from the Wortham Foundation went to, and continue going to, Houston's oldest mainstream arts institutions named in Wortham's letter to Carruth. In 1983, the Wortham Foundation provided the largest single donation for a theatre center to house the Houston Grand Opera and the Houston Ballet. The last of Houston's "lions," George Brown had personally visited Allen Carruth shortly before Brown's death to seek the original bequest for $15 million dollars. Another gift of $5 million came later. This has been the foundation's largest bequest to a single project.[42]

Gus Wortham's chief legacy, his foundation, is all that is left of the southwestern gentleman. His type no longer exists in Houston because of the growth he and others like him fostered. Two reasons for this are the vast political changes that have opened up the system to those previously excluded from gaining political power, and economic shifts that have turned former local business empires into components of huge international conglomerates.

While there are many corporate and civic leaders who support Houston institutions, the era of rule by a small coterie of socially and politically well connected business leaders is past. As one corporate leader said, it is no longer possible to gather the eight or ten most powerful men in the city together and ask them to throw in a few thousand dollars for a civic project or ensure the election of their chosen political candidate. Some lament their passing because these men seemed to be more personally invested in the city and its welfare. Others are not so sure.

In 1979 the *Houston Business Journal* carried a series of articles on "Houston's Founding Fortunes." It included features on Jesse Jones, Judge James Elkins, the Brown brothers, Will Clayton, and Wortham, among others. Writer Dana Blankenhorn described Wortham as the "embodiment of the Houston establishment," its "point man" who was one of the more visible, affable, and civic-minded of the group. Like the eulogy penned some fifty years earlier for John L. Wortham, this article celebrated a Wortham who was a smart businessman, a good friend, and a loyal and active Texan.[43]

The foundation for all this lay in a code of behavior that had been brought by Gus's grandfathers when they migrated to Texas from the old South. It was both a way of life and a personal demeanor that defined them as southern gentlemen. Faith in a ruling aristocracy and strict adherence to the rules of chivalry and noblesse oblige were the values. But these men had also searched for a better life on the western frontier, finally ending up in Texas. Thus John Wortham was born with a foot in each world. As his eulogizer R. B. Cousins put it, John L. Wortham was "[n]obly born of a family that was typical of the best in the Old South . . . [he] embodied and exemplified the traditional magnanimity and courage of that Old South that now lives only in song and story and united them with the nerve and alertness of the new South. . . ."[44]

And John's son, Gus Wortham, became an even more notable model of that blend. Gus's prominence and influence in business, in land matters, and in politics outdistanced his father's. He, even more distinctly than John, displayed the range of traits that defined the new southwestern gentleman.

Notes

PREFACE

1. Daniel Singal, *The War Within: Victorian to Modernist Thought in the South, 1919–1945*, 8–9, 11–13.
2. Singal, *The War Within*, 21–23.
3. Joe L. Dubbert, *A Man's Place: Masculinity in Transition*, 66, 122, 124.

CHAPTER 1. THE GREATEST BOY IN TEXAS

1. Gus S. Wortham to John L. Wortham, June, 1918, reprinted in "Inspiring Words of Soldier to Father," *Austin American*, June 22, 1918, Lyndall Wortham Seymour Papers.
2. John L. Wortham to Gus S. Wortham, June 18, 1918, reprinted in *Austin American*, June 22, 1918, Lyndall Wortham Seymour Papers.
3. Fanny Davis Diehl, telephone interview by author, March 16, 1990; John L. Wortham to Gus S. Wortham, various correspondence, John L. Wortham Papers and Wortham Correspondence Binders, American General Archives; Kenneth Fellows, "The Baby Is Born: The Story of American General's First Fifty Years," book MS written for American General Corp., 1976, American General Archives.
4. George Alice May Randolph, *Woodland Cousins: Their Kith and Kin*, 57; John L. Wortham, "To the Democracy of Texas," unpublished[?] announcement of candidacy, ca. 1912, John L. Wortham and Son Archives; Unidentified clipping, Gus S. Wortham Scrapbook no. 1, 4, American General Archives.
5. Freestone County Historical Commission, *History of Freestone County*, 645 (hereafter cited as Freestone County, *History*).
6. Randolph, *Woodland Cousins*, 57; John L. Wortham, "To the Democracy of Texas"; Unidentified clipping, Gus S. Wortham Scrapbook no. 1, 4.
7. Genealogical Society of Freestone County, *Freestone Frontiers* no. 1 (Feb. 1984), Freestone County Historical Museum; Program for Dedication of Historical Marker

for Woodland Cemetery, November 2, 1975, American General Archives; Freestone County, *History*, 645; Texas, Freestone County, County Clerk, *Deed Records*, Nov. 11, 1871, General Index nos. 2 and 3, 1871–1900.

8. Freestone County, *History*, 6–15, 18–20, 37–38, 51–52, 101–102; Barnes F. Lathrop, "Migration into East Texas, 1835–1860," *Southwestern Historical Quarterly* (July, 1948), 200–207; Betsy J. Powers, "'Gone to Texas,' The Impact of Southern Migration upon Antebellum Texas," M.A. thesis, University of Houston, 1990.

9. Some sources give Luther Rice Wortham's birth date as 1820 versus 1819 and date of death as 1875.

10. Texas, Freestone County, County Clerk, *Deed Records*, *General Index nos. 2 and 3*, 1871–1900; Texas, Freestone County, County Clerk, *Probate Minutes*, Vol. 1–5, #404, 745, 749, 920–933.

11. Baylor University, *Bulletin*, Ex-students directory, 23 (Waco: 1920); John L. Wortham, "To the Democracy of Texas"; Freestone County, *History*, p. 568; Carl B. Wilson, *A Registration of Baylor University, 1845–1935*.

12. Freestone County, *History*, p. 568

13. Ibid.; Texas, Freestone County, County Clerk, *Deed Records*, Jan. 14, 1887, General Index nos. 2 and 3, 1871–1900; Texas, Freestone County, County Clerk, *Deed Records*, 1900–1909; Texas, Limestone County, County Clerk, *Deed Records*, 1894–1905.

14. Randolph, *Woodland Cousins*, 38. J. R. Sessions, Jr., interview by author, September 10, 1990, Houston, Tex.

15. John L. Wortham, "To the Democracy of Texas"; J. R. Sessions interview; *Mexia (Tex.) Evening News*, March 7, 1899.

16. Texas. Limestone County, County Clerk, Birth Certificate for Gus S. Wortham; Bascom Timmons, *Jesse H. Jones: The Man and the Statesman*, 88; John L. Wortham to Henrietta Davie, February 28, 1902, Wortham Correspondence Binders; Fanny Davis Diehl telephone interview. John and Fannie had at least one other child who died as a baby. (John L. Wortham to Henrietta Davie, February 28, 1902, Wortham Correspondence Binders.)

17. John L. Wortham, "To the Democracy of Texas"; *Mexia (Tex.) Evening News*, various issues, Feb.–March, 1899.

18. John L. Wortham, "To the Democracy of Texas"; John L. Wortham to Lunie Lamb, May 20, 1908, William Wortham Papers; various Wortham Correspondence Binders; John L. Wortham to W. R. Davie, [no day or month], 1902, Wortham Correspondence Binders. Davie, himself, was active in politics and served as Texas' first state tax commissioner, and secretary of state from 1908 to 1910.

19. Gus S. Wortham, Notes of interview with Kenneth Fellows, Dec. 17, 1974, Kenneth Fellows Papers.

20. Benjamin N. Woodson, interview by author, no. 2, Feb. 26, 1990, Houston, Tex.; Allen Carruth, Interview by author, no. 1, Nov. 8, and 13, 1989, Houston Tex.; J. R. Sessions interview.

21. John L. Wortham, "To the Democracy of Texas."

22. Donald R. Walker, *Penology for Profit: A History of the Texas Prison System, 1867–1912*, 153–54.

23. Rupert N. Richardson, Ernest Wallace, and Adrian Anderson, *Texas: The Lone Star State*, 311–13; Walker, *Penology for Profit*, 154–56, 176, 150.

24. From 1868 until 1882, the prison system was "hired out" to private interests who, in turn, leased the prisoners out for hire. In 1883 the state regained control of the system, but still leased out convict labor. The legislature and the public, believing prisons should be self-supporting, provided no funding. Because the workshops at Huntsville and the relatively new iron foundry at Rusk could not employ all the convicts, many were leased to private contractors. Those in the system who believed the prisoners fared best under total state control bought farm land on which the prisoners worked. Many were still hired out to private contractors for farm, railroad, and road-building labor. The prison system was profitable but, especially under the lease system, little rehabilitation of prisoners was accomplished. (Herman L. Crow, "A Political History of the Texas Prison System, 1929–1951," Ph.D. diss., University of Texas, 1964, 170; Walker, *Penology for Profit*, 80–81.)

25. Crow, "History of the Texas Prison System," 173–81; Walker, *Penology for Profit*, 175–77, 188–89.

26. John L. Wortham, "To the Democracy of Texas"; Crow, "History of the Texas Prison System," 171–72.

27. Crow, "History of the Texas Prison System," 171–72; Walker, *Penology for Profit*, 186.

28. Walker, *Penology for Profit*, 183.

29. Walker, *Penology for Profit*, 189; "True to His Friends," *Houston Post*, Aug. 12, 1913. An investigation in 1909, spurred by a San Antonio newspaper exposé, led to reforms and the end of convict leasing. The three-man board had full-time jobs overseeing the system, thus taking the control out of the hands of political patrons and adding a measure of professionalism.

30. James A. Elkins, Jr., interview by author, no. 1, Oct. 25, 1985, Houston, Tex.; Fellows, "The Baby Is Born," 50–51.

James A. Elkins (1879–1972) was born in Huntsville, Texas, where he became city attorney and then county attorney in 1901, after having received his legal degree from the University of Texas. From 1903 until 1905 he was county judge of Walker County and practiced law there until 1917 when he went to Houston. He founded a law firm with William A. Vinson specializing in corporate law, especially oil-related enterprises. In 1924, he founded Guaranty Trust Company, which merged with Gulf State Bank and in 1934 became City National Bank. In 1956 it would again merge with First National Bank to become Houston's largest, First City National Bank. (Marcellus E. Foster and Alfred Jones, eds., *South and Southeast Texas: A Work for Newspaper and Library Reference*, 353; *Houston Chronicle*, May 8, 1972.

31. Jesse Holman Jones's (1875–1956) power and influence still pervade the city of Houston. One can go almost nowhere without finding some edifice named in his honor. Having initially started in the lumber business, Jones became best known for his real estate and building empire. At one time Jesse Jones was responsible for most of the buildings in the center of Houston. In time he acquired two institutions with vast power: the National Bank of Commerce and the *Houston Chronicle*. He served President Wilson as head of the Red Cross during World War I and was later named to the Reconstruction Finance Corporation (RFC) by President Hoover. Under FDR, Jones headed the RFC and was appointed secretary of commerce in 1940. (Fellows, "The Baby Is Born," 31–34; Walter M. Buenger and Joseph A. Pratt, *But Also Good Business: Texas Commerce Banks and the Financing of Houston and Texas, 1886–1986*, 75–77.)

32. John L. Wortham, "To The Democracy of Texas"; John L. Wortham to A. J. Harper, Sept. 15, 1909, John L. Wortham Papers; *Directory of the City of Houston 1911–1912*, 1,115; Timmons, *Jesse H. Jones*, 87–88; Fellows, "The Baby Is Born," 35; Jesse H. Jones Lumber Company, Minutes, vol. 10 (June 25, 1909–Nov. 28, 1920), Jesse H. Jones Lumber Company Collection, Houston Metropolitan Research Center.

33. Fellows, "The Baby Is Born," 51; John Tarleton College Football Team, framed photograph, Dec. 20, 1907, American General Archives.

34. Fellows, "The Baby Is Born," 52; University of Texas, College of Business Administration, "Interviews with Mr. Gus. Wortham of American General Life Insurance Company," Business Oral History Records (Austin, ca. 1970–71), Eugene Barker Texas History Center, University of Texas, 1–2 (hereafter cited as Gus S. Wortham Oral History).

35. Fellows, "The Baby Is Born," 53.

36. John L. Wortham to Mrs. Lunie Lamb, May 20, 1908; "The Martyrdom of Your Fads," typescript with photographs, n.d., John L. Wortham Papers.

37. John L. Wortham to A. J. Harper, Sept. 15, 1909, John L. Wortham Papers; Lewis L. Gould, *Progressives and Prohibitionists: Texas Democrats in the Wilson Era*, 16, 58–59; Sam Hanna Acheson, *Joe Bailey: The Last Democrat*, 260–61; Walter Prescott Webb, ed.-in-chief, *The Handbook of Texas* vol. 1, 772; A. J. Harper to John L. Wortham, September 13, 1909, John L. Wortham Papers; John L. Wortham to A. J. Harper, September 15, 1909; Gould, *Progressives and Prohibitionists*, 94.

Joseph Weldon Bailey (1863–1921) was a lawyer from Mississippi who moved to Texas in 1885. In 1891 he was elected to the U.S. Congress, serving until 1901 when he became U.S. senator from Texas. During his first term in the Senate, he was accused of taking money from the Waters-Pierce Oil Company, which was under state antitrust investigation. Bailey was also accused of questionable conduct in his involvements with Standard Oil and the interests of John Henry Kirby. He was exonerated and remained in the U.S. Senate until 1913, when he resigned to practice law in Washington, D.C. In 1921 he ran unsuccessfully for governor of Texas against Pat Neff. (Webb, *Handbook of Texas*, vol. 1, 95.)

38. Gould, *Progressives and Prohibitionists*, 274–75; John L. Wortham to W. E. Biggs, July 22, 1920, John L. Wortham Papers.

39. John L. Wortham to Gus S. Wortham, June 24, 1914, John L. Wortham Papers.

40. Gould, *Progressives and Prohibitionists*, 16, 58–59; Gus S. Wortham, Notes of interview by Kenneth Fellows, Nov. 15, 1974, Kenneth Fellows Papers (hereafter cited as Gus S. Wortham interview notes, various dates).

John Henry Kirby (1860–1940) is generally accepted as Texas' first captain of industry as well as its first millionaire. As a lawyer and lumberman, Kirby built out of the East Texas forest an empire which between 1910 and 1920 included vast timberland holdings, twelve mills, five logging camps and over 16,000 employees. He also built the Gulf, Beaumont and Kansas City Railroad to carry his lumber. In these operations he was instrumental in bringing investment dollars from the East Coast establishment into the Gulf Coast frontier. In 1890 he moved to Houston as a base of operations and opened his own law firm. He became an oil man, too, serving as president of the Southwestern Oil Company in Houston and founding the Kirby Oil Company in 1920. He was also president of the Planters and Mechanics National Bank. Kirby was active politically at all levels. He served two terms in the Texas House of Representatives and was a candidate for governor in 1914. (Webb, *Handbook of Texas*, vol. 2, 966; Fellows, "The Baby Is Born," 36–38.)

41. John L. Wortham, "To the Democracy of Texas"; S. G. Reed, *A History of the Texas Railroads and of the Transportation Conditions under Spain and Mexico and the Republic and the State*, 584; Richardson, Wallace, and Anderson, *Texas*, 344–46; James R. Norvell, "The Railroad Commission of Texas, Its Origin and History," *Southwestern Historical Quarterly* 68 (April, 1965): 465–80.

42. Norvell, "Railroad Commission of Texas," 468–72.

43. John L. Wortham, "To the Democracy of Texas"; C. S. Fiero to John L. Wortham, July 16, 1912, John L. Wortham Papers.

44. Fellows, "The Baby Is Born," 54.

45. John L. Wortham to F. M. Bralley; Webb, *Handbook of Texas* vol. 2, 901, and vol. 1, 320, 516; John L. Wortham Papers: John L. Wortham to J. D. Jackson, July 12, 1918; Clarence Ousley to John L. Wortham, June 4, 1924; John L. Wortham to E. A. DeWitt, July 12, 1918.

Only a year before he died, John Wortham wrote to Senator W. E. Doyle, asking him to join with his friend, Archie Parr, to get the needed appropriations for Kingsville Normal (South Texas Teachers College, later Texas A&I University), assuring him that the Klebergs (owners of King Ranch) wanted the school and would stock its ranch. Wortham said he had no "motive" because he had no financial interests in that area. Cousins had already been named the first president of the proposed college. The school was not begun until 1925, however, but Gus Wortham would serve on its first board of trustees from 1929 to 1935. (R. B. Cousins Papers, 1923 letters: John L. Wortham to W. E. Doyle, Apr. 23; R. B. Cousins to E. D. Dunlop, Apr. 24; A. Parr to John L. Wortham, Apr. 25; W. E. Doyle to R. B. Cousins with letter on back from John L. Wortham to R. B. Cousins, Apr. 26; R. B. Cousins to W. E. Doyle, Apr. 28.)

46. Freestone County, *History*, 645; John L. Wortham, "To the Democracy of Texas"; Edith Cousins, "R. B. Cousins Papers," n.d., R. B. Cousins Papers; John L. Wortham to R. B. Cousins, Sept. 27, 1918, R. B. Cousins Papers; W. S. Sutton to R. B. Cousins, c/o J. L. Wortham, Aug. 8, 1921, R. B. Cousins Papers.

47. "True to His Friends," *Houston Post*, Aug. 12, 1913.

48. Fellows, "The Baby Is Born," 60–61.

49. R. B. Cousins, "A High Priest In Friendship's Holy Temple," carbon typescript, n.d. [ca. Nov. 5, 1924], Kenneth Fellows Papers.

50. Cousins, "A High Priest" 54–55; Gus S. Wortham Oral History, 2–4; Gus S. Wortham interview notes, Dec. 17, 1974.

51. James A. Tinsley, "Texas Progressives and Insurance Regulation," *Southwest Social Science Quarterly* Dec., 1955: 244–46; Mary Jane Manford, *Insuring Texas' Future: A History of the Independent Insurance Agents of Texas*, 37–38. His job at the State Insurance Board was not Gus's first governmental job, for he had worked for the Department of Education under his father's friend, State Superintendent of Education F. M. Bralley, in 1910 or 1911.

52. John L. Wortham to F. M. Bralley, July 12, 1918, John L. Wortham Papers; Gus S. Wortham interview notes, Nov. 17, 1974; Fellows, "The Baby Is Born," 55–56.

53. Fellows, "The Baby is Born," 24–26; Allen Carruth interview oral history no. 1; Gus S. Wortham interview notes, Nov. 15, 1974; B. F. Carruth File, Gus S. Wortham Drawer, American General Archives.

54. Texas, Secretary of State Papers, John L. Wortham Bond for Secretary of State, Dec. 31, 1912, Texas State Archives; Webb, *Handbook of Texas* vol. 1, 66; Fellows, "The Baby Is Born," 96–97; D. A. Gregg to John L. Wortham, Nov. 5, 1914, Correspondence, Secretary of State Papers, Texas State Archives. Gregg's son, Leon, began his career with the State Insurance Board, joining John L. Wortham and Son and American General in 1929.

55. *Houston Chronicle,* May 24, n.d., O. B. Colquitt Papers, Eugene Barker Texas History Center, University of Texas.

56. Gus S. Wortham Oral History, 6; Harry V. Benedict and John A. Lomax, *The Book of Texas*, 201–205; John L. Wortham to R. B. Cousins, Oct. 26, 1914, R. B. Cousins Papers; John L. Wortham to Gus S. Wortham, June 27, 1914, Wortham Correspondence Binders; John L. Wortham to Gus S. Wortham, Nov. 3, 1914, Lyndall Wortham Seymour Papers.

57. John L. Wortham to Gus S. Wortham, Dec. 21, 1914, Lyndall Wortham Seymour Papers.

58. Gus S. Wortham interview notes, Nov. 15, 1974; Allen Carruth interview no. 1.

59. Gus S. Wortham Oral History, 6; Gus S. Wortham interview notes, Nov. 15, 1974.

60. Fellows, "The Baby Is Born," 56.

61. Gus S. Wortham interview notes Nov. 15, 1974; Fellows "The Baby Is Born," 56–57.

62. Fellows, "The Baby Is Born," 56–58, 62; Gus S. Wortham Oral History, 56–57.

63. Allen H. Carruth interview no. 1; Marvin Hand, "John L. Wortham and Son Partners," listing, Jan. 7, 1975, Kenneth Fellows Papers.

64. Fellows, "The Baby Is Born," 62–63; Fred Wallace, "History of John L. Wortham and Son," typescript, Oct. 3, 1983 (John L. Wortham and Son: 1983), John L. Wortham and Son Archives.

65. Timmons, *Jesse H. Jones*, 118; Fellows, "The Baby Is Born," 63–65; Gus S. Wortham interview notes, Nov. 15, 1974.

66. Fellows, "The Baby Is Born," 63–64; John L. Wortham Papers: W. B. Bizzell to John L. Wortham, Feb. 12, 1918; W. H. Draper to John L. Wortham, Feb. 28, 1918.

67. Fellows, "The Baby Is Born," 65; John L. Wortham to Gus S. Wortham, Aug. 20, 1918, Lyndall Wortham Seymour Papers.

68. Fellows, "The Baby Is Born," 24–26; Lyndall Wortham Seymour Papers, 1917 letters: A. R. Andrews to Whom It May Concern, Dec. 6; J. O. Masterson to Commanding Officer, Camp Kelly, Dec. 4; S. W. Inglish to Whom It May Concern, Dec. 8; W. P. Hobby to Commanding Officer, Dec. 8; Nelson Phillips to Commanding Officer, Dec. 8.

69 Fellows, "The Baby Is Born," 66–67; Gus S. Wortham interview notes, Nov. 15, 1974.

70. John L. Wortham to Gus S. Wortham, various correspondence, 1918, Lyndall Wortham Seymour Papers.

71. Fellows, "The Baby Is Born," 68; Gus S. Wortham interview notes, Nov. 15, 1974; Gus S. Wortham, Memorabilia, Gus S. Wortham Drawer, American General Archives.

72. Gus S. Wortham in front of barracks, framed photograph, American General

Archives; Fellows, "The Baby Is Born," 68–70; Gus S. Wortham interview notes, Nov. 15, 1974.

73. Gus S. Wortham Oral History, 8; Fellows, "The Baby Is Born," 70–71; Gus S. Wortham interview notes, Nov. 15, 1974.

74. Gus S. Wortham Oral History, 7–8; Fellows, "The Baby Is Born," 71–72.

75. Fellows, "The Baby Is Born," 72.

76. Lyndall Wortham Seymour Papers: John L. Wortham to Gus S. Wortham, Jan. 26, 1918, John L. Wortham to Gus S. Wortham, Jan. 24, 1918; B. F. Carruth to John L. Wortham, July 29, John L. Wortham Papers.

77. John L. Wortham to Gus S. Wortham, March 10, 1919, Lyndall Wortham Seymour Papers.

78. Memorabilia, Lyndall Wortham Seymour Papers.

79. John L. Wortham to Henrietta Davie, Jan. 19, 1924, Wortham Correspondence Binders; John L. Wortham to Marc Hubbart, n.d. [ca. 1921], John L. Wortham Papers.

80. J. W. Bailey to John L. Wortham, July 1, 1918, John L. Wortham Papers.

CHAPTER 2. COMING INTO HIS KINGDOM

1. Fellows, "The Baby Is Born," 74–75; Mamie Pace, Notes of interview with Kenneth Fellows, Feb. 24, 1976, Kenneth Fellows Papers; Wallace, "Wortham & Son" typescript. 45. Persevering in what was always a male-dominated environment, Pace was an example of the young working women of the era who were totally loyal to their employers—she was in Wortham's employ for forty-three years.

2. Fellows, "The Baby Is Born," 75, 77.

3. Allen Carruth, interview by author, no. 2, Feb. 13, 1990 Houston, Tex.; John Henry Kirby to Hugh B. Moore, Jan. 13, 1925, Lyndall Wortham Seymour Papers; John L. Wortham to R. B. Cousins, Sept. 27, 1918, R. B. Cousins Papers Wallace, "Wortham & Son" typescript, 46–47; John L. Wortham to Gus S. Wortham, April 30, 1919, Lyndall Wortham Seymour Papers.

4. [Willoughby Williams], typescript history of John L. Wortham and Son (John L. Wortham and Son: n.d.), John L. Wortham and Son Archives, 7; Fellows, "The Baby Is Born," 75–76.

5. Scrap of newspaper advertisement, n.d. 1923, American General Archives.

6. [Williams], typescript history of John L. Wortham and Son; Gus S. Wortham Oral History, 11.

7. Gus Wortham Oral History, 11–12; Gus S. Wortham interview notes, Jan. 22, 1976; Fellows, "The Baby Is Born," 6–9, 79–80.

8. Ellis A. Davis and Edwin H. Grobe, eds., *The New Encyclopedia of Texas*, 2, 122; Arthur S. Link and William B. Catton, *The American Epoch: A History of the United States Since the 1890s*, 134, 327; Allen Carruth interview no. 1; James T. DeShields, *They Sat in High Places: The Presidents and the Governors of Texas*, 419.

9. Gus S. Wortham to E. G. Quamme, Dec. 1, 1924, St. Paul Federal Land Bank File, John L. Wortham and Son Archives; "Analysis of Coverage Afforded by Blanket Bond as Compared with Present Schedule Bond," ca. 1924, Federal Land Bank Files, John L. Wortham and Son Archives. In addition, the three surety companies agreed to reduce the cost per employee each year for the five-year life of the bond.

10. Gus S. Wortham to E. G. Quamme, Dec. 1, 1924; "Analysis of Coverage Afforded . . ."; Federal Land Bank of St. Louis Newsletter "Service," Nov. 15, 1924, Federal Land Bank Files; Allen Carruth interview no. 2. John L. Wortham and Son partner Willoughby Williams wrote (and partner Leon Gregg told Kenneth Fellows) that Wortham and Carruth had carefully followed the legislation creating the federal land banks. They knew the banks would require some kind of fidelity or honesty bond. They "shuttled back and forth between Washington and New York City, riding herd on the legislation as it went through the Congressional mill, keeping in close touch to the bonding company and rating organization in New York in order to amend their proposed bond form in conformance with the frequent changes made to the land bank bill in the House and Senate." When the bill was signed into law, John L. Wortham and Son had just the right form and rates and the company was appointed agent to eight federal land banks for a five-year period. The Houston Land Bank was organized in 1917 and there is no documentation to prove Wortham and Carruth were active with these institutions this early. ([Williams], typescript history of John L. Wortham and Son, 1–3; Fellows, "The Baby Is Born," 77; Davis and Grobe, *New Encyclopedia of Texas*, 2,122.)

11. M. H. Gossett to E. H. Thomson, May 31, 1924, Federal Land Bank Files; Davis and Grobe, *New Encyclopedia of Texas*, 2,122.

12. Gus S. Wortham to E. H. Thomson, July 17, 1924, Federal Land Bank Files; Gus S. Wortham interview notes Jan. 22, 1976. On their trip to Washington, Wortham and Carruth had stayed at the Harrington, a small hotel within walking distance, but when the sale was made they moved to the more sumptuous Wardman Park Hotel to celebrate.

13. Fellows, "The Baby Is Born," 78–79; Gus S. Wortham interview notes, Jan. 22, 1976; Wallace, "Wortham & Son" typescript 45–46; Fellows, "The Baby Is Born," 6–9.

14. [Williams], typescript history of John L. Wortham and Son, 8.

15. Gus S. Wortham to Luther E. Mackall, Dec. 30, 1924; Allen Carruth interview no. 2.

16. "In the Estate of John L. Wortham, Deceased," inheritance tax document, Oct., 1925, with handwritten notes by Gus S. Wortham dated Sept. 28, 1931, John L. Wortham Papers, American General Archives; Fellows, "The Baby Is Born," 79; *A-General View*, 6 (Jan., 1972), 16.

17. Gus S. Wortham Oral History, 12.

18. Keith Bryant, Jr., and Henry C. Dethloff, *A History of American Business*, 210; James H. Robertson, quoted in Tinsley, "Texas Progressives," 241, 239–40, 243; American General Corporation, "A Sesquicentennial Commemorative," (Houston, ca. 1986), American General Archives, 40–41; Richardson, Wallace, and Anderson, *Texas* 316.

19. Tinsley, "Texas Progressives," 244–46; Texas Independent Insurance Agents, *Insuring Texas' Future*, 37–38, copy at J. L. Wortham & Son Library, Houston.

20. Wallace, "Wortham & Son" typescript, 46; Winifred Arndt Duffy, *John Wiley Link*; Fellows, "The Baby Is Born," 39; American General, Original Charter and By-Laws (Houston, 1926), American General Archives. John Wiley Link, Sr., had served as a bank president and mayor in Orange, Texas, before coming to Houston. There he organized the Houston Land Corporation, which developed the Montrose addition, building his own family mansion at the corner of Montrose Boulevard and Alabama

(later the Link-Lee House). He became involved in shipbuilding during World War I and oil afterward and took over John Henry Kirby's interests during a time when Kirby's financial fortunes were unsteady. In 1929, Link left Kirby Lumber to become president of the Dr. Pepper Company. (Fellows, "The Baby Is Born," 21–23.)

21. Fellows, "The Baby Is Born," 27; Gus S. Wortham Oral History, 13; American General, Original Charter and By-Laws.

22. American General, Original Charter and By-Laws; Gus S. Wortham Oral History, 14.

23. Gus S. Wortham Oral History, 14; Fellows, "The Baby Is Born," 11–12; Ed Kilman, "Hands Across the Canyon," *Texas Parade*, June, 1959, 35; *Houston Chronicle*, Nov. 13, 1965.

24. Gus S. Wortham Oral History, 12, 14; Fellows, "The Baby Is Born," 28–29; American General, Original Charter and By-Laws.

Joseph W. Evans (1877–1962) came to Houston in 1901, after studying briefly for the ministry and serving in the Spanish-American War. He went to work for Weld and Neville, an old cotton firm, but six years later left to start his own cotton merchandising and exporting firm, Evans and Company. It became one of the South's largest. Like Wortham's other backers, Evans was at the center of Houston's prime enterprises, serving as chairman of the Port Commission during the crucial years 1930–45 and as head of the Houston Cotton Exchange. He was also president of Manchester Terminal Corporation. (Earlier plans for construction of this terminal had caused a political fight over the port, involving John L. Wortham.) Evans's major civic involvements included the Chamber of Commerce and the Community Chest. He served on the boards of directors of both American General and Houston's other fledgling insurance company, Seaboard Life. (Fellows, "The Baby Is Born," 28–29).

25. Fellows, "The Baby Is Born," 43.

26. Manford, *Insuring Texas' Future*, 42; Mark Binkley to Charles Goosbee, Memorandum, July 21, 1976, Kenneth Fellows Papers; Texas, Texas Board of Insurance Commissioners, *53rd Annual Report of the Board of Insurance Commissioners for the Year Ending August 31, 1928*, 6; Fellows, "The Baby Is Born," 8; Wallace, "Wortham & Son" typescript, 9. The commission, in the case of Commercial Standard Insurance Company v. Moody, held that regulatory laws did not prevent a fire company from amending its charter to write casualty insurance also. The State Insurance Department thus said "there was no distinction which could properly be drawn under the laws between fire and casualty companies. . . ."

27. Fellows, "The Baby Is Born," 12, 13; *American General Journal*, 15 (Feb., 1975): 4; Harold S. Hook, interview by author, Nov. 7, 1991, Houston, Tex.

28. Fellows, "The Baby Is Born," 14; Kilman, "Hands Across the Canyon," 35–36. When it was formed in 1926, American General was one of 43 Texas insurance operations (including companies formed by stock, mutual, or fraternal charters) which provided fire, casualty, or life coverage. In 1926 there were 14 Texas-owned stock fire and marine companies: eight located in Dallas, two in Galveston, one each in Austin, Waco, and Fort Worth, and the American General in Houston. Clearly, Dallas was the center of insurance enterprise in Texas, signified by the number of home offices there, along with the fact that most "foreign" companies cited agents in Dallas as their Texas contacts. Of the 14 native firms, all except Republic of Dallas (by far the largest in assets) had been incorporated after the war, most in the 1920s, suggesting a particular

boom due to increased prosperity. Most of the out-of-state companies had entered Texas much earlier.

In addition to American General, the North American of Austin and Trinity Fire and Universal Automobile of Dallas were begun in 1926. Thirteen new Texas insurance companies of all kinds were listed in the 1926 commissioner's report, including Seaboard Life of Houston, which began operation in 1925, just a few months ahead of American General. (Texas, Department of Insurance, "List of Insurance Companies, 1925—1926"; Texas, Department of Insurance, *51st Annual Report of the Commissioner of Insurance for the Year Ending August 31, 1926*, 13; Texas, Board of Insurance Commissioners, *52nd Annual Report of the Commissioner of Insurance for the Year Ending August 31, 1927*, 16).

29. *Houston Post*, May 9, 1926, as quoted in Fellows, "The Baby Is Born," 19.

30. *Houston Post*, May 9, 1926, as quoted in Fellows, "The Baby Is Born," 19.

31. Fellows, "The Baby Is Born," 21–44; Gus S. Wortham interview notes, Nov. 15, 1974. Due to financial reverses, Kirby's reputation had lost some luster; but he was still, according to Wortham, a major behind-the-scenes player.

32. American General Insurance Company, Board of Directors, Minutes, May 13, 1926, Corporate Secretary, American General Corporation; American General Insurance Company, Management Contract, July 14, 1926, American General Archives; Allen Carruth interview no. 2; Fellows, "The Baby Is Born," 81–83.

33. Wallace, "Wortham & Son" typescript, 10.

34. *National Underwriter*, May 13, 1926; Fellows, "The Baby Is Born," 86; American General Insurance Company, Board of Directors, Minutes, July 14 and Dec. 15, 1926.

35. Gus S. Wortham Oral History, 13; Wallace, "Wortham & Son" typescript, 10;" "On the Production 'Firing Line,' Gus S. Wortham of Texas," *Eastern Underwriter*, 1935, 38; American General Insurance Company, Board of Directors, Annual Meeting, Minutes, Feb. 10, 1927; Fellows, "The Baby Is Born," 86.

36. Randolph, *Woodland Cousins*, 58–60; Gus S. Wortham and Lyndall Finley Wortham, various correspondence, Wortham Correspondence Binders; Eleanor Skaggs, interview by author, Oct. 3, 1989, Houston, Tex. James A. Elkins, Jr., interview no. 1; Laura Kirkland Bruce, interview by author, June 26, 1990, Houston, Tex. It had been Gus who had taught Judge Elkins's young son, Jim Jr., how to play cards when the boy's family lived at the Rice Hotel, before both families moved to the Warwick. (James A. Elkins, Jr., interview no. 1).

37. Lyndall Finley Wortham, interview by Kenneth Fellows, May 18, 1976; Gus S. Wortham to Lyndall Finley Davis, July 15, 1926, Correspondence Scrapbooks, American General Archives; "Social News, Wortham-Davis," *Galveston Daily News*, Oct. 15, 1926. Lyndall's only wedding attendants were six little boys, dressed in white, among them B. F. Carruth's son Allen, and James A. Elkins, Jr.

38. National Bank of Commerce, Board of Directors, Minutes, bk. 2, July 12 and Nov. 8, 1927, Texas Commerce Bank Archives. By the time Jones became president of the NBC in 1922, he had made a substantial fortune in lumber, real estate, and construction. He became NBC's head through acquiring a majority of its stock; additionally, he was involved with several other banks (Buenger and Pratt, *But Also Good Business*, 88–89).

39. Buenger and Pratt, *But Also Good Business*, 64–75.

40. Buenger and Pratt, *But Also Good Business*, 75–77, 88–89.

41. Ben F. Love, "People and Profits: A Bank Case Study," M.A. thesis, Southwest School of Banking, Dallas, 1967, 17; Buenger and Pratt, *But Also Good Business*, 75–89.

42. National Bank of Commerce, Board of Directors, Minutes, bk. 2, Jan. 8, 1929, June 12, 1934.

43. Gus S. Wortham, "Memorandum on Value of Atlas Realty Co. and Bayou Land Co.," Oct. 22, 1940, Wortham-Carruth Income Tax Files, American General Archives; Bayou Land Company to Internal Revenue Service, April 22, 1942, Wortham-Carruth Income Tax Files; Eric Gerber, "LaRue's Legacy," *Houston Post*, April 12, 1988; R. D. Walton to Gus S. Wortham and J. W. Link, Jr., Memorandum, March 27, 1941, A. H. Carruth Trustee File, American General Archives.

44. American General Insurance Company, Executive Committee, Minutes, Dec. 12, 1928, Feb. 16, 1929, Corporate Secretary, American General Corporation; American General Insurance Company, Board of Directors, Minutes, Feb. 14, 1929; Fellows, "The Baby Is Born," 87–89.

45. Benjamin Woodson, *A Financial Services Supermarket: The American General Story*, 19; Notes of Kenneth Fellows attached to notes of interview with Leon Gregg, Feb. 19, 1974, Kenneth Fellows Papers.

46. Gus S. Wortham Oral History, 18; Gus S. Wortham interview notes, Nov. 15, 1974.

47. *John L. Wortham and Son Insurance*, Advertising pamphlet, (Houston, ca. 1978), John L. Wortham and Son Archives; Fellows, "The Baby Is Born," 102–103.

48. American General Insurance Company, Board of Directors, Minutes, March 12, June 11, and Dec. 10, 1931; Dec. 14, 1932; Oct. 12, 1933.

49. American General Insurance Company, "Report to Stockholders," March 8, 1934, Stockholders Minutes, Corporate Secretary, American General Corporation.

50. Gus S. Wortham Oral History, 18.

CHAPTER 3. HOUSTON'S OWN

1. Richard Murray, "Power in the City: Patterns of Political Influence in Houston, Texas," in *Perspectives on American and Texas Politics: A Collection of Essays*, Donald S. Lutz and Kent Tedin, eds., 284; George Fuermann, *Houston: Land of the Big Rich*, 40–41. To make it into the highest echelons—what Houston newspaper columnist George Fuermann called "Proper Houstonians"—one also should possess such "disappearing refinements" as "good manners, good sense, and good talk"—attributes that few who had met Gus Wortham failed to note.

2. Joe R. Feagin, *Free Enterprise City: Houston in Political and Economic Perspective*, 152.

3. Harry Hurt III, "The Most Powerful Texans," *Texas Monthly*, April, 1976, 73ff; Robert D. Thomas and Richard W. Murray, *Pro-Growth Politics: Change and Governance in Houston*, 86–88.

4. Marvin Hurley, *Decisive Years for Houston*, 50; James A. Elkins, Jr., interview no. 1.

5. *Warwick Window*, Dec., 1926, 3; Warwick Hotel and Apartments brochure, 1931, Warwick Hotel File, Texas and Local History Room, Houston Public Library (quote). Although less than a year old, the Warwick had already become the center of fashionable life on the city's southern edge, Houston's "Art Centre," calling itself "the Finest

in the South." About the same time the Warwick was constructed, the Plaza Hotel was built a few blocks away, and Jesse Jones's Lamar Hotel, in which he would live, was built downtown. ("Lamar—Quiet Dowager of Houston Hotels," uncited news clipping, n.d., Lamar Hotel File, Texas and Local History Room, Houston Public Library).

6. Warwick Hotel and Apartments brochure; *Warwick Window*, Oct., 1928, 6 and Sept., 1927, 6. The Warwick became a place to see and be seen and hosted events of all kinds for residents and nonresidents: wedding receptions, civic banquets, religious events, civic club meetings, children's music recitals and birthday parties—even housing dignitaries for the 1928 Democratic Convention. Many prominent Houston names adorned the Warwick mail boxes: Neal, Abercrombie, Garwood, Hahlo, Holman, Gordon, and Foster.

7. Various letters, Wortham Correspondence Binders; *Warwick Window*, Dec., 1927, June 1928.

8. Lyndall Finley Wortham Correspondence, Wortham Correspondence Binders; *Warwick Window*, Nov. 15, 1926, 4–5, and "Social News, Wortham-Davis," Oct. 5, 1926.

9. Houston Country Club, Yearbooks, Texas and Local History Room, Houston Public Library; Gus S. Wortham to George G. Williams, Jan. 16, 1946, Rice University Files, American General Archives; "Biographical Sketch of Gus Sessions Wortham," ca. 1956, Gus Wortham Drawer, American General Archives; Feagin, *Free Enterprise City*, 131–32; "Houston Club History," *Houston Chronicle*, June 16, 1955.

10. Fellows, "The Baby Is Born," 106; *Houston Post*, April 21, 1935; *Houston*, April, 1935, 21.

11. American General Insurance Company, Advertising flyer, n.d., American General Scrapbook no. 1, 31, American General Archives.

12. Kenneth Fellows, Notes on A.G. Directorate and 13 Original Directors, n.d., Kenneth Fellows Papers; Gus S. Wortham interview notes, Nov. 8, 1975; Fellows, "The Baby Is Born," 41–47. One of the most striking things about Wortham's board choices is that not one was primarily an oil man. Wortham himself, through his father, held oil leases and most of the other directors were in the business to a variety of degrees, but none was known only for that enterprise. Wortham may have shied away consciously from naming men involved in an industry still perceived as reckless and unpredictable, or perhaps his connections did not include entre to this group.

13. John Henry Kirby to Col. Hugh B. Moore, Jan. 13, 1925; Feagin, *Free Enterprise City*, 114; Webb, *Handbook of Texas*, vol. 2, 966; Fellows, "The Baby Is Born," 36–38; Gus S. Wortham interview notes, Dec. 17, 1974. There is no doubt that Kirby trusted Wortham's abilities as he introduced Gus as the representative of a firm that could handle the entire extent of his own refinery's business.

14. Buenger and Pratt, *But Also Good Business*, 75–77; Fellows, "The Baby Is Born," 31–34; Clarence R. Wharton, *Texas Under Many Flags*, 222; Gus S. Wortham, Speech at Dedication of Jesse Jones High School, ca. 1956–57, Gus S. Wortham Drawer, American General Archives.

15. Fellows, "The Baby Is Born," 28; Gus S. Wortham interview notes re: Original Directors, n.d., Kenneth Fellows Papers; "Joseph W. Evans" biography, n.d., Joseph W. Evans Collection, Houston Metropolitan Research Center. Evans described his theory for success in life: "We all know the conventional route up the ladder—hard work,

forgetting about the clock and the practice of thrift. I believe, however, I would like to add to that something I have found worth while. I have a phrase for it, namely: 'The highest form of selfishness in the world is unselfishness . . . it enables one to acquire a great many friends and acquaintances . . . and that is a priceless asset."

16. Foster and Jones, *South and Southeast Texas*, 353; *Houston Chronicle*, May 8, 1972; Feagin, *Free Enterprise City*, 124.

17. Buenger and Pratt, *But Also Good Business*, 77.

18. "New Directors for Houston Service," *Houston*, Nov., 1932, 2; "Chamber of Commerce Budget Raise Sought," *Houston Press*, Dec. 20, 1932.

19. Houston Chamber of Commerce, various Scrapbooks; "Budget of 1936 Approved for Chamber Here," *Houston Post*, Jan. 16, 1936.

20. "Wortham is Honor Guest at Luncheon," *Houston Chronicle*, Dec. 20, 1933. Wortham's peers in the Insurance Exchange of Houston feted him at a luncheon following his election, which was broadcast over radio station KXYZ. Local insurance man W. Tucker Blaine gave some indication of the respect accorded Wortham by saying that, as head of one of Houston's largest agencies, Wortham "could demoralize the insurance business were it not operated on a highly ethical basis. Another evidence of his leadership is that the state official who supervises insurance recognizes his ability and respects his judgment." ("Insurance Men Laud Wortham," *Houston Post*, Dec. 21, 1933.)

21. "Gus S. Wortham Elected as Chamber of Commerce Head," *Houston Chronicle*, Dec. 8, 1933; Houston Chamber of Commerce Scrapbooks.

22. "Wortham Picks Chamber Aids," *Houston Post*, Jan. 5, 1934; "Chamber of Commerce Budget Raise Sought," *Houston Press*, Dec. 20, 1932.

23. *Houston Press*, Jan. 18, 1934; *Houston Post*, Jan. 7, 1934, Jan. 17, 1934; *Houston Chronicle*, Jan. 29, 1934.

24. *Houston Post*, Feb. 27, 1934. Wortham went to Mexico City in 1934, returning with, he felt, a better understanding of the country and its customs, announcing that just because a people were different did not mean they were uncivilized, and predicting more commerce between that country and Houston. ("Gus S. Wortham Reports on Trade Trip to Mexico," *Houston Post*, Oct. 20, 1934.)

25. Sibley, *Port of Houston*, 172; Port Section, *Houston*, Aug., 1934, 28; *Houston Chronicle*, Feb. 18, 1934; Feagin, *Free Enterprise City*, 54ff.

26. *Houston Chronicle*, April 29, 1934; *Houston Post*, April 29, 1934; *Houston Chronicle*, April 27, 1934; *Houston Press*, May 2 and 9, 1934; *Houston Post*, May 5, 1934. Later, as the result of yet another federal funding program for housing, into which the Chamber had launched the city, Houston opened the country's first federal subsistence homestead project, Houston Gardens, in 1935. (*Houston Post*, May 1, 1935.)

27. *Houston Post*, Feb. 20, and May 2, 3, and 8, 1934; *Houston Press*, May 7, 1934; *Houston Chronicle*, May 3, 1934.

28. *Houston Chronicle*, June 13, 1934; *Houston Post*, June 10, 16 and 19, 1934. Wortham noted that the industrial water business was "highly profitable and Houston can make money with an industrial rate lower than other cities." "Cheap government money" would provide a "handsome cash bonus" that would "give Houston its golden opportunity to accomplish a pressing objective."

29. *Houston Chronicle*, Dec. 22, 1934.

30. Houston Chamber of Commerce, "Deposit to Your Account," booklet published for 1934 Chamber of Commerce Banquet, Greater Houston Partnership Archives; *Houston Chronicle*, Dec. 12 and 22, 1934.

31. *Houston Post*, Dec. 3, 1934; *Houston Chronicle*, Dec. 22, 1934.

32. Houston Chamber of Commerce, *Annual Report, 1845–1935*, 3–4, Greater Houston Partnership Archives; David G. McComb, *Houston: The Bayou City*, 169–70; *Houston Post*, Dec. 12 and 29, 1935; "Biographical Sketch of Gus Sessions Wortham," n.d., ca. 1954, Biographical Data File, Gus S. Wortham Drawer. As Wortham and all were aware, Sam Houston Hall, which the new coliseum would replace, had been erected solely through Jones's efforts in getting the Democratic Convention of 1928 for Houston.

33. "Houston's Industrial Life is Well-Grounded," *Houston*, June, 1934, 3ff; *Houston Chronicle*, April 20, 1935; *Houston Post*, Nov. 2, 1934.

34. *Houston Chronicle*, Aug. 11, 1934; *Houston Post*, Sept. 10, 1934, and Dec. 12, 1935. Wortham personally had been actively behind getting the main celebration for Houston and had predicted "tragic results" would come out of Houston's failure to be chosen; that it would be a "disgrace" to be relegated to the second-place Texas city. "It is our big opportunity to forge farther ahead," Wortham said. But Houston's bid of $6 million lost out to Dallas's promise of $7,900,000. A possible reason for Houston's loss was a dispute between leaders of the two cities over control of centennial activities.

35. *Houston Post*, Dec. 10 and 12, 1935; *Houston Press*, Dec. 12, 1935.

36. *Houston Chronicle*, Dec. 12, 1935.

37. Feagin, *Free Enterprise City*, 55.

38. *Houston Chronicle*, Dec. 12, 1935; *Houston Post*, Dec. 12, 1935.

39. *Houston Post*, Jan. 25, 1936; *Houston Press*, Jan. 25, 1936; "Mefo," *Houston Press*, Jan. 27, 1936.

40. Fellows, "The Baby Is Born," 107–108; American General Insurance Company, Board of Directors, Minutes, Dec. 12, 1935, Sept. 10, and Nov. 30, 1936; American General Insurance Company, Stockholders Meeting, Minutes, March 11, 1937; American General Insurance Company, Board of Directors, Minutes, May 13, 1938.

41. American General Insurance Company, "Report to Stockholders," March 8, 1934; American General Insurance Company, "Report to Stockholders," March 11, 1937, Stockholders Minutes; American General Insurance Company, Board of Directors, Minutes, March 10, 1938; J. W. Evans to J. S. Kempner, July 22, 1958, J. W. Evans Collection; Various clippings, American General Scrapbook no. 10, American General Archives.

42. "On the Production 'Firing line,' Gus S. Wortham of Texas," *Eastern Underwriter*, 1935, 38.

43. Raymond Mauk, interview by author, Jan. 11, 1990; *Houston Post*, Dec. 24, 1935. When Mauk's term was up as commissioner, he also went to Wortham for advice in finding a position in the industry. Offered a job in Louisiana, Mauk queried Wortham on a suitable salary. Wortham's reply was $7,500. The Louisiana firm countered with $6,000 and Mauk told Wortham, who promptly offered Mauk a job with American General—but he, also, could pay only $6,000. Mauk eagerly took the AG job, glad to work for Wortham at any price. It was an example of the kind of trust and loyalty men felt for Wortham. (Raymond Mauk interview.)

44. Gus S. Wortham interview notes, Dec. 17, 1974; *Houston Chronicle*, Oct. 11, 1985.

45. George Norris Green, *The Establishment in Texas Politics: The Primitive Years, 1938–1957*, 17–18; Jimmy Banks, *Money, Marbles and Chalk: The Wondrous World of Texas Politics*, 131–32; Don E. Carleton, *Red Scare!* 64–72; Feagin, *Free Enterprise City*, 120–27; James Conaway, *The Texans*, 101–103; Craig Smyser, "Houston's Power: As It Was," *Houston Chronicle*, June 27, 1977; Harry Hurt III, "The Most Powerful Texans," in *Texas Monthly Political Reader*, 10–19; McComb, *Houston*, 111–12.

46. Dana Blankenhorn, "The Brown Brothers: Houston's Contracting and Energy Giants," *Houston Business Journal*, March 19, 1979; Conaway, *The Texans*, 93–95.

47. Conaway, *The Texans*, 93–95; Contribution Thank You Correspondence, Mayoral Campaign Files, Oscar Holcombe Collection, Houston Metropolitan Research Center.

48. *Houston Post*, May 18, 1947; *Houston Chronicle*, Nov. 21, 1963, and Feb. 15, 1966; Collection Notes, Albert Thomas Papers, Woodson Research Center, Fondren Library, Rice University.

49. Robert Dallek, *Lone Star Rising: Lyndon Johnson and His Times, 1908–1960*, 88–91.

50. Raymond Mauk interview.

CHAPTER 4. NEW DIRECTIONS

1. American General Insurance Company, Board of Directors, Minutes, May 13, 1938 and April 25 and May 9, 1939; American General Insurance Company, Stockholders, Minutes, May 9, 1939. *Houston*, Sept., 1939, 20; Aug., 1939, 18; Jan. 1940, 15.

2. American General Insurance Company, Board of Directors, Minutes, April 15, Sept. 20, and May 18, 1939; American General Insurance Company, Executive Committee, Minutes, April 19, 1939; American General Investment Corporation, Board of Directors, Minutes, July 11, 1939, Corporate Records, American General Investment Corporation. As he had done when founding American General, Wortham touted the new corporation's solid local foundation. "[T]he company was organized by Houston business men and with Houston capital, as it was felt that there was a definite need and place in a city the size of Houston that would operate under the general plan and principle followed by the national finance corporations." ("New Auto Insurance Firm Opens Here," no paper, n.d., American General Scrapbook no. 10, 131.)

3. American General Insurance Company, Board of Directors, Minutes, April 25 and May 9, 1939. *Houston*, 1936, 34–35; Jan. 1937, 9; May, 1937, 35; Sept. 1940, 32.

4. *Houston*, April, 1935, 23; Hurley, *Decisive Years for Houston*, 53–56; American General Investment Corporation, Board of Directors, Minutes, Aug. 17, 1939; "New Auto Finance Firm Opens Here." L. O. Benson, interview by author, Nov. 14, 1990, Conroe, Tex.; *Houston Chronicle*, Sept. 19, 1939.

5. *Houston*, Nov., 1939, 16, and Jan., 1940, 32.

6. American General Investment Corporation, Board of Directors, Minutes, Feb. 20, 1940.

7. American General Insurance Company, Board of Directors, Minutes, March 25 and May 23, 1940; Fellows, "The Baby Is Born," 116; American General Investment

Corporation, Board of Directors, Minutes, April 26, June 11, and Sept. 23, 1940. The board remained concerned through the fall, with Wortham even suggesting the investment operation move to offices more accessible to Houston's auto sales district.

8. American General Investment Corporation, Board of Directors, Minutes, July 16, Sept. 23, and Nov. 7, 1940. *Houston* magazine reported that "[c]apital throughout the country" was looking for Houston real estate investments and that "the local mortgage men have kept pace with Houston's growth and have developed throughout the country the greatest demand for Houston mortgages that has ever existed." Most of the mortgage lenders at this time were banking institutions or life insurance firms. (*Houston*, Sept., 1941, 35.)

9. American General Investment Corporation, Board of Directors, Minutes, July 16, Sept. 23, and Nov. 7, 1940; March 28, May 21, and Dec. 9, 1941; Jan. 15, 1942.

10. The city was already a strategically important oil, cotton, and transportation center, and its position as the hub of a vast area of natural resources coupled with the port made Houston the perfect place to locate such vital war industries as rubber, petrochemicals, shipbuilding, and industrial machines and tools of every variety. Two civic symbols of prosperity, both finished in 1939, were the new City Hall, built with WPA monies and the Sears, Roebuck store on South Main, featuring the city's first escalators. (*Houston*, Dec. 1939, 7.)

11. *Houston*, Dec., 1939, 7; Feb., 1941, 6; May, 1942, 16; June, 1942, 37; July, 1942, 8; May, 1945, 11.

12. American General Investment Corporation, Board of Directors, Minutes, April 16, 1946. AG Investment loaned the Oak Forest Corporation $400,000 to buy the acreage and $300,000 for developing its infrastructure, and $300,000 for the building of the Industrial Addition homes. Oak Forest received national attention as one of the huge housing "subdivisions" built expressly for returning veterans, and helped make Frank Sharp's career as a developer.

13. Fellows, "The Baby Is Born," 120–21; L. O. Benson interview; Charles Boswell, interview by author, Feb. 21, 1990, Houston, Tex.

14. Harry Standley, interview by author, Aug. 29, 1990, Houston, Tex.

15. *Houston*, Dec. 1936, 34; American General Insurance Company, Board of Directors, Minutes, Nov. 30, 1936; American General Insurance Company, 1939 Statement, n.d., Corporate Secretary, American General Corporation; American General Insurance Company, Board of Directors, Minutes, Aug. 20, 1940, Feb. 8, 1941, Feb. 18, 1943, and Feb. 17, 1944; *Milam Builder*, July, 1943, American General Scrapbook no. 10, 185.

16. "Gus S. Wortham Is Named Director of Southwestern Life," Uncited newspaper clipping, May 29, 1940, American General Scrapbook no. 10, 147; Raymond Mauk interview; "Texas Shows the Way to Succeed," *Insurance Age Journal*, April, 1944.

17. "Texas Shows the Way."

18. "Texas Shows the Way."

19. *National Underwriter*, May 18, 1940; Allen Carruth interview no. 1.

20. *Houston Post*, May 20, 1987, Vertical Biography File, Texas and Local History, Houston Public Library; Fellows, "The Baby Is Born," 33, 38–40; *John L. Wortham and Son*, Agency brochure (Houston: 1969), Kenneth Fellows Papers. A member of the law firm of Kayser, Liddell (which represented the National Bank of Commerce) when he joined the AG Board, Butler founded a new firm in 1941 with Jack Binion.

21. Morrison and Fourmey Directory Company, *Houston City Directory*; *Houston*, Sept., 1942, 1.

22. *Houston*, Nov., 1940, Feb., 1941, and Nov., 1943; Morrison and Fourmey, *Houston City Directory*. The award was presented at an impressive program, at which the colonel from the St. Louis army ordnance district praised McEvoy for its "ingenuity in improvising and using old machines and for its model labor-management relations." After the war years, Wortham was not a visible part of the company's operations, although it appears that George Butler succeeded him as president in 1953. (*Houston*, Nov., 1943; Morrison and Fourmey, *Houston City Directory*.

23. *Houston*, Nov., 1939; Jake Hershey, interview by author, Jan. 15, 1991, Houston, Tex.; Morrison and Fourmey, *Houston City Directory*. In 1939 the Port of Houston was ranked the nation's second largest port in tonnage behind New York City.

24. T. F. Smith, Notes of Interview with Kenneth Fellows, Feb. 19, 1976, Kenneth Fellows Papers; "In re: Gus S. Wortham, et ux., Summary," Mr. and Mrs. Gus S. Wortham 1937 Income Tax Return File, n.d., American General Archives; "Gus S. Wortham & B. F. Carruth Co-Partnership, Distribution of Assets, Jan. 2, 1937," Gus S. Wortham and B. F. Carruth Financial Statements and Accounts File, American General Archives; J. G. Beasley, Deposition, Nov. 6, 1935, Wortham/Carruth Files, American General Archives; Smith Brothers Properties, Financial Statement, Jan. 1, 1927, Early Personal Papers, Jesse Jones Papers, Eugene Barker Texas History Center; Unsigned, untitled memorandum re: history of "Longhorn Portland Cement Company (predecessor Republic Portland Cement Company)," n.d., WTB File, American General Archives. In 1929, Gus Wortham hired T. F. "Tuffy" Smith, the half-brother of Jim and Frank, to build up the agency's and the company's surety and performance bond business. Tuffy Smith's experience with his brother's contracting firm was of great benefit in securing bonding business from contractors. (Wallace, "Wortham & Son" typescript, 38.)

25. "In re: Gus S. Wortham, et ux., Summary." n.d.; Various documents, Smith Brothers Files, American General Archives.

26. Gus S. Wortham to C. F. Huffsmith, Sept. 18, 1936, Smith Brothers Data File, American General Archives.

27. J. G. Beasley to Sol Bromberg, Hyman Pearlstone, Receivers, June 23, 1933, Smith Brothers Data File; Gus S. Wortham and B. F. Carruth to W. L. McBride, June 7, 1935, Wortham and Carruth Partnership File, American General Archives. One plan called for Wortham to talk with Jones, then head of the RFC about the Smith Brothers Properties application for a loan, but despite the intimate business dealings between Wortham and Jones, Wortham made it clear that he could not ask for any special treatment. There is no indication whether such a loan was received. (Hyman Pearlstone to Gus S. Wortham, Dec. 12, 1933, Smith Brothers Data File.)

28. Gus S. Wortham, "Memorandum Regarding Smith Brothers Co-Partnership (In Receivership)," Feb. 10, 1936, Smith Brothers Files.

29. Gus S. Wortham, "Memorandum Regarding Smith Brothers Co-Partnership"; "To the Creditors of Smith Brothers Properties," April 16, 1936, Smith Brothers Data File; George A. Butler to Gus S. Wortham, Oct. 29, 1936, Smith Brothers Data File. Butler's involvement was due to a mortgage on the Plaza Hotel held by Jesse Jones's Bankers' Mortgage Company.

30. "In re: Gus S. Wortham, et ux, Summary"; J. E. Fortenberry, "To the Preferred

Stockholders of Smith Brother [*sic*] Properties Company of San Antonio, Texas," June 29, 1937, Smith Brothers Properties Stock, Preferred and Common File, American General Archives; Gus S. Wortham to William P. Hamblen, April 6, 1937, Smith Brothers Properties File, American General Archives.

31. Memorandum re: "Longhorn Portland Cement Company (predecessor Republic Portland Cement Company)" (see note 24).

32. George A. Butler, "In Re: WTB Corporation," Dec. 20, 1939, WTB Files, American General Archives. Century Investment Company (CIC)/General Investment File, American General Archives: Gus. S. Wortham to Jack Beasley, May 23, 1940; Century Investment Company, Stockholders Annual Meeting, Minutes, May 6, 1940; Gus S. Wortham to Nathan Adams, April 26, 1940. WTB Corporation/Reorganization and Acquisition File, American General Archives: Gus S. Wortham to Herman Brown, George Brown, W. M. Thornton, R. W. Briggs, George A. Butler, June 14, 1940; Gus S. Wortham to George A. Butler, Sept. 17, 1940; W. L. Moody, Jr., to Gus S. Wortham, 30 Oct. 1940. Harold Hyman, *Oleander Odyssey: The Kempners of Galveston, Texas, 1854–1980s*, 253–55.

33. Gus S. Wortham To R. W. Briggs, July 18, 1940, WTB/Reorganization and Acquisition File; Gus S. Wortham to Sol Bromberg, Oct. 24, 1940, WTB Files, American General Archives; Gus S. Wortham to WTB Stockholders, Oct. 31, 1940, WTB/Reorganization and Acquisition File; Various correspondence, WTB and CIC Files, American General Archives; Reagan Houston to Gus S. Wortham Nov. 23, 1942, CIC Special File, American General Archives; Gus S. Wortham to Ben Collins, Dec. 23, 1942, WTB Corp./General File, American General Archives.

34. Memorandum re: "Longhorn Portland Cement Company"; Gus S. Wortham to W. L. Moody, Jr., Oct. 31, 1940, WTB Reorganization Files, American General Archives; Kenneth Fellows, Notes of interviews with T. F. Smith and Leon Gregg, Feb. 17 and 19, 1976, Kenneth Fellows Papers.

35. Gus S. Wortham to Standard Statistics, April 24, 1940, Longhorn Portland Cement (LPC) Files, American General Archives; Dana Blankenhorn, "Gus Wortham: Insurance, Ranching and Civic Trend Setter Embodied Houston Establishment," *Houston Business Journal*, March 26, 1979, sec. 2, p. 1; Gus S. Wortham to W. B. Thornton, June 26, 1940, LPC Files; Robert Caro, *The Years of Lyndon Johnson: The Path to Power*, 1983), 377–79, 458–75. The Browns shared the dam construction with McKenzie Construction Company of San Antonio, which also held stock in the other Smith Brothers holdings and was an early John L. Wortham and Son customer.

36. LPC Files: Gus S. Wortham to G. A. Butler, Oct. 3, 1942; Gus S. Wortham to Nathan Wholfield, undated; A. M. Edwards to Gus S. Wortham, Memorandum, April 10, 1941; Gus S. Wortham to George T. Atkins, March 17, 1942; Longhorn Portland Cement to War Department, July 29, 1942; W. M. Thornton to War Dept., July 29, 1942; Gus S. Wortham to W. M. Thornton, Dec. 28, 1942. *Houston*, Aug., 1942, 18.

In December, 1941, Wortham and E. R. Barrow went on a hunting weekend with "people" from the Naval Air Station, probably the Corpus Christi Naval Air Station, on which Brown & Root and W. E. Bellows, both of Houston, had two-thirds of the construction contract. (E. R. Barrow to Gus S. Wortham, Dec. 5, 1941, LPC Files.)

37. LPC Files: Gus S. Wortham to Albert Thomas, n.d., Gus S. Wortham to Albert Thomas, May 28, 1943; W. M. Thornton to Gus S. Wortham, Nov. 4, 1942. Caro, *Years of Lyndon Johnson* (1983), 583.

38. LPC Correspondence File, American General Archives; Gus S. Wortham to W. M. Thornton, June 18 and 23, 1941; War Labor Board, New Case Committee, Minutes, sent to Gus S. Wortham by W. B. Bellows, March 31, 1943; W. M. Thornton to Gus S. Wortham, May 2, 1944 Gus S. Wortham to W. M. Thornton, May 5, 1944. Whether or not Wortham initiated it, the cement company was run like a "company town," providing housing and shopping for its employees. Wortham and Thornton continued to run it with a somewhat paternal outlook.

39. Gus S. Wortham to Standard Statistics, April 24, 1940; Gus S. Wortham to W. M. Thornton, July 30, 1942, LPC Correspondence File. During this same period, oil man Hugh Roy Cullen tried to mount a crusade against the War Production Board's order that no more cement be sold for oil wells. Wortham was well aware that commercial customers were upset and that the demand outweighed the supply. He told Thornton that the oil industry was important to the war effort and there must be a way Longhorn could help supply the special cement the oil man needed. He told Cullen that he and Thornton were going to Washington to see what could be done. (LPC Files, 1942 letters: H. R. Cullen to Office of Price Management, July 31; Gus S. Wortham to W. M. Thornton, Aug. 1; Gus S. Wortham to H. R. Cullen, Aug. 5,).

40. W. M. Thornton to Seeligson, Cox and Patterson, Attorneys, March 27, 1944 with attached statement, "The State of Texas vs San Antonio Portland Cement Company Et Al," Nov. 1939, LPC Files.

41. Gus S. Wortham to W. M. Thornton, March 30, 1944, LPC Files. Wortham wrote: ". . . the very fact that the price is the same will always be ample grounds for an Attorney General, who is in the mood to do so to file an anti-trust suit. We cannot so conduct our business that we will be relieved of even the probability of an anti-trust suit. What we can do is to conscientiously, and in a business like way, try to conduct our business so that we are not willfully or knowingly violating the anti-trust law, or the injunction. . . . [I]t is difficult, if not impossible, for cement prices to be competitive. Competition must be in the services rendered by the sales, shipping, laboratory, and other things . . . in connection with furnishing this standard product. If the cement business had always been conducted as it is now being . . . I do not believe that the industry would be confronted with anti-trust suits."

42. W. M. Thornton, "Memorandum," May 19, 1948, LPC Files; Charles I. Francis to W. M. Thornton, Oct. 3, 1945, LPC Files; Robert Caro, *The Years of Lyndon Johnson: Means of Ascent* (1990), 11, 122 W. M. Thornton to Vinson, Elkins, Nov. 28, 1945, LPC Files; Glenn Porter, ed., *Encyclopedia of American Economic History*, vols. 1, 2, esp. "Organized Business Groups," by Albert Steigerwalt and "Antitrust," by Ellis Hawley. In the Cement Institute Case of 1948, the system was deemed illegal by the Supreme Court, ending a decade of litigation.

43. LPC Files: [?] Bramlette to Gus S. Wortham, December 22, 1943, W. M. Thornton to Gus S. Wortham, Jan. 12, 1945; Gus S. Wortham, "Memorandum: Longhorn," Dec. 7, 1945; Gus S. Wortham to J. Cockrell, Dec. 8, 1945.

44. W. M. Thornton to Gus S. Wortham, June 21, 1945, and Gus S. Wortham to W. M. Thornton, June 25, 1945, both in LPC Files, American General Archives. Definitely not an 8F protégé, McCarthy overtly defied them by building his huge Shamrock Hotel, which he saw as the centerpiece of a new Houston, away from Jesse Jones's downtown. In 1945, Thornton complained that he had no luck in getting McCarthy to give Longhorn the business on his gas plant at Winnie, Texas. Wortham, in turn,

contacted Colonel William B. Bates, lawyer and chairman of the Second National Bank, in which McCarthy was the largest stockholder. Later, Wortham counseled Thornton to reduce their balance in Second National unless they received some of McCarthy's business. Wortham's reaction to McCarthy, also in his letter to Thornton, accurately reflected the apprehension of Houston's elite to this upstart: "I have now met McCarthy and it may be advisable for me to have a visit with him. He has made a lot of money and has a lot of big plans for the future. He is very active and he is not the type that will keep his money idle."

45. William N. Stokes, Jr., *Sterling C. Evans, Texas Aggie, Banker, Cattleman*, 47, 46; Sterling C. Evans, interview by author, no. 1, Nov. 16, 1989, Houston, Tex. Evans's investment money came from the sale of 180 acres he owned near College Station, a farm he called "Poor Acres."

46. Stokes, *Sterling C. Evans*, 23–32; Sterling C. Evans to author, April 17, 1991. As president of the Houston Land Bank, Evans had made a reputation for himself by developing the "Houston Plan," which was adopted by the 11 other land banks around the country. In the original organization of the land banks, local farmers would both borrow from and become stockholders of the local farm loan association. Five percent of the bank loan went for stock in the association; in turn the loan association guaranteed repayment. When their loans were repaid, the farmers retained the stock they had bought in the bank. However, defaults on loans were high during the depression, and associations used their capital to repay the land bank. Thus, many of the associations were practically defunct and the farmers who had borrowed from the association and repaid their loans found their stock worthless. Evans's plan restored the local farm loan associations to solvency by a new arrangement with the land bank, whereby the mineral interests owned by the associations were turned over to the bank in exchange for their debts. This complicated plan also allowed for the repayment of lost stock funds to thousands of farmers. In doing this, Evans also worked to keep the land bank and its associations out of federal government control. The land banks had been founded as private enterprise entities, but were capitalized by government funds to be used for selling bonds to investors. Evans believed the cooperatives could succeed only if run as private enterprise, with farmers as shareholders, and not run by the Department of Agriculture. As Wortham had, Evans recognized the importance of local ownership and ownership by the people directly involved in the enterprise.

47. Sterling Evans interview no. 1; Sterling C. Evans, interview with author, no. 2, Sept. 2, 1990, Houston, Tex.; Gus S. Wortham interview notes, Dec. 17, 1974; "To Record the initial partnership investment in 6 tracts of land in Milam Co., etc." May 4, 1944, Ledger, Sterling C. Evans Papers; Federal Land Bank, "Statement of Total Indebtedness on Baskin Loans as of May 3, 1944," n.d., Randle Lake File, American General Archives; Gus S. Wortham to Sterling C. Evans, July 18, 1945, Randle Lake File.

48. Sterling C. Evans to Houghton Brownlee, June 15, 1944, Randle Lake File; Ronnie Dugger, *The Politician: The Life and Times of Lyndon Johnson*, 197; Sterling C. Evans to U.S. District Engineer, July 19, 1990, Randle Lake File. Brownlee had been an unsuccessful candidate for the House of Representatives against Lyndon Johnson in 1937 and was obviously well known to Wortham.

49. Sterling C. Evans, notes of telephone interview by author, July 15, 1991. Randle Lake File: Sterling C. Evans to Gus S. Wortham, Memorandum, Oct. 3, 1944; Sterling

C. Evans to Houghton Brownlee, June 15, 1944; Sterling C. Evans to Gus S. Wortham, Monthly Report, Nov. 2, 1944; Sterling C. Evans, "Memorandum on Ranch for 1944," Jan. 6, 1945; Sterling C. Evans to Jackson and Dusek, Aug. 1, 1945; Sterling C. Evans to Gus S. Wortham, Aug. 6, 1945; Sterling C. Evans to V. G. Forrester, Dec. 27, 1945.

50. Randle Lake File: Sterling C. Evans to Gus S. Wortham, Jan 8, 1947; Gus S. Wortham to Sterling C. Evans, Jan. 9, 1947; J. F. Flack, "Financial Report, Special Report, Evans-Wortham Farm, December 31, 1948," May 27, 1949. The partnership was a comfortable business arrangement for both Evans and Wortham from the beginning. Correspondence shows that Evans was faithful in his reports to Wortham on the farm operations and had no hesitation in letting him know when additional monies were needed to be deposited to the farm's account. (Randle Lake File, 1947: Sterling C. Evans to Gus S. Wortham, Jan. 8; Gus S. Wortham to Sterling C. Evans, Jan. 9.)

51. Randle Lake File: Sterling C. Evans to Gus S. Wortham, March 10, 1949; Gus S. Wortham to Sterling C. Evans, Dec. 27, 1951. Agricultural sources predicted the insects would be a problem in the area and Evans told Wortham, sending him evidence from a Texas A&M professor that proved turkeys could eat a thousand grasshoppers a day. Indeed, the next month Wortham wrote to Evans that the papers were "full of the grasshopper plague" and that Milam County was to be hard hit. "Your far-sightedness in figuring out the grasshopper plague a year in advance is further evidence to me that you are the best agriculturalist in the world." (Gus S. Wortham to Sterling C. Evans, April 4, 1949, Randle Lake File.)

52. "What Is A Farm? A Story of Houston Men Who Are Farm Owners," *Houston*, Jan., 1946, 19ff.

53. Sterling C. Evans to Gus S. Wortham, Jan 19, 1953, Randle Lake File. The Randle Lake operation appeared in a 1954 issue of Humble Oil's magazine, *Humble Farm Family*, featuring the unique cattle feeding arrangement. Unlike other steer calf operations, no commercial feed was required; instead a four-field rotation system fattened nearly 700 steers for sale. ("Cattle Feeding—Texas Style," *Humble Farm Family*, Nov., 1954, 8–9.)

54. Gus S. Wortham interview notes, Dec. 17, 1974; "Santa Gertrudis at Nine Bar Ranch," *American Breeds*, March, 1960, 10ff; "Santa Gertrudis," *Humble Way*, May–June, 1953, 11–18.

55. Gus S. Wortham to Sterling C. Evans, Dec. 16, 1952, Randle Lake File. Wortham also told H. D. Reynolds, an American General employee who acted as his personal accountant, that there would be both a breeding and a commercial herd, even though for his purposes it would be better to put all the females in the breeding herd. Wortham was acquiescing to Evans on this point, because Evans wished to show that the partnership had made a profit. (Gus S. Wortham to H. D. Reynolds, Memorandum, Dec. 16, 1952, Randle Lake File.)

56. Sterling C. Evans interviews no. 1 and 2; Gus S. Wortham interview notes, Dec. 17, 1974; "Wortham and Evans Are Increasing the Size of their Santa Gertrudis Operation," *Santa Gertrudis Journal*, Jan., 1960, 8ff; Stokes, *Sterling C. Evans*, 48; Gus S. Wortham Oral History, 98, 110. Briscoe was a relative of Texas Governor Dolph Briscoe (1973–79.)

57. Sterling C. Evans to Gus S. Wortham, Jan. 19, 1953, Randle Lake File; Gus S. Wortham to R. O. Angell, Sept. 21, 1953, Randle Lake File; First Annual Sale Memorabilia, Gus S. Wortham Scrapbook, no. 1, 66ff.

58. Sterling C. Evans to Gus S. Wortham, Memorandum, Dec. 30, 1953, Randle Lake File; "Power of Attorney," Nov. 16, 1955, Sterling C. Evans Papers. They cultivated the land, but the house stood uncared for until the next spring. Then Wortham called Evans from Louisville, Kentucky, where he and his 8F cronies journeyed annually for the Kentucky Derby. He had made some good bets and they now had the money to restore the house to its former grandeur. Evans's wife, Catherine, spent the better part of two years finding period furnishings and making the house an area showplace. (Sterling C. Evans interview no. 1.)

59. *Houston Post*, Oct. 19, 1955; Photographs, Gus S. Wortham Scrapbook no. 1, 136ff. The partners had the houses and the church moved and renovated and in May, 1957, St. Simon's Baptist Church was rededicated. Wortham had photographs taken of the ceremony, at which he spoke. Newton Rayzor, E. R. Barrow, and E. D. Adams, all Wortham partners in various ventures, attended.

60. "Santa Gertrudis at Nine Bar Ranch," see n. 54.

61. "Santa Gertrudis at Nine Bar Ranch"; Sterling C. Evans interview no. 1. The finding and buying of good land offered Gus Wortham a new kind of business challenge. But he understood land was not just waiting out there to be bought and sold. Rather, as Wortham said in later years when discussing the price of land, someone had to want to sell it. "The more you offer the more he becomes determined to keep it. So there is no such thing as a price of land. It is so dependent upon circumstances." It was a tangible, which made it different from finances, but it required the same kind of astute prediction and bargaining. (Gus S. Wortham Oral History, 115.)

62. Gus S. Wortham Oral History, 115.

63. Gus S. Wortham Oral History, 22; Kenneth Fellows, "Seaboard and the Beginning of Life," Seaboard/Schuarte File, Kenneth Fellows Papers, 4. The government program allowed soldiers to purchase policies worth up to $10,000 backed by the U.S. Treasury.

64. Fellows, "Seaboard and the Beginning of Life," 2–14; "The Baby Is Born," 144–46. As assistant cashier of Jesse Jones's Texas Trust Company, Baker had also served as a personal assistant to Jones, finally rising to trust officer of Jones's Bankers' Trust Company. Later, he went into business for himself in Philadelphia, manufacturing coal briquets used for heating. In 1919 he returned to Texas to be an independent oil operator, which satisfied his entrepreneurial bent but worried his conservative nature.

65. [Kenneth Fellows], "Flirtation and Courtship," Seaboard/Schuarte File; Fellows, "The Baby Is Born," 137–39; Gus S. Wortham Oral History, 22; Mr. and Mrs. Rutherford Cravens, interview by the author, Jan. 18, 1991, Houston, Tex. Although Seaboard was run conservatively, its policies had created a company of the highest reputation. A December, 1944, comparison of some Texas life companies, taken from *Best's Life Insurance Reports*, showed that Seaboard, while not the leader in quantity, had the highest quality rating of the group. One sentence in the memo which Burke Baker sent with this listing to his directors gives evidence of the standards expected: "We wish to remind our Representatives that these comparative figures are furnished you for your own information, and are not to be used to disparage in any way any other company." (Burke Baker, "To Our Directors," Aug. 14, 1945, Seaboard Life Papers, American General Archives.)

66. [Fellows], "Flirtation and Courtship"; Seaboard Life Insurance Company, Board of Directors, Minutes, June 4, 1945, American General Archives.

67. American General Insurance Company, "Insurance Companies Merge," Press release, June 15, 1945, American General Scrapbook no. 10, 205; American General Insurance Company, Notice to Stockholders, June 12, 1945, American General Scrapbook no. 10, 203.

68. Gus S. Wortham Oral History, 43; Dan M. McGill, ed., *All Lines Insurance*, 2–13. Because of the very different natures of these kinds of insurance, however, most companies entered into all-lines carefully, and throughout the 1950s, all-lines insurance received scrutiny. Wortham was ahead of many other insurance men in realizing the greater profits to be made through all-lines organization. A 1958 talk by Wortham was cited in the Huebner insurance education text that duly noted the stiff competition which the all-lines entities were giving the traditionally organized companies.

69. *Houston Press*, June 15, 1945; Gus S. Wortham, Proposal, Seaboard Life Insurance Company, Board of Directors, Meeting of the Special Committee, Minutes, June 4, 1945, American General Archives.

70. Gus S. Wortham proposal, as in n. 69 above. For Baker, Seaboard was more than just a business. He believed that life insurance should serve to better humanity's tenure on earth and his direction of the company was as much a duty as it was a profession. Thus he viewed the merger with some sadness and even felt as if he were losing a part of himself. (Mr. and Mrs. Rutherford Cravens interview.)

71. Gus S. Wortham, Memorandum regarding exchange of stock, n.d., American General Scrapbook no. 10, 225. The importance of carefully handling the personal quotient in the merger was made clear to Wortham in a letter he received in August, 1945, from Seaboard director Walter H. Walne, a lawyer with one of the city's oldest firms, Baker, Botts, and active in civil pursuits, especially with Wortham's favorite, the Houston Symphony. Walne heartily approved the merger but felt it incumbent upon Wortham and perhaps J. W. Link, Jr., to attend the Seaboard annual convention at Waldemar, a resort on the Guadalupe River. This week-long retreat, which included spouses and children, was a combination of educational meetings and recreational and inspirational team-building which served as a kind of bonding experience for the small Seaboard sales force. Walne believed that nothing better could be done "to more effectually promote the objectives we have in mind." Wortham did attend, and told Burke Baker he had a "grand time" at the "most unusual and most successful" convention, and he praised the spirit and loyalty of Baker's employees. (Seaboard Life Papers, 1945: Walter Walne to Gus S. Wortham, Aug. 9; Gus S. Wortham to Burke Baker, Sept. 14.)

72. Gus S. Wortham Oral History, 23; Gus S. Wortham, Memorandum, Oct. 2, 1945, Seaboard Life Papers.

73. Gus S. Wortham to Burke Baker, Oct. 24, 1945, Seaboard Life Papers; Fellows, "Seaboard."

74. Seaboard Life Papers: Gus S. Wortham to Burke Baker, Memorandum, Nov. 20, 1945; Burke Baker, "To The Stockholders and Directors of American General Life Insurance Company," March 11, 1947. In December 1945, American General sold the life company nearly $600,000 in mortgage loans and the next year the life company purchased almost $1.25 million in mortgage loans from AG Investment, thus, "pretty well" solving the company's "investment problem."

75. Gus S. Wortham, Memorandum, Nov. 16, 1945, Seaboard Life Papers.

76. Gus S. Wortham to Davis Faulkner, Memorandum, Nov. 3, 1945, Seaboard Life Papers; Gus S. Wortham to Burke Baker, Nov. 20, 1945.

77. Burke Baker, "To All Members of the Seaboard Family," Nov. 14, 1945, Seaboard Life Papers; *Houston Chronicle*, Jan. 2, 1946; American General Life Insurance Company Board of Directors, Annual Meeting, Minutes, March 11, 1947, American General Archives.

78. American General Life Insurance Company, Board of Directors, Minutes, Dec. 22, 1947. Wortham had tried to put American General Life under the management contract by which John L. Wortham and Son managed American General, but by 1947 this had proven unworkable for a life insurance entity, and he proposed it be terminated. The firm was forgoing the expenses it had paid for the life company during this time and Wortham noted that the time of the firm had not been compensated.

CHAPTER 5. NOBLESSE OBLIGE

1. Murray, "Power in the City," 284; David Nevin, *The Texans: What They Are—and Why*, 188–89.

2. *Houston Post*, July 3, 8, and 9, 1937; Link and Catton, *American Epoch*, 436–40; *Houston Post*, June 20–28, 1937. In Houston in 1937, the Congress of Industrial Organization (CIO)-backed Oil Workers International was trying to make inroads at the Texas Oil Company at Galena Park. The city had numerous strikes involving electrical workers, auto mechanics, hotel employees, and women textile workers. The business establishment in general was leery of labor unions, especially those of the younger CIO, but claimed a good relationship with the older craft and trade groups of the American Federation of Labor.

Wortham was appointed to the city's Labor Relations Board by Mayor R. H. Fonville (1937–39, between terms of Oscar Holcombe). The group included K. E. Womack, vice president of the Cotton Exchange; W. W. Strong, a member of the Port Commission and state president of "organized labor's non-partisan league"; and A. S. McBride, president of the state federation of labor and president of the Houston Building and Trades Council. Womack and Wortham were to represent employers, the other two, labor. Former mayor A. E. Amerman was chosen by the four as a neutral fifth party to head the group. A *Post* editorial referred to those chosen as men known for their "honesty," with an "enlightened viewpoint"; men able to maintain the "industrial peace" in Houston. Houston City Council authorized the board to "iron out" labor disputes by hearing both sides of any dispute and trying to work out a compromise. However, the group was strictly advisory in nature.

3. Houston Chamber of Commerce, "Joint Meeting, May 10, 1939," Minutes, May 10, 1939, Greater Houston Partnership Archives; Carleton, *Red Scare!* 24–25.

4. Houston Chamber of Commerce, "Joint Meeting, May 10, 1939."

5. Houston Chamber of Commerce, "Joint Meeting, May 10, 1939."

6. Houston Chamber of Commerce, "Executive-Labor Committee Conference," Minutes, June 20, 1939, Greater Houston Partnership Archives; Carleton, *Red Scare!* 24–25. *Post* and *Chronicle* editorials promoted joint action between the county and city. On May 12 the papers announced an increase in police and sheriff's personnel while a grand jury investigation into labor unrest was set in motion. In June, a joint meeting of the Chamber's subcommittee and Wortham's Citizens' Committee heard Judge C. R. Wharton's report on his trip to Los Angeles where severe regulations regarding picketing had been enforced. (*Houston Post*, May 12, 1939; *Houston Chronicle*, May 12,

1939; Houston Chamber of Commerce, "Executive-Labor Committee Conference," Minutes, June 20, 1939.)

7. Benjamin N. Woodson, Daily Business Papers, March 3, 1954, Woodson Research Center, Fondren Library, Rice University; Edward Stumpf, interview by author, no. 2 June 19, 1990, Houston, Tex.; Chandler Davidson, *Race and Class in Texas Politics*, 128–30.

8. *Houston Press*, Jan. 31, 1941; *Houston Post*, Jan. 31, 1941; Houston, Housing Authority of the City of Houston, "Historical Sketch," *Houston's Public Housing Program*, Annual Report, 1939, Housing Authority Files, Texas and Local History Room, Houston Public Library.

Wortham was appointed to the commission by Mayor Neal Pickett (1941–43), who had been the first manager of the Houston Insurance Exchange, a trade association for property insurance agents. Wortham had known Pickett for almost fifteen years. In addition to the Houston Housing Authority position, Pickett appointed Wortham to the City of Houston Citizens Advisory Committee, where Wortham served as vice chairman under chairman Jesse Andrews, a well-known lawyer with the prominent firm of Baker and Botts. This latter group must have been put together in late 1941, and at least two of their areas of involvement included flood control and street rights-of-way. (Gus S. Wortham, "To Whom It May Concern," Dec. 28, 1941, Incoming Correspondence, Neal Pickett Collection, Houston Metropolitan Research Center; Jesse Andrews to Citizens Advisory Committee, Dec. 28, 1941, Incoming Correspondence, Neal Picket Collection.)

9. Houston, Housing Authority of the City of Houston, "Historical Sketch, 1939; *Houston Chronicle*, Jan. 16, 1940; *Houston Post*, Feb. 1, 1941. The projects included: Massive Cuney Homes and Cuney Homes Addition, 80 buildings for blacks only at Tierwester and Alabama Streets; Kelly Homes, 61 buildings for blacks in the Fifth Ward; San Felipe Courts, a white project on Buffalo Drive with nearly 1,000 units; a 25-building project at East Montgomery and Hayes Street; and a designated "Mexican project" of 35 buildings at Canal and 75th. When Wortham became a member, Cuney Homes was finished and inhabited, additions to Cuney and Kelly Courts were under construction, and the contract for construction of the San Felipe project had been awarded. (Housing Authority, Annual Report, 1939.)

The advent of such housing in Houston was somewhat unsettling for the thoroughly segregated city. Although the black community was getting some much-needed housing, it was upset that the HHA had first tried to name its Cuney Homes after Dick Dowling, naval hero of the Confederacy. Ironically, this decision also upset the local chapter of the Daughters of the Confederacy. More seriously, the black residents of the San Felipe district, which included the city's oldest black settlement, Freedmen's Town, deeply resented and vowed to fight the destruction of black homes and businesses for the building of the whites-only San Felipe Courts project. The HHA had no black or Hispanic members and neither ethnic group had much input in the selection or construction of the housing. (*Houston Chronicle*, June 18, 1940.)

10. *Houston Chronicle*, Jan. 15, and Feb. 13, 1941; *Houston Press* Jan. 23, 1941.

11. *Houston Chronicle*, Aug. 14, 1941; Houston, Housing Authority of the City of Houston, Minutes, 1941, Housing Authority of the City of Houston; *Houston Press*, Sept. 14, 1941.

For example, the debate over gas or electric refrigerators at Cuney Homes is illustrative of a number of political and cultural biases on the part of the members of the authority. The dispute pointed up the split between the regional director from Fort Worth and the local board. The Houstonians had already purchased several hundred electric refrigerators at a good price, but the director insisted on gas units because they could be operated at a cheaper rate. Biggers objected to uneducated people being allowed to have such sophisticated equipment. When proceedings appeared to reach an impasse, Wortham stepped in to call for further consideration at a later date. He counseled that the decision should be made in Texas, not by a trip to Washington, and asked a representative of Houston Natural Gas present at the meeting for rate clarification. It is not clear whether Wortham just wanted the proceedings to move along, or if he sought a working compromise. (Houston, Housing Authority of the City of Houston, Minutes, April 9, 1941.)

12. Robert D. Bullard, *Invisible Houston: The Black Experience in Boom and Bust*, 23; Feagin, *Free Enterprise City*, 242–43.

13. Cary D. Wintz, "Blacks in Houston," in *Ethnic Groups of Houston*, Fred R. von der Mehden, ed. 20–24.

14. Wintz, "Blacks in Houston," 29–30.

15. Lester Randle, interviews by author, no. 1, Oct. 23, 1989, and no. 2, Aug. 14, 1990, Houston, Tex. The grandson of slaves, Randle had been born in Fort Worth and spent his adolescence in a three-room shotgun house on Sauliner Street in Houston's Fourth Ward. He ended his education at the eighth grade at Gregory School and took an early job as water boy for workers building John Henry Kirby's mansion—one bucket and ladle for whites, a separate one for blacks. Later, he got a job at the River Oaks home of Steven Power Farish, for $10.50 per week. A falling out with Farish over a traffic ticket ended in a racist upbraiding, leading Randle to seek other employment. He learned from a friend that the Worthams needed a chauffeur—and would pay $15 a week. He joined the Worthams' household at the Warwick, which also included a cook, and was responsible for driving their Pierce Arrow and serving breakfast and dinner.

16. Lester Randle interviews.

17. Lester Randle interview no. 1; Gus S. Wortham Scrapbook no. 1, 136.

18. David C. Roller and Robert W. Twyman, eds. *The Encyclopedia of Southern History*, s.v. "Customs and Manners," by Clement Eaton.

19. Houston Symphony Orchestra Society, Scrapbooks, Houston Symphony Orchestra Collection, Houston Metropolitan Research Center.

20. Stanley Siegel, *Houston: A Chronicle of the Supercity on Buffalo Bayou* 143–44.

21. *Houston Press*, Nov. 11, 1937; *Houston Chronicle*, Nov. 12, 1939; *Houston Post*, Oct. 15, 1939, and Nov. 3, 1940; Houston Symphony, 1939–40 File, Leopold Meyer Collection, Houston Metropolitan Research Center. An indication of the Worthams' involvement and social prominence was the November 5, 1946, issue of the *Houston Post*, which had a featured drawing of the Symphony opening night gown of Lyndall Wortham. The same day, the *Press* featured pictures of the Worthams and Mrs. Wortham, her sister-in-law Fan Etta Hill, and Miss Ima at a Symphony Society coffee.

22. Gus S. Wortham Oral History, 120; Hubert Roussel, *The Houston Symphony Orchestra, 1913–1971*, 111, 194; Theodore H. White, "Texas: Land of Wealth and Fear," *The Reporter*, May 25, 1954. Cullen, a self-made man with little formal education, good native sense, and conservative politics, was then in the middle of donating

his vast oil-based fortune to various entities around town, including the University of Houston and the Texas Medical Center.

23. Roussel, *Houston Symphony Orchestra*, 112–13. There was no final decision on Hoffman's fate until early in 1947, when the board decided to ask for his resignation, shortly before he and the orchestra performed on an NBC radio national broadcast. Later that spring of 1947, Hogg, Wortham, and the new business manager, Francis Deering, set off to New York to woo the internationally known ballet conductor Efrem Kurtz to the Houston podium—supposedly with Cullen's assent. During their trip, however, Cullen sent a telegram telling Wortham he was quitting the Symphony altogether. Once again to appease Cullen, they did not hire Kurtz, but planned a season of guest conductors for 1947–48. (Roussel, *Houston Symphony Orchestra*, 117–18.)

24. Pamela F. Young, "History of the Houston Symphony Orchestra, 1913–1966," Master's thesis, University of Texas, 1970, 36.

25. Houston Symphony Orchestra Society, Scrapbook 1947–48, Houston Symphony Orchestra Collection; Houston Symphony Orchestra Society, Maintenance Fund Scrapbook, 1947–48, Houston Symphony Orchestra Collection.

26. Houston Symphony Orchestra Society, Joint Meeting of the Executive and Finance Committees, Minutes, Aug. 20, 1947, Scrapbook 1947–48.

27. *Houston Post*, Sept. 8, 1947.

28. *Houston Press*, Aug. 25 and Sept. 6, 1947; Houston Symphony Orchestra Society, Financial Brochure, Scrapbook 1947–48.

29. *Houston Post*, Sept. 7, 1947.

30. Houston Symphony Orchestra Society, Joint Meeting, Minutes, Aug. 20, 1947; Houston Symphony Orchestra Society, Information Sheet, n.d., Maintenance Fund Scrapbook 1947–48; Houston Symphony Orchestra Society, Gus S. Wortham to Women's Maintenance Fund Campaign, Aug. 26, 1947, Maintenance Fund Scrapbook 1947–48.

31. The Museum of the American West, "Robert Joy, Selected Paintings, 1927–1982," Exhibition catalog, 1984, American General Archives; Gus S. Wortham Oral History, 121; Houston Symphony Orchestra Society, Radio Script, Maintenance Fund Scrapbook 1947–48. Wortham's portrait, done in 1959, was part of a collection Joy called "The Power Brokers," which included Judge Elkins, Ima Hogg, Herman and George Brown, Leland Anderson, James Abercrombie, Leopold Meyer, Lamar Fleming, and Wharton Weems. (Museum of the American West, "Robert Joy, Selected Paintings" catalog.)

32. "$102,750.50 Collected to Aid Symphony," *Houston Chronicle*, Sept. 24, 1947.

33. Fanny Davis Diehl interview; Jean Gordon, interview by author, no. 2 Aug. 22, 1990, Houston, Tex.

34. Gus S. Wortham and American General Scrapbooks, American General Archives; *Houston Chronicle*, Nov. 10, 1963; Jean Gordon interview no. 2; *Houston Post*, Jan. 25, 1961.

35. *Houston Chronicle*, Nov. 11, 1963.

36. Various clippings, Gus S. Wortham and American General Scrapbooks; *Houston Chronicle*, Nov. 10, 1963; Jean Gordon interview no. 2.

37. Hal Shelton, Julie Kavitski, and Susanne Huxel, "The Wortham House: A History," MS, Program in Public History, 1987, 1–18, Institute for Public History, University of Houston; from Sterling Property, 1950–61 File, Museum of Fine Arts, Houston

Archives: Museum of Fine Arts, Resolution, Feb. 24, 1950; John Hamman, Jr. to Gus S. Wortham, March 3, 1950; John Hamman, Jr., to Thomas D. Anderson, March 5, 1951.

The house was not Gus's idea; he would have been perfectly happy to stay at the Warwick as he liked residence hotel living. It was Lyndall who wanted the house and she wanted it because of the children. By 1950, young Lyndall and Diana were active little girls, and Mrs. Wortham felt the family needed a house. Daughter Lyndall remembered the sisters' exploits in the residence hotel, not unlike those of the famed "Eloise" at New York's Plaza Hotel—including pouring water down the mail chutes. Mrs. Wortham liked to "show off" her daughters, dressing them up for her various parties or meetings. Daughter Lyndall remembered that her father set aside some time every evening upon coming home from work when he would play with her in the family's den. (Fanny Davis Diehl interview; Lyndall Wortham Seymour, interview by Judy Brumbelow and author, Oct. 1, 1990.)

38. Lyndall Finley Wortham interview, May 18, 1976; Gus S. Wortham and American General Scrapbooks, American General Archives.

Mrs. Wortham thought she handled the whole ordeal quite well, despite the year that had gone into the complete renovation. Although some local wags made jokes, the house was insured. Gus told Lyndall she could do whatever she wanted: find a new house, stay at the Warwick, or redo this one again. She decided upon the latter course, but during the second renovation received a phone call that the warehouse in New Orleans, which housed her antique furniture, had caught fire. This time, Lyndall did not take the news so well. Hysterical, she phoned Gus, crying the "devil is after us." She remembered his calm reply: "Well, I don't know about the devil, but I'd sure say we are snake-bit." (Lyndall Finley Wortham interview, May 18, 1976.)

39. "Wortham," *Rice University Review*, Spring, 1970, 5; Fredericka Meiners, *A History of Rice University, The Institute Years, 1907–1963*, 169; *Rice University Review*, Spring/Summer, 1968; Gus S. Wortham Oral History, 126. On retiring from the board in 1961, Wortham told the *Rice University Review* that his selection was done quietly by Brown, who did not want it known around town that he was looking for members for the Rice board. Wortham acknowledged that his own appointment was a complete surprise.

40. Joining the board with him in January, 1946, were banker William Kirkland, a former member of the Houston City Council and son-in-law of a retiring trustee; Dr. Frederick R. Lummis, chief of staff at Hermann Hospital and member of the clinical faculty at Baylor College of Medicine (Baylor College had relocated to Houston's brand new medical center in 1943); and Lamar Fleming, president of Anderson, Clayton and Company. These men, in the company of Brown and oil men Harry C. Hanszen and Harry C. Wiess, had clearly been chosen to help Rice enter a new era of adventure, risk and growth. (Meiners, *History of Rice University*, 137.)

41. Rice University General Correspondence File 1945–48, American General Archives: Rice Institute, Budget information for Board of Regents, May 21, 1946; and "Investment Problems of Rice University," Feb. 28, 1945. The new era at Rice had actually begun in 1942 with the institute's purchase, at the instigation of County Judge Roy Hofheinz, of an interest in the Rincon Oil Field, part of the unwieldy estate of W. R. Davis. The interest was too expensive for any corporation to take over, and Hofheinz worked with Brown and Wiess to arrange the deal with the trustees. Although its charter forbade the kind of financing that would be needed to carry through the

purchase, the institute received a district court ruling allowing this investment and such in the future, thus opening the way for Rice to "diversify the Institute's investments, no longer limited to those types of first mortgage loans and bonds that had characterized the cautious investments" of the previous Rice leadership. (Meiners, *History of Rice University*, 137.

42. Rice University General Correspondence File 1945–48: Rice Institute, Board of Trustees Special Meeting, Minutes, Jan. 14, 1946; and Gus S. Wortham to Harry Hanszen, Jan. 17, 1946. The Institute had earned under $100,000 per year for the years 1940 to 1943; in 1944 earnings were $163,000, and by 1945 had jumped to $322,800. But the February, 1945, "Investment Problems of Rice University" concluded that the institute should increase its investments in stock and decrease the municipal bonds in order to earn more on its investments (sources as in n. 41.)

43. "Wortham," *Rice University Review*, 6; Gus S. Wortham Oral History, 127. Wortham took no time in becoming active on the board—on January 17, 1946, he inspected and advised board chair Hanszen on an offer to buy property and on the agreement being drawn up with the architect to build the new library. Although Hanszen had agreed to okay the contract only after Wortham's study, Wortham was careful to remember his new status, cautioning Hanszen that he did not want to "inject myself too much into the completion of a contract which has been discussed . . . over a considerable period of time. . . . A new man coming into a situation that has been under consideration can frequently get in trouble and do more harm than good." (Gus S. Wortham to Harry Hanszen, Jan. 17, 1946, Rice University General Correspondence.)

44. Rice University General Correspondence File 1945–1948: Rice Institute, List of Stocks owned by Rice, Jan. 31, 1947; Rice Institute, List of Stocks, May 31, 1947; Rice Institute, Statement for Fiscal Year Ending 6/30/47 with memo by Chairman H. Hanszen, Aug. 6, 1947; Gus S. Wortham to C. A. Dwyer, Jan. 20, 1947. See also "Wortham," *Rice University Review*, 6.

45. Gus S. Wortham to Harry Hanszen, April 3, 1946, Rice University General Correspondence File 1947–48. Wortham confidentially told chairman Hanszen that while the bid of Warren Bellows for construction of the new library was "in line," he could be persuaded to do the job for less, and would agree to once he realized the public relations value of this contract.

46. "Retirement Plan for Rice Faculty Members Adopted," Uncited newspaper clip, Nov. 21, 1946, Rice Institute Retirement File, Vertical File, Texas and Local History Room, Houston Public Library; Various correspondence, 1949–1958, Papers of President William V. Houston, Rice University Archives, Woodson Research Center, Fondren Library, Rice University.

47. Wortham, as a member of the finance committee, advocated a 70 percent loan at a three percent rate and contacted Southwestern Life of Dallas to inquire about their possible participation in the loan. Although the loan was a mortgage, Wortham and the committee felt justified in its safety because it was in reality a "debenture, or an obligation of F. W. Woolworth and Company, with a mortgage on a very valuable piece of real estate as additional security." (Rice University General Correspondence File 1945–48: Gus S. Wortham to C. A. Dwyer, May 21, 1946, and Gus S. Wortham to T. L. Bradford, Jr., May 24, 1946 [quote].)

48. Rice University General Correspondence File 1945–48, 1946 letters: Gus S. Wortham to C. A. Dwyer, May 21; Gus S. Wortham to T. L. Bradford, Jr., May 24; Gus

S. Wortham to C. M. Malone, June 20; C. A. Dwyer to Gus S. Wortham, Oct. 20; Gus S. Wortham to C. A. Dwyer, Oct. 29.

49. Harry Hanszen to Rice Trustees, April 29, 1947, Rice University General Correspondence File 1945–48.

50. *Houston Post*, March 17 and April 17, 1938; Meiners, *History of Rice University*, 131–32; *Houston Chronicle*, Dec. 1948–Feb. 1949. In 1938, the old Rice stadium had been rehabilitated to seat 30,000 with funds raised in the community by the alumni. The largest donation had come from H. R. Cullen, and Gus S. Wortham had been a member of the Rice committee. The stadium, as everything else at the private school, was to remain solely the property of the trustees and the school. This stipulation perhaps had some bearing on the negotiations that began in the late 1940s about building a larger stadium for use by the whole community.

51. "Leaders in Drive for New Stadium Talk Finances," *Houston Chronicle*, April 6, 1949; *Houston Chronicle*, April–Nov. 1949.

52. "Rice Institute Is to Get 50,000 Seat Stadium," *Houston Chronicle*, Nov. 14, 1949.

53. "UH Rejects Rice Stadium Sharing Plan," *Houston Post*, Nov. 19, 1949.

54. Blankenhorn, "Gus Wortham."

55. Gus S. Wortham to Lenn Kelly, Dec. 1 and 12, 1947, Rice University General Correspondence File 1947–48; "Holcombe Pushes Stadium 'Peace,'" *Houston Post*, Nov. 18, 1949; Meiners, *History of Rice University*, 155–56.

56. *Houston Chronicle*, Nov. 20–Dec. 31, 1949.

57. *Houston Post*, Special Section, Sept. 26, 1950. The stadium opening was a major event for the city, heralded by special sections in the *Houston Press* and the *Houston Post*. Some 68,000 fans came to see the show, featuring 33 high school bands; Patti Page, currently appearing at the Shamrock Hotel, singing the National Anthem; and the Apache Belles from Tyler Junior College. Governor Shivers headed the list of notables. The game was broadcast over radio and television.

58. *Houston Chronicle*, Dec. 31, 1950.

59. Jack Mitchell to Gus S. Wortham, May 7, 1969, Rice University 1962–71 File, American General Archives. One sidelight of Wortham's devotion to Rice was his interest in the architecture program during the 1960s, based on his confidence in William Caudill, chairman of the department and a prominent Houston architect. Caudill asked Wortham for funds to attract top-quality students. In 1968 Wortham "earmarked" $600,000 to establish a graduate program, and made an anonymous donation to begin the school's urban design program. At one point, George Brown told Caudill that Wortham was the "key" to approaching the late Jesse Jones's Houston Endowment. Wortham was close to J. Howard Creekmore, the endowment's president, and American General had just purchased the endowment's stock in Texas Commerce Bank. His devotion to Caudill's program fits into Wortham's great interest in land, land development, and the growth of Houston. Given his belief that great institutions were necessary for a livable and economically prosperous environment, it is easy to see how Wortham felt Rice's architecture program was worth his care. (Gus S. Wortham to William W. Caudill, Feb. 27, 1962, Rice University 1962–71 File. From the Papers of President Kenneth Pitzer, Rice University Archives, Woodson Research Center, Fondren Library, Rice University: Bill Caudill to Bill Cannady, Memorandum, March 16, 1966; William Caudill to Gus S. Wortham, June 23, 1967; William W. Caudill to George R.

Brown, July 26, 1968; William Caudill to H. Malcolm Lovett, Oct. 16, 1968; William W. Caudill to Dean William E. Gordon, Memorandum, Nov. 7, 1968.)

60. Uncited clipping, n.d., Gus Wortham Scrapbook no. 1, 27.

61. Texas Children's Hospital "This is a Blueprint for Benevolent People!" brochure, ca. 1952, Texas Children's Hospital Archives; Russell J. Blattner, M.D., "History of the Development of the Texas Children's Hospital," Uncited magazine clipping, ca. 1955, Texas Children's Hospital Archives. Other members of the board included William A. Smith, Herman Brown, James A. Elkins, Jr., and J. W. Link, Jr.—all men with close ties to Wortham.

62. Gus S. Wortham to Talbot O. Freeman, Dec. 7, 1934, John L. Wortham and Son Archives; American General Archives: "Biographical Sketch of Gus Sessions Wortham," ca. 1956, Gus Wortham Drawer; Denton Cooley to Gus S. Wortham, Aug. 1, 1968, Gus S. Wortham Personal Contributions and Donations File; Gus S. Wortham, Notation on list dated April 19, 1974, Gus S. Wortham Personal Contributions and Donations 1974 File. Various correspondence, Houston Community Chest Files, Vertical Files, Texas and Local History Room, Houston Public Library; *Houston*, March, 1953, 18; Various correspondence, Leopold Meyer Collection; Houston Fat Stock Show/Houston Livestock and Rodeo Show Files, Vertical Files, Texas and Local History Room, Houston Public Library; Houston Chamber of Commerce, *Business Action*, Aug., 1950; *Houston Press*, March 2 and 8, 1954; *Houston*, May, 1953, 29.

63. *Houston Chronicle*, July 1, 1958; *Houston Post*, July 1, 1958; *Houston Press*, undated clip, Gus S. Wortham Scrapbook no. 6, 2.

64. Blankenhorn, "Gus Wortham," March 26, 1979.

CHAPTER 6. MIXING POLITICS WITH BUSINESS

1. *Houston*: April, 1946; June, 1946, 26, 50, 66; Aug., 1946, 6, 38; March, 1947, 8, 27; April, 1947, 53.

2. John Gunther, *Inside U.S.A.*, 827. In his article on Houston, right after calling it reactionary, Gunther (p. 827ff.) mentions the Texas Regulars; Judge T. [*sic*] A. Elkins, "head of one of the biggest legal firms in the world"; "distinguished women" like Oveta Culp Hobby; and Jesse Jones. Then he says: "But it also is the city of a splendid university—Rice Institute—and of people like Colonel J. W. Evans, the president of the Cotton Exchange and one of the creators of the port of Houston, who has held practically every job the community can bestow that calls for genuine civic spirit and bears no salary." Gunther mentions lunching with a group of "leading citizens" with Evans as host. It was very likely Wortham was at that lunch.

3. Hurt, "The Most Powerful Texans," 10.

4. Conaway, *The Texans*, 102.

5. Lester Randle interview no. 1.

6. Conaway, *The Texans*, 102.

7. Feagin, *Free Enterprise City*, 138–42; Davidson, *Race and Class*, 82–84, 92–95; Green, *The Establishment in Texas Politics*, 8; Murray, "Power in the City," 283–84.

8. Carleton, *Red Scare!* 71.

9. Feagin, *Free Enterprise City*, 154, 124; Carleton, *Red Scare!* 70; Smyser, "Houston's Power: As it was"; "Fat Cats Tie Oscar with Clasp of Gold," Uncited newspaper clipping, n.d., Gus S. Wortham Scrapbook no. 1, 95.

10. In *Free Enterprise City* (p. 153) Feagin says: "From 1947 to the early 1970s Houston had only four mayors, Oscar Holcombe, Lewis Cutrer, Roy Hofheinz, and Louie Welch, all of whom more or less depended on the Suite 8F crowd. Generally speaking the core of the business elite controlled the composition and major activities of the mayor's office."

11. Edward Stumpf, interview by author, no. 1, May 10, 1990, Houston, Tex.; Edward Stumpf interview no. 2; Johnnie Rogers, interview by author, Nov. 16, 1990, Houston, Tex.; Gus S. Wortham Oral History, 94–95, 131–32. According to Rogers, the group was afraid of being "raided" by the authorities, so one of the players who was on the legislative committee rewrote the penal code to protect this game.

12. Edward Stumpf interview no. 1; Frank Oltorf, telephone interview by author, Nov. 21, 1990.

13. Allen Carruth interviews no. 1 and 2; Feagin, *Free Enterprise City*, 7, 47, 171, 210; Barry J. Kaplan, "Houston: The Golden Buckle of the Sunbelt," in *Sunbelt Cities, Politics and Growth Since World War II*, ed. Richard M. Bernard and Bradley R. Rice, 200; Edward Stumpf interviews no. 1 and 2.

14. Searcy Bracewell, interview by author, no. 1, April 20, 1990, Houston, Tex.; *Houston Chronicle*, Biography of Searcy Bracewell, uncited, ca. 1958, "Bracewell," *Houston Chronicle* Microfiche File, Texas and Local History Room, Houston Public Library; *Houston Chronicle*, Uncited new clipping, ca. 1946, Vertical Biographical File, Texas and Local History Room; Davidson, *Race and Class*, 106.

15. Searcy Bracewell interview no. 1.

16. Edward Stumpf interview no. 2, Searcy Bracewell interview no. 1.

17. Searcy Bracewell interview no. 1.

18. Search Bracewell interview no. 1; Davidson, *Race and Class*, 106.

19. Robert Mehr and Emerson Cammack, *Principles of Insurance*, 787–88; Manford, *Insuring Texas' Future*, 60–61.

20. Manford, *Insuring Texas' Future*, 60–61; Douglas Caddy, *Understanding Texas Insurance*, 18; Chamber of Commerce of the U.S., Insurance Department, *Washington Insurance Notes*, June 23, 1944, Bailey–Van Nuys Files, American General Archives; American General Insurance Company, "Report to Stockholders," Feb. 23, 1945, Board of Directors, Minutes; Gus S. Wortham to Judge D. F. Strickland, Oct. 12, 1943, Bailey–Van Nuys Files; William S. Crawford, "Insurance People Must Get Active," mimeographed in *The Insurance Exchange of Houston*, Bulletin No. 103, Oct. 15, 1943, Bailey–Van Nuys Files.

21. Gus S. Wortham, "Memorandum on Federal Control of Insurance," Sept. 4, 1943, Bailey–Van Nuys Files.

22. Gus S. Wortham to Judge D. F. Strickland, Oct. 12, 1943.

23. Gus S. Wortham to Judge D. F. Strickland, Oct. 12, 1943.

24. Gus S. Wortham to Roy D. Montgomery, Oct. 18, 1943, Bailey–Van Nuys Files.

25. Bailey–Van Nuys Files, 1943: Gus S. Wortham to Lyndon B. Johnson, Oct. 18; Albert Thomas to Gus S. Wortham, Oct. 19; Gus S. Wortham to W. Lee O'Daniel, Nov. 15. Wortham also heard from "Cousin Nat" Patton, 7th District congressman, who praised "Cousin" Gus as "one of the soundest businessmen in Texas." Patton said the federal government had overstepped its bounds. (Nate Patton to Gus S. Wortham, Oct. 19, 1943, Bailey–Van Nuys Files.) The next month Wortham wrote to Johnson:

"It still gives me great pleasure to think of your fine response to my request for your assistance on Senate Bill 1362 . . . hope the bill will be reported out by the Committee this week. (Gus S. Wortham to Lyndon B. Johnson, Nov. 15, 1943, Bailey–Van Nuys Files.)

26. Gus S. Wortham to Fritz Lanham, Nov. 16, 1943, Bailey–Van Nuys Files.

27. Gus S. Wortham to Tom Connally, June 14, 1944, Bailey–Van Nuys Files.

28. Bailey–Van Nuys Files, 1944: Gus S. Wortham to Tom Connally, June 21; Gus S. Wortham to E. V. Williams, June 22.

29. American General Insurance Company, "Report to Stockholders," Feb. 23, 1945. In this report, Wortham recounted the Supreme Court decision and told of the impending state rate regulation legislation the company was helping to sponsor. He stressed that the company believed the added regulation was good and that, as the companies had always been able to sell at an equal rate, no business loss was expected.

30. Paul Benbrook, interview with author, Feb. 2, 1991, Houston, Tex.; Davidson, *Race and Class*, 103, 106; Searcy Bracewell interview no. 1.

31. Edward Stumpf interviews no. 1 and 2.

32. "Wortham Heads State Institutions Group," *Houston*, Oct. 1949; McComb, *Houston*, 158–59; "Wortham, Hess Named on New Group," *Houston Post*, Sept. 26, 1956; State of Texas, Certificate, Gus S. Wortham Scrapbook no. 2, 70.

33. Benjamin N. Woodson Papers, March 1, 1956; *Houston Press*, March 5, 1957; *Houston Post*, March 27, 1957; "Flexible Rates Stir Conflict," Uncited news clipping, ca. April, 1957, Gus S. Wortham Scrapbook no. 2, p. 135; *Texas Observer*, April 2, 1957.

34. "Flexible Rating Bill May be Buried for Session," *Houston Post*, April 8, 1959.

35. *Houston Post*, March 20, 1959; *Houston Chronicle*, March 20, 1959.

36. *Houston Post:* April 8 and 10, 1959. Wortham argued that if compulsory liability coverage worked it would have spread from Massachusetts, which had enacted the first such law 32 years earlier. Instead he advocated increasing the deposit from uninsured motorists involved in a collision and impounding their cars.

37. Democratic Party, National Campaign Committee, Receipt, 1940, Mr. and Mrs. Gus S. Wortham 1940 Income Tax File, American General Archives; Caro, *Years of Lyndon Johnson* (1983), 626–28.

38. Banks, *Money, Marbles and Chalk*, 84–85; Gus S. Wortham to C. A. Keppler, Telegram, Dec. 10, 1935, John L. Wortham and Son Archives; Gus S. Wortham to W. M. Thornton, June 26, 1940, Longhorn Portland Cement Files; Joe Flack interview with author, no. 1, Dec. 8, 1989, Houston, Tex.

39. U.S. House of Representative Papers 1937–48, Lyndon B. Johnson Archives (hereafter cited as LBJ Archives), Lyndon B. Johnson Library: Lyndon B. Johnson to Gus S. Wortham, telegram, March 4 and 5, 1941; John Connally to Gus S. Wortham, March 27, 1941; Lyndon B. Johnson to Gus S. Wortham, July 7 and 22, 1941.

40. Green, *The Establishment in Texas Politics*, 46, 110; Sam Kinch and Stuart Long, *Allan Shivers: The Pied Piper of Texas Politics*, 112; Harry S. Truman to Gus S. Wortham, Nov. 5, 1948, Framed letter, American General Archives.

41. Allen Carruth interview no. 1; Edward Stumpf interview no. 1; Lyndon B. Johnson to Gus S. Wortham, April 9, 1953, U.S. Senate Papers 1949–61, LBJ Archives. According to one account, there was no pressure for the employees to partici-

pate. Those who worked were given a leave of absence and assigned certain counties to canvas for Johnson. This included talking to voters, putting up posters, and collecting contributions.

42. Carleton, *Red Scare!* 68.

43. Arthur Perry to Gus S. Wortham, Dec. 21, 1953, Senate Papers, LBJ Archives; Link and Catton, *American Epoch*, 761.

44. Carleton, *Red Scare!* 256–57.

45. Dallek, *Lone Star Rising*, 435–37; Lyndon B. Johnson, Memorandum, n.d. Bricker Amendment File, Senate Papers, LBJ Archives.

46. Senate Papers, LBJ Archives: Gus S. Wortham to Lyndon B. Johnson, July 13, 1956 (Legislative Files); Lyndon B. Johnson to Gus S. Wortham, S. C. Evans, etc., telegram, July 15, 1956 (Legislative Files); Gus S. Wortham to Lyndon B. Johnson, telegram, April 8, 1959 (1959 Subject File Taxes/Insurance Cos.).

47. Gus S. Wortham to Lyndon B. Johnson, Feb. 4, 1958, 1958 Case Files, Wortham, G. S., Senate Papers, LBJ Archives.

48. Price Daniel to Gus S. Wortham, May 23, 1958, Gus S. Wortham Scrapbook no. 2, 7.

49. Richardson, Wallace, and Anderson, *Texas*, 404–405; Banks, *Money, Marbles and Chalk*, 60; Davidson, *Race and Class*, 29–30. The Senate seat Yarborough won had been the seat Daniel vacated when he became governor in 1956.

50. Kinch and Long, *Allan Shivers*, 118.

51. Houston Chamber of Commerce, various publication files, Greater Houston Partnership Archives.

52. *Houston Chronicle*, April 30, 1953; "New Leaders," *Nation's Business*, July, 1953; "Gus S. Wortham Named to U.S. Chamber of Commerce Board," *Houston Post*, April 29, 1953. In 1953 Wortham was one of 16 new officers and directors of the 58-man group and was elected a member-at-large. An insurance man, the head of Occidental Life, was chairman of the board, and the chairman of the executive committee was another Texan, D. A. Hulcy, president of Lone Star Gas in Dallas.

53. *Houston Press*, July 20, 1954; *Houston Post*, Aug. 8, 1954; *The Insurance Reporter*, Sept. 2, 1954.

54. Carleton, *Red Scare!* 74–75.

55. The article cited the port and oil as the main reasons behind the city's boom; mentioned Jones, the Hobbys, Cullen, McCarthy, and Holcombe as its superstars; and said the city was "essentially a big businessman's town."

56. "Southern City, Northern Pace: How Long Can It Last?" *Business Week*, Jan. 24, 1953, 76ff; Murphy, "Texas Business and McCarthy." In 1954, *Fortune* magazine carried a piece on Texas businessmen who supported Senator Joe McCarthy and his anticommunist vendettas. While some disapproved of McCarthy's tactics, several were glad someone was doing something about this danger. Among those mentioned as pro-McCarthy were Hugh Roy Cullen (who had invited McCarthy to speak at San Jacinto Day ceremonies that year) and close Wortham associates Jesse Jones and attorney Maurice Hirsch. (*Fortune*, May, 1954, 100ff; Carleton, *Red Scare!* 168–78 ff.)

57. Theodore H. White, "Texas: Land of Wealth and Fear, II: Texas Democracy—Domestic and Export Models," *The Reporter*, June 8, 1954, 31–32.

58. Arch Booth to Gus S. Wortham, June 12, 1958, Gus S. Wortham Scrapbook no. 2, 8; *Houston Chronicle*, July 12, 1958.

59. Gus S. Wortham Oral History, 130.

60. The national Chamber's monthly magazine, *Nation's Business*, reflected this philosophy. Almost every issue during Wortham's tenure, mid-1953 through 1959, included an article, editorial, or news mention about organized labor's attempts to raise wages and benefits and thereby wreak havoc on the free marketplace. Another major topic was the encroachment of government into realms—especially relating to social services—that rightly belonged to private enterprise or local government to handle, and handle better than big government. The arms race, and then after Sputnik in 1957, the space race with the Russians, were almost monthly topics. Rising taxes, higher Social Security benefits, and the danger of inflation from too much government spending were all "cutting down the supply of risk capital and endangering the future of our economy." (*Nation's Business*, Sept. 1953, 38.)

61. Fellows, *Baby Is Born*, p. 274.

CHAPTER 7. EXPANDING THE BUSINESS

1. American General Insurance Company, Board of Directors, Minutes, Feb. 20, 1947.

2. As above.

3. American General Insurance Company: "Report to Stockholders," Feb. 21, 1946, Stockholders, Minutes; Board of Directors, Minutes, Feb. 20, 1947; "Report to Stockholders of American General Insurance Company," Feb. 18, 1949, Stockholders, Minutes; "Report to Directors," May 22, 1951, Board of Directors, Minutes; "Report to the Directors," Sept. 12, 1951, Board of Directors, Minutes; "To Our Stockholders," Feb. 20, 1953, Stockholders, Minutes.

4. Raymond Mauk, telephone interview with author, March 5, 1991. Texas Advisory Committee File, American General Archives: Gus S. Wortham to Hal Conick, Nov. 13, 1944; Gus S. Wortham to Frank Christenson, Nov. 13, 1944; Gus S. Wortham to E. L. Williams, Nov. 13, 1944; Gus S. Wortham to Vinson, Elkins, Oct. 20, 1944.

5. Texas Advisory Committee File: Gus S. Wortham to T. R. Mansfield, Dec. 4, 1945 and Gus S. Wortham to R. B. Cousins, Jr., June 7, 1945.

6. Texas Advisory Committee File: Gus S. Wortham to R. B. Cousins, June 7, 1945, Gus S. Wortham to T. R. Mansfield, Dec. 4, 1945, and Gus S. Wortham to E. L. Williams, Nov. 13, 1944; Texas Insurance Advisory Association, *Texas Insurance Advisory Association*, Pamphlet (Austin: May 1990), Texas Insurance Advisory Association; "Wortham Re-Elected Texas Committee Head," *Journal of Commerce*, Nov. 21, 1952. Cousins, Jr., was the son of the educator, R. B. Cousins, John Wortham's friend and eulogizer. Cousins, Jr., later became manager of the TIAA.

7. American General Insurance Company, Board of Directors, Minutes: "Report to Stockholders and Directors," Feb. 16, 1951; "Report to Directors and Stockholders," Feb. 20, 1952; "To Our Directors," Sept. 5, 1952; "Report to the Directors," May 5, 1953; see also Charles Boswell interview.

8. "American General Life Insurance Total Passes $100 Million Mark," *Houston Post*, Sept. 29, 1949; American General Insurance Company, Stockholders and Directors Minutes, respectively: "Report to Stockholders," Feb. 20, 1948; 'Report to Directors," Nov. 18, 1949; "Report to Stockholders," Feb. 17, 1950; "Report to Stockholders and Directors," Feb. 16, 1951; "Report to the Directors," March 31, 1953.

9. Benjamin Woodson, interview by author, no. 1, Nov. 11, 1989, Houston, Tex.

10. Benjamin Woodson interview no. 1.

11. Woodson, *A Financial Services Supermarket*, 9–10.

12. Benjamin Woodson interview no. 1.

13. American General Insurance Company, "Memorandum," July 24, 1953, Board of Directors, Minutes.

14. American General Insurance Company, "To Our Directors," Oct. 12, 1954, Board of Directors, Minutes; "Woodson Chosen Head," *Louisville Courier-Journal*, n.d., American General Scrapbook no. 7, 4.

15. Benjamin N. Woodson Papers, May 12, 1954; Benjamin N. Woodson, Notes of Interview with Kenneth Fellows, May 12, 1976; Benjamin N. Woodson interview no. 1; Fellows, "The Baby Is Born," 179–81; Benjamin N. Woodson Papers, Jan. 2, 1955; American General Insurance Company, "To Our Stockholders," Feb. 15, 1957, Board of Directors, Minutes.

16. Benjamin N. Woodson, interview by author, no. 4 Aug. 9, 1991, Houston, Tex.

17. American General Insurance Company, "To Our Stockholders," Feb. 18, 1955, Stockholders, Minutes.

18. American General Insurance Company, "To Our Stockholders," Feb. 18, 1955; Lester Randle interview no. 1; "Page One Billboard," *Houston Press*, July 23, 1954; Benjamin N. Woodson Papers, July 20, 1954.

19. Benjamin N. Woodson Papers, February through July, 1955; American General Insurance Company, "To Our Directors," Nov. 22, 1955, Board of Directors, Minutes.

20. Fellows, "The Baby Is Born," 186–87; Benjamin N. Woodson Papers, October through December, 1955; "Local Firm Buys Hawaii Company," *Houston Post*, Jan. 13, 1956.

21. Benjamin N. Woodson Papers, various dates, 1955.

22. Gus S. Wortham and American General Scrapbooks, various clippings, 1955.

23. Fellows, "The Baby Is Born," 183–84; American General Insurance Company, "Report to Directors," Jan. 3, 1956, Board of Directors, Minutes; "AG One of Largest," *Houston Press*, Dec. 6, 1955; Benjamin N. Woodson Papers, Dec. 30, 1955.

24. Benjamin N. Woodson Papers, Jan. 3, 1956; American General Insurance Company, "Report to Directors," Jan. 3, 1956.

25. American General Insurance Company, "Report to Directors," Jan. 3, 1956.

26. American General Insurance Company, "Report to Directors," Jan. 3, 1956; "Insurance Firm Buys Big Company," *Houston Chronicle*, Jan. 9, 1956; "Local Firm Buys Big Hawaii Company," Jan. 13, 1956; American General Insurance Company, "To Our Stockholders," Feb. 15, 1957, Board of Directors, Minutes. At that same AG Board meeting, Judge Elkins received congratulations for the impending merger of his City National Bank with First National, making it the largest bank in Houston. (Benjamin N. Woodson Papers, Jan. 3, 1956.)

27. Ronnie Dugger, "What Corrupted Texas," *Harper's Magazine*, March, 1957, 68–74; Green, *The Establishment in Texas Politics*, 167–69.

28. Dugger, "What Corrupted Texas," 69–70.

29. Benjamin N. Woodson Papers: May 21 and 28, 1954; June 23 and 17, 1954; Nov. 16, 1954.

30. Benjamin N. Woodson Papers: May 2 and 3, 1955; Dec. 23, 24, and 25, Jan. 12, 1956; Dugger, "What Corrupted Texas," 69–70.

31. *Houston Chronicle*, Jan. 19, 1956; *Houston Post*, Jan. 18, 1956, reprinted in *Insurance Record*, Feb. 23, 1956.

32. Benjamin N. Woodson Papers, 1956: Jan. 30, Feb. 7, July 25, Oct. 15 and 25, Dec. 6, 7, and 14.

33. Benjamin N. Woodson Papers, 1956: Jan. 8, Feb. 6, 23, and 24, April 15 and 16, May 6 and 23.

34. Benjamin N. Woodson Papers: Various dates 1954 and 1955; July 1, 1955; Dec. 28, 1954; Dec. 10, 1955.

35. Benjamin N. Woodson interview no. 1.

36. Jesse H. Jones Papers, Personal File: Jesse H. Jones to Gus S. Wortham, Jan. 5, 1956, and Gus S. Wortham to Jesse H. Jones, Sept. 1, 1956; *Houston Post*, Feb. 23, 1956; Gus S. Wortham, Untitled speech at dedication of Jesse H. Jones Sr. High School, 1958, Speeches File, American General Archives.

37. American General Insurance Company, 1956 *Our 30th Anniversary AG Group*, 3; "American General Has Grown 30 Years," *Houston Press*, Aug. 21, 1956; *Houston Chronicle* Dec. 30, 1956.

38. Benjamin N. Woodson Papers: March 29–April 6, 1955; March 19, 1956; April 30, 1956; May 7, 14, and 31, 1956; June 1, 13, and 18, 1956; Jan. 21, 1957. Fellows, "The Baby Is Born," 218–20; Benjamin N. Woodson, "The Variable Annuity," reprinted in *The Variable Annuity Story*, Pamphlet (Houston: American General, 1967); Gus S. Wortham, Untitled speech on variable annuities, ca. 1960s, Gus S. Wortham Speeches File; "AG Acquires Two More," *Houston Chronicle*, May 6, 1967; *Wall Street Journal*, May 8, 1967.

39. Clinton Allen to Gus S. Wortham, March 13, 1958, Gus S. Wortham Scrapbook no. 2, 4.

40. Fellows, "The Baby Is Born," 188; American General Insurance Company, "To Our Directors," Aug. 23, 1957, Board of Directors, Minutes; Benjamin N. Woodson Papers: Benjamin N. Woodson to Gus S. Wortham, Memorandum, Dec. 24, 1956, and Benjamin N. Woodson, "Reflections on the Matter of the Knights Life Insurance Company," Feb. 21, 1957; Andrew Delaney, interview by author, May 10, 1991, Houston, Tex.; *National Underwriter*, Nov. 1, 1958; Benjamin N. Woodson Papers, Dec. 19, 22, 23, and 31, 1956, and Jan. 1 and 2 1957; American General Insurance Company, "Report to Directors," Nov. 14, 1959, Board of Directors, Minutes; Gus S. Wortham, "Report from the President," Feb. 19, 1960, American General Insurance Company, in *Annual Report to Stockholders, American General Companies, December 31, 1959* (Houston: 1960), 5.

41. "Union National/Knight's Life to Merge," *Houston Chronicle, Lincoln Star, Lincoln Journal*, Oct. 25, 1958; "Knights-Union Merger," *Eastern Underwriter*, Oct. 31, 1958; American General Insurance Company, "To Our Directors," Aug. 23, 1957, Board of Directors, Minutes; *Houston Post*, Jan. 17, and July 30, 1960; *Houston Chronicle*, Jan. 17, Feb. 21, and July 30, 1960.

42. Benjamin N. Woodson Papers, 1957: March 7, May 4, 20, and 27, July 2, 5, 9, 12, and 20–24, and Sept. 5, 9, 10, and 12, Oct. 1, 12, 23, and 25. American General Insurance Company, "A Report from the President," March 10, 1959, *Report to Stockholders*, Dec. 31, 1958, American General Records and Reports, American General Archives. Originally an "industrial" company, Home State became a "combination" company and retained its autonomy until 1962.

43. American General Investment Corporation, "Report to Directors of American General Investment Corporation," Aug. 26, 1958, Board of Directors, Minutes.

44. John Williams to Normal E. Risjord, Jan. 13, 1956, Gus S. Wortham Drawer; McGill, *All Lines Insurance*, 5.

45. Gus S. Wortham, "To Our Shareholders," Feb. 21, 1964 in *American General Group, Consolidated Statement, Annual Report, 31 December 1963* (Houston: 1964), 1.

46. *Annual Report*, 1963; Jesse H. Jones to Gus S. Wortham, July 15, 1952, Personal Files, Jesse H. Jones Papers.

47. Benjamin N. Woodson Papers: Sept. 4, 1954; May 26, 1956; July 26, 1957; Aug. 21, 1957. Late in 1957, George Butler brought Wortham, Barrow, and Woodson a proposal for the purchase of one of the Esperson Buildings in downtown Houston, and, although initially very interested in putting together a deal with Butler, Wortham decided it would cause bad feelings with Judge Elkins or the Jones's interest. (Benjamin N. Woodson Papers, Aug. 29 and 30, 1957)

48. "First City National Plans Huge Building, *Houston Post* and *Houston Chronicle*, July 13, 1958.

49. Kilman, "Hands Across the Canyon," 33–35; Carleton, *Red Scare!* 85.

50. "New Bank Building 'Expression of Faith,'" *Houston Post*, July 15, 1958.

51. "AG Builds New Building," *Houston Chronicle*, Aug. 26, 1960; *Houston Press*, Aug. 26, 1960; Gus S. Wortham, "To Our Stockholders," Feb. 17, 1961 in American General Group, *Consolidated Statement, American General Group, Annual Report*, Dec. 31, 1960 (Houston: 1961); "AG Looking Over Sites," *Houston Chronicle*, Sept. 25, 1960.

52. Christopher J. Castaneda and Joseph A. Pratt, *From Texas to the East: A Strategic History of Texas Eastern Corporation*, 132–35; *Houston Chronicle*, Feb. 21, 1956.

53. *Houston Post*, April 19, 1955; E. R. Barrow, Memorandum, May 17, 1955, Wortham Land and Cattle Co/Houston Country Club File, American General Archives; Jake Hershey, telephone interview with author, April 8, 1991, Houston, Tex.; L. O. Benson, telephone interview with author, April 30, 1991, Conroe, Tex.; *Houston Chronicle*, Oct. 5, 1952, March 14, 1954, and Aug. 24, Nov. 1, and March 14, 1960; American General Insurance Company, Memorandum to J. J. Hess from Executive Committee, Dec. 27, 1960, Merchants Park File, American General Archives; Milton Underwood to Gus S. Wortham, "Re: Merchants Park," etc.," Dec. 30, 1960, Merchants Park File. It was arranged that half of the sum for the Merchants Park purchase would be paid to Wortham through a six percent loan granted to Underwood by Knight's Life Insurance Company, the same Pittsburgh company that American General had acquired in June, 1960. Income tax records for Merchants Park, Inc. from the early 1970s show that while the corporation was still in existence, with Gus S. Wortham owning 100 percent of the stock, there had not been any activity with the corporation for some time.

54. DeWitt Gordon to H. D. Reynolds, July 17, 1957, Gus S. Wortham General Oil Information File, American General Archives; Various files related to oil properties ownership, American General Archives; Jean Gordon, interview with author, no. 1, March 26, 1990, Houston, Tex.

55. American General Archives: Gus S. Wortham to James A. Elkins, E. R. Barrow, A. H. Carruth, R. L. Mauk, H. D. Reynolds, Jan. 11, 1960, Jackrabbit II File; Gus S. Wortham to Herman and George Brown, Nov. 17, 1959, Jackrabbit File; Gus S. Wor-

tham to Leslie Appelt, Dec. 7, 1962, Parker Land File; E. R. Barrow to Gus S. Wortham, Dec. 9, 1959, Richard Rowles File.

56. E. R. Barrow to Gus S. Wortham, Dec. 9, 1959, Richard Rowles File; Wortham Land and Cattle Co. File; R-B-W Real Estate Syndicate, "Journal Entry to Set Up Land Cost and Notes Payable at 31 December 1956," Wortham Land and Cattle Co./Travis County Land File, American General Archives; "Wortham-Barrow Travis County Real Estate," n.d., Wortham Land and Cattle Co./Travis County Land File; David Barrow to E. R. Barrow, Aug. 9, 1958, Wortham Land and Cattle Co./Travis County Land File.

57. Wortham Land and Cattle Company File, American General Archives: R. H. Abercrombie to Pollard, Elkins, Smith, Wortham, Herman Brown, J. S. Abercrombie, Aug. 22, 1955, and J. C. Pollard to Gus S. Wortham. Invoice, Oct. 27, 1955.

58. Allen Carruth interview no. 1.

59. *Houston Post*, Aug. 16, 1955.

60. Auction Memorabilia, Gus S. Wortham Scrapbook no. 1, 66–68, 84; "Santa Gertrudis," *Humble Way*, 12–15.

61. Gus S. Wortham to R. W. Briggs, Jr., April 8, 1954, Nine Bar File, American General Archives; "Wortham and Evans . . . ," *Santa Gertrudis Journal*, 8–10.

62. Gus S. Wortham to J. F. Anderson, April 29, 1955, Randle Lake File; Gus S. Wortham Oral History, 97ff; Sterling C. Evans to Gus S. Wortham, 10/?/57, Wortham Land and Cattle Company File; "Investments, Wortham Land and Cattle Company," n.d., Wortham Land and Cattle Company, Nine Bar File.

63. Cover photograph, *Santa Gertrudis Journal*, Nov. 1959; *Houston Chronicle*, April 4, 1959; "Cattle Sale Draws Socialites," *Houston Chronicle*, April 14, 1959.

64. Gus S. Wortham to Sterling C. Evans, Oct. 25, 1960, Sterling C. Evans Papers.

65. "Wortham Foundation to Study Sterility in Beef Cattle," *American Breeds*, July, 1960, 24; *Houston Post*, July 8, 1960 (quote); *The Cattleman*, Aug., 1960.

66. Gus S. Wortham to Sterling C. Evans, Oct. 25, 1960.

67. *The Cattleman*, Aug., 1960.

68. *The Cattleman*, Aug., 1960; "Foundation is Announced by Gus S. Wortham," Unidentified newspaper clipping, n.d., Gus S. Wortham Scrapbook no. 2, 76; *Houston Post*, Sept. 28, 1961, July 13, 1985. The A&M connection was probably the result of Sterling Evans's strong ties with his alma mater as a member of the Texas A&M board, as well as of the location of the ranch.

CHAPTER 8. IN PURSUIT OF EMPIRES

1. In the early 1960s, Gus Wortham was trying to make two special acquisitions; one in insurance, the other in land. The two symbolized where he was going. The first was American General's successful pursuit of Commercial and Industrial Life, founded by Jesse H. Jones. Owning C&I made the circle complete, as Wortham now looked after his mentor's business. Wortham had become a builder, like Jones, seeking new opportunities for the expansion of his business. The second attempted acquisition was a piece of hallowed Texas land—ranch land of legendary writer J. Frank Dobie. Although his bid of $1.1 million for the 55,711 acres fell short, Wortham's attempt was part of his continuing search for and acquisition of large land holdings during this period.

These two events demonstrated the strength of Wortham's involvement in these pursuits, as well as his peculiar blend of southwestern and southern traits: an unflagging faith in growth and expansion motivated by ties of loyalty to men and to a place. (Fellows, "The Baby Is Born," 191–94; Pierre, S.D. *Weekly Reminder*, Jan. 26, 1961; *Houston Press*, Nov. 15, 1960.)

2. Gus S. Wortham, "To Our Stockholders," Feb. 16, 1962 in *Consolidated Statement, American General Group, Annual Report, 31 December 1961*, (Houston: 1962), 4.

3. *Annual Report*, 1961, 1, 7; *Consolidated Statement, American General Group, Annual Report, 31 December 1962*, (Houston: 1963) 1, 4–5; Benjamin N. Woodson, "The Back Page: Under One Flag," inserted in Benjamin N. Woodson Papers, Jan. 1, 1963.

4. "To Our Stockholders," Feb. 16, 1962, *Annual Report*, 1961, 7; "To Our Shareholders," Feb. 21, 1964, *Annual Report*, 1963, 6–7; Benjamin N. Woodson Papers, June 5, 1963.

5. Benjamin N. Woodson Papers, Feb. 16, 1961, Nov. 2, 1962, Jan. 1, 1963. Eventually, in 1984, American General did acquire Amicable, which was by then American-Amicable, as well as Republic Life of Dallas in its acquisition of Gulf United and its subsidiaries.

6. Benjamin N. Woodson Papers, Nov. 4, 1962; *Houston Post*, Nov. 14, 1962; *Houston Chronicle*, Nov. 14, 1962.

7. "To Our Shareholders," Feb. 21, 1964, *Annual Report*, 1963, 1; Fellows, "The Baby Is Born," 191–94; *Houston Post*, Sept. 2, 1964; *Houston Chronicle*, Sept. 2, 1964.

8. Fellows, "The Baby Is Born," 195–96; Benjamin N. Woodson, interview by author, no. 3, Aug. 9, 1991, Houston, Tex. During the depression the Maryland ran into great difficulty through too much business in one particular line. The company survived, however, through the offices of the Reconstruction Finance Corporation, headed by Jesse Jones. Many people believe that it was Jones's original prodding of Wortham that made Wortham finally go after the company in later years.

9. Fellows, "The Baby Is Born," 196.

10. Gus S. Wortham Oral History, 26.

11. Gus S. Wortham Oral History, 26; Benjamin N. Woodson Papers, Nov. 30, 1962.

12. Benjamin N. Woodson Papers, Jan. 19, 1963; Fellows, "The Baby Is Born," 199; "Stockholders Sought in Insurance Strategy," *Houston Chronicle*, May 20, 1964.

13. Andrew Delaney, Notes of interview with Kenneth Fellows, May 10, 1975, Kenneth Fellows Papers; Benjamin N. Woodson, Notes of Interview with Kenneth Fellows, May 12, 1976, Kenneth Fellows Papers; Benjamin N. Woodson Papers, June 28, 1963.

14. Benjamin N. Woodson Papers, Nov. 18, 19, and 21, 1963; Fellows, "The Baby Is Born," 196.

15. Benjamin N. Woodson interview notes, 12 May 1976; Benjamin N. Woodson Papers, Nov. 11 and 29 and Dec. 3, 1963.

16. Benjamin N. Woodson Papers, Dec. 11 and 13, 1963.

17. Benjamin N. Woodson Papers, Dec. 13 and 14, 1963.

18. Benjamin N. Woodson Papers, Dec. 27, 1963.

19. Benjamin N. Woodson Papers, Jan. 2, 1964; Fellows, "The Baby Is Born," 197–98.

20. Fellows, "The Baby Is Born," 197–98.

21. Fellows, "The Baby Is Born," 198–99; "Stockholders Sought in Insurance Strategy," *Houston Chronicle*, May 20, 1964.

22. Fellows, "The Baby Is Born," 199; Joe Flack interview no. 1.

23. Fellows, "The Baby Is Born," 200–201; *Houston Chronicle*, June 3, 1964; *Houston Post*, June 28, 1964; *Houston Post*, July 17, 1964; *Journal of Commerce*, July 28, 1964.

24. Fellows, "The Baby Is Born," 201; *Houston Chronicle*, "C&I Life and AG to Merge," Sept. 2, 1964, and "Congressman Critical of Insurance Merger," Sept. 3, 1964; "American General, Maryland Renew Negotiations," *Houston Post*, Oct. 2, 1964.

25. Fellows, "The Baby Is Born," 200–201; "American General Acquires Maryland Control," *Houston Post*, Sept. 12, 1964; *Houston Chronicle*, Aug. 12, 1964.

26. *Wall Street Journal*, Oct. 2, 1964; "AG, Md to Join," *Houston Chronicle*, Oct. 15, 1964; Fellows, "The Baby Is Born," 202.

27. "Formalities Over in Biggest Contested Stock Merger," Unidentified newspaper clipping, Nov. 22, 1964, Gus S. Wortham Scrapbook no. 3, 77.

28. "American General Acquires Maryland Control," Sept. 12, 1964, "Formalities Over in Biggest Contested Stock Merger," Nov. 22, 1964.

29. American General Group in New Home," *Insurance Graphic*, March 1965, Gus S. Wortham Scrapbook no. 3, 88.

30. "Annual Message from the Chairman," March 9, 1965 in *American General Insurance Company Annual Report 1964, 30 December 1964* (Houston: 1965), 14; "Annual Report of the Chairman, American General Insurance Company," April 12, 1966 in *American General Insurance Company Annual Report 1965* (Houston: 1966), 2–3, 15.

31. "To Our Stockholders," *Annual Report* 1965, 14–15.

32. "American General Plans Skyscrapers," *Insurance Graphic*, September, 1962; "Annual Message," *Annual Report*, 1964, 13. Of special concern to Wortham in the new building were the elevators. Reiterating the belief that the elevators gave a representative impression of the company, Wortham wanted them to have high ceilings, be well lighted, and have the look of prosperity. Also for the importance of first impressions, Wortham insisted on Italian marble for the entrance way and foyer of the building. (Fellows, "The Baby Is Born," 258–59.)

33. "Annual Message," *Annual Report*, 1964, 13.

34. "The Powers Behind American General," *Houston Chronicle*, March 14, 1965. In the story Wortham described himself as the "best picker of partners in the business," acknowledging the help and support he had received throughout his career from others. He valued the loyalty and continuity of personal relationships in the development of his business.

35. Clarence Hubbard, "A Breeze from the East," *Insurance Week*, March 26, 1965; *Southern Insurance*, July, 1965.

36. Dave Shanks, "A New Austin Investor, Or, Gus Wortham's Stake," *Austin American*, Sept. 20, 1962; *Houston Post*, Oct. 26, 1963.

37. Leslie Appelt, interview by author, Sept. 18, 1990, Houston, Tex.; *Houston Press*, March 6, 1964; *Houston Post*, March 6, 1964. Wortham later helped the man who was to develop the site, Leslie Appelt, secure other backers to bid successfully on the depot. And still later, Wortham would help bring together Appelt with the King Ranch interests and Exxon for the development of Kingwood, a planned community northeast of Houston.

38. Stokes, *Sterling C. Evans*, 59; Gus S. Wortham Oral History, 98.

39. *Alice (Tex.) Echo*, Sept. 23, 1962; *Texas Livestock Weekly*, Oct. 10, 1963; "Two

Texans Bid Spiritedly for Grazing Land in County," *The* (Santa Fe) *New Mexican*, Jan. 15, 1964; *Houston Post*, Jan 18, 1964; *Texas Livestock Weekly*, Jan. 23, 1964.

40. *West Texas Livestock Weekly*, April 23, 1964.

41. Will Harrison, "Inside the Capital," *The New Mexican*, n.d. March, 1964, Gus S. Wortham Scrapbook no. 3, 37; Robert Dietsch, "The Reason for so many 'affluent' new cattle raisers," *Houston Press*, n.d. March, 1964, Gus S. Wortham Scrapbook no. 3, 38.

42. Will Harrison, "Houston Tycoon Defaults Contracts," *The New Mexican*, Oct. 15, 1964; "Legal Issues Arise Out of Land Hearing," *The New Mexican*, July 12, 1967.

43. Sterling C. Evans interview no. 2.

44. "F&D Is Just Another Step in American Gen'l Growth," *Baltimore Sun*, March 19, 1969.

45. Gus S. Wortham Oral History, 98.

46. Gus S. Wortham to Sterling C. Evans, Oct. 25, 1960, Gus S. Wortham File, Sterling C. Evans Papers.

47. Jerri Jeidy, interview by author, no. 1, Oct. 20, 1989, Houston, Tex. By 1968, Wortham belonged to the Houston Club, Houston Country Club, Petroleum Club, Ramada Club, Coronado Club, Tejas Club, and Allegro Club, all in Houston; the Quarterback Club and Artillery Club of Galveston; and the Metropolitan Club of New York City. (*Houston Chronicle* Biographical Files, Feb. 1, 1968, Gus S. Wortham Drawer.)

48. "38 Santa Gertrudis Go for $116, 325 at Auction," *Houston Chronicle*, April 17, 1961; "Big Men, Big Money, Big Day at Nine Bar," *Houston Chronicle*, May 27, 1962.

49. *Houston Chronicle*, April 9, 1963, and April 13 and 14, 1964; *Houston Post*, April 14, 1964; *Denver Post*, April 14, 1964.

50. *Houston Chronicle*, April 13, 1965; "Chuck Wagon," *Fort Worth Star-Telegram*, n.d. April, 1965; *Houston Chronicle*, March 22, 1966; *Houston Post*, April 17 and 19, 1966; *Fort Worth Star-Telegram*, n.d., Gus S. Wortham Scrapbook no. 4, 10. The two-day event was being covered by journalist Hope Ridings Miller of *Diplomat* magazine, a friend of Mrs. Wortham's from Sherman.

51. *Houston Post*, April 18, 1967, and April 22 and 23, 1968; *Texas Magazine*, June 11, 1967; *Houston Chronicle*, April 22 and 23, 1968, and April 10, 14 and 15, 1969. Wortham had an excellent eye for cattle and took his purchasing seriously. In a 1962 memo he listed his opinions on the various auction bulls from the King Ranch. The memo provides a good indication of how much Wortham knew about the animals and how observant he was for the various traits that would indicate a good animal, such as blood line and weight gain. (Gus S. Wortham Memorandum, March 19, 1962, King Ranch Sale File, American General Archives.)

52. Fellows, "The Baby Is Born," 281; *Houston Chronicle*, Feb. 4 and April 29, 1962; *Houston Post*, 29 March and Sept. 28, 1961; *Fort Worth Star-Telegram*, Aug. 28, 1961; *Houston Post*, n.d., American General Scrapbook no. 2, American General Archives, 125.

53. *Houston Post*, Sept. 29, 1963, and September 10 and 26, 1964; *American Breeds*, May, 1964, 48. At the final session in 1964, Dr. Berry reported that his work had resulted in increasing the weaning weights of calves by 25 pounds through selection and improvement of the environment.

54. *Fort Worth Star-Telegram*, May 11, 1965; *San Antonio Enterprise*, May 18, 1965; *Houston Chronicle*, Aug. 18, 1965.

55. Allen Carruth interview no. 2.

56. University of Texas, *Daily Texan*, Oct. 19 and 20, 1962; Memorabilia, Gus S. Wortham Scrapbook no. 2, 141–42; *Houston Chronicle*, Nov. 20, 1962.

57. *Stephenville (Tex.) Empire*, Nov. 13, 1966; Morris Frank, *Houston Chronicle*, Nov. 9, 1966; "Gus Wortham: Beauty in a Sunset, a Sonnet or a Financial Statement," *Houston Chronicle*, Nov. 13, 1966.

58. "Woodson Elected President of American General," *Houston Post*, April 13, 1966.

59. Fellows, "The Baby Is Born," 212, 211–12, 215.

60. Fellows, "The Baby Is Born," 212–14.

61. Fellows, "The Baby Is Born," 214–16; *1966 Annual Report, American General Insurance Company* (Houston: 1967), 14. Acquisitions and mergers were increasing in the life insurance industry and American General was certainly riding that trend. In a piece for *Insurance* magazine on insurance marketing, Wortham, as might be expected, took in stride the changes occurring because of the "trend in business to ever-increasing bigness" and predicted "[w]e will see fewer—but stronger—better-equipped companies, and insurance agencies that will adapt to growing demands for larger and more complete insurance protection." ("Merger Process Is Dissected at Chicago Forum," *National Underwriter (Life)*, Nov. 7, 1964; *Insurance*, Jan. 28, 1967.)

62. "To Our Stockholders," March 22, 1968 in *1967 Annual Report, American General Insurance Company* (Houston: March 1968), 1.

63. "To Our Stockholders," March 22, 1968, *Annual Report*, 1967, 21; Benjamin N. Woodson Papers, April 22, 1967; *Houston Post*, April 26, 1967.

64. *Insurance Record*, May 18, 1967; *Wall Street Journal*, May 8, 1967; Fellows, "The Baby Is Born," 220; "VALIC Admitted Texas, Durrenberger Named," *Insurance*, March 9, 1968.

65. "To Our Stockholders," March 26, 1970 in *Forty-Fourth Annual Report to Stockholders, American General Insurance Company* [1969] (Houston: March 1970), 3; Gus S. Wortham Oral History, 39.

66. Fellows, "The Baby Is Born," 214–16; "A Big Board Stock Listing for American General," *Houston Chronicle*, Dec. 31, 1967.

67. "Success Story, Texas Style," *Finance*, December, 1967, 42–44; "The Spirit of 76," *Forbes*, June, 1968.

CHAPTER 9. SCOPE AND BREADTH

1. *New York Times*, June 11, 1967. This was a photo spread on the cattle auction at Winrock, Winthrop Rockefeller's Arkansas ranch.

2. Benjamin N. Woodson Papers, March 27, 1967.

3. Fellows, "The Baby Is Born," 237–41; "Success Story, Texas Style," *Finance*, December, 1967, 42; *Houston Post*, Aug. 17, 1967; "American General OKs Two Major Deals," *Houston Post*, Nov. 30, 1967.

4. Fellows, "The Baby Is Born," 242–43; "Cal-West Group to Fight Merger," *Houston Chronicle*, Aug. 22, 1967; "Cal-West Director Opposes AG Merger," *Houston Post*,

Aug. 23, 1967; "Cal-West Committee Opposes Merger Plan," *National Underwriter*, Sept. 16, 1967.

5. "Cal West Vote Opposes Firm's Sale," *Houston Chronicle*, Oct. 5, 1967; "Cal West Director Opposes AG Merger," Aug. 23, 1967; "AG Holders Back Mergers," *Wall Street Journal*, Nov. 30, 1967; "American General Oks Two Major Deals," *Houston Post*, Nov. 30, 1967; Fellows, "The Baby Is Born," 243.

6. Fellows, "The Baby Is Born," 243–44; "AG Lost $121 Million Bid to get Cal West," *Houston Chronicle*, Dec. 21, 1967; "Cal West Rejects AG Merger," *Houston Chronicle*, Dec. 26, 1967. Having learned a lesson, at their own next stockholders meeting in April, 1968, the management of American General pushed a vote on a measure to prevent the kind of action that Wortham believed had sunk the American General–Cal-West amalgamation. The AG stockholders voted to end cumulative voting rights for directors. Such rights allowed a shareholder to multiply his or her vote by the number of directorships being voted on and then cast the total number for one director or a selected group of directors. Woodson favored abolishing cumulative voting rights because he believed the majority should rule. ("AG Ends Cumulative Voting Rights," *Houston Chronicle*, April 23, 1968; "Co. of AG Faces Big Losses Because of Riots," *Houston Post*, April 24, 1968.)

7. "A Big Board Listing for AG," *Houston Chronicle*, Dec. 31, 1967; "Notable Gains of American General Cited in '67 Report," *Insurance Record*, Feb. 8, 1968; "To Our Stockholders," *Annual Report*, 1967, 1; *Annual Report*, 1967, 14.

8. "TX Firm Buys 500,000 Shares of Cal West," *Fresno (Calif.) Bee*, Feb. 16, 1968; *Wall Street Journal*, April 1, 1968; *Annual Report*, 1967, 15 (quote).

10. Buenger and Pratt, *But Also Good Business*, 185–202; John T. Jones, Jr., interview; Benjamin N. Woodson Papers, Jan 8 and July 17, 1963; John L. Whitmore, Interview by Walter Buenger, Sept. 17, 1982, Oral History of the Houston Economy, University of Houston; J. Howard Creekmore, Interview by Joseph Pratt and Walter Buenger, Sept. 17, 1982, Oral History of the Houston Economy; Thomas McDade, Interview by Joseph Pratt and Walter Buenger, June 22, 1983, Oral History of the Houston Economy. There was reason to believe that Wortham was behind the appointment of lawyer Marvin Collie to head the bank in 1958. But Collie, with no banking background, did not earn the confidence of the old guard running the bank and resigned two years later. Collie's father had worked with Gus Wortham at the State Insurance Board and later for John L. Wortham and Son. His son, a tax lawyer for Vinson, Elkins was well known and liked by Wortham. (Pratt/Buenger interview with Thomas McDade.)

11. John T. Jones, Jr., interview; Benjamin N. Woodson Papers, July 17, 1963; Buenger and Pratt, *But Also Good Business*, 203–206. Merger negotiations between the NBC and TNC groups were often held at Wortham's Lamar Hotel apartment. Arguments dragged on over succession and Wortham eventually got restless with Anderson's contentiousness over what Wortham thought were minor points. At one point, Wortham lost his temper with Anderson—the only time he could remember that happening in his whole business career.

12. Buenger and Pratt, *But Also Good Business*, 246–49; Benjamin N. Woodson, Interview by Joseph Pratt, June 18, 1985, Oral History of the Houston Economy.

13. "Insurance Firm Acquires Contract of Texas NB of C," *American Banker*, March

20, 1968; Buenger and Pratt, *But Also Good Business*, 252; Benjamin N. Woodson, Interview by Joseph Pratt.

14. *American Banker*, Dec. 28, 1970; Buenger and Pratt, *But Also Good Business*, 252–53; *Houston Chronicle*, March 1, 1972; *Temple (Tex.) Telegram*, March 2, 1972. In 1972, American General issued around 1.5 million nonvoting shares of a new class B stock which it exchanged for its voting shares in the Texas National Bank of Commerce. These shares were then sold to unrelated third parties who exchanged them for voting shares. ("To Our Stockholders," March 31, 1973 in *Forty-Seventh Annual Report to Stockholders, American General Insurance Company* [1972] [Houston: March, 1973], 3.)

15. "Company of AG Faces Big Losses Because of Riots," *Houston Post*, April 24, 1968; Joseph Califano to Lyndon B. Johnson, Oct. 7. 1968, Office Files of John Macy, Lyndon B. Johnson Library; "2 Texans Named to Riot Insurance Advisory Board," *Houston Chronicle*, Oct. 15, 1968; Gus S. Wortham Oral History, 52–53.

16. Fellows, "The Baby Is Born," 221–24. Begun in 1926, Van Strum and Towne was also a pioneer in the formation of a business conglomerate. After three decades of successful operation in investment advising, in 1950 the company merged several diverse companies under one holding company, including mutual funds. The mutual fund concept boomed and Van Strum and Towne began divesting Channing of all its non–mutual fund operations, consolidated the funds they owned, and by proxy fight, obtained another fund. Then in 1956, Channing acquired its own direct sales force, King Merritt and Company, the largest sales operation devoted to mutual fund shares. By 1965 it was the Channing Company, underwriter and distributor of the five domestic Channing Funds. In the late 1960s, as mutual funds and insurance companies were forming profitable alliances, Channing purchased the Tower Group of insurance companies.

17. Fellows, "The Baby Is Born," 221–24. In 1968 the Channing group included the Channing funds and their distributor, the Channing Company; a major share of the Canadian Channing Corp., Ltd., manager of the Canadian Channing Funds; Channing Service Corp., sponsor of the Variable Investment Plan; Emmett A. Larkin Co., Inc., a member of the Pacific Coast Stock Exchange; Chanstat Services, Inc., the stockholders service for Channing Company; Van Strum and Towne, Inc.,; a controlling interest in Federal Life and Casualty; and Agricultural Insurance Company. Between 1969 and 1976, AG divested itself of the two insurance companies, Emmett A. Larkin and Canadian Channing. (Fellows, "The Baby Is Born," 224–26; *Annual Report*, 1969, 17.)

18. Fellows, "The Baby Is Born," 225; American General Insurance Company Annual Reports to Stockholders [1970], 15; Forty-Seventh [1972], 10; Forty-Eighth, [1973], 10; Forty-Ninth, [1974], 12–13; Fiftieth, [1975], 8.

19. *Wall Street Journal*, July 10, 1968; *Houston Post*, July 10, 1968; *National Underwriter*, July 18, 1967, Benjamin N. Woodson Scrapbook, American General Archives; "Southwest Life's Plan Fought," *Dallas Morning News*, July 18, 1968; *Houston Post*, July 23, 1968. Gulf, headquartered in Dallas, had been ready to register its offer of stock for Southwestern shares when the AG deal was announced. The *Dallas Times Herald* declared it was a "sound decision" to drop the merger and that Dallas was now rivaling Hartford as an insurance capital. (*Dallas Times Herald*, July 25, 1968.)

20. *Wall Street Journal*, April 1 and 17, 1968; *Annual Report*, 1967, 15; *Annual Report*, 1968, 3; Fellows, "The Baby Is Born," 244–45; "Cal-West Bid Leak Hinted," *San Francisco Examiner*, Nov. 26, 1968. There was "nothing more fascinating" in local business circles, the *Sacramento Bee* claimed, than American General's position regarding Cal-West: AG's one-third ownership in effect barred anyone else from making a takeover while Wortham and Woodson denied they were trying to gain full control. The first ten percent was bought, Woodson told the press, because the stock was priced right, the second ten percent to protect the company from takeover by a third party, and after that, enough to protect the company from being acquired at too low a price. ("Texas Firm Puts Cal-West Away from Bidders Reach," *Sacramento Bee*, Nov. 17, 1968.)

21. "Texas Firm Buys Into Two Concerns," *San Francisco Examiner*, Aug. 7, 1968; *Wall Street Journal*, Sept. 11, 1968; "AG to Buy Channing Financial," *Los Angeles Times*, Sept. 11, 1968; "AG Considers Move Into Leasing," *Houston Post*, Oct. 6, 1968; "A Look at AG Life," *Baltimore Sun*, Oct. 22, 1968; "AG Will Seek NYSE Listing," *Houston Post*, Nov. 30, 1968; "AG Seeks Stock Exchange Listing," *Insurance Record*, Jan. 9, 1969 (quote).

22. "To Our Stockholders," March 24, 1969, *Annual Report*, 1968, 3; *Annual Report*, 1968, 13, 24.

23. Fellows, "The Baby Is Born," 227–30.

24. Fellows, "The Baby Is Born," 230–33. Woodson and Wortham determined to fly to Baltimore immediately upon talking to Neal. Both had forgotten, however, that a once-unfriendly stockholder of Cal-West was scheduled to be in Houston the next day to negotiate. So, Woodson stayed to woo the Cal-West man; Wortham went to Baltimore that very evening. Arriving at the airport at 10:30 P.M., Wortham met with Neal and his associates in his hotel room until 1:00 A.M. Sixteen phone calls between Baltimore and Houston were made as Woodson and Wortham conferred on the deal. By noon the following day, all had agreed to an affiliation of F&D with American General; at 5:00 P.M. the F&D board in Baltimore and the AG executive committee approved the merger.

25. Fellows, "The Baby Is Born," 233–35; *Wall Street Journal*, Feb. 14, 1969; "Security Quits Takeover," *Baltimore Sun*, Feb. 26, 1969; *Houston Post*, March 26, 1969; "F&D Plans Merger with Houston Firm," *Baltimore Sun*, Feb. 2, 1969; *Baltimore Daily Record*, n.d., American General Scrapbook no. 4, 113; "FTC Checks into Merger and Plan on F&D," *Baltimore Sun*, March 21, 1969.

26. Sam Weiner, "American General to Push Its Growth This Spring," *Houston Post*, March 23, 1969.

27. "AG Counts Its Blessings," *Sacramento Bee*, April 22, 1969.

28. *San Francisco Examiner*, March 27, 1969; *Houston Post*, May 9, 1969; "VALIC Moves Headquarters to Houston," *Washington Star*, May 13, 1969.

29. "AG to Participate in Industrial Park Development," *Houston Chronicle*, Oct. 6, 1969; "Two Big Firms Get Together," *Tacoma (Wash.) Tribune*, Oct. 5, 1969; "Amer. Genl.'s Net Edges Up," *National Underwriter*, Aug. 29, 1969; *Annual Report*, 1969, 17; "Insurance Firm's Earnings Down," *Houston Post*, Feb. 10, 1970; *Houston Chronicle*, Feb. 11, 1970.

30. *Houston Post*, May 25, 1968.

31. Feagin, *Free Enterprise City*, 142.

32. Benjamin N. Woodson Papers, April 18, 1967; Annual Report, 1967; WHCF Name File, LBJ Archives: Marvin Watson to Gus S. Wortham, Dec. 21, 1966; List of Stag Luncheon Guests, June 12, 1968, Joseph Califano to Lyndon B. Johnson, Jan. 22, 1968.

33. J. W. Macy to Lyndon B. Johnson, Memorandum, July 12, 1968, WHCF Name File, LBJ Archives; *Washington Daily News*, May 28, 1968; White House, Telegram to Gus S. Wortham, June 20, 1968, Gus S. Wortham Scrapbook no. 4, 90; Edward Stumpf interview no. 1; Hubert Humphrey to Gus S. Wortham, Aug. 5, 1968, American General Archives. One of the gifts sent Wortham was a pen like the one Johnson used to sign the bills from the first session of the "prudent and progressive" 89th Congress, which LBJ called the "greatest in American History."

34. Benjamin N. Woodson Papers, Feb. 15 and 18, 1966; Edward Stumpf interview no. 1.

35. Banks, *Money, Marbles and Chalk*, 195, 224, 195.

36. Conaway, *The Texans*, 34.

37. Edward Stumpf interview no. 1; John Connally to Gus S. and Lyndall Finley Wortham, Oct. 7, 1971, Gus S. Wortham Scrapbook no. 4, 124.

38. Conaway, *The Texans*, 13–14.

39. John Connally, Houston, Texas, Notes of telephone interview with author, Sept. 19, 1991.

40. Gus S. Wortham Oral History, 77, 139.

41. B. F. Godfrey to Gus S. Wortham, Sept. 15, 1969, North Texas State University File, American General Archives; Gus S. Wortham to Sam Winters, Sept. 10, 1970, North Texas State University File. Sam Winters, law partner of Ed Clark, sent Wortham a *Dallas News* editorial explaining an alleged radical pamphlet which included articles by Malcolm X and Herbert Marcuse, that was given to freshmen students at North Texas. "I am shocked to read 'A Shocking Start for a Freshman'—this would have been unbelievable a few years ago," Wortham replied. "I will urge the board to take positive action."

42. Gus S. Wortham Oral History, 80.

43. Gus S. Wortham Oral History, 134, 153–54.

44. Gus S. Wortham Oral History, 153–54.

45. Wintz, "Blacks in Houston," 34; Lester Randle interviews no. 1 and 2; Feagin, *Free Enterprise City*, 243–44. Another time, shortly before Houston integrated its public accommodations, Wortham had sent Randle to the Rice Hotel with a delivery for Jesse Jones. When the bellboy refused to allow Randle inside, he returned to Wortham, who immediately marched himself and Randle back to the hotel and spoke to the manager and Jones.

46. Gus S. Wortham Oral History, 153–54; Lester Randle interview no. 1; Francis Lowenheim, "False Crescendo," *Texas Monthly*, February, 1986, 168; Feagin, *Free Enterprise City*, 242.

47. Gus S. Wortham Oral History, 141. *Houston Chronicle*, July 7, 1966; *Houston Post*, Sept. 27, 1967. Jones Hall, the home of the Houston Symphony, was built by Jesse Jones's Houston Endowment and then given to the city. Because there had been no suitable venue before for such attractions as the Bolshoi Ballet or the Berlin Phil-

harmonic, they bypassed the city, "detracting," said arts critic Ann Holmes, "from its reputation as a metropolitan center." The SPA would not only bring such events, but keep Jones Hall occupied for the city.

48. Roussel, *Houston Symphony Orchestra*, 87, 218–23.

49. *Houston Chronicle*, July 2, 1969; Roussel, Houston Symphony 187. Holmes pointed out the executive committee was a group elected from the board, while the other was appointed. But Hubert Roussel rationalized in his history of the symphony that the finance committee was the "administrative core of the symphony enterprise." Gus Wortham had been involved with that committee and served as its chairman from 1947 to 1970. "It was a record unique for the venture. Mr. Wortham's contributions to the symphony cause, both material and advisory have been vital, and the orchestra has not known a more faithful or generous friend," Roussel said. It was well understood that for many years, Gus Wortham would write a check to cover all or part of the orchestra's deficit at the end of the season.

50. "Suit by SEC Charges American General Ads Broke Security Laws," *Wall Street Journal*, Jan. 16, 1970; "Of Ads and Equities," *National Underwriter*, Feb. 21, 1970; "SEC Settles Its Suit Over Ads of American General Insurance Company," *Wall Street Journal*, Dec. 18, 1970. The SEC claimed that, rather than just corporate advertisements announcing American General's ownership of Channing, these ads were in fact sales prospectuses, but without the required financial statements.

51. "FTC Hits Insurance Merger," *Baltimore News-American*, Feb. 4, 1971; "FTC Action is Surprise," *Baltimore Sun*, Feb. 4, 1971; *Houston Chronicle*, Feb. 4, 1971; "American General Bucks FTC on F&D Merger," *National Underwriter*, Oct. 8, 1971; *Baltimore Sun*, March 17 and 18, 1972.

52. "To Our Stockholders," March 24, 1972, *Forty-Sixth Annual Report to Stockholders American General Insurance Company* [1971] (Houston: March 1972), 3; *Annual Report*, 1972, 12; *Annual Report*, 1974, 13; *American General Insurance Company 1976 Annual Report* (Houston: March 1977), 6. By 1976, American General owned 17 open end funds and three closed end funds.

53. "New, Different Bond Funds Stirs Interest," *Baltimore Sun*, Sept. 27, 1970; *Houston Chronicle*, Aug. 6, 1970; *Houston Chronicle*, Dec. 6, 1970; "American General Plans to Add to 33.3% of State in Cal-West," *Wall Street Journal*, Dec. 7, 1970; *Journal of Commerce*, Dec. 8, 1970.

54. Harold S. Hook interview.

55. Benjamin N. Woodson interview no. 3, Notes of Interview by author, July 31, 1991; Harold S. Hook interview; Fellows, "The Baby Is Born," 245.

56. "Cal West Profit Up Sharply," *San Francisco Chronicle*, Jan. 27, 1971; "AG Plan for Cal West Okeyed by California Insurance Commissioner," *Wall Street Journal*, Feb. 3, 1971; *Wall Street Journal*, July 20, 1971; *Modesto (Calif.) Bee*, July 29, 1971; "AG Owns 37% of Cal West," *San Francisco Chronicle*, Dec. 22, 1971; "AG Begins to Buy Cal West," *Sacramento Bee*, Nov. 22, 1971; "AG Near Control of Cal Western," *Los Angeles Times*, Dec. 27, 1971.

However involved in Cal-West, American General was still looking for companies in Texas. The *Wall Street Journal*, in June, 1971, reported that a feasibility "study" was being conducted on a proposed affiliation of American General with its neighboring insurance giant, American National in Galveston. The combination would result in an entity with over $22 million of life insurance in force. *Chronicle* journalist Tommy

Thompson speculated that the merger would create a holding company worth about $3.5 billion; a big company able to better compete with other, even bigger companies. Each company named a panel to study such an affiliation. By October, however, talks had broken off between the two companies. ("American General and American National Affiliation Feasibility Study," *Wall Street Journal*, May 28, 1971; *Houston Chronicle*, May 28, 1971.)

57. "AG Earnings Up," *Insurance Record*, Feb. 17, 1972; "To Our Stockholders," March 24, 1972, *Annual Report*, 1971, 3; "AG Investment Expands Operations in Dallas–Ft. Worth," *Financial Trend*, March 4, 1971; "To the Shareowners," March 19, 1973, *1972 Annual Report, California-Western States Life Insurance Company*, March, 1972, 3.

58. *Houston Chronicle*, Aug. 2, 1972; "American General Earnings Hit Record $45 Million," *Journal of Commerce*, Nov. 1, 1972; "AG Insurance Begins 2nd Building," *Houston Post*, July 30, 1972.

59. *Houston Post*, May 8, 1972; *Wall Street Journal*, Aug. 2, 1972; *Annual Report*, 1972, 3; Harold S. Hook interview.

60. "Program for Dedication," Gus S. Wortham Scrapbook no. 4, 141.

61. Sterling C. Evans interview no. 3.

62. Harold S. Hook interview.

63. Allen Carruth, interview by author, no. 3, Aug. 12, 1991, Houston, Tex.

64. Gus Wortham Oral History, 134.

65. *Southern Insurance*, Nov. 1972; "Retirement at 81 Won't Slow Down Life of Insurance Executive Wortham," *Houston Chronicle*, Nov. 5, 1972; Harold S. Hook interview.

66. "Elizabeth Reap Named Assistant Secretary at AG," *Houston Chronicle*, Nov. 26, 1972; *Houston Chronicle*, Dec. 28, 1972.

67. "3000 at Birthday Party for Ima Hogg," *Houston Post*, Dec. 16, 1972; *Houston Chronicle*, Dec. 16, 1972.

CHAPTER 10. DEATH OF A SOUTHWESTERN GENTLEMAN

1. Lyndall Finley Wortham Interview, May 18, 1976; Dr. Lloyd Gregory, interview by author, Sept. 12, 1990, Houston, Tex.

2. Lloyd Gregory interview. Lyndall Wortham, too, had had several health-related problems, including operations on her arthritic knees, and in 1974 she had a pacemaker inserted.

3. "FTC Says Has Jurisdiction," *Baltimore Sun*, Dec. 13, 1972; "FTC Reasserts Antitrust Power in Insurance Merger," *Wall Street Journal*, Dec. 14, 1972; *Insurance Advocate*, Dec. 23, 1972; *Houston Post*, June 6, 1973. In 1973, American General tried to get an injunction to keep the FTC from pressing its antitrust complaint, but U.S. District Court Judge Woodrow Seals of Houston refused to grant the injunction, saying it was the FTC's duty to protect the public from mergers which might prove monopolistic.

Mayo Thompson, a Houston maritime lawyer from Newton Rayzor's firm, was appointed an FTC commissioner 1973. Thompson was one of Wortham's young protégés, a Santa Gertrudis breeder and involved in the Nine Bar operations. Thompson had himself removed from any of the commission's dealings with American General and said that, although they talked often, Wortham never discussed the pending case with him. (Mayo Thompson, interview by author, May 1, 1990.)

4. *Houston Post*, Jan. 16, 1973.

5. "AG Seeks Cal-West Stock," *Journal of Commerce*, Feb. 7, 1973; *Wall Street Journal*, Feb. 5 and 7, 1973; "Cal-West Again at Crossroads," *Sacramento Bee*, Feb. 7, 1973; "Texas Firm Wins Control of Cal-West," *Sacramento Bee*, Feb. 17, 1973; "And the Cal-Western Stock Fight," *Houston Post*, March 4, 1973.

6. Benjamin N. Woodson interview no. 3; *Sacramento Bee*, April 25, 1973; *Fresno (Calif.) Bee*, March 25, 1973; *Annual Report*, 1972, 37.

7. "AG Buys Ten Percent of Own Common," *Wall Street Journal*, April 16, 1973; "AG Insurance Says SEC Clears Tender Bid," *Wall Street Journal*, April 18, 1973; *Annual Report*, 1973, 3; *Baltimore Sun*, Jan. 3, 1974.

8. "$39 Million Total Community Planned for NW Harris County," *Houston Chronicle*, March 11, 1973; "AG's Oldest Subsidiary," *A-G View*, April–May, 1972, American General Archives.

9. Fred Nahas, "Tribute to Gus S. Wortham," May 22, 1973, Gus S. Wortham Drawer, American General Archives.

10. "Gus S. Wortham Named Key Houstonian of the Year," *Houston Post*, May 25, 1968. At the 1967 fete his friend and partner Wright Morrow said Gus Wortham had been an important citizen for 40 years. Wortham responded humbly by claiming that Houston had been "abundantly good," rewarding him "a hundredfold for anything I have done or tried to do."

11. Gus S. Wortham to Allen Carruth, Feb. 27, 1973, American General Archives.

12. Sterling C. Evans interview no. 1. Wortham tried to secure the financial prosperity of his daughter's marriages, too. Doing what he knew how to do best for them, he was instrumental in funding business propositions for both of their young husbands. Lyndall and her husband went into the grain elevator business in Tallulah, Louisiana, as partners with Sterling Evans. Wortham and Evans also sold the young couple the Crescent plantation. For Diana, who had also married young and precipitously, Wortham backed a real estate development project her husband was involved with in Charlotte, North Carolina.

13. Gus S. Wortham, "Memorandum," March 2, 1973, Gus S. Wortham Financial Papers Files, American General Archives.

14. Gus S. Wortham to Edward C. Davis, Nov. 19, 1973, Gus S. Wortham Files, American General Archives.

15. *Houston Post*, Jan. 29, 1973.

16. Jake Hershey interview.

17. Marie Phelps McAshan, *On the Corner of Main and Texas, A Texas Legacy*, 58–59; Allen Carruth interview no. 1; Sterling C. Evans interview no. 1; Gus S. Wortham Donation Files, American General Archives; Jake Hershey interview. In his later years, records show that Wortham financed the college education of a number of young people who were either children of friends or employees, or were recommended to him by Sterling Evans or others. He was particularly interested in young people who had specific goals in mind; practical careers and courses of study rather than general humanities programs.

18. Theodore Law to L. F. McCollum, Dec. 23, 1969, 1969 Contributions File, Gus S. Wortham Drawer, American General Archives; Barbecue for Racial Harmony Crusade, 1969 Contributions File; Dr. Harry Ransom to Mr. and Mrs. G. S. Wortham, June 19, 1969, 1969 Contributions File; Various correspondence, 1969 Contributions File;

1971 Donations File, Gus S. Wortham Drawer; Gus S. Wortham 1973 Contributions File, Gus S. Wortham Drawer.

19. Contributions Lists and Files, 1971, 1972, 1973, 1974, Gus S. Wortham Drawer, American General Archives.

20. Invitation, Newcomen Dinner, April 29, 1974, Gus S. Wortham Scrapbook no. 4, 163. Woodson's history, *A Financial Services Supermarket*, began with the story of his "long lunch hour" with Wortham in 1953. It concentrated on the company's founding and on Wortham's abilities and the favorable choices he made in building the company Woodson calling Wortham both his "mentor and guide."

21. Woodson, *A Financial Services Supermarket*, 26; *Houston Chronicle*, ? May, 1974, Gus S. Wortham Scrapbook no. 5, 164.

22. Rev. John Lancaster, "Pastor's Letter," *First Presbyterian*, May 10, 1974, American General Archives; Gus S. Wortham to Rev. John W. Lancaster, Dec. 1, 1969, Personal Contributions and Donations, 1969 File, American General Archives.

23. "Cowboy Boots and Cacharels," *Houston Post*, Oct. 10, 1974; "From Quiche to Barbecue—That's a Wortham Cattle Auction Weekend, *Houston Chronicle*, Oct. 8, 1974; "Gus S. Wortham Sells Nine Bar to Cox Enterprises," *Houston Post*, Dec. 29, 1974; *Houston Chronicle*, Dec. 29, 1974; "Cox Enterprises Purchases Wortham's 9 Bar Ranch," *Weekly Western Livestock Journal*, Jan. 13, 1975.

24. "To Our Stockholders," *Annual Report*, 1974, 3, 52; *Anaheim (Calif.) Bulletin*, Sept. 17, 1974; *Financial Trend*, Jan. 20, 1975.

25. "AG Asks Stock Swap with Cal-West," *Houston Chronicle*, June 11, 1975; Harold S. Hook interview; *Insurance*, July, 1975.

26. Harold S. Hook interview.

27. *Houston Chronicle*, Feb. 21, 1975. And Wortham demonstrated his loyalty to friends when he and Ben Woodson joined other well-wishers who welcomed Connally home in April after his trial and acquittal on charges of accepting a political bribe. ("John F. Connally Acquitted," *Houston Chronicle*, April 19, 1975.)

28. "Houston Group Unites to back Amendment 4," *Houston Post*, Oct. 27, 1972; "Pro-revision donations low," *Houston Post*, October 7, 1975. The 1972 committee also included representatives of the AFL–CIO, the League of Women Voters, and State Senator Barbara Jordan.

29. Lyndall was neither the only, nor the most accomplished writer in the Wortham clan. June Davis Arnold, daughter of Gus's youngest sister, Cad (called "The Baby" by the family), published *Applesauce*, a somewhat autobiographical novel, in 1967. Gus and Lyndall were prominent in the local press publicity for the book. Arnold, who had lived away from Houston for a number of years, returned in the 1980s to write *Baby Houston*, based on her mother's life and the almost obsessively close relationship between "the Baby," called Eudora Yancey in the book, and her youngest daughter, Hallie (June Arnold herself). Although the characters' names are changed, the book follows June's mother's life after her first husband died in the late 1930s and she returned to Houston with her two small daughters. Gus Wortham, Oscar Yancey in the book, is a central character and comes across as a rather staid wheeler-dealer and Houston business tycoon upon whom the Baby depends for financial support and to whom she looks for guidance. Oscar is often thwarted by his nieces and his sister, but remains close to and supportive of his family. Lyndall Wortham, "the Duchess," does not come off so well; Arnold portrays her as self-involved and jealous of Oscar's relationship with his

sister and nieces. The book was published after Arnold's death in 1987. (*Houston Chronicle*, Feb. 26, 1967, May 18, 1987.)

30. Lyndall Finley Wortham Interview, May 18, 1976; *Houston Post*, March 31, 1930.

31. "Wortham Honored at Big Club Party," *Houston Post*, Sept. 30, 1975.

32. "They Built Houston: Portrait of an Optimist," *Houston Town and Country*, Dec., 1975, 18ff.

33. "They Built Houston," *Houston Town and Country*, Dec., 1975; Benjamin N. Woodson interview no. 3. *Houston Chronicle*, Sept. 16 and 18, 1975. During the park construction in 1975, however, relatives of people buried in Magnolia disputed the fact that there were no graves in the north end and five citizens filed suit to stop the park construction, claiming there were graves on the site.

34. Lyndall Finley Wortham Interview, May 18, 1976.

35. Gus S. Wortham, Various Medicare and Personal Bills Files, American General Archives; Lloyd Gregory interview. History.

36. Harold S. Hook interview.

37. Harold S. Hook interview.

38. Harold S. Hook interview.

39. "Gus Wortham, Longtime Civic Leader, Dies at 85," *Houston Chronicle*, Sept. 2, 1976; *Galveston Daily News*, Sept. 2, 1976; "Leaders Mourn Death of Gus S. Wortham, *Houston Post*, Sept. 2, 1976.

40. "Lyndall Wortham," *Houston Post*, July 17, 1980.

41. "Arts Panel Rejects Wortham Fountain," *Houston Chronicle*, Nov. 22, 1977; "Water Works, Wortham Fountain," *Houston Chronicle*, May 31, 1981; "Wortham Funds Benefit the Arts," *Chronicle*, July 13, 1985.

42. Allen Carruth interview no. 3.

43. Blankenhorn, "Gus Wortham."

44. Cousins, "A High Priest," see n. 49, ch. 1.

Bibliography

BIBLIOGRAPHIC ESSAY

By far the largest and most valuable collection of information and documentation concerning Gus S. Wortham and the institutions with which he was involved is contained in the archives of the American General Corporation, under the direction of corporate archivist Judy Brumbelow. This collection includes the official records of all the various corporate entities which became part of American General; all corporate publications produced by American General and its subsidiaries; required government documents, such as Convention Statements, 10K Forms and state papers; shareholder materials; statistical supplements; schedules of securities and security portfolios; press releases from 1968 to the present; Records and Reports, 1953–67; personal and corporate photographs; acquisition and merger correspondence files; corporate memorabilia; and materials relating to Wortham's successors, Benjamin N. Woodson and Harold S. Hook.

One large filing cabinet drawer labeled "Gus S. Wortham" contains biographical sketches, papers from his ranches, correspondence, contributions files, and assorted letters, documents, or memorabilia associated with Wortham.

Some of this material comes from the contents of almost a dozen and half record boxes containing correspondence and personal and business documents of Wortham and his father that are also part of the archives. These boxes were held in storage at American General for several years. This group includes records regarding: the myriad of Wortham's land holdings and oil lease properties, including those he owned with the R-B-W Syndicate and others, Houston

Country Club, land at FM 1960, and land owned with B. F. Carruth; Wortham Land and Cattle Company files with information on Randle Lake, Nine Bar, and other ranching properties, and files regarding Santa Gertrudis cattle breeding activities; various companies owned by Wortham or in which he was involved, including Longhorn Portland Cement, Merchants Park, and files regarding the various Smith Brothers' entities including Century Investment Corporation; private income tax returns and related documents; papers regarding Wortham's partnership with B. F. Carruth; securities files; trust papers for family members; stock holdings; medical expenses and financial statements; and papers and correspondence about the Southeast Underwriters' case, Bailey–Van Nuys Bill, and Texas Insurance Advisory Committee. Two boxes contain papers and letters belonging primarily to John L. Wortham, and these are listed as the John L. Wortham Papers in this bibliography. These papers date primarily from the mid-1910s to the 1920s. This is a truncated listing of topics of the documents, correspondence, memoranda, and related materials in these boxes. The bulk of this material dates from the 1940s through the 1960s.

The archives also have eleven Wortham Correspondence Binders containing letters from and to Gus S. Wortham, John L. Wortham, and Lyndall Finley Wortham and her family, dating from 1864 through 1930. Much of this material was given to the archives by a relative of Mrs. Wortham and provides insight into her life before her marriage.

Another source of information is the Lyndall Wortham Seymour collection, a group of letters, most of them from John L. Wortham to Gus S. Wortham, formerly in the possession of Wortham's daughter. These letters have been integrated into the correspondence binders, but are cited in this text separately.

Of central importance to the writing of this manuscript have been the dozen Gus S. Wortham Scrapbooks, Nine Bar and ranch scrapbooks, and related photographic scrapbooks and the twenty American General Scrapbooks contained in the archives. The primary contents of these scrapbooks are clippings dating from the founding of American General through the present, from newspapers and periodicals all over the country. In addition, especially in the Wortham and early American General volumes, some documents and memorabilia are also included. The bulk of these clippings are dated from the 1940s through the present, and all significant events in the history of American General are covered. The newspapers and periodicals from which articles were included in these books, and which the author has used most significantly in this manuscript, are:

Austin American
American Banker
American Breeds
Austin Statesman
Baltimore News-American
Baltimore Sun
Best's Fire and Casualty News
Best's Life Insurance Reports
Best's Review
Business Action (Houston)

Business Week
Cattleman, The
Dallas Morning News
Dallas Times-Herald
Eastern Underwriter
Financial Trend
Financial World
Forbes
Fortune
Fort Worth Star-Telegram
Fresno (Calif.) *Bee*
Galveston Daily News
Houston (Chamber of Commerce publication)
Houston Action
Houston Business Journal
Houston Chronicle
Houston Post
Houston Press
Insurance
Insurance Advocate
Insurance Age Journal
Insurance Graphic
Insurance Record
Insurance Reporter
Insurance Week
Journal of Commerce
Life Insurance News
Lincoln (Nebr.) *Journal*
Los Angeles Herald-Examiner
Los Angeles Times
Louisville Courier-Journal
Mexia Evening News
Nashville Banner
Nashville Tennessean
National Underwriter variously titled: Life, Fire, and Casualty
Nation's Business
New Mexican, The
New York Times
Omaha World-Herald
Sacramento Bee
Sacramento Union
San Francisco Chronicle
San Francisco Examiner
Santa Gertrudis Journal
Southern Insurance
Southwest Insuror
Texas Insuror
Texas Livestock Weekly
Texas Observer
Texas Parade
U.S. Investor
U.S. Review
Wall Street Journal
Washington Daily News
Washington Post
Washington Star
Weekly Underwriter
Weekly Western Livestock Journal
West Texas Livestock Weekly

Most of the newspaper citations in the text and all of the insurance publication citations are from these scrapbooks.

Kenneth Fellows's manuscript history of American General, "The Baby Is Born," is also housed in the archives, along with several other insurance company histories and some of the Fellows's files from his research work at American General from 1974 to 1976.

At the time this manuscript was being researched and written, an exhibition in honor of the hundredth birthday of Gus Wortham was researched, organized, and displayed under the direction of Ms. Brumbelow. The work on this exhibition greatly helped the author not only in locating material, but in establishing chronology.

The minute books of the American General Company board of directors, stockholders, and executive committee, housed in the corporate secretary's office, provided more information than might be expected such corporate records, on the growth and development of American General Insurance and its subsidiaries. This was also true for the minutes of the American General Investment Corporation.

A few boxes of records, memoranda, and various documents remain at John L. Wortham and Son, including early ledger books and files from the federal land bank bonding business. Two documents which provide historical information and anecdotes on the early years of the agency are found here, too: one by the late Willoughby Williams and another, which includes Fellows's and Williams's material, by Fred Wallace. Both Williams and Wallace were John L. Wortham and Son partners.

After the American General archival material, the greatest asset to this work was the papers of Kenneth Fellows. Fellows was hired to write a corporate history of American General in 1974 and his papers, which he loaned to the author before his death in early 1992, include his own interview notes with early and significant employees of the agency and corporation, copies of documents, notes of interviews with Gus and Lyndall Wortham, all the material used in the preparation of the company's Newcomen history, and Fellows's manuscript, "The Baby Is Born." This manuscript and its related documents proved to be a bedrock upon which could be built a comprehensive story of Wortham's insurance career, especially in the later years. Fellows's document accurately and clearly defines the various acquisitions of American General and puts them in an understandable chronology and context. The numerous additions to the American General family have never been ordered, listed, and thoroughly explained before, except in some annual reports. Fellows's copious work saved this author much time and provided much content for this project.

The fifty or so interviews conducted by the current author for this work serve as sources of facts, opinions, lore, and viewpoints that, put together, created a context against which the author was able to define Gus Wortham's institutional involvement. Most provide information about the interviewees' institutional relationships with Wortham and their perceptions about him as a businessman, rancher, and/or civic leader.

Benjamin N. Woodson, Gus Wortham's successor at American General, has a collection of papers at Rice University containing memoranda, correspondence, files, a business diary, and notes. These materials provided data about Gus Wortham's involvement with the company, as well as his governmental and civic involvements, and serve as valuable sources for the history of business development at American General.

Housed at the Eugene Barker Texas History Center at the University of Texas are the audio tapes, individual tape transcripts, and edited and combined transcript of several oral history sessions with Gus Wortham conducted in 1970 as part of a collection of oral histories done by the UT College of Business Administration. The edited version of this oral history provided the author with the story of Gus Wortham as he remembered it and obviously was a very valuable source for this work.

A fascinating collection of information is available at the Freestone County Museum in Freestone, Texas, under the direction of Sylvia Childs. The county has produced an excellent local history, now on its third volume, and the museum, housed in an old jail, contains a caliber of documents and artifacts not often found in such local repositories.

The papers of individuals and collections of organizations were helpful in providing information on Wortham's involvement in Houston. These were found in several repositories including: the Houston Metropolitan Research Center at the Houston Public Library, under the direction of Dr. Louis Marchiafava, and the Texas and Local History Room of the library; Woodson Research Center, under the direction of Nancy Boothe, at Rice University; Special Collections, headed by Patricia Bozeman, at the University of Houston; the Eugene Barker Texas History Center at the University of Texas, under the direction of Dr. Don Carleton; and the Lyndon Baines Johnson Archives located at the Lyndon B. Johnson Library in Austin, Texas.

Several books and articles about Houston and Texas proved very useful in connecting Wortham to larger contexts. They include *Houston, The Bayou City* by David McComb; *Red Scare! Right-Wing Hysteria, Fifties Fanaticism and their Legacy in Texas* by Don E. Carleton; *Free Enterprise City, Houston in Political and Economic Perspective* by Joe R. Feagin; *Money, Marbles and Chalk, The Wondrous World of Texas Politics* by Jimmy Banks; *The Texans* by James Conaway; *The Establishment in Texas Politics, the Primitive Years 1938–1957* by George Norris Green; *Race and Class in Texas Politics* by Chandler Davidson; the series of articles on "Houston's Power" by Craig Smyser in the *Houston Chronicle*, June-July, 1977; and Harry Hurt's "The Most Powerful Texans," in *Texas Monthly Political Reader*.

SOURCES

Manuscripts and Manuscript Collections

American General Archives. American General Corporation. Houston, Tex.
Acquisition Files.
American General Annual Reports and Statements.
American General and Subsidiaries. 10K Forms.
American General Press Releases.
American General Quarterly Reports.
American General Proxy Statements.
American General Records and Reports.
American General and Subsidiaries. Corporate Publications.
A-General View
AG Life Lines
American General Journal

The Home Port
American General Scrapbooks. ca. 1926-present.
American General Shareholders Material.
American General Securities Portfolios and Schedule of Securities.
American General Statistical Supplements.
Benjamin N. Woodson Scrapbooks.
Brochures.
Gus S. Wortham Drawer.
Gus S. Wortham Papers.
Gus S. Wortham Scrapbooks. ca. 1875–1987.
John L. Wortham Papers.
Seaboard Life Insurance Company Papers. ca. 1920s-1940s.
Wortham Correspondence Binders. ca. 1860–1933.

American General Corporation. Corporate Secretary. Houston, Tex.
Minutes, Board of Directors.
Minutes, Executive Committee.
Minutes, Stockholders' Meetings.
Report to Stockholders.

American General Investment Corporation. Houston, Tex. Minutes, Board of Directors.

Castaneda, Christopher J., and Joseph A. Pratt. "From Texas to the East: A Strategic History of Texas Eastern Corporation." College Station: Texas A&M University Press, 1993.

Chamber of Commerce Scrapbooks. 1932–36. Houston Metropolitan Research Center. Houston Public Library.

O. B. Colquitt Papers, Eugene Barker Texas History Center. University of Texas. Austin.

R. B. Cousins Papers. Eugene Barker Texas History Center. University of Texas. Austin.

Creekmore, J. Howard. Interview by Joseph Pratt and Walter Buenger, Sept. 17, 1982. Oral History of the Houston Economy, University of Houston.

Crow, Herman L. "A Political History of the Texas Prison System, 1929–1951." Ph.D. diss., University of Texas, Austin, 1964.

Joseph W. Evans Collection. Houston Metropolitan Research Center. Houston Public Library.

Sterling C. Evans Papers. Castroville, Tex.

Fellows, Kenneth. "The Baby Is Born, The Story of American General's First Fifty Years." MS written for American General Corporation, Houston, 1976. Copy in AG Archives.

Kenneth Fellows Papers for 'The Baby Is Born." Houston, Tex.

Freestone County Historical Museum. Fairfield, Tex. *Freestone Frontiers*,. Genealogical Society of Freetone County.

Greater Houston Partnership Archives. Houston, Tex.

Oscar Holcombe Collection. Houston Metropolitan Research Center. Houston Public Library.

Houston Chamber of Commerce Scrapbooks. 1929–ca. 1940. Houston Metropolitan Research Center. Houston Public Library.

Houston Symphony Orchestra History Files. Houston, Tex.
Houston Symphony Orchestra Collection. Houston Metropolitan Research Center. Houston Public Library. Houston Symphony Orchestra Society Scrapbooks.
Jesse H. Jones Papers. Eugene Barker Texas History Center. University of Texas. Austin.
John L. Wortham and Son Archives. Houston, Tex. Federal Land Bank Files.
Love, Ben. "People and Profits: A Bank Case Study." M.A. thesis, Southwest School of Banking, 1967.
Lyndon B. Johnson Archives. Lyndon B. Johnson Library. Austin, Tex.
Appointment Files.
House of Representatives Papers.
LBJ Post-Presidential Files.
Office Files of John Macy.
Presidential Papers.
Senate Papers.
Social Files—Alpha File.
Vice-Presidential Papers.
WHCF Name File.
Jesse H. Jones Lumber Company Collection. Houston Metropolitan Research Center. Houston Public Library.
Mary Lasswell Papers. Eugene Barker Texas History Center. University of Texas. Austin.
McDade, Thomas. Interview by Joseph Pratt and Walter Buenger, June 22, 1983. Oral History of the Houston Economy, University of Houston.
Leopold Meyer Collection. Houston Metropolitan Research Center. Houston Public Library.
Museum of Fine Arts, Houston Archives. Houston, Tex.
Neal Pickett Collection. Houston Metropolitan Research Center. Houston Public Library.
Powers, Betsy J. "'Gone to Texas,' The Impact of Southern Migration Upon Antebellum Texas." M.A. thesis, University of Houston, 1990.
Rice University. Woodson Research Center. Fondren Library. Rice University. Houston, Tex.
Presidents' Papers, Houston and Pitzer.
University Archives.
Shelton, Hal, Julie Kavitski, and Susanne Huxel. "The Wortham House: A History." MS. Program in Public History, University of Houston, 1987.
Lyndall Wortham Seymour Papers. Tallulah, La.
Texas A&I University Archives. Kingsville, Tex.
Texas and Local History Room. Houston Public Library.
Biographical Scrapbooks. Houston and Texas.
Houston Chronicle Microfiche Collection.
Houston Scrapbooks.
Texas Scrapbooks.
Vertical Files
Houston Community Chest.
Houston Fat Stock Show/Livestock and Rodeo Show Files.

Rice University.
Warwick Window.
Texas Children's Hospital Archives. Houston, Tex.
Texas Commerce Bancshares Archives. Houston, Tex.
Interviews by Bill Allison.
Gus S. Wortham. May 11, 1972.
Minutes, Board of Directors.
Texas Insurance Advisory Association. Austin.
Texas State Archives. Austin.
Secretary of State Papers.
Railroad Commission of Texas Papers.
Governors' Records. O. B. Colquitt.
Albert Thomas Papers, Woodson Research Center. Fondren Library. Rice University. Houston, Tex.
Tucker, Leah Brooke. "The Houston Business Community, 1945–1965." Ph.D. diss., University of Texas, Austin, 1979.
University of Houston. M. D. Anderson Library. Special Collections. Houston, Tex.
University of Houston Archives.
Houston Gargoyle. 1928–32.
Benjamin N. Woodson Papers. Woodson Research Center. Fondren Library. Rice University. Houston, Tex.
Wallace, Fred, ed. "History of John L. Wortham & Son." Typescript, Houston: John L. Wortham and Son, 1983. Kenneth Fellows Papers.
Whitmire, John L. Interview by Walter Buenger, Sept. 17, 1982. Oral History of the Houston Economy, University of Houston.
[Williams, Willoughby]. Typescript history of John L. Wortham and Son, Houston: John L. Wortham and Son, n.d. John L. Wortham and Son Archives.
Woodson, Benjamin N. Interview by Joseph A. Pratt, June 18, 1985. Oral History of the Houston Economy, University of Houston.
Wortham, Gus S. "Interviews with Mr. Gus S. Wortham of American General Life Insurance. Business Oral History Records." College of Business Administration, University of Texas, Austin. 1970–71. (Combined, rough edited transcript only used.)
———. Interview by Kenneth Fellows, for "The Baby is Born." Dec. 17, 1974.
Wortham, Lyndall Finley. Interview by Kenneth Fellows, for "The Baby Is Born." May 18, 1976.
William Wortham Papers. Bryan, Tex.
Young, Pamela F. "History of the Houston Symphony Orchestra, 1913–1966." Master's thesis, University of Texas, Austin, 1970.

Government Documents/Publications

Houston. Housing Authority of the City of Houston, Tex. Board of Directors Minutes.
Texas. Department of Insurance. *51st Annual Report of the Commissioner of Insurance for the Year Ending August 31, 1926.* Austin: A. C. Baldwin, 1926.
———. Department of Insurance. *52nd Annual Report of the Commissioner of Insurance for the Year Ending August 31, 1927.* Austin: A. C. Baldwin, 1927.

———. Department of Insurance. *53rd Annual Report of the Commissioner of Insurance for the Year Ending August 31, 1928*. Austin: 1928.

Texas. Freestone County. Freestone, Tex.

Probate Minutes. County Clerk.

Deed Records. County Clerk

Texas. Limestone County. Groesbeck, Tex.

Deed Records. County Clerk.

Probate Minutes. County Clerk.

Texas. State Board of Insurance. Austin, Tex.

Books

Acheson, Sam Hanna. *Joe Bailey: The Last Democrat*. Freeport, N.Y.: Books for Libraries Press, 1932.

Bainbridge, John. *The Super Americans*. New York: Holt, Rinehart and Winston, 1972.

Banks, Jimmy. *Money, Marbles and Chalk. The Wondrous World of Texas Politics*. Austin: Texas Publishing Company, 1971.

Benedict, Harry V., and John A. Lomax. *The Book of Texas*. Garden City, N.J.: Doubleday, Page and Co., 1916.

Big Town, Big Money. The Business of Houston. Houston: Cordovan Press, 1973.

Bryant, Keith, Jr., and Henry C. Dethloff, *A History of American Business*. Englewood Cliffs, N.J.: Prentice-Hall, 1983.

Buenger, Walter M., and Joseph A. Pratt, *But Also Good Business. Texas Commerce Banks and the Financing of Houston and Texas, 1886–1986*. College Station: Texas A&M University Press, 1986.

Bullard, Robert. *Invisible Houston: The Black Experience in Boom and Bust*. College Station: Texas A&M University Press, 1987.

Caddy, Douglas. *Understanding Texas Insurance*. College Station: Texas A&M University Press, 1984.

Carleton, Don E. *Red Scare! Right-wing Hysteria, Fifties Fanaticism and their Legacy in Texas*. Austin: Texas Monthly Press, 1985.

Caro, Robert A. *The Years of Lyndon Johnson. The Path to Power*. New York: Vintage Books 1983.

———. *The Years of Lyndon Johnson. Means of Ascent*. New York: Alfred A. Knopf, 1990.

Cochrane, Willard W. *The Development of American Agriculture. A Historical Analysis*. Minneapolis: University of Minnesota Press, 1979.

Conaway, James. *The Texans*. New York: Alfred A. Knopf, 1976.

Dallek, Robert. *Lone Star Rising: Lyndon Johnson and His Times, 1908–1960*. New York: Oxford University Press, 1991.

Daniel, L. E., ed. *Personnel of the Texas State Government with Sketches of Distinguished Texans, Embracing the Executive and Staff, Heads of Departments, U.S. Senators and Representatives, Members of the XXth Legislature*. Austin: City Printing Company, 1887.

Davidson, Chandler. *Biracial Politics, Conflict and Coalition in the Metropolitan South*. Baton Rouge. Louisiana State University Press, 1972.

———. *Race and Class in Texas Politics*. Princeton: Princeton University Press, 1990.

Davis, Ellis, A. and Edwin H. Grobe, eds. *The New Encyclopedia of Texas*. Dallas: Texas Development Bureau, 1925.

DeShields, James T. *They Sat in High Places. The Presidents and Governors of Texas*. San Antonio: The Naylor Company, 1940.

Directory of the City of Houston 1911–12. Houston: Texas Publishing Company, 1911.

Dubbert, Joe L. *A Man's Place: Masculinity in Transition*. Englewood Cliffs, N.J.: Prentice-Hall, 1979.

Duffy, Winifred Arndt. *John Wiley Link*. Houston: Harold Link (privately published), 1974.

Dugger, Ronnie. *The Politician: The Life and Times of Lyndon Johnson—The Drive for Power, from the Frontier to Master of the Senate*. New York: W.W. Norton and Company, 1982.

Eaton, Clement. *The Waning of the Old South Civilization*. New York: Pegasus, 1968.

Feagin, Joe R. *Free Enterprise City: Houston in Political and Economic Perspective*. New Brunswick, N.J.: Rutgers University Press, 1988.

Fehrenbach, T. R. *Lone Star: A History of Texas and the Texans*. New York: American Legacy Press, 1983.

Foster, Marcellus E., and Alfred Jones, eds. *South and Southeast Texas: A Work for Newspaper and Library References*. Texas Biographical Association, 1928.

Fox, Stephen. *Houston Architectural Guide*. Houston: American Institute of Architects, Houston Chapter and Herring Press, 1990.

Freestone County Historical Commission. *History of Freestone County*. 1st ed. Preservation Publishers, 1978.

Fuermann, George. *Houston: Land of the Big Rich*. Garden City, N.J.: Doubleday, 1951.

———. *Reluctant Empire*. Garden City, N.J.: Doubleday, 1957.

Goodwyn, Frank. *Lone-Star Land: Twentieth Century Texas in Perspective*. New York: A. A. Knopf, 1955.

Gould, Lewis L. *Progressives and Prohibitionists. Texas Democrats in the Wilson Era*. Austin: University of Texas Press, 1973.

Grantham, Dewey, Jr., ed. *The South and the Sectional Image: The Sectional Theme Since Reconstruction*. New York: Harper and Row, 1967.

———. *Southern Progressivism: the Reconciliation of Progress and Tradition*. Knoxville: University of Tennessee Press, 1983.

Gray, Kenneth E. A *Report on the Politics of Houston*. 2 vols. Cambridge, Mass.: Joint Center for Urban Studies, Massachusetts Institute of Technology and Harvard University, 1960.

Green, George Norris. *The Establishment in Texas Politics: The Primitive Years, 1938–1957*. Westport, Conn.: Greenwood Press, 1979.

Gunther, John. *Inside U.S.A.* New York: Harper and Brothers, 1947.

Hurley, Marvin. *Decisive Years for Houston*. Houston: Houston Chamber of Commerce, 1966.

Hyman, Harold. *Oleander Odyssey: The Kempners of Galveston, Texas, 1854–1980s*. College Station: Texas A&M University Press, 1990.

Kane, Harnett T. *Gone Are the Days: Illustrated History of the Old South*. New York: Bramhall House, 1960.

Key, V. O. *Southern Politics in State and Nation*. New York: Alfred A. Knopf, 1949.

Kinch, Sam, and Stuart Long. *Allan Shivers: The Pied Piper of Texas Politics*. Austin: Shoal Creek Publishers, 1973.

Johnston, Marguerite. *Houston: The Unknown City, 1836–1946*. College Station: Texas A&M University Press, 1991.

Lamare, James W. *Texas Politics, Economics, Power, and Policy*. St. Paul: West Publishing Co., 1985.

Lasswell, Mary. *John Henry Kirby, Prince of the Pines*. Austin: Encino Press, 1967.

Link, Arthur S., and William B. Catton. *The American Epoch: A History of the United States Since the 1890s*. 2nd ed. New York: Alfred A. Knopf, 1965.

Lutz, Donald S., and Kent L. Tedin. *Perspectives on Amerian and Texas Politics: A Collection of Essays*. Dubuque, Iowa: Kendall/Hunt, 1987.

Manford, Mary Jane. *Insuring Texas' Future: A History of the Independent Insurance Agents of Texas*. Project of the IIAT Sesquicentennial Committee. Austin: Insurance Publishing House, 1987.

McAshan, Marie Phelps. *On the Corner of Main and Texas: A Houston Legacy*. Mary Jo Bell, ed. Houston: Hutchins House, 1985.

McComb, David G. *Houston. The Bayou City*. Austin: University of Texas Press, 1969.

McGill, Dan M., ed. *All Lines Insurance*. The S. S. Huebner Foundation for Insurance Eduation. Homewood, Ill.: Richard D. Irwin, 1960.

McKay, Seth, and Odie Faulk. *Texas After Spindletop*. Austin: Steck-Vaughn, 1965.

Mehr, Robert, and Emerson Cammack. *Principles of Insurance*. 5th ed. Homewood, Ill.: Richard D. Irwin, 1972.

Meiners, Fredericka. *A History of Rice University: The Institute Years, 1907–1963*. Houston: Rice University Studies, 1982.

A Memorial Biographical History of Navarro, Henderson, Anderson, Limestone, Freestone and Leon Counties, Texas. Chicago: Lewis Publishing Company, 1893.

Meyer, Leopold L. *The Days of My Years: Autobiographical Reflections of Leopold L. Meyer*. Houston: Universal Printers, 1975.

Miner, H. Craig. *The Re-Birth of the Missouri Pacific, 1956–1983*. College Station: Texas A&M University Press, 1983.

Morrison and Fourmey Directory Company. *Houston City Directory*. Vols. 1920–52, Houston: R. L. Polk and Company.

Nevin, David. *The Texans: What They Are — And Why*. New York: Bonanza Books, 1968.

Orum, Anthony M. *Power, Money and the People: The Making of Modern Austin*. Austin: Texas Monthly Press, 1987.

Porter, Glenn, ed. *Encyclopedia of American Economic History*. Vols. 1, 2. New York: Charles Scribner's Sons, 1980. S. v. "Organized Business Groups" by Albert Steigerwalt and "Antitrust" by Ellis Hawley.

Presley, James. *A Saga of Wealth: An Anecdotal History of the Texas Oilmen*. Austin: Texas Monthly Press, 1983.

Pugh, David. *Sons of Liberty: The Masculine Mind in Nineteenth Century America*. Westport, Conn.: Greenwood Press, 1983.

Randolph, George Alice May. *Woodland Cousins, Their Kith and Kin*. Austin: By the author, 1974.

Ray, Edgar W. *The Grand Huckster: Houston's Judge Roy Hofheinz, Genius of the Astrodome*. Memphis: Memphis State University Press, 1980.

Reed, S. G. *A History of the Texas Railroads and of the Transportation Conditions under Spain and Mexico and the Republic and the State*. Houston: St. Clair Publishing Co., 1941.

Reston, James, Jr. *The Lone Star: The Life of John Connally*. New York: Harper and Row, 1989.

Richardson, Rupert N., Ernest Wallace, and Adrian Anderson. *Texas: The Lone Star State*. 5th ed. Englewood Cliffs, N.J.: Prentice Hall, 1988.

Roller, David C., and Robert W. Twyman, eds. *The Encyclopedia of Southern History*. Baton Rouge: Louisiana State University, 1979. S. v. "Customs and Manners" by Clement Eaton.

Roussel, Hubert. *The Houston Symphony Orchestra, 1913–1971*. Austin: University of Texas Press, 1972.

Sheehy, Sandy. *Texas Big Rich: Exploits, Eccentricities, and Fabulous Fortunes Won and Lost*. New York: William Morrow and Company, 1990.

Sibley, Marilyn McAdams. *The Port of Houston: A History*. Austin: University of Texas Press, 1968.

Siegel, Stanley E. *Houston: A Chronicle of the Supercity on Buffalo Bayou*. Woodland Hills, Calif.: Windsor Hill Publications, 1983.

Singal, Daniel J. *The War Within: Victorian to Modernist Thought in the South, 1919–1945*. Chapel Hill: University of North Carolina Press, 1982.

Spratt, John Stricklin. *The Road to Spindletop: Economic Change in Texas, 1875–1901*. Austin: University of Texas Press, 1955.

Steen, Ralph W. *Twentieth Century Texas, An Economic and Social History*. Austin: The Steck Company, 1942.

Stephens, A. Ray, and William M. Homes. *Historical Atlas of Texas*. Norman, Okla.: University of Oklahoma Press, 1984.

Stokes, William N., Jr. *Sterling C. Evans: Texas Aggie, Banker, Cattleman*. Friends of the Sterling C. Evans Library and the Federal Land Bank of Texas, 1985.

Taylor, William R. *Cavalier and Yankee: The Old South and American National Character*. Cambridge, Mass.: Harvard University Press, 1979.

Texas Monthly's Political Reader. 1st ed. Austin: Texas Monthly Press and Sterling Swift Publishing Company, 1978.

Thomas, Robert D., and Richard W. Murray. *Progrowth Politics, Change and Governance in Houston*. Berkeley: IGS Press, 1991.

Timmons, Bascom N. *Jesse H. Jones: The Man and the Statesman*. New York: Henry Holt, 1956.

Walker, Donald R. *Penology for Profit: A History of the Texas Prison System, 1867–1912*. College Station: Texas A&M University Press, 1988.

Webb, Walter Prescott, editor-in-chief. *The Handbook of Texas*. 2 vols. Austin: Texas State Historical Association, 1952.

Wharton, Clarence R. *Texas Under Many Flags*. Chicago: American Historical Society, 1930.

Wilson, Charles Reagan, and William Ferris, eds., *The Encyclopedia of Southern Culture*. Center for the Study of Southern Culture, University of Mississippi. Chapel Hill:

University of North Carolina Press, 1989. S.v. "Belles and Ladies" by Ann Goodwyn Jones.

Woodson, Benjamin N. *A Financial Services Supermarket: The American General Story*. New York: Newcomen Society, 1974.

Woodward, C. Vann. *Origins of the New South, 1877–1913*. Vol. 9. *A History of the South*, Wendell Holmes Stephenson and E. Merton Coulter eds. Littlefield Fund for Southern History of the University of Texas. Baton Rouge: Louisiana State University Press, 1951.

Wortham, Louis J. *A History of Texas: From Wilderness to Commonwealth*. Vol. 5. Fort Worth: Wortham-Molyneaux Co., 1924.

Wright, Gavin. *Old South, New South, Revolutions in the Southern Economy Since the Civil War*. New York: Basic Books, 1986.

Articles

Blankenhorn, Dana. "The Brown Brothers; Houston's Contracting and Energy Giants." *Houston Business Journal*, March 19, 1979.

———. "Gus Wortham: Insurance, Ranching and Civic Trend Setter Embodied Houston Establishment." *Houston Business Journal*, March 26, 1979, Sec. 2, 1.

Boal, Sam. "Treatise on Texas and the Texans." *New York Times Magazine*, May 15, 1949, 13ff.

"Cattle Feeding—Texas Style." *Humble Farm Family*, Nov. 1954, 8–9.

Chapman, Belin B. "The Claim of Texas to Greer County, Part III." *Southwestern Historical Quarterly* 53 (April, 1950): 404–21.

Dugger, Ronnie. "What Corrupted Texas." *Harper's Magazine*, March, 1957, 69–7?.

Franks, Zarko. "Gus Wortham: Beauty in a Sunset, a Sonnet or a Financial Statement." *Houston Chronicle*, Nov. 13, 1966, Sec. 2, 1ff.

Gaston, Paul B. "New South Creed: A Study in Mythmaking." In *Myth and Southern History; The New South*, Patrick Gerster and Nicholas Cords, eds., 49–64. Chicago: Rand McNally, 1974.

Gordon, Lila Humphries. "They Built Houston: Portrait of an Optimist." *Houston Town and Country*, Dec. 1975, 18ff.

Hardeman, D. B. "Shivers of Texas, a tragedy in three acts." *Harper's* Nov., 1956, 50ff.

Harrison, Will. "Houston Tycoon Defaults Contracts." *The New Mexican*. Oct. 15, 1964.

"Houston." *Town and Country*, March 6, 1969, 89ff.

Hurt, Harry III. "The Most Powerful Texans." In *Texas Monthly's Political Reader*. 1st ed. Austin: Texas Monthly Press, 1978, 10–19.

Irons, Peter W. "American Business and the Origins of McCarthyism: The Cold War Crusade of the United States Chamber of Commerce." In *The Specter: Original Essays on the Cold War and the Origins of McCarthyism*, Robert Griffith and Athan Theoharis, eds., 74–89. New York: Franklin Watts, 1974.

Kaplan, Barry J. "Houston, The Golden Buckle of the Sunbelt." In *Sunbelt Cities, Politics and Growth Since World War II*, Richard M. Bernard and Bardley R. Rice, eds., 196–212. Austin: University of Texas Press, 1983.

Kilman, Ed. "Hands Across the Canyon." *Texas Parade*, June, 1959, 33–35.

Lathrop, Barnes F. "Migration into East Texas, 1835–1860." *Southwestern Historical Quarterly* (July, 1948): 200–207.

Lowenheim, Francis. "False Crescendo." *Texas Monthly*, Feb., 1986, 168.

Mezerick, A. G. "Journey in America: III." *The New Republic*, Nov. 27, 1944, 684–87.

Murphy, Charles J. V. "Texas Business and McCarthy," *Fortune*, May, 1954, 100ff.

Murray, Richard. "Power in the City: Patterns of Political Influence in Houston, Texas." In *Perspectives on American and Texas Politics: A Collection of Essays*, Donald S. Lutz and Kent Tedin, eds. 277–93. Dubuque, Iowa: Kendall/Hunt, 1989.

Norvell, James R. "The Railroad Commission of Texas, Its Origin and History." *Southwestern Historical Quarterly* 68 (April, 1965): 465–80.

Perry, George Sessions. "Houston, Texas." *Saturday Evening Post*, Nov. 29, 1947, 22ff.

"Santa Gertrudis." *Humble Way*, May-June, 1953, 11–18.

"Santa Gertrudis at Nine Bar Ranch." *American Breeds*, March, 1960, 10ff.

Shanks, Dave. "A New Austin Investor, Or, Gus Wortham's Stake." *Austin American*, Sept. 20, 1962.

Smyser, Craig. "Houston's Power: As It Was." *Houston Chronicle*. June 27, 1977.

———. "Houston's Power: The "Top 20." *Houston Chronicle*, June 28, 1977.

———. "Houston's Power: Law, Banks, Oil." *Houston Chronicle*, June 29, 1977.

———. "Houston's Power: Taking a Share." *Houston Chronicle*, June 30, 1977.

———. "Houston's Power: How It's Won." *Houston Chronicle*, July 1, 1977.

"Something for Everybody." *The New Yorker*, March 13, 1948, 82ff.

"Southern City, Northern Pace: How Long Can It Last?" *Business Week*, Jan. 24, 1953, 77ff.

Stillwell, Hart. "Texas, Owned by Oil and Interlocking Directorates." In *Our Sovereign State*, Robert Allen, ed., 314–44. New York: Vanguard Press, 1949.

"Success Story, Texas Style." *Finance*, Dec. 1967, 42–44.

Swanson, Bert E. "Discovering an Economic Clique in the Development and Growth of Houston." In *Essays in Economic and Business History: Selected Papers from the Economic and Business Historical Society*, 1986, vol. 5, 101–14. History Department, University of Southern California for Economic and Business Historical Society, 1987.

"Texas." *Fortune*, Dec., 1939, 80ff.

Tindall, George B. "Mythology: A New Frontier in Southern History." In *Myth and Southern History; The New South*, Patrick Gerster and Nicholas Cords, eds. 1–31. Chicago: Rand McNally, 1974.

Tinsley, James A. "Texas Progressives and Insurance Regulation." *Southwest Social Science Quarterly* (Dec. 1955): 241–46.

Weems, John Edward. "Houston." *Marathon World*, Winter, 1966, 2–9.

Weiner, Sam. "American General to Push Its Growth This Spring." *Houston Post*, March 23, 1969.

White, Theodore H. "Texas; Land of Wealth and Fear, I: Blowing the Bass Tuba the Day It Rained Gold." *The Reporter*, May 25, 1954, 10–17.

———. "Texas: Land of Wealth and Fear, II: Texas Democracy—Domestic and Export Models." *The Reporter*, June 8, 1954, 30–37.

Wintz, Cary D. "Blacks in Houston." In *Ethnic Groups of Houston*, Fred R. von der Mehden, ed. 4–90. Houston: Rice University Press, 1984.

"Wortham." *Rice University Review*. Spring, 1970, 6ff.

"Wortham and Evans are Increasing the Size of their Santa Gertrudis Operation." *Santa Gertrudis Journal*, Jan., 1960, 8ff.

Index

CPSIA information can be obtained at www.ICGtesting.com
Printed in the USA
LVOW03s0013220314

378458LV00002B/3/P

9 781623 491543